# Black Book

# AFC

**Clayton Walnum**

### AFC Black Book

**Limits of Liability and Disclaimer of Warranty**

The author and publisher of this book have used their best efforts in preparing the book and the programs contained in it. These efforts include the development, research, and testing of the theories and programs to determine their effectiveness. The author and publisher make no warranty of any kind, expressed or implied, with regard to these programs or the documentation contained in this book.

The author and publisher shall not be liable in the event of incidental or consequential damages in connection with, or arising out of, the furnishing, performance, or use of the programs, associated instructions, and/or claims of productivity gains.

**Trademarks**

Trademarked names appear throughout this book. Rather than list the names and entities that own the trademarks or insert a trademark symbol with each mention of the trademarked name, the publisher states that it is using the names for editorial purposes only and to the benefit of the trademark owner, with no intention of infringing upon that trademark.

The Coriolis Group, Inc.
An International Thomson Publishing Company
14455 N. Hayden Road, Suite 220
Scottsdale, Arizona 85260

602.483.0192
FAX 602.483.0193
http://www.coriolis.com

Library of Congress Cataloging-In-Publication Data
Walnum, Clayton.
    Afc black book / by Clayton Walnum.
       p.   cm.
    Includes index.
    ISBN 1-57610-235-1
     1. Java (Computer program language)   2. Microsoft AFC.   3. User interfaces
(Computer systems)   I. Title.
QA76.73.J38W345   1998
005.13'3–dc21                                 98-12320
                                               CIP

Printed in the United States of America
10 9 8 7 6 5 4 3 2 1

**Publisher**
Keith Weiskamp

**Aquisitions Editors**
Stephanie Wall
Jeff Duntemann

**Project Editor**
Mariann Hansen Barsolo

**Production Coordinator**
Michael Peel

**Cover Design**
Anthony Stock

**Layout Design**
April Nielsen

**CD-ROM Development**
Robert Clarfield

*an International Thomson Publishing company* I(T)P®

Albany, NY • Belmont, CA • Bonn • Boston • Cincinnati • Detroit • Johannesburg • London
Madrid • Melbourne • Mexico City • New York • Paris • Singapore • Tokyo • Toronto • Washington

*To Lynn, my life partner and best friend.*

# Acknowledgments

I'd like to thank all the fine folks whose touch made this book as good as it could be. Special thanks go to Ann Waggoner Aken, Shari Jo Hehr, Mariann Barsolo, and Don Eamon, all of whom not only did their part to ensure this book's quality, but also made this project a joy to work on. Thanks also to Production Coordinator Michael Peel, Cover Designer Anthony Stock, Interior Designer April Nielsen, typesetter Deb Shenenberg and proofreader Laura Poole. Additional thanks to Chris Rouviere for the cool artwork in some of the screen shots.

And, as always, thanks goes to my family, Lynn, Christopher, Justin, Stephen, and Caitlynn, who, when the deadlines get tight, have to watch TV without Dad.

# Table Of Contents

## Chapter 4   Edit, List, Choice, And Group Components   121

## Practical Guide To Using Edit, List, Choice, And Group Components   145

# Introduction

It wasn't too long ago that Java was a fledgling language, trying to gain a foothold in the Internet development market. Now, everywhere you look, the name Java pops up, having become one of the most popular programming languages in the world for creating Internet content. With the language's popularity, of course, comes hundreds of third-party add-ons, not the least of which is Microsoft's Application Foundation Classes (AFC), which provides not only an extensive library of new components that you can add to your Java applets and applications, but also extends graphics classes that give your Java programs more graphics power.

Just as with any new library, however, learning to use AFC takes time and a little patience. The documentation that comes with the package is sparse at best, leaving the programmer to figure out the details, a task that doesn't always lead to success. *AFC Black Book* is designed to reduce the time it takes for you to get up and running with AFC, so you can get started using this powerful class library in your Java projects as soon as possible. Your humble author has already spent many hours digging through the libraries, figuring out how to program the classes and looking for problems that you, the reader, may run into as you program AFC.

*AFC Black Book* takes a somewhat unconventional approach to teaching programming. Many programming books feature several large applets or applications that, while they present real-world program examples, may bury the programming details in hundreds of lines of irrelevant code. This book, instead, includes more than 150 tiny applets or applications, most of which demonstrate a single AFC programming technique. In most cases, you can see at a glance how a specific sample program works. Just as importantly, you can—and indeed are encouraged to—take an active, "hands-on" approach to each sample. That is, load each sample program into your text editor and modify it to see how your changes affect the program. Because each concept is presented in a working applet or application, you'll know immediately if your changes work properly. And because the programs are, in most cases, so small, you don't have to wonder whether some other part of the program is affecting your modifications.

Some of the sample applets may, in fact, seem trivial at first. But once you see how quickly this approach gets you up to speed with AFC, you'll appreciate the conciseness of the samples. And, yes, it would be even more concise to skip the applets completely and just present code snippets as examples. However, it's this author's opinion that context is everything. How may times have you studied a programming example only to find that you couldn't get the example code snippets to work? By demonstrating each AFC concept in its own tiny applet, you get to see each programming concept in the context of a functioning program. Instead of spending valuable time trying to figure out why you can't get a code snippet to work, you can spend your time experimenting with functioning code.

## Prerequisites

*AFC Black Book* is an intermediate-level programming tutorial. To understand the presented topics, you must already have a good grasp of general Java programming. You don't necessarily have to be a Java expert, but you should understand how to build Java applets and applications, have a good grasp of object-oriented programming concepts, and be reasonably familiar with Java's commonly used classes. This book does, however, review important advanced Java concepts such as creating layouts and responding to events. In the case of events, this book covers both the Java 1.0 and Java 1.1 event models (called the propagation and delegation event models, respectively).

## Technical Support

If you have comments about this book, both positive or negative, feel free to contact me at my Web site. Just point your browser to www.connix.com\~cwalnum. If you discover errors in the book, especially feel free to contact me. However, please don't ask me to debug your AFC programming projects. Not only does this type of request take great chunks of time away from my own work, but it's an almost impossible task to start with, since I can't possibly re-create your exact system settings on my computer.

If you have problems with the CD (for example, it won't install properly or is damaged), you should contact Coriolis Group's technical department at techsupport@coriolis.com.

# Introducing The Application Foundation Classes

*Without music to decorate it, time is just a bunch of boring production deadlines or dates by which bills must be paid.*
—*Frank Zappa, The Real Frank Zappa Book*

# Notes...

# Chapter 1

Do you ever tap your foot to the music coming from an elevator's overhead speaker? Probably not. Elevator music is as bland—and as safe—as any music can possibly be. This is because the folks who produce this so-called music must be sure not to offend anyone's musical sensibilities. The problem with such a task is its impossibility. In an effort to please everyone, elevator musicians produce forgettable sounds that vertical travelers barely notice.

Sun Microsystems found itself in the same position as elevator-music composers when it decided to create a platform-independent programming language called Java. Suddenly, Sun had to find a way to please programmers of Windows 95, Windows NT, Solaris, Macintosh, and possibly other computers. Unfortunately for Sun, all these computer systems have their own strengths and weaknesses. To create a language that would run well on all systems, Sun had to determine what all the systems had in common and then write Java to meet these minimal requirements.

This try-to-please-everyone philosophy resulted in a bland language. Although Java programs can perform all the tasks needed to create applications that run reasonably well under today's sophisticated, graphical operating systems, they don't take advantage of the special features of a particular operating system. Taking advantage of these features is left to the programmers of those systems—which is where Microsoft's *Application Foundation Classes* (AFC) come in.

Like many Java programmers struggling to create modern-looking applications, Microsoft's programmers devised a set of Java *class libraries* that enabled them to write the types of applications they were used to seeing. These class libraries, which make up AFC, included classes for graphical objects such as progress bars, sliders, spinners, status bars, toolbars, and more. Moreover, the young AFC libraries enhanced the many standard Java classes, providing programmers with more power over their Java applications and applets. Now, Microsoft has graciously released AFC to the rest of us.

Of course, AFC represents Microsoft's vision of how applications should look and act, which is a lot like elevator composers saying, "Look, we don't care if you like Mozart or Elton John. In this elevator, you will listen to AC/DC!" But that's okay; the AFC set of classes is so powerful, it's hard to imagine that programmers of non-Windows systems could be offended. Anyone who is offended can build his or her own class libraries.

In fact, AFC isn't the only Java class library out there. Many third-party developers have put together class libraries that make it easier for Java programmers to include special features such as tables, 3D graphics, database displays, and animation in Java programs. AFC, however, is one of the most complete of these classes, providing not only additional component classes, but also improving upon many original Java classes. Moreover, AFC has Microsoft's not insignificant development muscle behind it—you can expect to see the library flourish and continually improve. Someday, AFC may be as sophisticated as Microsoft Foundation Classes (MFC) for C++ is today.

## AFC From The Inside Out

So, what exactly is AFC? You already know that AFC is a Java class library that extends the standard Java language. More specifically, AFC consists of five Java packages that do everything from provide custom button objects to offer support for resource and cabinet (CAB) files. Along the way, AFC manages to tuck in some special graphical effects that can spice up your Java projects like a dash of hot pepper on pizza. All told, AFC features the following packages:

- **com.ms.fx** is AFC's graphics package, which features caret, curve, ellipse, font, color, pen, texture, and brush classes; it also provides classes for managing text.

- **com.ms.ui** is AFC's interface control package, which contains classes for components such as buttons, menus, scroll bars, lists, trees, spinners, sliders, and more. This package also includes window classes for message boxes, wizards, and property sheets, and also many custom layout classes.

- **com.ms.ui.event** is AFC's event package, which supports the new event model introduced with Java 1.1. This event model, called the *delegation event model*, broadcasts events from an event source to a listener object. (AFC also supports the original Java 1.0 event model, called the *propagation event model*.)

- **com.ms.ui.resource** is AFC's resource support package, which enables Windows resources to be accessed from Java applets and applications.

- **com.ms.util.cab** is AFC's cabinet support class, which enables Java programs to read and write CAB files.

In the following sections, you examine AFC's five Java packages and see how the AFC library can make your Java programs more powerful. Along the way, you may discover that there is an alternative to elevator music, after all.

## The **com.ms.fx** Package

If you've done any Visual C++ MFC programming, you're familiar with the many classes MFC provides for Graphics Device Interface (GDI) objects like pens, brushes, and fonts. The classes in the **com.ms.fx** package take their cue from MFC, delivering similar graphical objects that you can use to create your program's display. Because the classes in the **com.ms.fx** package are fully Java-compatible, you can use them much as you use traditional graphical classes—such as **Color**—in Java programs.

For example, to draw more interesting lines, you can create and select an AFC **FxPen** object before drawing a shape. You can create a pen that draws a single-pixel-width line as happens in Java, or you can create a pen of any width. You have similar control over fonts, brushes, and other graphical objects. To get this power, you need only call upon one of AFC's classes. To see how this works, first look at the traditional Java code you might use to draw a rectangle in an applet's **paint()** method, shown in Listing 1.1.

## Listing 1.1   Drawing a Java rectangle.

```
///////////////////////////////////////////////
// RectApplet.java
//
// An applet that draws with an AWT pen.
///////////////////////////////////////////////

import java.awt.*;
import java.applet.*;

public class RectApplet extends Applet
{
    public void paint(Graphics g)
    {
        g.setColor(Color.red);
        g.drawRect(20, 20, 100, 100);
    }
}
```

This Java code draws a rectangle with a one-pixel-wide line, as shown in Figure 1.1. If you want to draw a rectangle with thicker lines, you have to draw several rectangles.

Now look at Listing 1.2, which uses the AFC **FxPen** class:

## Listing 1.2   Drawing an AFC rectangle.

```
///////////////////////////////////////////////
// AFCRectApplet.java
//
// An applet that draws with an AFC pen.
///////////////////////////////////////////////

import java.awt.*;
import java.applet.*;
import com.ms.fx.*;

public class AFCRectApplet extends Applet
{
    public void paint(Graphics g)
    {
        FxPen pen = new FxPen(5, FxColor.red);
        g.setColor(pen);
        g.drawRect(20, 20, 100, 100);
    }
}
```

Here, the program creates an AFC **FxPen** object to use in place of the standard Java **Color** object. This pen draws a line five pixels wide in the color red. Figure 1.2 shows the result. Notice that, although the previous example uses an AFC object, the method call to draw the rectangle is exactly the same. The **FxPen** object simply takes the place of the color you would ordinarily pass to the **setColor()** method.

The **FxPen** object is an example of AFC's *extensible objects*. These extensible objects are graphical objects based on the standard Java **Color** and **Font** classes, but which enable you to do much more than ever before with colors and text. You can even select an image as a color, after which all drawing operations use the image as a

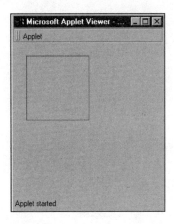

**Figure 1.1**

*RectApplet displaying a rectangle.*

**Figure 1.2**

*AFCRectApplet displaying a rectangle drawn with an AFC pen.*

texture. Don't believe it? Look at Listing 1.3, and then look at Figure 1.3. *Voilà*—a textured rectangle. And it's just as easy to use textures in window backgrounds and other places.

**Listing 1.3   An applet that draws a textured rectangle.**

```
/////////////////////////////////////////////////
// TextureRectApplet.java
//
// An applet that draws with a texture.
/////////////////////////////////////////////////

import java.awt.*;
import java.applet.*;
import java.net.*;
import com.ms.fx.*;

public class TextureRectApplet extends Applet
{
    public void paint(Graphics g)
    {
        URL url = getCodeBase();
        Image image = getImage(url, "sglass.gif");
        FxTexture texture = new FxTexture(image);
        FxPen pen = new FxPen(20, texture);
        g.setColor(pen);
        g.drawRect(20, 20, 100, 100);
    }
}
```

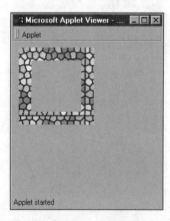

**Figure 1.3**

*TextureRectApplet displaying a textured rectangle.*

There's more to the **com.ms.fx** package, though, than pens, colors, and fonts. Also included is the AFC extended graphics object, represented by the **FxGraphics** class, which you can use in place of Java's standard **Graphics** object. Because **FxGraphics** extends, but fully supports, Java's **Graphics** class, the basic drawing methods you use to create a display are the same regardless of which graphics object you use. The **FxGraphics** class, however, gives you much more power over your display.

If you're working with an AFC component, such as an object of the **UICanvas** class, the component's **paint()** method automatically gets an **FxGraphics** object as a parameter, rather than receiving a standard Java **Graphics** object. However, you can harness the power of **FxGraphics** at any time in your Java programs by calling the **FxGraphics.getExtendedGraphics()** static method to convert a Java **Graphics** object to an AFC **FxGraphics** object. Listing 1.4, for example, shows an applet that uses an **FxGraphics** object to draw text at a 45-degree angle. Figure 1.4 shows the resulting display. Try this trick with Java's standard **drawString()** method!

### Listing 1.4   An applet that draws angled text.

```
//////////////////////////////////////////////////
// AngleTextApplet.java
//
// An applet that draws angled text.
//////////////////////////////////////////////////

import java.awt.*;
import java.applet.*;
import com.ms.fx.*;

public class AngleTextApplet extends Applet
{
    public void paint(Graphics g)
    {
        FxGraphics fxGraphics = FxGraphics.getExtendedGraphics(g);
        Font font = new Font("TimesRoman", Font.BOLD, 24);
        fxGraphics.setFont(font);
        fxGraphics.drawString("Angled Text!", 60, 180, 45);
    }
}
```

Now that you have an idea of what you can do with the **com.ms.fx** package, you may want to see all the goodies it contains. Table 1.1 lists the classes included in the **com.ms.fx** package. In following chapters of this book, you explore many of these classes in greater detail.

**Figure 1.4**

*AngleTextApplet displaying angled text.*

**Table 1.1   Classes in the AFC com.ms.fx package.**

| Class | Description |
| --- | --- |
| **FloatPoint** | Represents a point on the screen |
| **fullTxtRun** | Manages formatted strings of text |
| **FxBrushPen** | Represents a graphics component used for drawing and filling |
| **FxCaret** | Represents a caret object |
| **FxColor** | Represents extendable color objects |
| **FxComponentImage** | Provides images for display components |
| **FxComponentTexture** | Provides textures for display components |
| **FxCurve** | Provides a base class for AFC curve classes |
| **FxEllipse** | Represents ellipse objects |
| **FxFill** | Represents fill objects |
| **FxFont** | Represents user-defined fonts |
| **FxFontMetrics** | Manages font metrics objects |

*(continued)*

**Table 1.1   Classes in the AFC com.ms.fx package *(continued)*.**

| Class | Description |
| --- | --- |
| FxFormattedText | Provides multilingual text layout and formatting |
| FxGraphicMetaFile | Manipulates Windows metafiles |
| FxGraphics | Extends the Java **Graphics** object |
| FxMapFont | Validates mapping between strings and fonts |
| FxMapFontMapping Section | Represents part of a **FxMapFont** buffer |
| FxOutlineFont | Supports outline font objects |
| FxPen | Provides an extendable pen object |
| FxRubberPen | Supports "rubber band" line drawing |
| FxStateConfigurableImage | Provides images that represent system states |
| FxStateConfigurableUIImage | Provides images that represent UI component states |
| FxStyledPen | Represents dotted, dashed, and other styled lines |
| FxSystemFont | Manages system fonts |
| FxSystemIcon | Provides images for AFC |
| FxText | Supports text operations on strings |
| FxTexture | Represents texture objects |
| FxToolkit | Represents a generic AFC toolkit class |
| GlyphMetrics | Represents character outline metrics |
| GlyphOutline | Contains character outline information |
| OutlineCurve | Defines curves of an outline |
| OutlinePolygon | Supplies outline arrays to the **GlyphOutline** class |
| Region | Represents the coordinates of a region |
| txtRun | Manipulates text runs |

# The com.ms.ui Package

One of the biggest advantages of using AFC in Java program development is the availability of many custom components that can make your applications look more attractive and professional. You can find these custom components—including buttons, status bars, message boxes, trees, lists, progress bars, menus, spinners, and sliders—in the **com.ms.ui** package. This huge package boasts well over 100 classes and interfaces that work together to provide your Java programs with a modern user interface.

Some components in the **com.ms.ui** package are more sophisticated than others. For example, although it takes only a couple of code lines to add a status bar to an applet, it may take dozens of lines to create the tree view display you need. Still, creating these advanced components is a snap compared with the effort required to roll your own. After you get started with AFC's components, you'll thank Microsoft for doing most of the work.

Before you dig deeper into **com.ms.ui**, why don't you look at how a couple of the components work? You can easily add a status bar to an AFC applet with only two lines of code. To prove this claim, Listing 1.5 shows the source code for a simple AFC applet that displays a basic status bar.

**Listing 1.5   The source code for a simple AFC applet with a status bar.**

```
/////////////////////////////////////////////////
// StatusApplet.java
//
// An AFC applet that displays a status bar.
/////////////////////////////////////////////////

import com.ms.ui.*;

public class StatusApplet extends AwtUIApplet
{
    public StatusApplet()
    {
        super(new AppletImplementation());
    }
}

class AppletImplementation extends UIApplet
{
    public void init()
    {
```

```
        UIBorderLayout layout = new UIBorderLayout();
        setLayout(layout);
        UIStatus status = new UIStatus("An AFC Status Bar!");
        add(status, "South");
        setValid(true);
    }
}
```

Notice that the applet in Listing 1.5 extends the AFC **AwtUIApplet** class (which itself extends the Java **Applet** class). The applet must extend **AwtUIApplet** because Java's **Applet** class does not, for obvious reasons, know how to add AFC components to the applet's display. The **AwtUIApplet** class provides the link between old-fashioned Java applets and those that can take advantage of AFC's custom components. The **com.ms.ui** package also features the **UIFrame** class, which enables you to create standalone applications that can contain AFC components. You could say that **UIFrame** is **AwtUIApplet**'s counterpart.

In Listing 1.5, the **StatusApplet** class, which extends **AwtUIApplet**, acts as a bridge between AFC and Java's AWT. This class has only a constructor that passes the program's applet class on to the **AwtUIApplet** superclass (also known as a base class). Listing 1.5 implements the actual applet in the **AppletImplementation** class, which extends AFC's **UIApplet**. This is where all the applet code in an AFC applet lives, so it's here that the applet creates its status bar in only two lines of code.

Also in Listing 1.5, notice that the applet's layout manager is an AFC **UIBorderLayout** object. The **com.ms.ui** package features many layout managers, some of which are enhanced versions of standard Java layout managers (like **UIBorderLayout** is an enhanced version of Java's **BorderLayout** class) and others, like **UIBarLayout**, that work in conjunction with AFC's custom components.

Figure 1.5 shows the applet running under Microsoft Applet Viewer. (Keep in mind that you're seeing a basic status bar. You can do a lot to beef up the program, as you discover in later chapters.)

A handy object for organizing data is the **UITree** component, which is also easy to get up on the screen in its basic form. Listing 1.6 shows the source code for an applet that displays a basic tree component. Although the tree that's created in the applet is mundane, you can, with a little extra effort, add graphics and other components to produce a more professional look. The thing to notice here is how easy it is to create and display a tree component.

## Figure 1.5

*An AFC applet with a basic status bar.*

### Listing 1.6   An applet that displays a tree component.

```
///////////////////////////////////////////////
// TreeApplet.java
//
// An AFC applet that displays a tree component.
///////////////////////////////////////////////

import com.ms.ui.*;

public class TreeApplet extends AwtUIApplet
{
    public TreeApplet()
    {
        super(new AppletImplementation());
    }
}

class AppletImplementation extends UIApplet
{
    public void init()
    {
        UIBorderLayout layout = new UIBorderLayout();
        setLayout(layout);
        UITree tree = new UITree("A Sample Tree");
        tree.add("Child Entry 1");
        tree.add("Child Entry 2");
        tree.add("Child Entry 3");
        tree.add("Child Entry 4");
```

```
        add(tree, "Center");
        setValid(true);
    }
}
```

Figure 1.6 shows the applet running under Applet Viewer. When the applet first appears, you can see only the root tree item, which has the text string "A Sample Tree". If you double-click the root item, the child items appear, as shown in the figure. You can collapse the tree—and so hide the child items—by double-clicking the root item again.

I could go on for pages, demonstrating the many components included in the **com.ms.ui** package, but now you should have a general idea of how easily you can add these components to your applets. As I mentioned previously, the components you've seen so far are in their basic forms. With a little extra work, you can create sophisticated displays that rival those created with other languages, such as C++. The many upcoming examples in this book show how to create such sophisticated displays. For now, look over Table 1.2, which lists the main classes included in the **com.ms.ui** package. Note that many of the classes listed are support classes for other classes. That is, you probably won't have occasion to use all the **com.ms.ui** classes directly. If you want to see how fancy some of these components can get, look at Figure 1.7.

Table 1.2 lists only about half the classes in the **com.ms.ui** package. The package also includes a set of "compatibility" classes that support the use of AFC components as

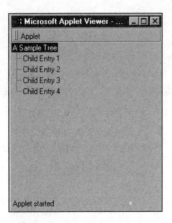

**Figure 1.6**

*TreeApplet displaying a simple tree component.*

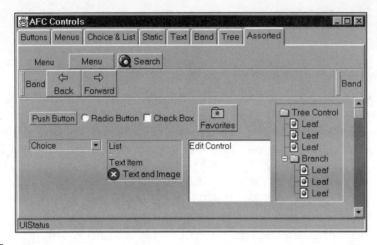

**Figure 1.7**

*AFC components on display.*

**Table 1.2   Main classes in the AFC com.ms.ui package.**

| Class | Description |
|---|---|
| **UIApplet** | Represents an AFC applet |
| **UIAwtHost** | Enables AWT components to be used in an AFC program |
| **UIBand** | Represents a movable band of buttons |
| **UIBandBox** | Represents a band box component |
| **UIBandThumb** | Represents a thumb control for a band |
| **UIBarLayout** | Represents a bar layout manager |
| **UIBorderLayout** | Enhances the Java **BorderLayout** layout manager |
| **UIButton** | Represents a base button component |
| **UIButtonBar** | Represents a container for **UIPushButton** objects |
| **UICanvas** | Represents a canvas component |
| **UICardLayout** | Enhances the Java **CardLayout** layout manager |
| **UICheckButton** | Represents a checkbox component |

*(continued)*

**Table 1.2   Main classes in the AFC com.ms.ui package (continued).**

| Class | Description |
|---|---|
| UICheckGroup | Represents a group component for checkboxes |
| UIChoice | Represents a combo box component |
| UIColorDialog | Represents a dialog box for selecting colors |
| UIColumnHeader | Manipulates column headers |
| UIColumnViewer | Represents a column-viewer component |
| UIComponent | Represents a stateless component |
| UIContainer | Represents a stateless container |
| UIContextMenu | Represents a context menu |
| UIDialog | Represents a dialog box |
| UIDialogMapping | Maps pixels to dialog logical units |
| UIDrawText | Manipulates and displays read-only text |
| UIEdit | Represents an edit component |
| UIEditChoice | Represents a combo box |
| UIExpandButton | Represents a tree component's expand button |
| UIFindReplaceDialog | Represents a find/replace dialog box |
| UIFixedFlowLayout | Represents a **FlowLayout** manager with a set width |
| UIFlowLayout | Enhances the Java **FlowLayout** layout manager |
| UIFontDialog | Represents a dialog box for selecting fonts |
| UIFrame | Represents a frame window |
| UIGraphic | Represents a static graphic component |
| UIGridBagConstraints | Holds layout values for the **UIGridBagLayout** class |
| UIGridBagLayout | Enhances the Java **GridBagLayout** class |

*(continued)*

**Table 1.2  Main classes in the AFC com.ms.ui package *(continued)*.**

| Class | Description |
|---|---|
| **UIGridLayout** | Enhances the Java **GridLayout** class |
| **UIGroup** | Represents a group box component |
| **UIHeaderRow** | Represents a row header |
| **UIItem** | Represents a static item component |
| **UILayoutManager** | Represents a base layout manager |
| **UILine** | Represents a line |
| **UIList** | Represents a list component |
| **UIMarquee** | Represents a marquee component |
| **UIMenuButton** | Represents a menu button component |
| **UIMenuItem** | Represents a menu item component |
| **UIMenuLauncher** | Represents a base menu launcher component |
| **UIMenuList** | Represents a menu list component |
| **UIMessageBox** | Represents a message box window |
| **UIPanel** | Represents a container that can hold multiple components |
| **UIProgress** | Represents a progress bar component |
| **UIPropertyDialog** | Represents a property sheet window |
| **UIPropertyPage** | Represents a base property page object |
| **UIPushButton** | Represents a push button component |
| **UIRadioButton** | Represents a radio button component |
| **UIRadioGroup** | Represents a group box for radio buttons |
| **UIRepeatButton** | Represents a repeating push button component |
| **UIRoot** | Links Java's AWT classes to AFC |

*(continued)*

**Table 1.2  Main classes in the AFC com.ms.ui package _(continued)_.**

| Class | Description |
|---|---|
| **UIRow** | Represents a row component |
| **UIRowLayout** | Represents a row layout manager |
| **UIScroll** | Represents a scroller track component |
| **UIScrollBar** | Represents a scroll bar component |
| **UIScrollThumb** | Represents a scroller thumb component |
| **UIScrollViewer** | Represents a scroll viewer component |
| **UISelector** | Represents a base selector component |
| **UISingleContainer** | Represents a single-header-component container |
| **UISlider** | Represents a slider component |
| **UISpinner** | Represents a spinner component |
| **UISpinnerEdit** | Represents a spin box component with an edit box |
| **UISplitLayout** | Represents a split-viewer-component layout manager |
| **UISplitViewer** | Represents a split viewer component |
| **UIStateComponent** | Represents a component with states |
| **UIStateContainer** | Represents a container with states |
| **UIStatic** | Represents a base static component |
| **UIStatus** | Represents a status bar component |
| **UITab** | Represents a tab component |
| **UITabLayout** | Represents a layout manager for tabbed pages |
| **UITabList** | Manipulates a set of tabs |
| **UITabListLayout** | Represents a layout manager for tab components |
| **UITabViewer** | Represents a tab viewer component |

_(continued)_

**Table 1.2   Main classes in the AFC com.ms.ui package (continued).**

| Class | Description |
|---|---|
| **UIText** | Represents a static text component |
| **UIThreePanelLayout** | Represents a three-panel layout manager |
| **UIThumb** | Represents a thumb component |
| **UITree** | Represents a tree component |
| **UITreeLayout** | Represents a tree-node layout manager |
| **UIVerticalFlowLayout** | Represents a vertical flow layout manager |
| **UIViewer** | Represents a viewer component |
| **UIWindow** | Implements a top-level window |
| **UIWinEvent** | Implements a way for objects to receive window event notifications |
| **UIWizardStep** | Represents a page in a wizard |

JavaBeans in Java applications. These compatibility component classes have the same names as the classes shown in Table 1.2, except with the prefix **Awt**. For example, the AWT compatibility class for **UIChoice** is **AwtUIChoice**.

**AwtUIApplet** and **UIFrame** are two other classes in **com.ms.ui** that are not listed in Table 1.2. As you learned previously in this chapter, you use **AwtUIApplet** to create applets that incorporate AFC components. Similarly, you use **UIFrame** to create standalone applications that incorporate AFC components.

# The com.ms.ui.event Package

When Java was first released, it used the propagation event model (Java 1.0 event model), which broadcasts event messages throughout a class's hierarchy. When you use the event propagation model, you often wrote an **action()** method to capture user actions. If **action()** didn't meet your needs, you could override the **handleEvent()** method, through which all events were processed. Listing 1.7 shows the source code for a simple applet that responds to a single button component using the propagation event model. If you've done any Java programming, you should be familiar with this event model.

**Listing 1.7  The source code for ButtonApplet.**

```java
//////////////////////////////////////////////////
// ButtonApplet.java
//
// An applet that demonstrates the propagation
// event model.
//////////////////////////////////////////////////

import java.awt.*;
import java.applet.*;

public class ButtonApplet extends Applet
{
    private Button button;
    String displayString;

    public void init()
    {
        button = new Button("Test Button");
        add(button);
        displayString = "";
    }

    public void paint(Graphics g)
    {
        g.drawString(displayString, 20, 100);
    }

    public boolean action(Event event, Object object)
    {
        if (object == "Test Button")
        {
            displayString = "Button clicked!";
            repaint();
            return true;
        }
        return false;
    }
}
```

When Sun Microsystems developed Java 1.1, it came up with a more flexible event model, one that enabled any class to receive messages from an event source like a button. To implement the new delegation event model (Java 1.1 event model), a class that wants to receive events (the *listener* class) registers with the event source. Then, when the event occurs, the event source broadcasts the event to all registered listener classes.

Many Java programmers are not yet familiar with the delegation event model and still use the propagation model. This is rarely a problem because Java fully supports both event models. Sun, however, strongly advises programmers to learn and use the new model, because it's the event model that makes JavaBeans possible. Listing 1.8 shows the source code for a version of ButtonApplet (Listing 1.7) that implements the delegation event model. ButtonApplet2 looks and acts exactly like its predecessor, ButtonApplet, except that it uses the new event model.

### Listing 1.8   The source code for ButtonApplet2.

```
import java.awt.*;
import java.awt.event.*;
import java.applet.*;

public class ButtonApplet2 extends Applet
    implements ActionListener
{
    private Button button;
    String displayString;

    public void init()
    {
        button = new Button("Test Button");
        button.addActionListener(this);
        add(button);
        displayString = "";
    }

    public void paint(Graphics g)
    {
        g.drawString(displayString, 20, 100);
    }

    public void actionPerformed(ActionEvent event)
    {
        String arg = event.getActionCommand();
        if (arg == "Test Button")
        {
            displayString = "Button clicked!";
            repaint();
        }
    }
}
```

Why all this talk of Java event models? AFC supports both the propagation and delegation event models. To use the propagation model, you just write your applets as you always have. AFC, however, features a group of new classes that provides support for Java's delegation event model. You can find these classes in the **com.ms.ui.event** package, which also defines the interfaces that listener classes must implement.

The **com.ms.ui.event** package also features a set of abstract classes for developing *event adapters*. Event adapters are described in the JavaBeans API Specification. Simply put, an event adapter is a method that sits between an event source and an event listener. The adapter receives events from the source, processes them in some way, and then passes the events on to the listener. A programmer might use an event adapter to add behaviors to an event, filter out events that shouldn't be passed to listeners, or any number of other reasons.

Table 1.3 lists the classes and interfaces—along with their descriptions—in the **com.ms.ui.event** package. If you've used the delegation event model, you're already familiar with the Java versions of the classes and interfaces listed in the table. If not, you can look forward to Chapter 15.

**Table 1.3   Classes in the AFC com.ms.ui.event package.**

| Class | Description |
| --- | --- |
| IUIActionListener | An AFC version of Java's **ActionListener** interface |
| IUIAdjustmentListener | An AFC version of Java's **AdjustmentListener** interface |
| IUIBaseEventListener | A base event interface |
| IUIComponentListener | An AFC version of Java's **ComponentListener** interface |
| IUIContainerListener | An AFC version of Java's **ContainerListener** interface |
| IUIFocusListener | An AFC version of Java's **FocusListener** interface |
| IUIItemListener | An AFC version of Java's **ItemListener** interface |
| IUIKeyListener | An AFC version of Java's **KeyListener** interface |
| IUIMouseListener | An AFC version of Java's **MouseListener** interface |
| IUIMouseMotionListener | An AFC version of Java's **MouseMotionListener** interface |
| IUITextListener | An AFC version of Java's **TextListener** interface |
| UIActionAdapter | An adapter class for action events |
| UIActionEvent | An AFC version of Java's **ActionEvent** class |

*(continued)*

**Table 1.3   Classes in the AFC com.ms.ui.event package _(continued)_.**

| Class | Description |
| --- | --- |
| **UIAdjustmentAdapter** | An adapter class for adjustment events |
| **UIAdjustmentEvent** | An AFC version of Java's **AdjustmentEvent** class |
| **UIBaseEvent** | An event base class |
| **UIContainerAdapter** | An adapter class for container events |
| **UIContainerEvent** | An AFC version of Java's **ContainerEvent** class |
| **UIEvent** | An event base class |
| **UIFocusAdapter** | An adapter class for focus events |
| **UIFocusEvent** | An AFC version of Java's **FocusEvent** class |
| **UIInputEvent** | An AFC version of Java's **InputEvent** class |
| **UIItemAdapter** | An adapter class for item events |
| **UIItemEvent** | An AFC version of Java's **ItemEvent** class |
| **UIKeyAdapter** | An adapter class for key events |
| **UIKeyEvent** | An AFC version of Java's **KeyEvent** class |
| **UIMouseAdapter** | An adapter class for mouse events |
| **UIMouseEvent** | An AFC version of Java's **MouseEvent** class |
| **UITextAdapter** | An adapter class for text events |
| **UITextEvent** | An AFC version of Java's **TextEvent** class |
| **UIWindowEvent** | A class that represents window events |

# The **com.ms.ui.resource** Package

As if you didn't know, Microsoft's current major entry into the OS race (this is a race?) is Windows 95. It shouldn't surprise anyone, then, that Microsoft not only modeled AFC's components on Windows 95 controls, but also that Microsoft provided support for other Windows-centric concepts. One of these concepts is the resource file, which holds information about an application's menus, dialog boxes, controls, and other objects. With all the resource files that must be floating around on Microsoft programmers' hard disks, it's only logical that the AFC programmers would come up with Java classes that enable Java applications and applets to access Windows resource files. So logical, in fact, that this is exactly what Microsoft's programmers did. You can find the results of this choice in the **com.ms.ui.resource** package. Table 1.4 lists the classes included in the **com.ms.ui.resource** package.

## The **com.ms.util.cab** Package

Often, components and other objects created with Microsoft development tools are distributed in a special compressed file format called a cabinet (CAB) file. The **com.ms.util.cab** package features classes that enable Java programs to read and write CAB files. There's not a heck of a lot to say about these classes. Take a glance at Table 1.5, which lists all the classes in the **com.ms.util.cab** package.

## Summary

And there you have it: a quick look at all the wonderful things in AFC—and I do mean a quick look! There's much more to cover, so don't nod off. In the rest of this book, you learn to incorporate AFC into your programming projects to produce the kind of professional applets and applications that'll make your programming buddies turn green with envy. First, however, you need to know how to get started with AFC.

**Table 1.4   Classes in the AFC com.ms.ui.resource package.**

| Class | Description |
| --- | --- |
| DataBoundInputStream | Reads Java data types |
| ResourceDecoder | Reads resource files |
| ResourceFormattingException | Reports resource read errors |
| UIDialogLayout | Supports dialog logical units in a layout manager |
| Win32ResourceDecoder | Supports Win32 resource files |

**Table 1.5  Classes in the AFC com.ms.util.cab package.**

| Class | Description |
|---|---|
| CabCorruptException | Signals a corrupted CAB file |
| CabCreator | Creates a CAB file |
| CabDecoder | Decodes a CAB file |
| CabEnumerator | Accesses items in a CAB file |
| CabException | Signals miscellaneous CAB errors |
| CabFileEntry | Represents a CAB file entry |
| CabFolderEntry | Represents a CAB folder entry |

# Practical Guide To

# Setting Up AFC

- Getting Your Copy Of AFC
- Installing AFC
- Compiling And Running An AFC Program

As you've seen, AFC provides many ways to get the most out of Java. Before you can take advantage of AFC's extras, you need to get a copy of the library. AFC is currently available on Microsoft's Java Web pages, free for the downloading. In the following sections, you learn exactly where to get your copy of AFC and how to get it up and running on your system.

## Getting Your Copy Of AFC

You can download the AFC library by itself, or, if you're programming under Windows 95, you can download the entire Microsoft SDK for Java 2.0, which includes AFC. Because Microsoft SDK for Java includes a complete suite of development tools, you might want to download the entire package, which you can find at www.microsoft.com/java. The programs and examples in this book were developed with Microsoft SDK for Java 2.0.

## Installing AFC

To install AFC and the core Microsoft Java SDK 2.0, hop onto Microsoft's Web site and download at least the Microsoft Java SDK 2.0 (which includes AFC), the Microsoft virtual machine for Java, and the SDK documentation. When you've retrieved these executable files, run the file containing the SDK first, which installs the SDK on your computer. Then install the virtual machine and the documentation.

## Compiling And Running An AFC Program

With the SDK installed, you're ready to write and run your first AFC program. If you chose the default selections during the installation procedure, you have a directory called SDK-Java.20 on your hard drive. Your copy of AFC lives here. All the Microsoft SDK for Java 2.0 development tools also resides here, in the bin directory. The first step, then, is to add the SDK-Java.20\bin directory to your path. You can do this easily by running SYSEDIT.EXE (found in your Windows\System directory) and adding the SDK path to your AUTOEXEC.BAT file. Remember to reboot your system so that the new path takes effect.

After adding the SDK tools to your path, you're ready to compile and run your first AFC applet, named appropriately enough, FirstAFCApplet. Listing 1.9 shows the applet's complete source code. Type the listing (or copy it from this book's CD-ROM), and save it to the directory into which you'll save the other projects from this book. Then, bring up a DOS window, change to the applet's directory, and compile the applet with this command:

```
jvc FirstAFCApplet.java
```

The jvc application is the SDK's Java compiler. If all goes well, after compilation, the files FirstAFCApplet.class and MyCanvas.class appear in your applet's directory. Copy FirstAFCApplet.html from this book's CD-ROM to the applet's directory. Load FirstAFCApplet.html into your Web browser, and the applet shown in Figure 1.8 should appear. FirstAFCApplet may not be fancy, but it proves your AFC installation is ready to go.

### Listing 1.9 Source code for FirstAFCApplet.

```
/////////////////////////////////////////////////
// FirstAFCApplet.java
//
// A basic AFC applet.
/////////////////////////////////////////////////

import java.awt.*;
import com.ms.ui.*;
import com.ms.fx.*;

public class FirstAFCApplet extends AwtUIApplet
{
    public FirstAFCApplet()
    {
        super(new AppletImplementation());
    }
}

class AppletImplementation extends UIApplet
{
    public void init()
    {
        UIBorderLayout layout = new UIBorderLayout();
        setLayout(layout);
        setValid(true);
    }

    public void paint(FxGraphics graphics)
    {
        graphics.drawString("Hello from AFC!", 20, 20);
    }
}
```

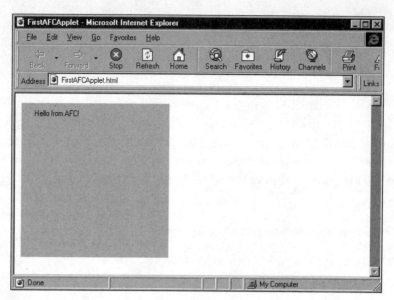

**Figure 1.8**

*FirstAFCApplet running in Applet Viewer.*

# Applets And Applications

> An empty house is like
> a stray dog or a body from
> which life has departed.
> —Samuel Butler,
> The Way of All Flesh

# Notes...

# Chapter 2

One day, I was driving down the highway, making my way to the local mall, when traffic slowed to a crawl. As I approached the bottleneck, I saw cars in the right-hand lane trying to get around what turned out to be one half of a house on a flatbed truck. Yep, half a house on a flatbed truck. The other half of the house sat on a second truck, just in front of the first. When I managed to stop cursing about the holdup, it occurred to me what an amazing thing it was to build a house and then, after it's finished, to decide where to put it.

As all Java programmers know, Java programs come in two varieties: applets and applications. An applet is a lot like the house on the flatbed trucks. It can't stand alone, but you can put it wherever there's a suitable foundation. An application, on the other hand, is more like a conventional house. It's built upon the foundation with which it'll be joined for all its lifetime. Both types of Java programs have their advantages and disadvantages. However, if you judged by the applet's popularity, it would seem that Java programmers like to keep their traveling options open.

When programming under straight vanilla Java, an applet is represented by the **Applet** class, which enables you to create a mini-application that you can place on Web pages or inside a Java frame widow. In the case of an applet, the Web page or frame window is the foundation that supports the applet. A standalone application, on the other hand, is represented by the **Frame** class, which enables you to create a window that can be displayed on the user's desktop. Although a frame window can act as the

33

foundation for an applet, you can't place a frame window into a Web page or other container. A frame window comes with its own foundation.

AFC fully supports the applet/application design philosophy, but it does so with panache. AFC takes the Java **Applet** and **Frame** classes and expands on them to create custom classes for creating super applets and standalone applications. The **AwtUIApplet** class is derived directly from its Java cousin, so inherits all the functionality of the Java **Applet** class. **AwtUIApplet**, however, adds extra capabilities to its superclass, not the least of which is the capability to host AFC components.

On the other hand, although AFC's **UIFrame** provides the same type of user-interface element that Java's **Frame** class does (a frame window for standalone applications), **UIFrame** has no connection with Java's AWT. **UIFrame**'s long ancestry extends up through AFC superclasses, from **UIWindow** to **UIRoot** to **UIPanel** and so on, all the way back to **UIComponent**. Still, this AFC ancestry notwithstanding, you can think of **UIFrame** as an enhanced version of Java's **Frame** class.

AFC applets and applications are a little more complicated than Java applets and applications, because both **AwtUIApplet** and **UIFrame** rely on two other classes to display and manage their user interfaces. These two other classes are **AwtUIHost** and **UIRoot**. Every applet and application creates objects of the **AwtUIHost** and **UIRoot** classes. The **AwtUIHost** object is associated with the applet or application. Similarly, the **AwtUIHost** object contains the **UIRoot** object, which itself can contain AFC components.

The **AwtUIApplet** class, along with its **AwtUIHost** and **UIRoot** objects, acts as a bridge between AWT and AFC. (In case you've forgotten, AWT is Java's standard library of graphical classes.) For this reason, **AwtUIApplet** is often referred to as a *bridge class*. You don't place much of your program's code in this class. Instead, you do little more in **AwtUIApplet** than create an object of the applet's implementation class.

This brings you to the **UIApplet** class. In an AFC program, the **UIApplet** class represents the applet's implementation. That is, nearly all of the applet's code appears in the implementation class, an object of which gets created in the class you extend from **AwtUIApplet**.

The only snag in the proceedings is when you implement scriptable methods, such as **getAppletInfo()** and **getParameterInfo()**. Because these methods must be exposed to objects outside of the applet, you must provide "pass-through" methods in your **AwtUIApplet**-derived class. These methods respond to calls from the object hosting the applet by passing the requests on to the applet's implementation.

Because **AwtUIHost** extends Java's **Panel** class, it can work closely with AWT to enable communications between AWT and AFC components. **UIRoot**, on the other hand, extends **UIPanel**—which has no Java classes in its ancestry. **UIRoot** depends upon **AwtUIHost** to keep it posted on what's happening in the AWT. **AwtUIHost** receives events from AWT and dispatches them as appropriate to the **UIRoot** container. Together, **AwtUIApplet**, **AwtUIHost**, and **UIRoot** make up the connection between AFC and Java's AWT in an AFC applet.

The good news: You don't need to be concerned with the applet's host or root objects, which are handled internally by AFC. You never access the host or root objects directly, nor do you ever create these objects explicitly in your AFC programs. Still, it's always nice to know what's going on behind your back, right?

# The **AwtUIApplet** Class

As I stated previously, the **AwtUIApplet** class extends Java's **Applet** class and so inherits a lot of functionality from **Applet**. Because **AwtUIApplet** extends **Applet**, it can do nearly anything an **Applet** object can do (but rarely needs to). However, in addition to the methods **AwtUIApplet** inherits from **Applet**, the class also adds a couple of its own. The **getRoot()** method returns the applet's root object, whereas the **getUIApplet()** method returns the applet's implementation object.

You will probably never need to call **getRoot()**. You do, however, need to call **getUIApplet()** now and then. For example, if a script calls a scriptable method in your **AwtUIApplet** class (such as **getAppletInfo()**), you must pass that request on to the applet's implementation class. You call **getUIApplet()** to obtain a reference to the implementation class.

# The **UIApplet** Class

As you now know, the **UIApplet** class represents an AFC applet's implementation. That is, you extend **UIApplet** in your program to create your applet. The **AwtUIApplet** bridge class creates an object of this implementation class and acts as a bridge between the applet's implementation and AWT. (Guess that's why they call **AwtUIApplet** a bridge class, eh?)

All the data fields and methods that make up your applet should be defined in your **UIApplet** class. This rule includes scriptable methods, even though scripts can call only methods defined in the **AwtUIApplet** object. The **AwtUIApplet** object must pass these calls on to the **UIApplet** object.

**UIApplet** has no direct connection to Java's AWT. Instead, it relies upon the bridge class—extended from **AwtUIApplet**—to keep things rolling. **UIApplet** has no direct connection with AWT because it has only AFC classes in its ancestry, its immediate superclass being **UIPanel**. The **UIApplet** class inherits many methods from its super-classes, but it also defines its own methods.

Table 2.1 lists **UIApplet**'s methods and their descriptions.

**Table 2.1   Methods of the UIApplet class.**

| Method | Description |
|---|---|
| destroy() | Called by a browser when the applet is to be destroyed |
| getApplet() | Gets a reference to the underlying AWT applet |
| getAppletContext() | Gets a reference to the applet's container, usually a browser |
| getAppletInfo() | Called by an applet's container to get information about the applet |
| getAudioClip() | Gets a reference to an audio clip |
| getCodeBase() | Gets the URL from which the applet was loaded |
| getDocumentBase() | Gets the URL from which the applet's container was loaded |
| getImage() | Loads an image from the given URL |
| getParameter() | Gets a parameter value from the applet's HTML tag |
| getParameterInfo() | Called by an applet's container to get information about the applet's parameters |
| init() | Called when the applet first loads |
| isActive() | Returns **true** if the applet is active |
| play() | Plays an audio clip |
| setStub() | Sets the applet's stub |
| showStatus() | Displays text in the status window |
| start() | Called by a browser when the applet should begin execution |
| stop() | Called by a browser when the applet should stop executing |

Listing 2.1 shows the source code for an AFC applet that displays three buttons. This listing illustrates how to implement the applet's bridge and implementation objects. Notice how the bridge class (**CompApplet**, which extends **AwtUIApplet**) only creates an object of the implementation class and passes that object on to the **AwtUIApplet** superclass. Figure 2.1 shows the applet running in Microsoft Applet Viewer.

## Listing 2.1   An AFC applet.

```
//////////////////////////////////////////////////
// CompApplet.java
//
// An AFC applet that demonstrates how to create
// an applet's bridge and implementation objects.
//////////////////////////////////////////////////

import com.ms.ui.*;

public class CompApplet extends AwtUIApplet
{
    public CompApplet()
    {
        super(new AppletImplementation());
    }
}

class AppletImplementation extends UIApplet
{
    public void init()
    {
        UIBorderLayout layout = new UIBorderLayout();
        setLayout(layout);
        UIPushButton button1 =
            new UIPushButton(new UIText("AFC Button1"));
        add(button1, "North");
        UIPushButton button2 =
            new UIPushButton(new UIText("AFC Button2"));
        add(button2, "Center");
        UIPushButton button3 =
            new UIPushButton(new UIText("AFC Button3"));
        add(button3, "South");
        setValid(true);
    }
}
```

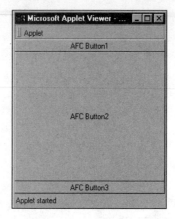

## Figure 2.1

*CompApp running in Applet Viewer.*

# The **UIFrame** Class

If you want to write an AFC standalone application, you must use **UIFrame** as the application's window. Just like **AwtUIApplet**, **UIFrame** replaces a Java class. In this case, the class is **Frame**. Because **UIFrame** replaces **Frame** as the frame window class, AFC's **UIFrame** defines or inherits many of the same methods as **Frame**. **UIFrame** inherits methods from its superclasses, which include **UIWindow**, **UIRoot**, **UIPanel**, **UIStateContainer**, **UIContainer**, and **UIComponent**. In other words, **UIFrame** can do nearly anything **Frame** can do. However, a **UIFrame** object can contain AFC components. Table 2.2 lists **UIFrame**'s methods and their descriptions.

The biggest difference between creating an applet and a standalone application is that you initialize an applet in the class's **init()** method, and you initialize a standalone application in its **main()** method. This difference is true for Java applets and applications, as well as for AFC applets and applications.

Listing 2.2 shows a standalone application version of the applet in Listing 2.1. Figure 2.2 shows the running application.

### Listing 2.2   The standalone application version of CompApplet.

```
//////////////////////////////////////////////////
// CompApp.java
//////////////////////////////////////////////////

import java.awt.*;
import com.ms.ui.*;
import com.ms.fx.*;
```

```
public class CompApp
{
    public static void main(String args[])
    {
        CompFrame frame = new CompFrame("Component App");
    }
}

class CompFrame extends UIFrame
{
    public CompFrame(String title)
    {
        super(title);

        UIBorderLayout layout = new UIBorderLayout();
        setLayout(layout);

        UIPushButton button1 =
            new UIPushButton(new UIText("AFC Button1"));
        add(button1, "North");

        UIPushButton button2 =
            new UIPushButton(new UIText("AFC Button2"));
        add(button2, "Center");

        UIPushButton button3 =
            new UIPushButton(new UIText("AFC Button3"));
        add(button3, "South");

        setSize(240, 240);
        setVisible(true);
        setValid(true);
    }

    public boolean handleEvent(Event event)
    {
        switch (event.id)
        {
            case Event.WINDOW_DESTROY:
                System.exit(0);
                return true;

            default:
                return super.handleEvent(event);
        }
    }
}
```

**Table 2.2  Methods of the UIFrame class.**

| Method | Description |
| --- | --- |
| forwardEvent() | Forwards events to the parent container |
| getFrame() | Gets a reference to the underlying AWT **Frame** object |
| getInsets() | Gets the window's margins |
| getMenuBar() | Gets a reference to the window's menu bar |
| getTitle() | Gets the window's title |
| layout() | Lays out the window and its components |
| setMenuBar() | Sets the window's menu bar |
| setName() | Sets the window's name |
| setResizable() | Toggles the window's resizable flag |
| setTitle() | Sets the window's title |

## The **AwtUIHost** Class

An AFC applet's or application's **AwtUIHost** object sits comfortably between the applet or application and the root container. Almost everything that comes to the applet or application from AWT gets filtered through the host object. **AwtUIHost** extends Java's **Panel** class, which means that **AwtUIHost** inherits all the functionality of a Java panel. However, **AwtUIHost** extends the class with its own methods. These methods make

**Figure 2.2**

*CompApp running under Windows 95.*

up the link between AFC and AWT, including the processing of incoming AWT events. Table 2.3 lists **AwtUIHost**'s methods and their descriptions.

**Table 2.3  Methods of the AwtUIHost class.**

| Method | Description |
| --- | --- |
| add() | Adds a component to the root container |
| addComponentListener() | Adds a listener for component events |
| addContainerListener() | Adds a listener for container events |
| addFocusListener() | Adds a listener for focus events |
| addKeyListener() | Adds a listener for key events |
| addMouseListener() | Adds a listener for mouse events |
| addMouseMotionListener() | Adds a listener for mouse motion events |
| addNotify() | Calls **addNotify()** for all components in the root container |
| disable() | Disables the host object |
| disableHostEvents() | Disables the given events |
| enable() | Enables the host object |
| enableHostEvents() | Enables the specified events |
| getComponent() | Returns a component in the root container |
| getComponentIndex() | Gets the index of a component in the root container |
| getHeader() | Returns the root container's header component |
| getPreferredSize() | Returns the root container's preferred size |
| getRoot() | Returns the host object's root container |
| getUIComponent() | Returns the component at the given index in the root container |
| getUIComponentCount() | Returns the number of components in the root container |
| handleEvent() | Dispatches incoming events |

(continued)

**Table 2.3  Methods of the AwtUIHost class (continued).**

| Method | Description |
|---|---|
| hide() | Hides the host object and its root container |
| invalidate() | Causes the root container to redraw itself and its components |
| layout() | Lays out the root container's components |
| paint() | Draws the host object's root container |
| paintAll() | Draws the host object's root container and all its components |
| postEvent() | Posts an event |
| preferredSize() | Returns the root container's preferred size |
| processComponentEvent() | Processes component events |
| processContainerEvent() | Processes container events |
| processComponentEvent() | Processes component events |
| processEvent() | Posts the given event |
| processFocusEvent() | Processes focus events |
| processHostEvent() | Converts **Event** objects to **AwtEvent** objects and posts the event |
| processKeyEvent() | Processes key events |
| processMouseEvent() | Processes mouse events |
| processMouseMotionEvent() | Processes mouse motion events |
| remove() | Removes a component from the root container |
| removeAll() | Removes all components from the root container |
| removeComponentListener() | Removes the given component listener |
| removeContainerListener() | Removes the given container listener |

(continued)

**Table 2.3  Methods of the AwtUIHost class (continued).**

| Method | Description |
|---|---|
| **removeFocusListener()** | Removes the given focus listener |
| **removeKeyListener()** | Removes the given key listener |
| **removeMouseListener()** | Removes the given mouse listener |
| **removeMouseMotionListener()** | Removes the given mouse motion listener |
| **removeNotify()** | Calls **removeNotify()** for all components in the root container |
| **setBackground()** | Sets the host object's background color |
| **setFont()** | Sets the host object's font |
| **setForeground()** | Sets the host object's foreground color |
| **setHeader()** | Sets the root container's header component |
| **setLayout()** | Sets the root container's layout manager |
| **show()** | Shows the host object and its root container |
| **update()** | Redraws the root container and all its components |
| **validate()** | Validates the host object and the root container |
| **validateTree()** | Validates the host objects, all the host object's descendants and the root container |

Because the **AwtUIHost** object is used internally by AFC, you shouldn't deal with it directly. In fact, the only way to get a reference to the host is to first get a reference to the root container and then get the host through the root's **getHost**() method. As with **AwtUIApplet**, many of the method calls you make on the host object result in equivalent calls to the root container. Listing 2.3 illustrates this chain of events. The HostApp application gets a reference to the host object and creates its user interface through host method calls. (Remember that this program is meant only to illustrate a concept and is not an example of good AFC programming.)

**Listing 2.3   Creating a user interface through the host object.**

```java
/////////////////////////////////////////////////
// HostApp.java
//
// An AFC standalone application that illustrates
// the connection between an applet or application
// and its root and host objects.
/////////////////////////////////////////////////

import java.awt.*;
import com.ms.ui.*;
import com.ms.fx.*;

public class HostApp
{
    public static void main(String args[])
    {
        CompFrame frame = new CompFrame("Host App");
        frame.setSize(240, 240);
        frame.setVisible(true);
    }
}

class CompFrame extends UIFrame
{
    public CompFrame(String title)
    {
        super(title);

        IUIRootContainer root = getRoot();
        AwtUIHost host = (AwtUIHost)root.getHost();

        UIBorderLayout layout = new UIBorderLayout();
        host.setLayout(layout);

        UIPushButton button1 =
            new UIPushButton(new UIText("AFC Button1"));
        host.add(button1, "North");

        UIPushButton button2 =
            new UIPushButton(new UIText("AFC Button2"));
        host.add(button2, "Center");

        UIPushButton button3 =
            new UIPushButton(new UIText("AFC Button3"));
        host.add(button3, "South");
```

```
        setValid(true);
    }

    public boolean handleEvent(Event event)
    {
        switch (event.id)
        {
            case Event.WINDOW_DESTROY:
                System.exit(0);
                return true;

            default:
                return super.handleEvent(event);
        }
    }
}
```

# The **UIRoot** Class

**UIRoot** has no direct connection to AWT, thanks to the fact that it extends AFC's
**UIPanel** class, which has no AWT ancestry. The root container is all AFC and couldn't
function if it weren't for its associated host object. The **UIRoot** methods that add
components to the root container are inherited from **UIPanel**, which **UIPanel** inherits from a rich set of base classes, from **UIStateContainer** to **UIContainer** and,
finally, to **UIComponent**. A complete list of **UIRoot** methods you can call is immense.
(You can learn more about **UIRoot**'s base classes in Chapter 12.

Because the **UIRoot** container is used internally by AFC, you won't deal with it directly. Usually, you make method calls in your applet class and let AFC route those
calls through the host object to the root container. Still, it can be handy to know
what goes on in each of the classes. You never know when you might need to dig a
little deeper.

# Practical Guide To

# Creating AFC Applets And Applications

- Creating A Basic AFC Applet
- Creating A Basic AFC Application
- Creating An AFC Applet That Also Runs As An Application
- Adding Components To An Applet Or Application
- Setting Background Colors For Applets And Components
- Setting Layout Managers
- Implementing Dynamic Controls
- Implementing Scriptable Methods

## Creating A Basic AFC Applet

Creating a basic AFC applet is much like creating a standard Java applet. The main difference is that—because you want to take advantage of other AFC classes—you must derive your applet's class from **AwtUIApplet** rather than from **Applet**. This establishes the bridge between Java's AWT and the applet's implementation, while enabling your applet to host AFC components. You define the applet's implementation in a class derived from **UIApplet**, as described previously in this chapter. Listing 2.4 shows a basic, do-nothing AFC applet.

### Listing 2.4   A basic AFC applet.

```
/////////////////////////////////////////////////
// AFCApplet.java
//
// The skeleton of an AFC applet.
/////////////////////////////////////////////////

import com.ms.ui.*;

public class AFCApplet extends AwtUIApplet
{
    public AFCApplet()
    {
        super(new AppletImplementation());
    }
}

class AppletImplementation extends UIApplet
{
    public void init()
    {
        // Initialize the applet and its components here.
    }

    public void start()
    {
        // Start code goes here.
    }

    public void stop()
    {
        // Stop code goes here.
    }
```

```
    public void destroy()
    {
        // Put cleanup code here.
    }
}
```

Although Listing 2.4 shows the applet's **init()**, **start()**, **stop()**, and **destroy()**, only **init()** is required. You may or may not need to supply the others, depending on how your applet works. You should already be familiar with these four methods, which represent an applet's life cycle. If not, use the following list as a quick refresher:

- **init()**—Called when the applet is first loaded. You should perform your applet's initialization here, including setting the layout manager and adding components. You can initialize the class's data fields in **init()** or in the class's constructor.

- **start()**—Called when the applet should start running. This call occurs when the applet becomes visible in the currently displayed Web page. The **start()** method is typically where the applet runs threads.

- **stop()**—Called when the applet should stop running. This call occurs when the user switches away from the Web page that displays the applet. The **stop()** method is typically where the applet suspends all running threads.

- **destroy()**—Called when the applet is about to be removed from memory. Use the **destroy()** to clean up after the applet. It's your last chance to do something before the applet goes away.

## Creating A Basic AFC Application

Creating an AFC application is a little more complicated than creating an applet; you must create a frame window to host the application's user interface. The process, however, is virtually identical to creating a Java application. The difference between a Java application and an AFC application is the class that the frame window extends. A Java application will extend the **Frame** class, whereas an AFC application will extend the **UIFrame** class. Listing 2.5 shows a basic AFC application.

### Listing 2.5   A basic AFC application.
```
/////////////////////////////////////////////////
// AFCApp.java
//
```

```
// The skeleton of an AFC standalone application.
///////////////////////////////////////////////

import java.awt.*;
import com.ms.ui.*;

public class AFCApp
{
    public static void main(String args[])
    {
        AFCFrame frame = new AFCFrame("AFC Application");
        frame.setSize(500, 350);
        frame.setVisible(true);
    }
}

class AFCFrame extends UIFrame
{
    public AFCFrame(String title)
    {
        super(title);

        // Add components here.

        setValid(true);
    }

    public boolean handleEvent(Event event)
    {
        switch (event.id)
        {
            case Event.WINDOW_DESTROY:
                System.exit(0);
                return true;

            default:
                return super.handleEvent(event);
        }
    }
}
```

As you can see from the listing, to gain control over the frame window, you must create your own frame window class extended from **UIFrame**. This action enables you to set up a message handler so the window can respond to the **WINDOW_ DESTROY** message. If you don't explicitly call **System.exit(0)** to close the application when the user clicks the window's close button or selects the system menu's

Close command, the window ignores the message. Your application's users won't be too thrilled about a window that they can't close!

The application's **main()** function, which is the entry point for the application, only creates an instance of the window class, and then sizes and displays the window. Everything else happens in the frame window class. You must be sure to size the window. Otherwise, your application's user will see only a tiny title bar on the screen, forcing him to resize the window manually. Also, if you don't call **setVisible()** to display the window, the window won't appear at all. Figure 2.3 shows the frame window created by Listing 2.5.

## Creating An AFC Applet That Also Runs As An Application

A handy Java trick that also works well with AFC is to create a program that runs both as an applet and an application. You accomplish this snappy bit of Java prestidigitation by providing a **main()** method, as well as the applet's **init()** method. When the program runs as an applet, **main()** is completely ignored, and **init()** gets things going. When the applet runs as an application, **main()** is the program's entry point. In **main()**, the program creates a frame window and adds the applet part of the program to the window. Listing 2.6 shows how this programming technique works.

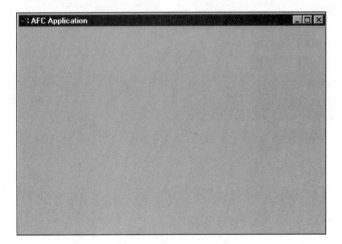

**Figure 2.3**

*AFCApp's frame window.*

**Listing 2.6   An AFC program that runs as either an applet or an application.**

```java
/////////////////////////////////////////////////
// AFCAppApplet.java
//
// An AFC program that can run as either an
// applet or an application.
/////////////////////////////////////////////////

import java.awt.*;
import com.ms.ui.*;

public class AFCAppApplet extends AwtUIApplet
{
    public AFCAppApplet()
    {
        super(new AppletImplementation());
    }

    // Entry point, when running as an application.
    public static void main(String args[])
    {
        AFCAppletFrame frame =
            new AFCAppletFrame("AFC Applet/Application");
        frame.setSize(240, 240);
        frame.setVisible(true);
    }
}

class AppletImplementation extends UIApplet
{
    // Entry point, when running as an applet.
    public void init()
    {
        UIPushButton button =
            new UIPushButton(new UIText("Test Button"));
        add(button);
    }
}

class AFCAppletFrame extends UIFrame
{
    public AFCAppletFrame(String title)
    {
        super(title);
        AppletImplementation applet =
            new AppletImplementation();
```

```
        applet.init();
        add(applet, "Center");
        setValid(true);
    }

    public boolean handleEvent(Event event)
    {
        switch (event.id)
        {
            case Event.WINDOW_DESTROY:
                System.exit(0);
                return true;

            default:
                return super.handleEvent(event);
        }
    }
}
```

Figure 2.4 shows AFCAppApplet running as an application, where the frame window displays the applet. The frame window class, **AFCAppletFrame**, creates the applet object and places it in the center position of its layout manager. Figure 2.5 shows AFCAppApplet running in Applet Viewer, as a normal applet. In this case, both the frame window class and the **main()** method are ignored and have no effect on the applet.

## Adding Components To An Applet Or Application

If you've written other Java applets, you've no doubt added your share of components to an applet's user interface. Adding components to an AFC applet or

**Figure 2.4**

*The AFCAppApplet, running as an application.*

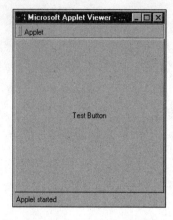

**Figure 2.5**

*The AFCAppApplet, running as an applet.*

application works in much the same way. You shouldn't, however, attempt to mix AWT components with AFC components. Many AFC containers require AFC components anyway, and they don't even have **add()** methods for standard AWT components.

Although you can add components directly to the applet's root container, it's often more elegant to create a control set by adding components to a panel and then adding the panel to the applet. In this way, you can come up with some great layouts because each container can have its own layout manager. Listing 2.7, for example, creates a panel containing three buttons organized in a grid layout manager. The program places this control set in the north position of the root container's border layout. The buttons control the color of the canvas that the program places in the center position of the applet's border layout.

**Listing 2.7   An applet that uses a control set to organize buttons.**

```
/////////////////////////////////////////////////
// ButtonApplet.java
//
// An AFC applet that demonstrates how to create
// a set of components on a panel.
/////////////////////////////////////////////////

import com.ms.ui.*;
import com.ms.fx.*;
import java.awt.*;

public class ButtonApplet extends AwtUIApplet
{
```

```
    public ButtonApplet()
    {
        super(new AppletImplementation());
    }
}

class AppletImplementation extends UIApplet
{
    public void init()
    {
        UIBorderLayout layout = new UIBorderLayout();
        setLayout(layout);
        DrawingCanvas canvas = new DrawingCanvas();
        ButtonPanel panel = new ButtonPanel(canvas);
        add(panel, "North");
        add(canvas, "Center");
        setValid(true);
    }
}

class DrawingCanvas extends UICanvas
{
    public DrawingCanvas()
    {
        setBackground(FxColor.red);
    }

    public void paint(FxGraphics graphics)
    {
        graphics.setColor(FxColor.white);
        graphics.drawString("An AFC Canvas", 85, 100);
        graphics.drawRect(70, 80, 102, 32);
    }
}

class ButtonPanel extends UIPanel
{
    private DrawingCanvas canvas;
    private UIPushButton redButton;
    private UIPushButton greenButton;
    private UIPushButton blueButton;

    public ButtonPanel(DrawingCanvas canvas)
    {
        UIGridLayout layout = new UIGridLayout(1, 3);
        setLayout(layout);
        this.canvas = canvas;
```

```
        redButton = new UIPushButton(new UIText("Red"));
        add(redButton);
        greenButton = new UIPushButton(new UIText("Green"));
        add(greenButton);
        blueButton = new UIPushButton(new UIText("Blue"));
        add(blueButton);
    }

    public boolean action(Event event, Object obj)
    {
        if (event.target == redButton)
        {
            canvas.setBackground(FxColor.red);
            canvas.repaint();
            return true;
        }
        else if (event.target == greenButton)
        {
            canvas.setBackground(FxColor.green);
            canvas.repaint();
            return true;
        }
        else if (event.target == blueButton)
        {
            canvas.setBackground(FxColor.blue);
            canvas.repaint();
            return true;
        }
        return false;
    }
}
```

Figure 2.6 shows the running applet. When you click one of the color buttons at the top of the display, the canvas's color changes. Notice in the listing how the button panel's constructor receives a reference to the canvas as a parameter. This reference gives the class access to the canvas object, so that the panel's event handler can call the canvas object's methods.

## Setting Background Colors For Applets And Components

In the preceding section, you saw how to change the background color of a canvas component. What you didn't see there was that, when you set the background color of a container, the color of the container's components are set to match. This component color change may not be what you want. For example, while you might want

**Figure 2.6**

*ButtonApplet running in Applet Viewer.*

a panel to have a blue background, you may want the buttons on the panel to remain light gray. Luckily, the solution is easy. Just call the **setBackground()** methods for both the components and the container.

Listing 2.8 shows an applet that places two light-gray buttons on a dark-gray panel. To set up this color scheme, the applet calls the **setBackground()** method for the panel and for both buttons. Figure 2.7 shows the resulting display. If the applet doesn't set the buttons' background color, the buttons take on the color of the panel, as shown in Figure 2.8.

**Figure 2.7**

*ColorApplet running in Applet Viewer.*

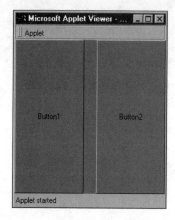

**Figure 2.8**

*ColorApplet without setting the button colors.*

**Listing 2.8   An applet that sets up a panel and button color scheme.**

```java
/////////////////////////////////////////////////
// ColorApplet.java
//
// An applet that demonstrates setting background
// colors.
/////////////////////////////////////////////////

import com.ms.ui.*;
import com.ms.fx.*;

public class ColorApplet extends AwtUIApplet
{
    public ColorApplet()
    {
        super(new AppletImplementation());
    }
}

class AppletImplementation extends UIApplet
{
    public void init()
    {
        UIBorderLayout layout = new UIBorderLayout();
        setLayout(layout);

        ColorPanel panel = new ColorPanel();
        add(panel, "Center");
```

```
            setValid(true);
        }
}

class ColorPanel extends UIPanel
{
        private UIPushButton panelButton1;
        private UIPushButton panelButton2;

        public ColorPanel()
        {
            UIGridLayout layout = new UIGridLayout(1, 2, 20, 20);
            setLayout(layout);

            panelButton1 = new UIPushButton(new UIText("Button1"));
            add(panelButton1);

            panelButton2 = new UIPushButton(new UIText("Button2"));
            add(panelButton2);

            setBackground(FxColor.gray);
            panelButton1.setBackground(FxColor.lightGray);
            panelButton2.setBackground(FxColor.lightGray);
        }
}
```

## Setting Layout Managers

Dealing with layout managers is an important part of programming Java and AFC applications. Layout managers control the position and size of components that you place into a container object. AFC layout managers range from the simple **UIFlowLayout**, which simply positions controls one after the other, to more sophisticated layout managers such as **UIGridBagLayout**, which enables you to position controls just about anywhere. You learn a lot about AFC's layout managers in Chapter 9, but to get you started, this section shows how you can use layout managers to create just about any component layout you like.

There's a key to creative component layout design—each container in your applet can have its own layout manager. When you add several containers, each with its own layout manager, to your applet's display, you can come up with some snazzy user interfaces. You can even place containers within containers within containers—if you like—to do such things as creating rows of border layouts.

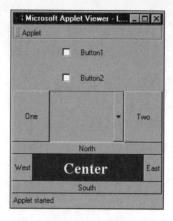

## Figure 2.9

*LayoutApplet running in Applet Viewer.*

Listing 2.9 shows the source code for an applet with a fairly complex user interface. Figure 2.9 shows the applet that results. The applet uses various levels of nested components (usually panels) to organize the checkbox, button, choice, and canvas components that form the applet's user interface. The three main panels are defined in their own classes, making the applet's **init()** method clean and easy to follow.

### Listing 2.9   An applet that sets up panels for a complex user interface.

```
/////////////////////////////////////////////////
// LayoutApplet.java
//
// An AFC applet that demonstrates using panels
// to create a user interface.
/////////////////////////////////////////////////

import com.ms.ui.*;
import com.ms.fx.*;

public class LayoutApplet extends AwtUIApplet
{
    public LayoutApplet()
    {
        super(new AppletImplementation());
    }
}
```

```
class AppletImplementation extends UIApplet
{
    public void init()
    {
        UIGridLayout layout = new UIGridLayout(3,1);
        setLayout(layout);

        PanelOne panelOne = new PanelOne();
        add(panelOne);

        PanelTwo panelTwo = new PanelTwo();
        add(panelTwo);

        PanelThree panelThree = new PanelThree();
        add(panelThree);

        setValid(true);
    }
}

class PanelOne extends UIPanel
{
    public PanelOne()
    {
        UIRowLayout rowLayout = new UIRowLayout(3);
        setLayout(rowLayout);

        UIPanel panel = new UIPanel();
        UIGridLayout gridLayout = new UIGridLayout(2, 1);
        panel.setLayout(gridLayout);

        UICheckButton button =
            new UICheckButton(new UIText("Button1"));
        panel.add(button);

        button = new UICheckButton(new UIText("Button2"));
        panel.add(button);

        UICanvas canvas = new UICanvas();
        add(canvas);
        add(panel);

        canvas = new UICanvas();
        add(canvas);

        setValid(true);
    }
}
```

```java
class PanelTwo extends UIPanel
{
    public PanelTwo()
    {
        UIRowLayout layout = new UIRowLayout(3);
        layout.setWidth(0, 60);
        layout.setWidth(1, 120);
        layout.setWidth(2, 60);
        setLayout(layout);

        UIPushButton button =
            new UIPushButton(new UIText("One"));
        add(button);

        UIChoice choice = new UIChoice();
        for (int x=0; x<10; ++x)
        {
            String str = "Selection " + String.valueOf(x);
            choice.addString(str);
        }
        add(choice);

        button = new UIPushButton(new UIText("Two"));
        add(button);

        setValid(true);
    }
}

class PanelThree extends UIPanel
{
    public PanelThree()
    {
        UIBorderLayout layout = new UIBorderLayout();
        setLayout(layout);

        UIPushButton button =
            new UIPushButton(new UIText("North"));
        add(button, "North");

        button = new UIPushButton(new UIText("South"));
        add(button, "South");

        button = new UIPushButton(new UIText("East"));
        add(button, "East");

        button = new UIPushButton(new UIText("West"));
        add(button, "West");
```

```
            CenterCanvas canvas = new CenterCanvas();
            add(canvas, "Center");

            setValid(true);
        }
    }

class CenterCanvas extends UICanvas
{
    private FxFont font;

    public CenterCanvas()
    {
        font = new FxFont("TimesRoman", FxFont.BOLD, 24);
        setFont(font);
        setBackground(FxColor.blue);
    }

    public void paint(FxGraphics graphics)
    {
        graphics.setColor(FxColor.white);
        graphics.drawString("Center", 50, 30);
    }
}
```

## Implementing Dynamic Controls

Sometimes, the controls you want to display in an applet or application depend upon options that the user selects. In such cases, when the user selects a new option, you need to display a different set of controls. You can achieve this effect by using the **add()** and **remove()** methods. You also can call on **removeAll()** to remove all components from a container. The following steps implement dynamic controls:

1.  Create panel classes for the sets of components you want to switch. These classes should extend the **UIPanel** class.

2.  Add components to their appropriate panel classes. You would do this in the classes' constructor.

3.  In your program, create instances of the panel classes, but add only the first instance to the display (although you could start with no panels displayed if you want).

4.  When the user performs the action that signals a change of the available controls, call **remove()** to hide the currently displayed panel.

5.  Call **add()** to display the new set of components.

Listing 2.10 shows the source code for an applet that employs the dynamic-controls technique to switch between two canvas components when the user clicks the Click Me! button. (The example uses canvases instead of panels to simplify the program; the technique is exactly the same when you use panels.) Figure 2.10 shows the applet running in Microsoft Applet Viewer. Figure 2.11 shows the applet after the user clicks the button, causing the applet to display a different canvas component. Note that you can create a similar set of controls using the **UICardLayout** layout manager, described in Chapter 9.

### Listing 2.10   An applet with dynamic controls.

```
/////////////////////////////////////////////////
// DynamicApplet.java
//
// An AFC applet that demonstrates switching
// between controls.
/////////////////////////////////////////////////

import java.awt.*;
import com.ms.ui.*;
import com.ms.fx.*;

public class DynamicApplet extends AwtUIApplet
{
    public DynamicApplet()
    {
        super(new AppletImplementation());
    }
}

class AppletImplementation extends UIApplet
{
    private UIPushButton button;
    private CanvasOne canvasOne;
    private CanvasTwo canvasTwo;
    private UICanvas currentCanvas;

    public void init()
    {
```

```
        UIGridLayout layout = new UIGridLayout(2, 1);
        setLayout(layout);

        button = new UIPushButton(new UIText("Click Me!"));
        FxFont font = new FxFont("TimesRoman", FxFont.PLAIN, 24);
        button.setFont(font);
        add(button);

        canvasOne = new CanvasOne();
        add(canvasOne);

        canvasTwo = new CanvasTwo();
        currentCanvas = canvasOne;

        setValid(true);
    }

    public boolean action(Event event, Object obj)
    {
        if (event.target == button)
        {
            if (currentCanvas == canvasOne)
            {
                remove(canvasOne);
                add(canvasTwo);
                currentCanvas = canvasTwo;
                return true;
            }
            else
            {
                remove(canvasTwo);
                add(canvasOne);
                currentCanvas = canvasOne;
                return true;
            }
        }
        return false;
    }
}

class CanvasOne extends UICanvas
{
    private FxFont font;

    public CanvasOne()
    {
```

```
            font = new FxFont("TimesRoman", FxFont.BOLD, 24);
            setFont(font);
            setBackground(FxColor.blue);
        }

        public void paint(FxGraphics graphics)
        {
            graphics.setColor(FxColor.white);
            graphics.drawString("Canvas One", 60, 65);
        }
    }

    class CanvasTwo extends UICanvas
    {
        private FxFont font;

        public CanvasTwo()
        {
            font = new FxFont("Courier", FxFont.BOLD, 36);
            setFont(font);
            setBackground(FxColor.red);
        }

        public void paint(FxGraphics graphics)
        {
            graphics.setColor(FxColor.white);
            graphics.drawString("Canvas", 55, 55);
            graphics.drawString("Two", 90, 85);
        }
    }
```

**Figure 2.10**

*DynamicApplet, running in Applet Viewer.*

**Figure 2.11**

*DynamicApplet, with the second canvas displayed.*

 Implementing Scriptable Methods

Java applets can expose methods to scripts, which enables scripts to manipulate the applet in some way. The most common applet methods called by scripts are **getAppletInfo()** and **getParameterInfo()**. While the **getAppletInfo()** method returns a string that contains information about the applet's author and copyright, **getParameterInfo()** returns strings that describe the applet's parameters. Usually, you implement these functions by overriding the superclass's versions in your applet class.

But AFC throws in a monkey wrench because of the way in which the **AwtUIApplet** bridge object sits between the AWT and the applet's implementation object. Scripts can call methods in the bridge object but cannot get to the implementation object. Still, AFC programming rules dictate that you implement all your applet's methods in the implementation class, and this rule includes scriptable methods. What to do?

For a solution, create scriptable methods in the bridge class that call the scriptable methods of the same name in the implementation class. In this way, the bridge class continues to act as a bridge between the applet's implementation and the outside world, and you can still place all your applet's code in the implementation class. Listing 2.11 shows a simple applet that implements the **getAppletInfo()** method. Scripts can call **getAppletInfo()** in the bridge class (**InfoApplet**). When they do, the bridge class's **getAppletInfo()** passes the call on to the implementation class's **getAppletInfo()**, which returns the information string to the bridge class.

## Listing 2.11  An applet with a scriptable method.

```
/////////////////////////////////////////////////
// InfoApplet.java
//
// An AFC applet that demonstrates implementing
// scriptable methods.
/////////////////////////////////////////////////

import java.awt.*;
import com.ms.ui.*;
import com.ms.fx.*;

public class InfoApplet extends AwtUIApplet
{
    public InfoApplet()
    {
        super(new AppletImplementation());
    }

    public String getAppletInfo()
    {
        UIApplet applet = getUIApplet();
        String str = applet.getAppletInfo();
        return str;
    }
}


class AppletImplementation extends UIApplet
{
    public void init()
    {
        setValid(true);
    }

    public String getAppletInfo()
    {
        String str = "InfoApplet info goes here";
        return str;
    }
}
```

# Chapter 3

# Button Components

# Notes...

# Chapter 3

They say you can choose your friends, but you can't choose your relatives. I guess that's an obvious statement. Still, with continual advances in genetics, the day may come when you really can choose your relatives—or at least who didn't exist before you were born (or cloned or hatched or whatever they'll do in those days). Choosing enemies is a whole other matter. I suggest you stick with friends.

Luckily when you're programming a Java applet or application, you don't have to make choices that involve such deep philosophical considerations. You do, however, have to give your user ways to choose program functions, and buttons are one of the components that enable the user to make such choices. Plain old Java has buttons—yes, indeed—but AFC adds a plethora of cool components that shove the idea of buttons a bit into the future.

AFC buttons include not only buttons as you know them, they also include buttons that pop up when the mouse pointer passes over them, buttons that display menus, buttons that contain images, and even normal buttons (such as checkboxes and radio buttons). All AFC buttons, however (even those that seem to be clones of Java buttons), have additional abilities that make your Java programs more appealing.

Most AFC buttons trace their ancestry back to the **UIButton** class. However, one class (although it contains a button object) is more akin to drop-down menus. Still, because the user launches the menu by clicking a button, this class also is covered in this chapter. The main button classes covered in this chapter include:

- **UIButton**—An abstract class that most button classes extend
- **UIPushButton**—A standard pushbutton object
- **UIRepeatButton**—A pushbutton that continually generates events as long as the button is pressed
- **UICheckButton**—A checkbox component
- **UIRadioButton**—A radio button component
- **UIMenuButton**—A button that displays a menu when clicked

You learn about these main button classes, as well as about the **UIMenuButton** support classes, **UIMenuList**, **UIMenuItem**, and **UIMenuLauncher**. As you can guess, the **UIMenuButton** class can't count **UIButton** among its base classes.

## The **UIButton** Class

**UIButton** is the patriarch of the button clan. In less metaphoric terms, all button classes, except **UIMenuButton**, trace their ancestry back to **UIButton**. **UIButton** itself extends no Java AWT class. Instead, its ancestry winds back through a long line of AFC superclasses, starting with **UISingleContainer** and going back through **UIStateContainer**, **UIContainer**, and **UIComponent**.

With this long family line, you can imagine that **UIButton**—and all button classes that extend **UIButton**—inherit a boatload of methods. (See Chapter 12 for an indepth look at **UIButton**'s superclasses.) The methods that make a button a button are defined in **UIButton**, as shown in Table 3.1.

Because **UIButton** is an abstract class, you can't create a **UIButton** object. **UIButton** simply provides the basic functionality that all buttons require. AFC incorporates this basic functionality into its buttons by extending the **UIButton** class with the nonabstract button classes. You create button objects from the nonabstract classes.

## The **UIPushButton** Class

The most obvious type of button is the standard pushbutton that most computer users have seen and used a billion times. A standard pushbutton generates an event

**Table 3.1  Methods of the UIButton class.**

| Method | Description |
|---|---|
| addActionListener() | Registers a class as a listener for action events |
| doDefaultAction() | Executes the button's default action |
| getDefaultAction() | Gets the button's default action, which is "press" |
| getStyle() | Gets the buttons current style settings |
| keyDown() | Watches the spacebar and Enter and Esc keys |
| keyUp() | Watches the spacebar and Enter key |
| mouseClicked() | Delivers the button's action event |
| processActionEvent() | Dispatches action events to registered listeners |
| processEvent() | Calls the appropriate event-processing method for an event |
| removeActionListener() | Removes an action listener from the button's list of listeners |
| setHot() | Toggles the button's hot tracking in response to the mouse |
| setStyle() | Sets the button's style |

when the user clicks it. Your application responds to the event, performing the task the button represents. You can create a **UIPushButton** object exactly as you're used to creating a plain Java **Button** object, by calling the class's constructor with the button's text string:

```
UIPushButton button = new UIPushButton("An AFC Push Button");
```

The resultant button, however, behaves differently than you may expect. Figure 3.1 shows the button created with the previous line. The button was added to the center of a border layout, but you see only the button's text. When the pointer passes over the button, the button pops out from the applet, as shown in Figure 3.2.

If you're used to Java buttons, AFC's plain pushbutton can be perplexing. To make the button work more normally, you must tell AFC that you want the button to be

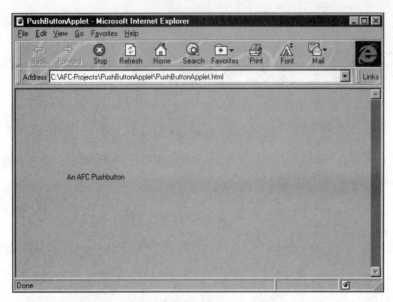

**Figure 3.1**

*An AFC pushbutton in an applet.*

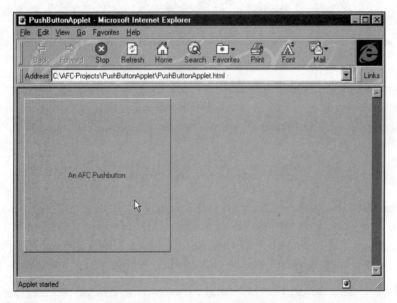

**Figure 3.2**

*The pushbutton as the mouse pointer passes over.*

raised. You perform this step by providing the **UIPushButton.RAISED** style constant to the button object's constructor, as follows:

```
UIPushButton button =
    new UIPushButton("An AFC Push Button", UIPushButton.RAISED);
```

Now you will get a normal looking button.

Listing 3.1 is the source code for a simple applet that displays a pushbutton component. Figure 3.3 shows the applet running in Microsoft Applet Viewer.

### Listing 3.1 The source code for PushButtonApplet.

```
/////////////////////////////////////////////////
// PushButtonApplet.java
//
// An applet that displays an AFC pushbutton.
/////////////////////////////////////////////////

import com.ms.ui.*;
import com.ms.ui.event.*;

public class PushButtonApplet extends AwtUIApplet
{
    public PushButtonApplet()
    {
        super(new AppletImplementation());
    }
}

class AppletImplementation extends UIApplet
{
    public void init()
    {
        UIText text = new UIText("An AFC Pushbutton");
        UIPushButton button =
            new UIPushButton(text, UIPushButton.RAISED);
        add(button);
        setValid(true);
    }
}
```

The **UIPushButton** class defines a set of methods in addition to the methods it inherits from **UIButton**. In fact, some **UIPushButton** methods override **UIButton** methods. Table 3.2 lists **UIPushButton**'s methods and their descriptions.

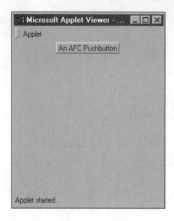

**Figure 3.3**

PushButtonApplet running in Microsoft Applet Viewer.

**Table 3.2  Methods of the UIPushButton class.**

| Method | Description |
|---|---|
| addActionListener() | Registers a class as a listener for action events |
| getInsets() | Gets the button's insets |
| getRoleCode() | Gets the button's role code, which is **ROLE_SYSTEM_PUSHBUTTON** |
| paint() | Draws the button |
| processActionEvent() | Dispatches action events to registered listeners |
| processEvent() | Calls the appropriate event-processing method for an event |
| removeActionListener() | Removes an action listener from the button's list of listeners |
| setChecked() | Toggles the button's checked state |
| setFocused() | Toggles the button's focus state |
| setHot() | Toggles the button's hot tracking in response to the mouse |
| setPressed() | Toggles the button's pressed state |
| setStyle() | Sets the button's style |

**UIPushButton**'s constructor is overloaded several times to enable you to create buttons in various ways. The constructors' signatures look like this:

```
public UIPushButton();
public UIPushButton(String text);
public UIPushButton(String text, int style);
public UIPushButton(IUIComponent comp);
public UIPushButton(IUIComponent comp, int style);
```

As you see, you can create a button object that contains two types of objects: a text string or a component. Usually, the component you provide to **UIPushButton**'s constructor is an object of the **UIText**, **UIGraphic**, or **UIItem** class. You can also provide style flags to the constructor. These flags are defined as follows:

- **RAISED**—The button initially appears raised with a 3D border.

- **TOGGLE**—The button toggles between its raised (called *unchecked*) and depressed (called *checked*) states.

- **TRITOGGLE**—The button switches between three states: raised (unchecked), depressed (checked), and indeterminate.

- **THICK**—The button has a thick border.

- **FLAT_PRESSED**—The button looks flat when pressed, rather then indented.

You use the flags by combining them with the OR operator. For example, to create a raised toggle button, you construct the pushbutton like this:

```
UIPushButton button = new UIPushButton(text,
    UIPushButton.RAISED | UIPushButton.TOGGLE);
```

## The **UIRepeatButton** Class

The **UIRepeatButton** class represents a special type of pushbutton that continually issues action events while the button is in its pressed state. You create a **UIRepeatButton** object in exactly the same way you create a **UIPushButton** object. The only difference—a pushbutton generates only a single event when it's pressed and held down, whereas a repeat button generates a stream of events. Here's an example of creating a repeat button:

```
UIRepeatButton button =
    new UIRepeatButton("An AFC Repeat Button", UIPushButton.RAISED);
```

This repeat button looks exactly like a normal pushbutton and differs only in the way it generates events.

The **UIRepeatButton** class extends **UIPushButton**. Because a repeat button is so similar to a pushbutton, the only extra methods it requires are the ones that handle the repeating events. Table 3.3 describes these methods. You probably will never call these methods directly.

**UIRepeatButton**'s constructor is overloaded so you can create repeat buttons in various ways. The constructors' signatures look like this:

```
public UIRepeatButton();
public UIRepeatButton(String text);
public UIRepeatButton(String text, int style);
public UIRepeatButton(IUIComponent comp);
public UIRepeatButton(IUIComponent comp, int style);
```

Just as with a pushbutton, you can create a repeat button object that contains two types of objects—a text string or a component. Usually, the component you provide to **UIPushButton**'s constructor is an object of the **UIText**, **UIGraphic**, or **UIItem** class. You can also provide the same style flags—**RAISED**, **TOGGLE**, and **TRITOGGLE**, **THICK**, **FLAT_PRESSED**—used with pushbuttons. A repeat button, however, ignores the **TOGGLE** and **TRITOGGLE** flags (or at least the flags don't change the button's behavior), so there's little point in specifying any style but **RAISED**, **THICK**, or **FLAT_PRESSED** when constructing the button.

## The **UICheckButton** Class

The **UICheckButton** class creates a check button that looks and acts much like a standard Java check button. The AFC check button, however, supports extras that you get when you create an AFC button. To create a check button object, just call the

**Table 3.3  Methods of the UIRepeatButton class.**

| Method | Description |
| --- | --- |
| mouseClicked() | Delivers the button's action event |
| setPressed() | Toggles the button's pressed state and starts the repeat timer |
| timeTriggered() | Delivers a timed action event |

class's constructor, as you do with any button, and then add the button to your applet's layout. Listing 3.2 shows the source code for a quickie applet that displays a check button. Figure 3.4 shows the applet running in Applet Viewer.

### Listing 3.2 The source code for CheckButtonApplet.

```
/////////////////////////////////////////////////
// CheckButtonApplet.java
//
// An applet that displays an AFC check button.
/////////////////////////////////////////////////

import com.ms.ui.*;

public class CheckButtonApplet extends AwtUIApplet
{
    public CheckButtonApplet()
    {
        super(new AppletImplementation());
    }
}

class AppletImplementation extends UIApplet
{
    public void init()
    {
        UIFlowLayout layout = new UIFlowLayout();
        setLayout(layout);

        UICheckButton button =
            new UICheckButton("An AFC Check Button");
        add(button);

        setValid(true);
    }
}
```

Because check buttons look and act quite differently from other types of buttons, the **UICheckButton** class defines many methods, most of which AFC calls internally. Of course, **UICheckButton** inherits methods from its base classes, including **UIButton**. Table 3.4 lists **UICheckButton**'s methods along with their descriptions.

**UICheckButton**'s constructor is overloaded, so you can create repeat buttons in various ways. The constructors' signatures look like this:

**Figure 3.4**

*CheckButtonApplet running in Microsoft Applet Viewer.*

```
public UICheckButton();
public UICheckButton(String name);
public UICheckButton(String name, int style);
public UICheckButton(IUIComponent comp);
public UICheckButton(IUIComponent comp, int style);
```

As is typical with AFC buttons, you can create a check button object that contains one of two types of objects: a text string or a component. Usually, the component you provide to **UIPushButton**'s constructor is an object of the **UIText**, **UIGraphic**, or **UIItem** class. You also can specify style flags—**TOGGLE** or **TRITOGGLE**—although **TOGGLE** is the button's default behavior.

Usually, when the user clicks a check button, AFC takes care of checking or unchecking the button. In programs that incorporate check buttons, however, you may want to explicitly check or uncheck the button. You can do this by calling the button's **setChecked()** method, as follows:

```
UICheckButton button = new UICheckButton("An AFC Check Button");
button.setChecked(true);
```

The **setChecked()** method takes a **boolean** value as its single argument. A value of **true** checks the button, and a value of **false** unchecks the button.

You can get the check button's state by calling its **isChecked()** method (as shown in the following example), which the **UICheckButton** class inherits from its **UIStateContainer** ancestor:

```
boolean checked = button.isChecked();
```

A return value of **true** means that the button is checked, whereas **false** means the button is not checked.

## The **UIRadioButton** Class

**UIRadioButton**'s immediate base class is **UICheckButton**. This isn't surprising when you consider that a radio button is just a check button with a round box instead of a square

**Table 3.4   Methods of the UICheckButton class.**

| Method | Description |
| --- | --- |
| **addItemListener()** | Registers a class as a listener for item events |
| **getInsets()** | Gets the button's insets |
| **getMinimumSize()** | Gets the checkbox's minimum size |
| **getPreferredSize()** | Gets the checkbox's preferred size |
| **getRoleCode()** | Gets the button's role code, which is **ROLE_SYSTEM_CHECKBUTTON** |
| **paint()** | Draws the button |
| **paintCheck()** | Draws the button's checkbox |
| **processEvent()** | Calls the appropriate event-processing method for an event |
| **processItemEvent()** | Dispatches item events to registered listeners |
| **removeItemListener()** | Removes an item listener from the button's list of listeners |
| **setChecked()** | Toggles the button's checked state |
| **setHot()** | Toggles the button's hot tracking in response to the mouse |
| **setID()** | Sets the component's ID |
| **setIndeterminate()** | Toggles the button's indeterminate state |
| **setName()** | Sets the component's name |
| **setPressed()** | Toggles the button's pressed state |
| **setSelected()** | Toggles the button's selected state |

one. Traditionally, radio buttons are used in a group in which only one radio button at a time can be selected. The button's name comes from the buttons you have on your car radio, with which you can select only a single station at a time. Often, however, developers use radio buttons only as a different style of check button.

To create a radio button object, call the class's constructor just as you would with a check button, and then add the button to your applet's layout. Listing 3.3 shows the source code for an applet that displays a check button. Figure 3.5 shows the applet running in Applet Viewer.

### Listing 3.3  The source code for RadioButtonApplet.

```
/////////////////////////////////////////////////
// RadioButtonApplet.java
//
// An applet that displays a radio button.
/////////////////////////////////////////////////

import com.ms.ui.*;

public class RadioButtonApplet extends AwtUIApplet
{
    public RadioButtonApplet()
    {
        super(new AppletImplementation());
    }
}

class AppletImplementation extends UIApplet
{
    public void init()
    {
        UIFlowLayout layout = new UIFlowLayout();
        setLayout(layout);

        UIRadioButton button =
            new UIRadioButton("An AFC Radio Button");
        add(button);

        setValid(true);
    }
}
```

A radio button looks a little different than a check button, even though they operate similarly. For this reason, **UIRadioButton** overrides a couple of the methods the class inherits from **UICheckButton**. Table 3.5 lists these methods and their descriptions.

**Figure 3.5**

*RadioButtonApplet running in Microsoft Applet Viewer.*

**Table 3.5   Methods of the UIRadioButton class.**

| Method | Description |
| --- | --- |
| getRoleCode() | Gets the button's role code, which is **ROLE_SYSTEM_RADIOBUTTON** |
| paintCheck() | Draws the button's checkbox |

As with most AFC buttons, **UIRadioButton**'s constructor is overloaded so you can create radio buttons in various ways. The constructors' signatures look like this:

```
public UIRadioButton();
public UIRadioButton(String name);
public UIRadioButton(String name, int style);
public UIRadioButton(IUIComponent comp);
public UIRadioButton(IUIComponent comp, int style);
```

As the constructors show, you can create a radio button object that contains a text string or a component. Usually, the component you provide to **UIRadioButton**'s constructor is an object of the **UIText**, **UIGraphic**, or **UIItem** class. You can also specify style flags—**TOGGLE** or **TRITOGGLE**. The **RAISED**, **THICK**, and **FLAT_ PRESSED** style flags are not defined for a radio button.

When the user clicks a radio button, AFC takes care of selecting (checking) or deselecting (unchecking) the button. However, you can explicitly check or uncheck the button by calling the button's **setChecked()** method:

```
UIRadioButton button = new UIRadioButton("An AFC Radio Button");
button.setChecked(true);
```

The **setChecked()** method takes a **boolean** value as its single argument. A value of **true** checks the button, and a value of **false** unchecks the button.

You can get the radio button's state by calling its **isChecked()** method (as shown in the following syntax), which the **UIRadioButton** class inherits from its **UIStateContainer** ancestor:

```
boolean checked = button.isChecked();
```

A return value of **true** means that the button is checked; a **false** value means the button is unchecked.

# The **UIMenuButton** Class

The **UIMenuButton** class represents a button object that, as compared with Java, is unique to AFC. A menu button looks like a standard pushbutton. However, when the user clicks a menu button, the button launches a pop-up menu from which the user can select a command.

Creating a menu button requires a little more work than creating other types of buttons, because you also have to create the menu and associate it with the button. To create a menu button, you must perform the following steps:

1. Create a **UIMenuList** object:

   ```
   UIMenuList menuList = new UIMenuList();
   ```

2. Add menu items to the **UIMenuList** object:

   ```
   menuList.add("Menu Item 1");
   menuList.add("Menu Item 2");
   ```

3. Create a **UIMenuButton** object, passing the **UIMenuList** object to the class's constructor:

   ```
   UIMenuButton menuButton =
       new UIMenuButton("AFC Menu Button", menuList);
   ```

Listing 3.4 contains a short applet that demonstrates creating and displaying a menu button. Figure 3.6 shows the applet before the user clicks the menu button; Figure 3.7 shows the applet with the pop-up menu launched.

**Figure 3.6**

*MenuButtonApplet running in Microsoft Applet Viewer.*

**Figure 3.7**

*The activated menu button.*

### Listing 3.4 An applet that creates and displays a menu button.

```
/////////////////////////////////////////////////
// MenuButtonApplet.java
//
// An applet that demonstrates AFC menu buttons.
/////////////////////////////////////////////////

import com.ms.ui.*;

public class MenuButtonApplet extends AwtUIApplet
{
```

```
    public MenuButtonApplet()
    {
        super(new AppletImplementation());
    }
}

class AppletImplementation extends UIApplet
{
    public void init()
    {
        UIFlowLayout layout = new UIFlowLayout();
        setLayout(layout);

        UIMenuList menuList = new UIMenuList();
        menuList.add("Menu Item 1");
        menuList.add("Menu Item 2");
        menuList.add("Menu Item 3");
        menuList.add("Menu Item 4");
        menuList.add("Menu Item 5");
        UIMenuButton menuButton =
            new UIMenuButton("AFC Menu Button", menuList);
        add(menuButton);

        setValid(true);
    }
}
```

**UIMenuButton** doesn't extend the **UIButton** class. Instead, its immediate base class is **UIMenuLauncher**. This means **UIMenuButton** inherits methods not only from **UIMenuLauncher**, but also from **UISingleContainer**, **UIStateContainer**, **UIContainer**, and **UIComponent**. The **UIMenuButton** class defines methods in addition to those it inherits. Table 3.6 lists these methods and their descriptions, although you probably won't need to call any of these methods directly.

The **UIMenuButton** class overloads its constructor, giving you four ways to create a **UIMenuButton** object. The constructors' signatures look like this:

```
public UIMenuButton(String string, UIMenuList menu);
public UIMenuButton(String string, int style, UIMenuList menu);
public UIMenuButton(IUIComponent comp, UIMenuList menu);
public UIMenuButton(IUIComponent comp, int style, UIMenuList menu);
```

As you see, you can create a menu button using a text string or component as content. Moreover, you can specify style flags that dictate how the button looks and acts.

**Table 3.6  Methods of the UIMenuButton class.**

| Method | Description |
|---|---|
| action() | Launches or cancels the button's pop-up menu |
| ended() | Clears the menu's launched state and the pushbutton's checked state |
| getPlacement() | Gets the menu's bounding rectangle |
| keyDown() | Launches the menu when the keyboard's down-arrow key is pressed |
| launch() | Launches the button's pop-up menu |
| mouseDown() | Launches or cancels the button's menu in response to a mouse click |
| mouseUp() | Launches or cancels the button's menu in response to a mouse click |
| requestFocus() | Requests focus for the button control |

The default style is **RAISED**, so you don't need to specify this style. The only other style is a flat button, which you select with a style value of zero.

## The **UIMenuList** Class

The **UIMenuList** class has a longer ancestry than **UIMenuButton**, being derived from **UIList**, whose family tree extends from **UISelector** to **UIPanel** to **UIStateContainer** and so on down the line. (Please refer to Chapter 4 for more information on the **UIList** class.) The **UIMenuList** class adds several of its own methods, which are listed in Table 3.7.

**UIMenuList** overloads its constructor, giving you two ways to create a **UIMenuList** object. The constructors' signatures follow:

```
public UIMenuList();
public UIMenuList(int layoutStyle);
```

In the second version of the constructor, you can specify a menu layout style. Because the menu list organizes its entries with a **UIVerticalFlowLayout** layout manager, the style values are defined in that class. The possible values are **UIVerticalFlowLayout. MULTICOLUMN** (creates a multicolumn menu) and **UIVerticalFlowLayout.FILL** (forces menu entries to the width of the menu).

Table 3.7  Methods of the **UIMenuList** class.

| Method | Description |
| --- | --- |
| action() | Displays the currently selected item |
| getMenuLauncher() | Gets a reference to the menu launcher |
| gotFocus() | Requests focus for the component |
| keyDown() | Launches the menu when the keyboard's down-arrow key is pressed |
| lostFocus() | Called when the component loses the focus |
| mouseClicked() | Handles mouse button releases |
| mouseEnter() | Selects items over which the mouse pointer passes |
| setMenuLauncher() | Assigns a menu launcher to the component |

## The **UIMenuItem** Class

The menus that you associate with menu buttons (and other types of menus) can be snazzy objects that contain other types of components. Sometimes, you may want to add a **UIText** item to a menu—rather than a plain text string—to acquire more control over the text displayed in the menu. However, you can add almost any type of AFC component to the menu list.

To add components to the menu, you create **UIMenuItem** objects as the menu entries. These **UIMenuItem** objects can hold other components. You give the component to the **UIMenuItem** when you construct it. You then add the **UIMenuItem** object to the menu list and add the list to the menu button. The entire process looks like this:

```
UICheckButton button1 = new UICheckButton("Button 1");
UIMenuItem menuItem1 = new UIMenuItem(button1);
UIMenuList menuList = new UIMenuList();
menuList.add(menuItem1);
UIMenuButton menuButton =
    new UIMenuButton("AFC Menu Button", menuList);
```

Listing 3.5 reveals a short applet that creates a menu button whose menu list contains check buttons. Figure 3.8 shows the applet running in Applet Viewer.

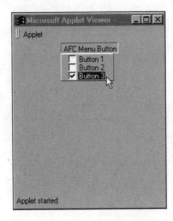

**Figure 3.8**

*MenuButtonApplet2, showing off its check button menu items.*

### Listing 3.5   An applet that creates and displays a menu button.

```
/////////////////////////////////////////////////
// MenuButtonApplet2.java
//
// An applet that shows how to add components to
// a menu button.
/////////////////////////////////////////////////

import com.ms.ui.*;

public class MenuButtonApplet2 extends AwtUIApplet
{
    public MenuButtonApplet2()
    {
        super(new AppletImplementation());
    }
}

class AppletImplementation extends UIApplet
{
    public void init()
    {
        UIFlowLayout layout = new UIFlowLayout();
        setLayout(layout);

        UICheckButton button1 = new UICheckButton("Button 1");
        UICheckButton button2 = new UICheckButton("Button 2");
        UICheckButton button3 = new UICheckButton("Button 3");
```

```
        UIMenuItem menuItem1 = new UIMenuItem(button1);
        UIMenuItem menuItem2 = new UIMenuItem(button2);
        UIMenuItem menuItem3 = new UIMenuItem(button3);

        UIMenuList menuList = new UIMenuList();
        menuList.add(menuItem1);
        menuList.add(menuItem2);
        menuList.add(menuItem3);

        UIMenuButton menuButton =
            new UIMenuButton("AFC Menu Button", menuList);
        add(menuButton);

        setValid(true);
    }
}
```

**UIMenuItem** extends the **UIMenuLauncher** class, which extends **UISingleContainer**. Besides the methods it inherits from **UIMenuLauncher** and its other ancestors, **UIMenuItem** defines the five methods shown in Table 3.8.

## The **UIMenuLauncher** Class

It's the **UIMenuLauncher** class that gives **UIMenuItem** some of its special capabilities, not the least of which is the capability to display submenus. (You will learn about submenus in the following Practical Guide.) You're not likely to call any **UIMenu Launcher** methods directly—and because it's an abstract class, you won't create objects from it—but (for the sake of completeness) Table 3.9 lists the class's methods and their descriptions. **UIMenuItem** inherits each of these methods.

**Table 3.8   Methods of the UIMenuItem class.**

| Method | Description |
| --- | --- |
| action() | Called in response to a component event |
| getInsets() | Gets the menu item's insets |
| getRoleCode() | Gets the button's role code, which is **ROLE_SYSTEM_MENUITEM** |
| keyDown() | Launches or cancels a menu in response to the right- or left-arrow keys |
| paint() | Draws the menu item |

**Table 3.9   Methods of the UIMenuLauncher class.**

| Method | Description |
|---|---|
| cancel() | Cancels the control's pop-up menu |
| ended() | Called when the menu is canceled. |
| fitToScreen() | Gets the menu's bounding rectangle |
| getDisplayer() | Gets a reference to the menu's displayer |
| getMenu() | Gets the menu's content |
| getPlacement() | Gets the menu's position by calling **fitToScreen()** |
| isLaunched() | Gets the menu's launched state |
| launch() | Launches the pop-up menu |
| postEvent() | Posts the given event |
| raiseEvent() | Called by the menu in response to an event |
| setFocused() | Toggles the menu launcher's (and its content component's) focus state |
| setHot() | Toggles the menu launcher's (and its content component's) hot tracking |
| setMenu() | Associates a menu with the launcher control |
| setSelected() | Toggles the menu launcher's (and its content component's) selected state |

# Practical Guide To

# Creating And Using AFC Buttons

- Responding To Pushbutton Components
- Creating Graphical Buttons
- Using Repeat Buttons
- Responding To Check Buttons
- Using Radio Buttons
- Using Radio Buttons Without A Group Box
- Displaying Submenus
- Responding To Menu Selections
- Enabling And Disabling Components

## Responding To Pushbutton Components

Creating and displaying a button is only half the battle. Your program also must respond to the button when it's clicked. How you respond to a button depends on the event model you decide to use in your applet or application. For a detailed look at AFC and Java events, check out Chapter 15. You can, however, choose between the older Java 1.0 propagation model and the newer Java 1.1 delegation model. Because you've probably written many applets before reading this book, you should at least be familiar with the propagation event model (although you may not know it by that name).

AFC pushbuttons, just like their AWT counterparts, generate action events when clicked. In other words, when you use the propagation event model, you can capture the button click in the applet's **action()** method. However, the arguments sent to action on behalf of an AFC button are very different from those sent for AWT buttons.

You may recall that, with AWT button action events, the second parameter received by **action()** is the button's label. When an AFC button generates the action event, the second **action()** parameter is a reference to the button object itself, rather than just the button's label. To determine which button is clicked, the program must compare the object received as **action()**'s second parameter with the button objects.

Listing 3.6 shows the source code for an applet that demonstrates how to respond to AFC button clicks, using the propagation event model. When you run the applet, you see one large button with the caption, "An AFC Pushbutton", as shown in Figure 3.9. Click the button, and the caption changes to "Thanks for the click!" You can find the program's important details in the **action()** method, which determines whether the button was clicked; it also calls the button's **getName()** method to retrieve the button's label and calls **setName()** to change the button's label.

### Listing 3.6   An applet that responds to button clicks.

```
/////////////////////////////////////////////////
// PushButtonApplet2.java
//
// An applet that responds to AFC button events.
/////////////////////////////////////////////////

import com.ms.ui.*;
import java.awt.*;
```

```java
public class PushButtonApplet2 extends AwtUIApplet
{
    public PushButtonApplet2()
    {
        super(new AppletImplementation());
    }
}

class AppletImplementation extends UIApplet
{
    UIPushButton button;

    public void init()
    {
        UIBorderLayout layout = new UIBorderLayout();
        setLayout(layout);

        UIText text = new UIText("An AFC Pushbutton");
        button = new UIPushButton(text, UIPushButton.RAISED);
        add(button, "Center");

        setValid(true);
    }

    public boolean action(Event event, Object arg)
    {
        if (arg == button)
        {
            String name = button.getName();
            if (name == "An AFC Pushbutton")
                button.setName("Thanks for the click!");
            else
                button.setName("All right, already!");
            return true;
        }
        return false;
    }
}
```

If you're not familiar with the delegation event model, the next sample program may be a little hard to follow because this model, while more up-to-date, is a little trickier to implement. (Again, you may want to read Chapter 15 to uncover the details.)

In any case, Listing 3.7 is the same applet as that shown in Listing 3.6, except this version uses the delegation event model instead of the propagation model. Because

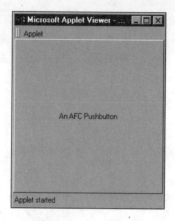

**Figure 3.9**

*PushButtonApplet2, running in Microsoft Applet Viewer.*

the button generates action events, the applet must implement the **IUIActionListener** interface, which is the AFC version of Java's **ActionListener** interface.

The **IUIActionListener** interface dictates that the applet must provide the **actionPerformed()** method, which the event source calls to deliver the event to the applet. The **actionPerformed()** method receives a single parameter, which is a **UIActionEvent** object. (Just for comparison purposes, the Java version of **actionPerformed()** receives an **ActionEvent** object. Beginning to see a pattern here?) The **UIActionEvent** object's **getActionCommand()** method gets the clicked button's label.

**Listing 3.7   An applet that responds to button clicks using the delegation event model.**

```
/////////////////////////////////////////////////
// PushButtonApplet3.java
//
// An applet that uses the delegation event
// model to respond to a button press.
/////////////////////////////////////////////////

import com.ms.ui.*;
import com.ms.ui.event.*;

public class PushButtonApplet3 extends AwtUIApplet
{
```

```
        public PushButtonApplet3()
        {
            super(new AppletImplementation());
        }
    }

    class AppletImplementation extends UIApplet
        implements IUIActionListener
    {

        UIPushButton button;

        public void init()
        {
            UIBorderLayout layout = new UIBorderLayout();
            setLayout(layout);

            UIText text = new UIText("An AFC Pushbutton");
            button = new UIPushButton(text, UIPushButton.RAISED);
            button.addActionListener(this);
            add(button, "Center");

            setValid(true);
        }

        public void actionPerformed(UIActionEvent event)
        {
            String str = event.getActionCommand();
            if (str == "An AFC Pushbutton")
                button.setName("Thanks for the click!");
            else
                button.setName("All right, already!");
        }
    }
```

##  Creating Graphical Buttons

They say a picture is worth a thousand words. If this is true, adding an image to a pushbutton should be equivalent to displaying two pages of the software's manual. Anyone who's tried to decipher the meaning of an icon in a toolbar knows that an image is barely worth one word, let alone a thousand. Still, buttons with images sure are nice to look at.

Thanks to the different constructors provided by the **UIPushButton** class, it's easy to create buttons that display images. You can even create buttons that display both images and text, which, those thousand words notwithstanding, is a great way to create attractive buttons that don't confuse the user with cryptic icons.

To create a graphical button, first load the image that will appear on the button:

```
URL codeBase = getCodeBase();
Image image = getImage(codeBase, "image.ext");
```

Then create an AFC **UIGraphic** object from the image:

```
UIGraphic graphic = new UIGraphic(image);
```

Because a **UIGraphic** object is an AFC component, you can use it with the **UIPushButton** constructor that accepts a **UIComponent** object, as follows:

```
UIPushButton button = new UIPushButton(graphic, UIPushButton.RAISED);
```

Presto! You have a button that displays an image.

If you want to add both an image and text label to a button, first create a **UIItem** object that holds the image and the text string, as follows:

```
UIItem item = new UIItem(image, "Button Label");
```

Then, pass the **UIItem** object to the **UIPushButton** constructor:

```
UIPushButton button = new UIPushButton(item);
```

To see graphical buttons in action, try the applet shown in Listing 3.8, which creates a graphical button with only an image as well as a button with both an image and a label. Figure 3.10 shows the applet running in Microsoft Applet Viewer.

## Listing 3.8   An applet with graphical buttons.

```
/////////////////////////////////////////////////
// GraphicButtonApplet.java
//
// An AFC applet that displays graphical buttons.
/////////////////////////////////////////////////

import com.ms.ui.*;
import java.awt.*;
import java.net.*;

public class GraphicButtonApplet extends AwtUIApplet
{
```

```
    public GraphicButtonApplet()
    {
        super(new AppletImplementation());
    }
}

class AppletImplementation extends UIApplet
{
    public void init()
    {
        UIGridLayout layout = new UIGridLayout(2, 1);
        setLayout(layout);

        URL codeBase = getCodeBase();
        Image image = getImage(codeBase, "sunburst.gif");
        UIGraphic graphic = new UIGraphic(image);

        UIPushButton button1 =
            new UIPushButton(graphic, UIPushButton.RAISED);

        UIItem item = new UIItem(image, "Graphical Button");
        UIPushButton button2 = new UIPushButton(item);

        add(button1);
        add(button2);

        setValid(true);
    }
}
```

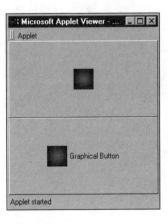

## Figure 3.10

*Two graphical buttons in an applet.*

## Using Repeat Buttons

Repeat buttons enable you to create controls that perform a task repeatedly. For example, you can use a repeat button to construct a control that—when pressed—continually increments or decrements a value, much like a spinner component. As long as the user keeps the button pressed, the button continues to generate action events.

Because the repeat button generates action events, you handle the button press much like you handle a regular pushbutton component. That is, when using the propagation event model, you write an **action()** method for the applet. For the delegation event model, you implement the **IUIActionListener** interface and add the applet to the button's listener list.

Listing 3.9 contains an applet that demonstrates a repeat button, using the delegation event model. When you press and hold the repeat button, the number displayed in the canvas component continues to increment. Figure 3.11 shows the applet running in Applet Viewer. If you want to use the propagation event model, modify the applet by taking out the **IUIActionListener** stuff and adding the **action()** method (don't forget to add the line **import java.awt.\*** to the top of the applet) as shown in the following example:

```
public boolean action(Event event, Object arg)
{
    if (arg == button)
    {
        canvas.count();
        return true;
    }
    return false;
}
```

**Listing 3.9   An applet that gathers events from a repeat button.**
```
///////////////////////////////////////////////////
// RepeatButtonApplet.java
//
// An AFC applet that demonstrates repeat buttons.
///////////////////////////////////////////////////

import com.ms.ui.*;
import com.ms.ui.event.*;
import com.ms.fx.*;

public class RepeatButtonApplet extends AwtUIApplet
{
```

```
    public RepeatButtonApplet()
    {
        super(new AppletImplementation());
    }
}

class AppletImplementation extends UIApplet
    implements IUIActionListener
{
    UIRepeatButton button;
    CountingCanvas canvas;

    public void init()
    {
        UIBorderLayout layout = new UIBorderLayout();
        setLayout(layout);

        UIText text = new UIText("An AFC Repeat Button");
        button = new UIRepeatButton(text, UIPushButton.RAISED);
        button.addActionListener(this);
        add(button, "North");

        canvas = new CountingCanvas();
        add(canvas, "Center");

        setValid(true);
    }

    public void actionPerformed(UIActionEvent event)
    {
        String command = event.getActionCommand();
        if (command == "An AFC Repeat Button")
            canvas.count();
    }
}

class CountingCanvas extends UICanvas
{
    int count;
    String displayString;

    public CountingCanvas()
    {
        setBackground(FxColor.blue);
        count = 0;
        displayString = "0";
    }
```

```
public void paint(FxGraphics graphics)
{
    FxFont font =
        new FxFont("TimesRoman", FxFont.PLAIN, 72);
    graphics.setFont(font);
    graphics.setColor(FxColor.white);
    graphics.drawString(displayString, 85, 130);
}

public void count()
{
    ++count;
    displayString = String.valueOf(count);
    repaint();
}
}
```

## Responding To Check Buttons

Check buttons, like all buttons when clicked, generate events. Unlike pushbuttons, however (which generate action events), a check button generates item events. This means that, with the delegation event model, you must implement the **IUIItemListener** interface, which is the AFC version of Java's **ItemListener** interface. You propagation event model fans must write an **action()** method.

Listing 3.10 is the source code for an applet that demonstrates check buttons and their events. The applet displays a check button, whose state is displayed in a canvas

**Figure 3.11**

*RepeatButtonApplet running in Applet Viewer.*

**Figure 3.12**

*CheckButtonApplet2, running in Applet Viewer.*

component, as shown in Figure 3.12. The applet uses the delegation event model and, therefore, implements the **IUIItemListener** interface.

The **IUIItemListener** interface requires that the applet define the **itemStateChanged()** method, which the button object calls when the user clicks the button. The **itemStateChanged()** method receives a **UIItemEvent** object as its single parameter. In the applet's **itemStateChanged()**, the program first calls the **UIItemEvent** object's **getItemSelectable()** method to retrieve a reference to the component that issued the event. If the component is the check button, the program calls the event object's **getStateChange()** method to get the button's new state, which can be **UIItem.SELECTED** or **UIItem.DESELECTED**.

If you prefer the propagation event model, the equivalent **action()** method might resemble Listing 3.11.

**Listing 3.10   An applet that demonstrates a check button.**

```
//////////////////////////////////////////////////
// CheckButtonApplet2.java
//
// An AFC applet that demonstrates how to respond
// to check buttons using the delegation event
// model.
//////////////////////////////////////////////////

import com.ms.ui.*;
import com.ms.ui.event.*;
import com.ms.fx.*;
```

```
public class CheckButtonApplet2 extends AwtUIApplet
{
    public CheckButtonApplet2()
    {
        super(new AppletImplementation());
    }
}

class AppletImplementation extends UIApplet
    implements IUIItemListener
{
    UICheckButton button;
    MessageCanvas canvas;

    public void init()
    {
        UIGridLayout gridLayout = new UIGridLayout(2,1);
        setLayout(gridLayout);

        UIPanel panel = new UIPanel();
        UIFlowLayout flowLayout = new UIFlowLayout();
        panel.setLayout(flowLayout);
        add(panel);

        button = new UICheckButton("An AFC Check Button");
        button.addItemListener(this);
        panel.add(button);

        canvas = new MessageCanvas("Unchecked", 36, 40, 70);
        add(canvas);

        setValid(true);
    }

    public void itemStateChanged(UIItemEvent event)
    {
        IUIComponent comp = event.getItemSelectable();
        if (comp == button)
        {
            int state = event.getStateChange();
            if (state == UIItemEvent.SELECTED)
                canvas.showMessage("Checked");
            else
                canvas.showMessage("Unchecked");
        }
    }
}
```

```
class MessageCanvas extends UICanvas
{
    String displayString;
    int pointSize;
    int col, row;

    public MessageCanvas(String msg, int points, int x, int y)
    {
        displayString = msg;
        pointSize = points;
        col = x;
        row = y;
        setBackground(FxColor.blue);
    }

    public void paint(FxGraphics graphics)
    {
        FxFont font =
            new FxFont("TimesRoman", FxFont.PLAIN, pointSize);
        graphics.setFont(font);
        graphics.setColor(FxColor.white);
        graphics.drawString(displayString, col, row);
    }

    public void showMessage(String str)
    {
        displayString = str;
        repaint();
    }
}
```

**Listing 3.11   An action() method for the CheckButtonApplet2 applet.**

```
public boolean action(Event event, Object arg)
{
    if (event.target instanceof UICheckButton)
    {
        UICheckButton button = (UICheckButton)event.target;
        boolean checked = button.isChecked();
        if (checked)
            canvas.showMessage("Checked");
        else
            canvas.showMessage("Unchecked");
        return true;
    }
    return false;
}
```

## Using Radio Buttons

As you know, radio buttons are usually organized into groups in which only a single button at a time can be selected. You can handle the radio buttons on your own, if you like, as you'll discover in the next section. However, AFC features the **UIRadioGroup** class, which automatically handles a group of radio buttons for you, ensuring that only one button at a time is in its selected state. To create a group of radio buttons, you first create an object of the **UIRadioGroup** class, like this:

```
UIRadioGroup radioGroup = new UIRadioGroup("Group Label");
```

The constructor's single argument is the string that'll appear as the group's label.

After constructing the **UIRadioGroup** object, construct your radio button objects and add them to the group:

```
UIRadioButton button1 = new UIRadioButton("Button Label 1");
button1.setChecked(true);
radioGroup.add(button1);
UIRadioButton button2 = new UIRadioButton("Button Label 2");
radioGroup.add(button2);
```

Notice the call to the first button's **setChecked()** method. Remember that one button in a radio button group must always be selected.

After you've added all your buttons to the group, add the group to its container:

```
add(radioGroup);
```

The radio button, like its check button cousin, generates item events. So, to handle radio buttons in a modern applet, you must implement the **IUIItemListener** interface. The methods of determining which button has been clicked is identical to the methods used with check buttons.

Listing 3.12 is an applet that demonstrates the management of radio buttons, using the delegation event model. (The **MessageCanvas** class referenced in the applet is exactly the same as the **MessageCanvas** class in Listing 3.10, and so is not shown here.) When you run the applet, you see three radio buttons, with the canvas component at the bottom of the applet reporting the selected button. You can select one—and only one—radio button in the group, as shown in Figure 3.13.

**Figure 3.13**

*RadioButtonApplet2, running in Applet Viewer.*

## Listing 3.12   The RadioButtonApplet2 applet.

```
//////////////////////////////////////////////////
// RadioButtonApplet2.java
//
// An AFC applet that demonstrates how to use
// a UIRadioGroup component to organize a set of
// radio buttons.
//////////////////////////////////////////////////

import com.ms.ui.*;
import com.ms.ui.event.*;
import com.ms.fx.*;

public class RadioButtonApplet2 extends AwtUIApplet
{
    public RadioButtonApplet2()
    {
        super(new AppletImplementation());
    }
}

class AppletImplementation extends UIApplet
{
    public void init()
    {
        UIGridLayout layout = new UIGridLayout(2,1);
        setLayout(layout);

        MessageCanvas canvas =
            new MessageCanvas("Button 1", 36, 60, 70);
```

```
                RadioPanel panel = new RadioPanel(canvas);
                add(panel);
                add(canvas);

                setValid(true);
        }
}

class RadioPanel extends UIPanel
        implements IUIItemListener
{
        MessageCanvas canvas;
        UIRadioButton button1;
        UIRadioButton button2;
        UIRadioButton button3;

        public RadioPanel(MessageCanvas c)
        {
                canvas = c;
                UIFlowLayout layout = new UIFlowLayout();
                setLayout(layout);

                UIRadioGroup group = new UIRadioGroup("Radio Buttons");

                button1 = new UIRadioButton("Radio Button 1");
                button1.setChecked(true);
                button1.addItemListener(this);
                group.add(button1);

                button2 = new UIRadioButton("Radio Button 2");
                button2.addItemListener(this);
                group.add(button2);

                button3 = new UIRadioButton("Radio Button 3");
                button3.addItemListener(this);
                group.add(button3);

                add(group);
        }

        public void itemStateChanged(UIItemEvent event)
        {
                UIRadioButton comp = (UIRadioButton)event.getItemSelectable();

                if (comp == button1)
                    canvas.showMessage("Button 1");
```

```
        else if (comp == button2)
            canvas.showMessage("Button 2");
        else
            canvas.showMessage("Button 3");
    }
}
```

## Using Radio Buttons Without A Group Box

Normally, you would use a **UIRadioGroup** object to organize radio buttons into a group, but there may be times when you want to manage the radio buttons on your own, without the help of a group box. This task is easy to accomplish thanks to the **setChecked()** method. Just remember that one button in the group, and only one button, must always be selected.

Listing 3.13 is an applet that demonstrates the management of radio buttons without a group box, using the delegation event model. (The **MessageCanvas** class referenced in the applet is exactly the same as the **MessageCanvas** class in Listing 3.10, and so is not shown here.) When you run the applet, you see three radio buttons, with the canvas component at the bottom of the applet reporting the selected button. You can select one—and only one—radio button in the group, as shown in Figure 3.14.

If you prefer to use the propagation event model, Listing 3.14 shows an equivalent **action()** method.

**Figure 3.14**

*RadioButtonApplet3, running in Applet Viewer.*

## Listing 3.13   An applet that manages a group of radio buttons.

```
/////////////////////////////////////////////////
// RadioButtonApplet3.java
//
// An AFC applet that manages radio buttons
// without a radio button group box.
/////////////////////////////////////////////////

import com.ms.ui.*;
import com.ms.ui.event.*;
import com.ms.fx.*;

public class RadioButtonApplet3 extends AwtUIApplet
{
    public RadioButtonApplet3()
    {
        super(new AppletImplementation());
    }
}

class AppletImplementation extends UIApplet
{
    public void init()
    {
        UIGridLayout layout = new UIGridLayout(2,1);
        setLayout(layout);

        MessageCanvas canvas =
            new MessageCanvas("Button 1", 36, 60, 70);
        RadioPanel panel = new RadioPanel(canvas);
        add(panel);
        add(canvas);

        setValid(true);
    }
}

class RadioPanel extends UIPanel
    implements IUIItemListener
{
    MessageCanvas canvas;
    UIRadioButton button1;
    UIRadioButton button2;
    UIRadioButton button3;
    UIRadioButton currentButton;

    public RadioPanel(MessageCanvas c)
    {
```

```
            canvas = c;
            UIGridLayout layout = new UIGridLayout(1, 3);
            setLayout(layout);

            button1 = new UIRadioButton("Button 1");
            button1.setChecked(true);
            currentButton = button1;
            add(button1);
            button1.addItemListener(this);

            button2 = new UIRadioButton("Button 2");
            add(button2);
            button2.addItemListener(this);

            button3 = new UIRadioButton("Button 3");
            add(button3);
            button3.addItemListener(this);
        }

    public void itemStateChanged(UIItemEvent event)
    {
        UIRadioButton comp = (UIRadioButton)event.getItemSelectable();
        currentButton.setChecked(false);
        comp.setChecked(true);
        currentButton = comp;

        if (comp == button1)
            canvas.showMessage("Button 1");
        else if (comp == button2)
            canvas.showMessage("Button 2");
        else
            canvas.showMessage("Button 3");
    }
}
```

## Listing 3.14  An **action()** method for the **RadioButtonApplet3** applet.

```
public boolean action(Event event, Object arg)
{
    UIRadioButton comp = (UIRadioButton)event.target;
    currentButton.setChecked(false);
    comp.setChecked(true);
    currentButton = comp;

    if (comp == button1)
        canvas.showMessage("Button 1");
    else if (comp == button2)
        canvas.showMessage("Button 2");
```

```
    else
        canvas.showMessage("Button 3");

    return true;
}
```

##  Displaying Submenus

Previously in this chapter, you discovered that the **UIMenuItem** class extends **UIMenuLauncher**, which gives **UIMenuItem** the ability to launch menus. This ability is the key to creating submenus within menu buttons. All you need to do is create a **UIMenuItem** that contains a menu list.

The first step is to create the menu list, which is an object of the **UIMenuList** class, and add menu commands to the list:

```
UIMenuList subMenuList = new UIMenuList();
subMenuList.add("Sub Item 1");
subMenuList.add("Sub Item 2");
```

Next, create a **UIMenuItem** object, passing the menu list to the **UIMenuItem** constructor:

```
UIMenuItem menuItem = new UIMenuItem("Menu Item", subMenuList);
```

Here, the constructor's first argument is the text string that'll represent the submenu in the main menu list, and the second argument is the menu list that represents the submenu connected to the menu item object.

Now, add the new menu item object to the main menu list, just like any other menu list item:

```
UIMenuList menuList = new UIMenuList();
menuList.add(menuItem);
```

Finally, add the main menu list to the menu button:

```
UIMenuButton menuButton =
    new UIMenuButton("AFC Menu Button", menuList);
```

Listing 3.15 is an applet that creates and displays a menu that contains a submenu. When you run the applet, click the menu button. The main menu appears. One of the menu items is indented and is marked with a small arrow. select this menu item, and the submenu appears, as shown in Figure 3.15.

**Figure 3.15**

*MenuButtonApplet3 displaying a submenu.*

## Listing 3.15   An applet that creates a menu with a submenu.

```
///////////////////////////////////////////////
// MenuButtonApplet3.java
//
// An AFC applet that demonstrates how to create
// menus with submenus.
///////////////////////////////////////////////

import com.ms.ui.*;

public class MenuButtonApplet3 extends AwtUIApplet
{
    public MenuButtonApplet3()
    {
        super(new AppletImplementation());
    }
}

class AppletImplementation extends UIApplet
{
    public void init()
    {
        UIFlowLayout layout = new UIFlowLayout();
        setLayout(layout);

        UIMenuList subMenuList = new UIMenuList();
        subMenuList.add("Sub Item 1");
        subMenuList.add("Sub Item 2");
        subMenuList.add("Sub Item 3");
        UIMenuItem menuItem = new UIMenuItem("Menu Item 4", subMenuList);
```

```
        UIMenuList menuList = new UIMenuList();
        menuList.add("Menu Item 1");
        menuList.add("Menu Item 2");
        menuList.add("Menu Item 3");
        menuList.add(menuItem);
        menuList.add("Menu Item 5");

        UIMenuButton menuButton =
            new UIMenuButton("AFC Menu Button", menuList);
        add(menuButton);

        setValid(true);
    }
}
```

## Responding To Menu Selections

In previous programs, you saw how to create and display menu buttons and their associated menus and submenus. What happens now is that, when the user selects a menu item, the menu generates an action event.

When programming menus with the propagation event model, the **action()** method receives the event, with the menu button object passed in the event object's **target** field and the selected item component in the **Object** passed as the **action()** method's second parameter. By checking these values, you can easily determine the selected menu item and respond accordingly.

Listing 3.16, for example, is an applet (shown in Figure 3.16) that demonstrates how to respond to menu selections. (The **MessageCanvas** class referenced in the applet is exactly the same class as the **MessageCanvas** class referred to in Listing 3.10.) The program uses the propagation event model and so supplies an **action()** method.

The **action()** method examines the event object's **target** field to determine the menu button selected (in this case, there's only one possibility, but often, you need to differentiate between several menu buttons). The **action()** method then examines **arg** to determine the exact menu item selected.

If you want to use the newer delegation event model, the program must implement the **IUIActionListener** interface:

```
public class MenuButtonApplet4 extends AwtUIApplet
    implements IUIActionListener
```

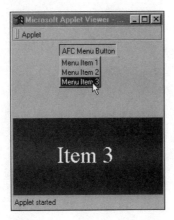

**Figure 3.16**

*MenuButtonApplet4 responds to menu selections.*

Then you must register the applet as an action listener with the **UIMenuList** object:

```
UIMenuList menuList = new UIMenuList();
menuList.addActionListener(this);
```

Finally, you must provide the **actionPerformed()** method, which may look like the following:

```
public void actionPerformed(UIActionEvent event)
{
    String str = event.getActionCommand();
    canvas.showMessage(str);
}
```

**Listing 3.16   An applet that responds to menu selections.**
```
/////////////////////////////////////////////////
// MenuButtonApplet4.java
//
// An AFC applet that responds to menu selections.
/////////////////////////////////////////////////

import com.ms.ui.*;
import com.ms.fx.*;
import java.awt.*;

public class MenuButtonApplet4 extends AwtUIApplet
{
    public MenuButtonApplet4()
    {
```

```
            super(new AppletImplementation());
        }
    }

    class AppletImplementation extends UIApplet
    {
        IUIComponent item1;
        IUIComponent item2;
        IUIComponent item3;
        UIMenuButton menuButton;
        MessageCanvas canvas;

        public void init()
        {
            UIGridLayout layout = new UIGridLayout(2, 1);
            setLayout(layout);

            UIPanel panel = new UIPanel();
            UIMenuList menuList = new UIMenuList();
            item1 = menuList.add("Menu Item 1");
            item2 = menuList.add("Menu Item 2");
            item3 = menuList.add("Menu Item 3");
            menuButton =
                new UIMenuButton("AFC Menu Button", menuList);
            panel.add(menuButton);
            add(panel);

            canvas = new MessageCanvas("None", 36, 70, 70);
            add(canvas);

            setValid(true);
        }

        public boolean action(Event event, Object arg)
        {
            if (event.target == menuButton)
            {
                if (arg == item1)
                    canvas.showMessage("Item 1");
                else if (arg == item2)
                    canvas.showMessage("Item 2");
                else if (arg == item3)
                    canvas.showMessage("Item 3");
                return true;
            }
            return false;
        }
    }
```

# Enabling And Disabling Components

Often in your programs, you need to enable or disable components based on the state of other components. You may have a check button, for example, that when selected, makes some options appropriate and others inappropriate. A good way to handle this situation is to disable the options that are no longer suitable, and to enable the new options. You can do this easily by tracking the state of the controlling component and calling the other components' **setEnabled()** methods as needed.

The **setEnabled()** method takes a single argument, which is a **boolean** value specifying whether the component should be enabled (**true**) or disabled (**false**). To create a disabled button component, for example, you might write these lines:

```
UIPushButton button = new UIPushButton("Button", UIPushButton.RAISED);
button.setEnabled(false);
```

Listing 3.17 is an applet that demonstrates how you can *subjugate* a set of components to another component. The subjugated pushbuttons are enabled or disabled based on the state of the "boss" check button. When you run the applet in Applet Viewer, you see the window shown in Figure 3.17. The check button is unchecked, and as a result, the subjugated pushbuttons are disabled. To correct this sorry situation, select the check button. When you do, the pushbuttons become enabled and ready to click, as shown in Figure 3.18.

Listing 3.18 shows an **action()** method that EnableButtonApplet might use if it processed events by using the propagation event model.

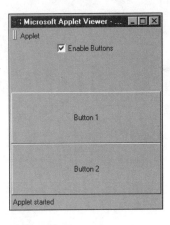

**Figure 3.17**

*The EnableButtonApplet applet, running in Applet Viewer.*

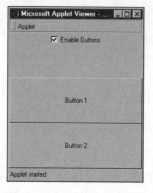

**Figure 3.18**

*The EnableButtonApplet applet, after enabling the buttons.*

**Listing 3.17   An applet that enables and disables buttons.**

```
///////////////////////////////////////////////
// EnableButtonApplet.java
//
// An AFC applet that demonstrates enabling and
// disabling components.
///////////////////////////////////////////////

import com.ms.ui.*;
import com.ms.ui.event.*;

public class EnableButtonApplet extends AwtUIApplet
{
    public EnableButtonApplet()
    {
        super(new AppletImplementation());
    }
}

class AppletImplementation extends UIApplet
    implements IUIItemListener
{
    UICheckButton enableButton;
    UIPushButton button1;
    UIPushButton button2;

    public void init()
    {
        UIGridLayout layout = new UIGridLayout(3, 1);
        setLayout(layout);
```

```
        UIPanel panel = new UIPanel();
        enableButton = new UICheckButton("Enable Buttons");
        enableButton.addItemListener(this);
        panel.add(enableButton);
        add(panel);

        button1 = new UIPushButton("Button 1", UIPushButton.RAISED);
        button1.setEnabled(false);
        add(button1);

        button2 = new UIPushButton("Button 2", UIPushButton.RAISED);
        button2.setEnabled(false);
        add(button2);

        setValid(true);
    }

    public void itemStateChanged(UIItemEvent event)
    {
        IUIComponent comp = event.getItemSelectable();
        if (comp == enableButton)
        {
            boolean checked = enableButton.isChecked();
            button1.setEnabled(checked);
            button2.setEnabled(checked);
        }
    }
}
```

## Listing 3.18   An **action()** method for EnableButtonApplet.

```
public boolean action(Event event, Object arg)
{
    if (event.target == enableButton)
    {
        boolean checked = enableButton.isChecked();
        button1.setEnabled(checked);
        button2.setEnabled(checked);
        return true;
    }
    return false;
}
```

# Chapter 4

# Edit, List, Choice, And Group Components

# Notes…

# Chapter 4

Words are the most powerful tools ever invented by the human race. Words have the power to soothe a child or to destroy entire nations, to create art or to evoke hate and fear. As Philip K. Dick said, words can even manipulate reality, changing the way people think, act, and feel. Words are everywhere: in newspapers, on cereal boxes, on billboards, on trash, on clothes, on TV, in the sink, and, yes, even in our minds.

Words are, of course, in AFC programs. Chances are the words in your next AFC program won't win the Nobel peace prize or cure cancer, but they sure can help you to communicate with the user. One of the most powerful tools AFC provides for working with words is the edit box, represented in AFC by the **UIEdit** class. Your application can use an edit box to obtain single-line responses from the user or to create a mini word processor. You can set text alignments, manipulate text selections, mask out unwanted characters, and more.

**UIEdit** is only one of the AFC classes you'll discover in this chapter. You also get a look at AFC's list and choice components, represented by the **UIList** and **UIChoice** classes, respectively. These two classes enable you to arrange items into lists from which users can make one or more selections. Often, these components contain a list of—you guessed it—words (in this case, words that represent objects or commands).

This chapter also covers the group components, represented in AFC by the **UIGroup**, **UICheckGroup**, and **UIRadioGroup** classes. These components help you to design attractive and easy-to-comprehend user interfaces, by grouping related controls into separate boxes. Finally, although it's true that the group components don't manipulate words...well, they do all have text labels!

## The **UIEdit** Class

One main way a user enters data into an application is through the keyboard. Most often, the user enters text into a dialog box or some other type of form that contains editable text boxes. Applets, too, can take advantage of text boxes, by using them to obtain information from the user. In AFC, the **UIEdit** class represents edit boxes. This class enables the user not only to enter and edit text information, it also supports various types of text alignment. You can even set up an edit box to handle multiple lines of text, complete with word wrapping.

The **UIEdit** class extends the **UIDrawText** class, which represents the text contained in an edit box. **UIDrawText** extends **UICanvas** and so traces its ancestry up through **UIStateComponent** to **UIComponent**. **UIEdit** inherits methods from all of these superclasses, but it also defines its own set of methods, as shown in Table 4.1.

Creating an edit box is a simple matter of calling the class's constructor, like this:

```
UIEdit edit = new UIEdit();
```

**Table 4.1   Methods of the UIEdit class.**

| Method | Description |
| --- | --- |
| **addActionListener()** | Registers an object as an action listener |
| **addTextListener()** | Register an object as a text listener |
| **append()** | Adds a character to the end of the text in the control |
| **clear()** | Clears all text from the control |
| **clearUndo()** | Clears undo and redo information for the component |
| **getBackground()** | Gets the component's background color |
| **getMaskChars()** | Gets the component's mask characters |
| **getMaskMode()** | Gets the component's character mask mode |

*(continued)*

Table 4.1 Methods of the **UIEdit** class *(continued).*

| Method | Description |
| --- | --- |
| getMaxBufferSize() | Gets the maximum number of characters that the control can hold |
| getRoleCode() | Returns the **ROLE_SYSTEM_TEXT** role code |
| insert() | Inserts text into the control |
| isReadOnly() | Returns **true** if the control is read-only |
| isRedoable() | Returns **true** if the component can redo the last undo |
| isUndoable() | Returns **true** if the component can undo the last change |
| keyDown() | Processes the key-down event |
| processActionEvent() | Broadcasts action events to all registered action listener objects |
| processEvent() | Calls the appropriate event method for a received event |
| processTextEvent() | Broadcasts text events to registered text listener objects |
| redo() | Reverses the last undo |
| remove() | Removes characters from the control |
| removeActionListener() | Removes an action listener object from the listener list |
| removeTextListener() | Removes a text listener from the listener list |
| setBackground() | Sets the component's background color |
| setMaskChars() | Sets the component's mask characters |
| setMaskMode() | Sets the component's character mask mode |
| setMaxBufferSize() | Sets the maximum number of characters that the control can hold |
| setReadOnly() | Toggles the control's read-only state |
| setValueText() | Sets the component's contents |
| undo() | Restores the previous changes |

**Figure 4.1**

*EditApplet, running in Microsoft Applet Viewer.*

You don't even need to supply arguments. However, if you want the edit box to start off containing text, you could construct the control like this:

```
UIEdit edit = new UIEdit("This text will be in the edit box");
```

You can also specify various attributes for the edit box, including a border, read-only state, background color, text color, font, alignment, single-line text entry, and word wrapping. You set some of these attributes by calling methods defined in **UIEdit**. **UIEdit** inherits other attributes from **UIDrawText**.

Listing 4.1 presents a small applet that creates and displays an edit box with a border, a Courier font, and single-line text entry. Figure 4.1 shows the applet running in Microsoft Applet Viewer.

### Listing 4.1   The source code for EditApplet.

```
///////////////////////////////////////////////////
// EditApplet.java
//
// An AFC applet that creates and displays an
// edit box with a border, a custom font, and
// single-line text entry.
///////////////////////////////////////////////////

import com.ms.ui.*;
import com.ms.fx.*;

public class EditApplet extends AwtUIApplet
```

```
{
    public EditApplet()
    {
        super(new AppletImplementation());
    }
}

class AppletImplementation extends UIApplet
{
    public void init()
    {
        UIBorderLayout layout = new UIBorderLayout();
        setLayout(layout);

        UIEdit edit =
            new UIEdit("This text will be in the edit box");
        FxFont font = new FxFont("Courier", FxFont.PLAIN, 12);
        edit.setFont(font);
        edit.setBordered(true);
        edit.setSingleLine(true);
        add(edit, "North");
        edit.requestFocus();

        setValid(true);
    }
}
```

# The **UIDrawText** Class

Most of the control an applet has over the text in an edit box comes from the
**UIDrawText** class. This class features methods that enable the applet to set text align-
ment, colors, word wrapping, single- or multiline text entry, and other text attributes.
The class also has methods for obtaining both the current attribute settings and
information about the portion of the text the user may have selected. Table 4.2 lists
**UIDrawText**'s methods.

You can create **UIDrawText** objects in your AFC programs to have text displays that
you can manipulate programmatically. Normally, however, you'll create **UIEdit** objects, which inherit from the **UIDrawText** class, so that the text is editable both by
the user and by the program. The **UIEdit** class also adds support for the **IUIAction-
Listener** and **IUITextListener** interfaces, providing a mechanism for responding to
text control events.

**Table 4.2  Methods of the UIDrawText class.**

| Method | Description |
|---|---|
| addNotify() | Called to notify the object that the graphics context is available |
| ensureNotDirty() | Updates text |
| ensureVisible() | Displays the text at the given index, point, or rectangle |
| eoln() | Gets the position of the end-of-line character |
| getCharFromScreen() | Gets the character at the given position |
| getCharLocation() | Gets the location at which a character will be drawn |
| getCurrIndex() | Gets the caret's position |
| getHorizAlign() | Gets the text's horizontal alignment setting |
| getIndexHeight() | Gets the height of a font |
| getLength() | Gets the number of characters in the text |
| getMinimumSize() | Gets the control's minimum size in pixels |
| getOutline() | Gets the control's outline |
| getPasswordChar() | Gets the control's password character |
| getPreferredSize() | Gets the controls preferred size |
| getRoleCode() | Returns the ROLE_SYSTEM_STATICTEXT role code |
| getSelectedText() | Gets the control's selected text |
| getSelectionEnd() | Gets a selection's ending position |
| getSelectionStart() | Gets a selection's starting position |
| getValueText() | Gets the control's contents |
| getVertAlign() | Gets the component's vertical alignment setting |
| getWordEdge() | Gets the position of a word's first or last character |
| getWordWrap() | Gets the control's word-wrap style |

*(continued)*

Table 4.2 Methods of the **UIDrawText** class *(continued)*.

| Method | Description |
|---|---|
| gotFocus() | Called when the control gets the focus |
| hideCaret() | Hides the control's caret |
| isAutoResizable() | Returns **true** if the control's auto-resize setting is set to on |
| isBordered() | Returns **true** if the control has a border |
| isSingleLine() | Returns **true** if the control displays only a single text line |
| keyDown() | Processes key-down events |
| lostFocus() | Called when the control loses the focus |
| mouseDown() | Processes mouse-down events |
| mouseDrag() | Processes mouse-drag events |
| paint() | Draws the control or the control's text |
| processKeyEvent() | Processes key events |
| selectAll() | Selects all the control's text |
| setAutoResizable() | Toggles the control's auto-resize feature |
| setBackground() | Sets the control's background color |
| setBorder() | Toggles the control's border |
| setBounds() | Positions and sizes the control |
| setCurrIndex() | Positions the caret |
| setFont() | Sets the font used to display text |
| setForeground() | Sets the control's text color |
| setHorizAlign() | Sets the control's horizontal text alignment |
| setInputMethod() | Sets the component's InputMethodListener |
| setLocation() | Positions the control |

*(continued)*

**Table 4.2  Methods of the UIDrawText class (continued).**

| Method | Description |
| --- | --- |
| setOutline() | Sets the control's outline |
| setPasswordChar() | Sets the control's password character |
| setRefresh() | Toggles the control's refresh flag |
| setSelection() | Selects a range of text in the control |
| setSingleLine() | Toggles the control's single-line feature |
| setSize() | Sets the control's size |
| setTabs() | Sets the component's tab stops |
| setTextCallback() | Sets the control's text callback interface |
| setValueText() | Sets the control's contents |
| setVertAlign() | Sets the control's vertical text alignment |
| setWordWrap() | Toggles the control's word-wrap feature |
| showCaret() | Displays the control's caret |
| update() | Redraws the component |

# The UIList Class

The **UIList** class represents a list of items in a program. The class provides methods for adding items to the list, selecting items, and removing items. **UIList** extends the **UISelector** class, from which **UIList** inherits the methods that enable the user or the program to select items in the list, as well as methods for setting selection modes. **UISelector** extends **UIPanel**, and so traces its ancestry up through **UIStateContainer** and **UIContainer** to **UIComponent**. In addition to the classes **UIList** inherits from its superclasses, it also defines its own method—**add()**—which enables a program to add items to the list.

To create a list, you call the class's constructor and then call **add()** to add items to the list, as in the following:

```
UIList list = new UIList();
list.add("First Item");
```

You can also specify a selection mode and a layout style when you create the list control. Please refer to this chapter's Practical Guide for more information on selection modes and layout styles. Listing 4.2 presents a short applet that displays a list component. Figure 4.2 shows the applet running in Applet Viewer. When you run the applet, notice how you can select items either with the mouse or by pressing your keyboard's up- and down-arrow keys.

### Listing 4.2 The source code for ListApplet.

```
/////////////////////////////////////////////////
// ListApplet.java
//
// An AFC applet that shows how to create a list
// component.
/////////////////////////////////////////////////

import com.ms.ui.*;
import com.ms.ui.event.*;
import com.ms.fx.*;

public class ListApplet extends AwtUIApplet
{
    public ListApplet()
    {
        super(new AppletImplementation());
    }
}

class AppletImplementation extends UIApplet
{
    public void init()
    {
        UIFlowLayout layout = new UIFlowLayout();
        setLayout(layout);

        UIList list = new UIList();
        list.add("List Item 1");
        list.add("List Item 2");
        list.add("List Item 3");
        list.add("List Item 4");
        add(list);
        list.requestFocus();
    }
}
```

**Figure 4.2**

*ListApplet, running in Microsoft Applet Viewer.*

## The **UISelector** Class

The **UISelector** class supplies most of a list's functionality; it enables items to be selected, and it processes the events that these selections generate. As mentioned in the preceding section, **UISelector** extends **UIPanel**, which means it also counts **UIStateContainer**, **UIContainer**, and **UIComponent** among its superclasses. Besides the methods it inherits from these superclasses, **UISelector** defines a rich set of its own methods. Table 4.3 lists these methods and their descriptions.

Note that **UISelector** is an abstract class—you cannot directly create objects from it. Rather, you must create objects from classes that extend **UISelector**, including **UIList**, **UITabList**, and **UITree**.

## The **UIChoice** Class

The **UIChoice** class represents an object similar to a Windows combo box. The component comprises a text box with an associated list of menu items. The user clicks the arrow next to the text box to display the menu from which the user can select an item. **UIChoice** extends **UIPanel**, which means that it also inherits methods from **UIStateContainer**, **UIContainer**, and **UIComponent**. Additionally, **UIChoice** defines the methods shown in Table 4.4. These methods enable a program to set the component's attributes, handle item selection, respond to events, and obtain information about the component.

**Table 4.3   Methods of the UISelector class.**

| Method | Description |
| --- | --- |
| addActionListener() | Registers an object as an action listener |
| addItemListener() | Registers an object as an item listener |
| addSelectedIndex() | Selects the item at the given index |
| addSelectedIndices() | Selects the items at the given indexes |
| addSelectedItem() | Selects the given item |
| addSelectedItems() | Selects the given items |
| find() | Finds a component, given the component's name |
| getAnchorItem() | Gets the anchor component |
| getExtensionItem() | Gets the extension component |
| getRoleCode() | Returns the component's role code, which is **ROLE_SYSTEM_LIST** |
| getSelectedIndex() | Returns a selected item's index |
| getSelectedIndices() | Returns the indexes of multiple selected items |
| getSelectedItem() | Gets the selected component |
| getSelectedItems() | Gets all selected components |
| getSelectionMode() | Gets the current selection mode, which can be **SINGLESELECT**, **MULTISELECT**, **EXTENDSELECT**, or **NOSELECT** |
| getStateCode() | Gets the control's state |
| gotFocus() | Called when the control gets the focus |
| keyDown() | Processes key-down events |
| lostFocus() | Called when the control loses the focus |
| mouseDown() | Processes mouse-down events |
| mouseDrag() | Processes mouse-drag events |

*(continued)*

**Table 4.3  Methods of the UISelector class _(continued)._**

| Method | Description |
|---|---|
| processActionEvent() | Processes action events |
| processEvent() | Processes the given event |
| processItemEvent() | Processes item events |
| remove() | Removes a component from the control |
| removeActionListener() | Removes action event listeners from the component's list of listeners |
| removeItemListener() | Removes item event listeners from the component's list of listeners |
| removeSelectedIndex() | Deselects the item at the given index |
| removeSelectedIndices() | Deselects the items at the given indexes |
| removeSelectedItem() | Deselects the given item |
| removeSelectedItems() | Deselects the given items |
| setAnchorItem() | Sets the component's anchor item |
| setExtensionItem() | Sets the component's extension item |
| setSelected() | Toggles the control's selected state |
| setSelectedIndex() | Selects the item at the given index |
| setSelectedIndices() | Selects the items at the given indexes |
| setSelectedItem() | Selects the given item |
| setSelectedItems() | Selects the given items |
| setSelectionMode() | Sets the component's selection mode; can be **SINGLESELECT**, **MULTISELECT**, **EXTENDSELECT**, or **NOSELECT** |
| timeTriggered() | Stops incremental searches in the component |

**Table 4.4  Methods of the UIChoice class.**

| Method | Description |
| --- | --- |
| action() | Redraws the control to show the selected component |
| add() | Adds a component to the control |
| addActionListener() | Registers an object as an action listener |
| addItemListener() | Registers an object as an item listener |
| addNotify() | Called when the graphics context becomes available |
| addSelectedIndex() | Selects the item at the given index |
| addSelectedIndices() | Selects the items at the given indexes |
| addSelectedItem() | Selects the given item |
| addSelectedItems() | Selects the given items |
| addString() | Adds text to the component |
| getAnchorItem() | Gets the anchor component |
| getExtensionItem() | Gets the extension component |
| getMenu() | Gets a reference to the component's menu list |
| getPreferredSize() | Gets the component's preferred size |
| getRoleCode() | Returns the component's role code, which is **ROLE_SYSTEM_COMBOBOX** |
| getSelectedIndex() | Returns a selected item's index |
| getSelectedIndices() | Returns the indexes of multiple selected items |
| getSelectedItem() | Gets the selected component |
| getSelectedItems() | Gets all selected components |
| getSelectionMode() | Gets the current selection mode, which can be **SINGLESELECT**, **MULTISELECT**, or **EXTENDSELECT** |
| getStyle() | Gets the component's style |

(continued)

**Table 4.4  Methods of the UIChoice class (continued).**

| Method | Description |
|---|---|
| getValueText() | Gets the selected item's name |
| handleEvent() | Keeps the component updated |
| keyDown() | Processes key-down events |
| layout() | Lays out the component |
| mouseDown() | Processes mouse-down events |
| postEvent() | Posts the given event to the component |
| processEvent() | Processes the given event |
| processItemEvent() | Processes item events |
| remove() | Removes a component from the control |
| removeActionListener() | Removes action event listeners from the component's list of listeners |
| removeItemListener() | Removes item event listeners from the component's list of listeners |
| removeSelectedIndex() | Deselects the item at the given index |
| removeSelectedIndices() | Deselects the items at the given indexes |
| removeSelectedItem() | Deselects the given item |
| removeSelectedItems() | Deselects the given items |
| requestFocus() | Requests the input focus for the control |
| setAnchorItem() | Sets the component's anchor item |
| setExtensionItem() | Sets the component's extension item |
| setSelectedIndex() | Selects the item at the given index |
| setSelectedIndices() | Selects the items at the given indexes |
| setSelectedItem() | Selects the given item |

*(continued)*

**Table 4.4** Methods of the **UIChoice** class *(continued)*.

| Method | Description |
| --- | --- |
| setSelectedItems() | Selects the given items |
| setSelectionMode() | Sets the component's selection mode; must be **SINGLESELECT** |
| setStyle() | Sets the component's style, which can be 0 (the default) or **THICK** |
| setValueText() | Selects the given item if it exists in the component |

To create a **UIChoice** component, call its constructor, and then call the **add()** or **addString()** methods to populate the component with menu items, as shown in the following:

```
UIChoice choice = new UIChoice();
choice.addString("First Menu Item");
```

Listing 4.3 presents an applet that creates and displays a choice component that contains four menu items. Figure 4.3 shows the applet as it first appears. When you click the component's arrow, the menu list (from which you can select an item) appears, as shown in Figure 4.4.

**Figure 4.3**

*ChoiceApplet, running in Microsoft Applet Viewer.*

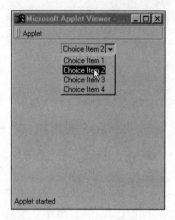

**Figure 4.4**

*ChoiceApplet with its menu displayed.*

**Listing 4.3   The source code for ChoiceApplet.**

```
//////////////////////////////////////////////////
// ChoiceApplet.java
//
// An AFC applet that creates and displays a
// choice component.
//////////////////////////////////////////////////

import com.ms.ui.*;
import com.ms.fx.*;

public class ChoiceApplet extends AwtUIApplet
{
    public ChoiceApplet()
    {
        super(new AppletImplementation());
    }
}

class AppletImplementation extends UIApplet
{
    public void init()
    {
        UIFlowLayout layout = new UIFlowLayout();
        setLayout(layout);
        UIChoice choice = new UIChoice();
        choice.addString("Choice Item 1");
        choice.addString("Choice Item 2");
        choice.addString("Choice Item 3");
        choice.addString("Choice Item 4");
```

```
        add(choice);
        choice.requestFocus();

        setValid(true);
    }
}
```

# The **UIEditChoice** Class

The preceding section described a **UIChoice** object as being similar to a Windows combo box. The difference is that, in a Windows combo box, the user can edit the text in the component's text box. A combo box can even automatically complete an entry that the user starts typing, provided that the typed characters match an existing item in the combo box's list. No object of the **UIChoice** class has these capabilities.

The **UIEditChoice** class, on the other hand, combines the best of an edit control with a choice control, creating a component that better matches Windows' combo box control. **UIEditChoice** extends the **UIChoice** class, but it also implements the **IUITextListener** interface. Implementing this interface enables the component to monitor the characters the user types in the text box. This implementation enables the component to automatically complete entries for the user, when the user has entered only the first few characters of an existing item in the component's list. Table 4.5 lists the methods of the **UIEditChoice** class.

In an AFC program, you create and manipulate a **UIEditChoice** object exactly as you do a **UIChoice** object. The components even look almost the same on screen, the difference being that the **UIEditChoice** component enables the user to type a selection into the associated edit box. Here's an example of creating and populating a **UIEditChoice** component:

```
UIEditChoice choice = new UIEditChoice();
choice.addString("Choice Item 1");
choice.addString("Choice Item 2");
choice.addString("Choice Item 3");
```

# The **UIGroup** Class

Often, when designing a user interface, you're faced with dozens of components that you need to organize in a logical way. You want to fit as many options as you can on the screen, but you don't want to confuse or overwhelm the program's eventual user. Group boxes provide a great way to organize related components into a single unit. Previously in this book, you saw group boxes used to organize radio buttons,

**Table 4.5   Methods of the UIEditChoice class.**

| Method | Description |
|---|---|
| action() | Redraws the control to show the selected component |
| getValueText() | Gets the selected item's name |
| gotFocus() | Called when the component gets the input focus |
| keyDown() | Processes key-down events |
| layout() | Lays out the component |
| lostFocus() | Called when the component loses the input focus |
| requestFocus() | Gives the component the input focus |
| setValueText() | Selects the given item if it exists in the component |
| textValueChanged() | Responds to text events |

which are almost always placed into a group. AFC's **UIGroup** class enables you to organize any set of components into a group.

**UIGroup** is the superclass for the other group classes, **UICheckGroup** and **UIRadioGroup**. By itself, **UIGroup** extends the **UIPanel** class, which means that it inherits methods not only from **UIPanel** but also from **UIStateContainer**, **UIContainer**, and **UIComponent**. Table 4.6 shows the methods defined in the **UIGroup** class. As

**Table 4.6   Methods of the UIGroup class.**

| Method | Description |
|---|---|
| adjustLayoutSize() | Adjusts the group box's layout size |
| getInsets() | Gets the group box's insets (margins) |
| isWidthRelative() | Returns **true** if the layout manager lays out components by using the container's width |
| layout() | Lays out the group box |
| paint() | Draws the group box |
| setName() | Sets the group box's label |

you can see, **UIGroup** has only a few of its own methods, getting most of its functionality from its base classes.

To create a group box, call its constructor and then call the **add()** method to add components to the box, as in the following syntax:

```
UIGroup group = new UIGroup("Group Box Label");
UIPushButton button = new UIPushButton("Button Label");
group.add(button);
```

The constructor's single argument is the group box's text label, which can be a string or a **UIText** object. You also can create a group box without specifying a label. In this case, you would call **setName()** to specify the label, as in the following:

```
UIGroup group = new UIGroup();
group.setName("Group Box Label");
```

Listing 4.4 presents a short applet that creates and displays a group box that contains several buttons.

### Listing 4.4   The source code for GroupApplet.

```
/////////////////////////////////////////////////
// GroupApplet.java
//
// An AFC applet that creates and displays a
// Group component that contains three buttons.
/////////////////////////////////////////////////

import com.ms.ui.*;
import com.ms.fx.*;

public class GroupApplet extends AwtUIApplet
{
    public GroupApplet()
    {
        super(new AppletImplementation());
    }
}

class AppletImplementation extends UIApplet
{
    public void init()
    {
        UIFlowLayout layout = new UIFlowLayout();
        setLayout(layout);

        UIGroup group = new UIGroup("Button Group");
```

```
UIPushButton button =
    new UIPushButton("   Button 1    ",
    UIPushButton.RAISED);
group.add(button);

button = new UIPushButton("    Button 2     ",
    UIPushButton.RAISED);
group.add(button);

button =
    new UIPushButton("    Button 3     ",
        UIPushButton.RAISED);
group.add(button);

add(group, "North");
setValid(true);
    }
}
```

Figure 4.5 shows the applet running in Applet Viewer.

## The **UICheckGroup** Class

Although you can place check buttons into a generic **UIGroup** group box, AFC defines a special class for this task, named **UICheckGroup**. The truth is, though, that there's no difference between how check buttons look and work when placed in a **UIGroup** box, as compared with a **UICheckGroup** box. **UICheckGroup** is meant to

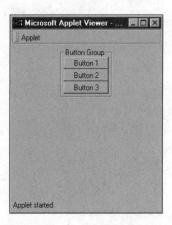

**Figure 4.5**

*GroupApplet with its menu displayed.*

replace AWT's **CheckboxGroup** class, except the AFC version doesn't treat check boxes as radio buttons (like the AWT version does). AFC provides the **UIRadioButton** class for managing radio buttons.

**UICheckGroup** extends the **UIGroup** class, but defines only three methods of its own—**add()**, **handleEvent()**, and **setHeader()**—all of which override methods in its superclasses. You create and populate a **UICheckGroup** box just as you do a **UIGroup** box. However, you can place only **UICheckButton** components into a **UICheckGroup** box. If you try to add other types of components, your program will not compile.

## The **UIRadioGroup** Class

**UIRadioGroup** is the last type of AFC group box. Its task is to manage radio buttons to ensure that only a single button is selected simultaneously. **UIRadioGroup** extends **UICheckGroup**, but defines only two methods of its own—**add()** and **handleEvent()**. Both of these methods override methods in the **UIGroup** superclass. For an example of using radio buttons with the **UIRadioGroup** class, refer to Chapter 3's Practical Guide.

# Practical Guide To

## Using Edit, List, Choice, And Group Components

- Responding To Edit-Box Events
- Masking Edit-Box Input
- Creating Read-Only Edit Boxes
- Managing Text Selection In An Edit Box
- Managing Text Alignment In An Edit Box
- Responding To List Selections
- Managing Multiple List Selections
- Responding To Choice Events
- Adding And Removing Choice Items
- Handling A Group Box That Contains Different Component Types
- Customizing A Group Box's Layout

## Responding To Edit-Box Events

After you have your edit boxes on screen, the user can enter whatever data your program requests. As the user enters text into the control, however, your program must have some way of extracting the resulting input. One way to do this is to respond to text events that Java generates every time the user enters or deletes a character in the edit box.

AFC provides the **IUITextListener** interface for responding to these text events. To use this interface, declare the container class (the component that contains the edit box) as implementing the **IUITextListener** interface. Then call the edit box's **addTextListener()** method to register the container as a text listener. The **IUITextListener** interface declares the **textValueChanged()** method, which you must define in the container class. When the user types data into the edit box, Java calls **textValueChanged()** for every object that registered itself with the edit box.

Listing 4.5 introduces an applet that shows how to use text events to gather input from an edit box. When you run the applet, select the edit box and start typing. In the canvas at the bottom of the applet, the applet mirrors everything you type. You can delete text from your keyboard or click the Clear button to start over. Figure 4.6 shows the applet after the user has entered a line of text.

**Figure 4.6**

*EditEventApplet, running in Applet Viewer.*

## Listing 4.5  The source code for EditEventApplet.

```
///////////////////////////////////////////////////
// EditEventApplet.java
//
// An AFC applet that shows how to respond to
// edit-box events.
///////////////////////////////////////////////////

import com.ms.ui.*;
import com.ms.ui.event.*;
import com.ms.fx.*;

public class EditEventApplet extends AwtUIApplet
{
    public EditEventApplet()
    {
        super(new AppletImplementation());
    }
}

class AppletImplementation extends UIApplet
{
    MessageCanvas canvas;

    public void init()
    {
        UIGridLayout layout = new UIGridLayout(2, 1);
        setLayout(layout);

        canvas = new MessageCanvas("", 12, 20, 40);
        EditPanel panel = new EditPanel(canvas);
        add(panel);
        add(canvas);

        setValid(true);
    }
}

class EditPanel extends UIPanel
    implements IUITextListener, IUIActionListener
{
    UIEdit edit;
    MessageCanvas msgCanvas;

    public EditPanel(MessageCanvas canvas)
    {
        msgCanvas = canvas;
```

```
        UIBorderLayout panelLayout = new UIBorderLayout();
        setLayout(panelLayout);

        edit = new UIEdit();
        edit.setBordered(true);
        edit.setSingleLine(true);
        edit.addTextListener(this);
        add(edit, "North");

        UIPushButton button =
            new UIPushButton("Clear", UIPushButton.RAISED);
        button.addActionListener(this);
        add(button, "Center");
    }

    public void textValueChanged(UITextEvent e)
    {
        String str = edit.getValueText();
        msgCanvas.showMessage(str);
    }

    public void actionPerformed(UIActionEvent e)
    {
        edit.clear(true);
    }
}

class MessageCanvas extends UICanvas
{
    String displayString;
    int pointSize;
    int col, row;

    public MessageCanvas(String msg, int points, int x, int y)
    {
        displayString = msg;
        pointSize = points;
        col = x;
        row = y;
        setBackground(FxColor.blue);
    }

    public void paint(FxGraphics graphics)
    {
        FxFont font =
            new FxFont("TimesRoman", FxFont.PLAIN, pointSize);
        graphics.setFont(font);
```

```
        graphics.setColor(FxColor.white);
        graphics.drawString(displayString, col, row);
    }

    public void showMessage(String str)
    {
        displayString = str;
        repaint();
    }
}
```

 ## Masking Edit-Box Input

Each edit box in an application requests a certain type of information from the user. For example, one edit box might accept the user's name, while another might accept the user's ZIP code. When the user enters a name, certain characters—such as numbers—aren't valid for the input. On the other hand, a ZIP code requires only numbers (and maybe a hyphen). You can always validate a text line after the user enters it, but this process requires extra work on your part. You can take advantage of **UIEdit**'s built-in masking, a simpler way to prevent the user from entering invalid characters.

To incorporate masking into a program, first set the edit box's masking mode to **EXCLUDE** or **INCLUDE**, depending on whether the mask will represent valid characters or invalid characters. Then, create the edit box's mask string by calling its **setMaskChars()** method. If, for example, you want to prevent the user from entering numbers, start by setting the mask mode to **EXCLUDE**, as in the following example:

```
edit.setMaskMode(UIEdit.EXCLUDE);
```

Then, create the mask string, as follows:

```
edit.setMaskChars("1234567890");
```

Now, the user will be unable to enter numbers into the edit box.

To allow only numbers, you use the same mask string, but you set the mode to **INCLUDE**, as shown in the following example:

```
edit.setMaskMode(UIEdit.INCLUDE);
edit.setMaskChars("123456789");
```

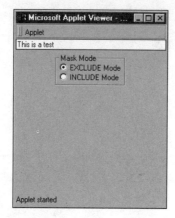

**Figure 4.7**

*EditMaskApplet, running in Applet Viewer.*

Listing 4.6 is the source code for an applet that demonstrates using masks to filter text input. When you run the applet, type text into the edit box. Notice that the box will not accept numbers or the letters X, Y, or Z (upper- and lowercase). Next, click the **INCLUDE** mode button to change the mask mode. Now, the edit box accepts only numbers and the letters X, Y, and Z. Figure 4.7 shows the applet after the user has entered a line of text into the edit box.

**Listing 4.6   The source code for EditMaskApplet.**

```
/////////////////////////////////////////////////
// EditMaskApplet.java
//
// An AFC applet that demonstrates using masks
// with an edit box.
/////////////////////////////////////////////////

import com.ms.ui.*;
import com.ms.ui.event.*;
import com.ms.fx.*;

public class EditMaskApplet extends AwtUIApplet
{
    public EditMaskApplet()
    {
        super(new AppletImplementation());
    }
}
```

```
class AppletImplementation extends UIApplet
    implements IUIItemListener
{

    UIEdit edit;
    UIRadioButton excludeButton;
    UIRadioButton includeButton;

    public void init()
    {
        UIBorderLayout layout = new UIBorderLayout();
        setLayout(layout);

        edit = new UIEdit();
        edit.setBordered(true);
        edit.setSingleLine(true);
        edit.setMaskMode(UIEdit.EXCLUDE);
        edit.setMaskChars("1234567890xyzXYZ");
        add(edit, "North");

        excludeButton = new UIRadioButton("EXCLUDE Mode");
        excludeButton.setChecked(true);
        excludeButton.addItemListener(this);

        includeButton = new UIRadioButton("INCLUDE Mode");
        includeButton.addItemListener(this);

        UIRadioGroup group = new UIRadioGroup("Mask Mode");
        group.add(excludeButton);
        group.add(includeButton);

        UIPanel panel = new UIPanel();
        UIFlowLayout panelLayout = new UIFlowLayout();
        panel.setLayout(panelLayout);
        panel.add(group);

        add(panel);
        edit.requestFocus();

        setValid(true);
    }

    public void itemStateChanged(UIItemEvent event)
    {
        edit.clear();
        edit.requestFocus();

        UIRadioButton comp =
            (UIRadioButton)event.getItemSelectable();
```

```
        if (comp == excludeButton)
            edit.setMaskMode(UIEdit.EXCLUDE);
        else
            edit.setMaskMode(UIEdit.INCLUDE);
    }
}
```

## Creating Read-Only Edit Boxes

After users enter information into a form, the program usually extracts the text from the form and stores it someplace. Later, when users view the information they entered, you may not want them to edit the information. To keep them from attempting an edit, you can display the users' information as static text on the screen. However, you already designed an attractive form for entering the information, so why not use the same form to display the information?

In this situation, you can take advantage of an edit box's read-only state. By restoring the users' information to the edit boxes, you can display the information exactly as the users remember seeing it. By setting the edit boxes' read-only states, you disable the boxes' editing features, preventing users from changing the information.

To change an edit box to read-only, call the **setReadOnly()** method with a value of **true**, as follows:

```
edit = new UIEdit("This is a test");
edit.setReadOnly(true);
```

To restore the box's editing functions, call **setReadOnly(false)**.

Listing 4.7 presents an applet that displays an edit box and enables you to switch on and off its read-only state. Figure 4.8 shows the applet when it first runs, with the edit box's read-only state turned off. Figure 4.9 shows the applet with the read-only state turned on.

### Listing 4.7   The source code for ReadOnlyEditApplet.
```
/////////////////////////////////////////////////
// ReadOnlyEditApplet.java
//
// An AFC applet that demonstrates read-only
// edit boxes.
/////////////////////////////////////////////////
```

```java
import com.ms.ui.*;
import com.ms.ui.event.*;
import com.ms.fx.*;

public class ReadOnlyEditApplet extends AwtUIApplet
{
    public ReadOnlyEditApplet()
    {
        super(new AppletImplementation());
    }
}

class AppletImplementation extends UIApplet
    implements IUIItemListener
{
    UIEdit edit;
    UICheckButton readOnlyButton;

    public void init()
    {
        UIBorderLayout layout = new UIBorderLayout();
        setLayout(layout);

        edit = new UIEdit("This is a test");
        edit.setBordered(true);
        edit.setSingleLine(true);
        add(edit, "North");

        readOnlyButton = new UICheckButton("Read-Only Mode");
        readOnlyButton.addItemListener(this);

        UIPanel panel = new UIPanel();
        UIFlowLayout panelLayout = new UIFlowLayout();
        panel.setLayout(panelLayout);
        panel.add(readOnlyButton);

        add(panel);
        edit.requestFocus();

        setValid(true);
    }

    public void itemStateChanged(UIItemEvent event)
    {
        edit.requestFocus();
```

```
        UICheckButton comp =
            (UICheckButton)event.getItemSelectable();
        int state = event.getStateChange();

        if (state == UIItemEvent.SELECTED)
            edit.setReadOnly(true);
        else
            edit.setReadOnly(false);
    }
}
```

**Figure 4.8**

*ReadOnlyEditApplet, running in Applet Viewer.*

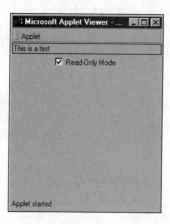

**Figure 4.9**

*ReadOnlyEditApplet with a read-only edit box.*

## Managing Text Selection In An Edit Box

An edit box can be more than just a way to get text input from the user. You can set up the edit box to be a kind of mini word processor that not only accepts multiple lines of text, but also enables the user to select text blocks. Using text selection techniques, your program can, for example, incorporate a simple cut-and-paste feature.

The **UIDrawText** class, from which AFC derives **UIEdit**, provides methods for implementing text selection in an edit box. The most important of these methods are **getSelectedText()**, **getSelectionStart()**, and **getSelectionEnd()**. The **getSelectedText()** method returns the text the user has selected in the edit box, whereas **getSelection Start()** and **getSelectionEnd()** return the starting and ending indexes (character positions) of the selection.

You do nothing to enable the user to select text; this capability is built into the component. Users can select text by highlighting it with the mouse or keyboard. After the user selects the text, however, it's up to your program to decide what to do with it.

Listing 4.8 shows the source code for an applet that demonstrates text selection in an edit box. When you first run the applet, you see the window shown in Figure 4.10 (assuming, of course, that you run the applet with Applet Viewer, rather than loading it into a browser). At the top of the applet, you see a multiline edit box from which you can select text. Select text in the edit box, and click the Select button. When you do, the selected text appears in the yellow edit box (shown as a light gray here), and the starting and ending indexes appear in the canvas component, as shown in Figure 4.11.

### Listing 4.8 The source code for SelectionEditApplet.

```
/////////////////////////////////////////////////
// SelectionEditApplet.java
//
// An AFC applet that shows how to manage
// selected text in an edit box.
/////////////////////////////////////////////////

import com.ms.ui.*;
import com.ms.ui.event.*;
import com.ms.fx.*;

public class SelectionEditApplet extends AwtUIApplet
{
    public SelectionEditApplet()
    {
```

```
                super(new AppletImplementation());
        }
    }

    class AppletImplementation extends UIApplet
        implements IUIActionListener
    {
        UIEdit edit1;
        UIEdit edit2;
        UIPushButton selectionButton;
        SelectionCanvas canvas;

        public void init()
        {
            UIGridLayout layout = new UIGridLayout(4,1);
            setLayout(layout);

            edit1 = new UIEdit("This is a test of text ");
            edit1.append("selection inside an edit box ");
            edit1.append("component. Select some text in ");
            edit1.append("this box, and then click the ");
            edit1.append("select button. Your text selection ");
            edit1.append("will appear below, and the starting ");
            edit1.append("and ending indexes will appear in ");
            edit1.append("the blue canvas.");
            edit1.setBordered(true);
            edit1.setWordWrap(UIEdit.wwKeepWordIntact);
            add(edit1);

            edit2 = new UIEdit();
            edit2.setBordered(true);
            edit2.setReadOnly(true);
            edit2.setWordWrap(UIEdit.wwKeepWordIntact);
            edit2.setBackground(FxColor.yellow);
            add(edit2);

            canvas = new SelectionCanvas();
            add(canvas);

            selectionButton =
                new UIPushButton("Select", UIPushButton.RAISED);
            selectionButton.addActionListener(this);
            add(selectionButton);

            edit1.requestFocus();
            setValid(true);
        }
```

```
    public void actionPerformed(UIActionEvent event)
    {
        edit1.requestFocus();

        String str = event.getActionCommand();
        if (str == "Select")
        {
            String text = edit1.getSelectedText();
            edit2.setValueText(text);
            int start = edit1.getSelectionStart();
            int end = edit1.getSelectionEnd();
            canvas.showSelection(start, end);
        }
    }
}

class SelectionCanvas extends UICanvas
{
    int start;
    int end;

    public SelectionCanvas()
    {
        setBackground(FxColor.blue);
        setForeground(FxColor.white);
        FxFont font =
            new FxFont("TimesRoman", FxFont.PLAIN, 24);
        setFont(font);

        start = 0;
        end = 0;
    }

    public void showSelection(int start, int end)
    {
        SelectionCanvas.start = start;
        SelectionCanvas.end = end;
        repaint();
    }

    public void paint(FxGraphics fxGraphics)
    {
        String str = "START: " + String.valueOf(start);
        fxGraphics.drawString(str, 65, 35);
        str = "END: " + String.valueOf(end);
        fxGraphics.drawString(str, 89, 60);
    }
}
```

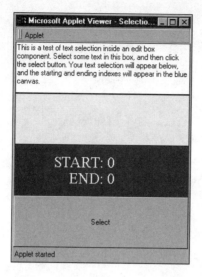

**Figure 4.10**

*SelectionEditApplet, running in Applet Viewer.*

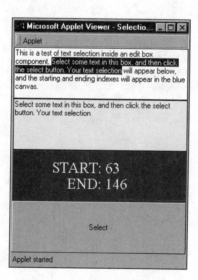

**Figure 4.11**

*SelectionEditApplet after the user makes a selection.*

## Managing Text Alignment In An Edit Box

In its default state, an edit box aligns its text to the left and top, in the same way you expect to see text on screen. However, the edit box isn't limited to left alignment. By setting the component's horizontal and vertical alignment attributes, you can align text in various ways, including left, center, right, top, and bottom.

The two methods that make text alignments possible are **setHorizAlign()** and **setVertAlign()**. AFC defines a set of constants that you can use with these functions to set the appropriate alignments. These constants are shown in the following list:

- **htaCenter**—Aligns text horizontally, centered

- **htaJustified**—Justifies text horizontally (not currently supported)

- **htaLeft**—Aligns text horizontally, left

- **htaRight**—Aligns text horizontally, right

- **htaScriptDefault**—Uses the script default alignment

- **htaStretch**—Uses horizontal stretch alignment (not currently supported)

- **vtaBaseline**—Aligns text vertically to the character baseline

- **vtaBottom**—Aligns text vertically to the bottom

- **vtaCenter**—Aligns text vertically, centered

- **vtaStretch**—Uses vertical stretch alignment (not currently supported)

- **vtaTop**—Aligns text vertically to the top

Notice that several of the alignments are described as not currently supported. If you try to use these alignments, AFC sets the component's alignment to its default value.

In Listing 4.9, you see the source code for an applet that demonstrates text alignment in an edit box. When you run the applet, you see the window shown in Figure 4.12. In the figure, the text in the edit box is aligned horizontally left and vertically to the top. By selecting radio buttons in the Horizontal Alignment and Vertical Alignment button groups, you can set various alignment combinations. Figure 4.13, for example, shows the text centered both horizontally and vertically, whereas Figure 4.14 shows the text with right and bottom alignment.

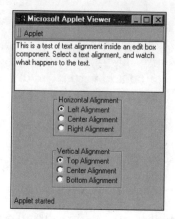

**Figure 4.12**

*EditAlignApplet set to left and top alignment.*

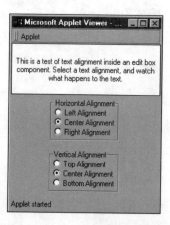

**Figure 4.13**

*EditAlignApplet with text vertically and horizontally centered.*

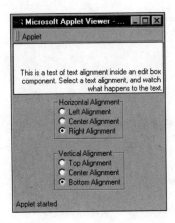

## Figure 4.14

*EditAlignApplet set to right and bottom alignment.*

### Listing 4.9   The source code for EditAlignApplet.

```
/////////////////////////////////////////////
// EditAlignApplet.java
//
// An AFC applet that demonstrates the use of
// various text alignments in an edit box.
/////////////////////////////////////////////

import com.ms.ui.*;
import com.ms.ui.event.*;
import com.ms.fx.*;

public class EditAlignApplet extends AwtUIApplet
{
    public EditAlignApplet()
    {
        super(new AppletImplementation());
    }
}

class AppletImplementation extends UIApplet
    implements IUIItemListener
{
    UIEdit edit;
    UIRadioButton leftButton;
    UIRadioButton centerButton;
    UIRadioButton rightButton;
    UIRadioButton topButton;
    UIRadioButton vCenterButton;
```

```
UIRadioButton bottomButton;

public void init()
{
    UIGridLayout layout = new UIGridLayout(3,1);
    setLayout(layout);

    edit = new UIEdit("This is a test of text ");
    edit.append("alignment inside an edit box ");
    edit.append("component. Select a text alignment, ");
    edit.append("and watch what happens to the text.");
    edit.setBordered(true);
    edit.setWordWrap(UIEdit.wwKeepWordIntact);
    edit.setVertAlign(UIEdit.vtaStretch);
    add(edit);

    leftButton = new UIRadioButton("Left Alignment");
    leftButton.setChecked(true);
    leftButton.addItemListener(this);

    centerButton = new UIRadioButton("Center Alignment");
    centerButton.addItemListener(this);

    rightButton = new UIRadioButton("Right Alignment");
    rightButton.addItemListener(this);

    UIRadioGroup group = new UIRadioGroup("Horizontal Alignment");
    group.add(leftButton);
    group.add(centerButton);
    group.add(rightButton);

    UIPanel panel = new UIPanel();
    UIFlowLayout panelLayout = new UIFlowLayout();
    panel.setLayout(panelLayout);
    panel.add(group);
    add(panel);

    topButton = new UIRadioButton("Top Alignment");
    topButton.setChecked(true);
    topButton.addItemListener(this);

    vCenterButton = new UIRadioButton("Center Alignment");
    vCenterButton.addItemListener(this);

    bottomButton = new UIRadioButton("Bottom Alignment");
    bottomButton.addItemListener(this);
```

```
        group = new UIRadioGroup("Vertical Alignment");
        group.add(topButton);
        group.add(vCenterButton);
        group.add(bottomButton);

        panel = new UIPanel();
        panelLayout = new UIFlowLayout();
        panel.setLayout(panelLayout);
        panel.add(group);
        add(panel);

        edit.requestFocus();

        setValid(true);
    }

    public void itemStateChanged(UIItemEvent event)
    {
        edit.requestFocus();

        UIRadioButton comp =
            (UIRadioButton)event.getItemSelectable();
        if (comp == leftButton)
            edit.setHorizAlign(UIEdit.htaLeft);
        else if (comp == centerButton)
            edit.setHorizAlign(UIEdit.htaCenter);
        else if (comp == rightButton)
            edit.setHorizAlign(UIEdit.htaRight);
        else if (comp == topButton)
            edit.setVertAlign(UIEdit.vtaTop);
        else if (comp == vCenterButton)
            edit.setVertAlign(UIEdit.vtaCenter);
        else if (comp == bottomButton)
            edit.setVertAlign(UIEdit.vtaBottom);
    }
}
```

## Responding To List Selections

When your AFC program displays a list of items using a **UIList** object, users can use
the mouse to select one or more items in the list. When this happens, your program
needs a way to determine the selected item. The program can do this by responding
to the action event that occurs when the user makes the selection. This technique
requires (for the delegation event model) that the list's container implement the
**IUIActionListener** interface with the **actionPerformed**() method.

**Figure 4.15**

*ListEventApplet, running in Applet Viewer.*

The **actionPerformed()** method receives a **UIActionEvent** object as its single parameter. Your program can get the selected item in the list by calling the event object's **getActionCommand()** method. Listing 4.10 shows the source code for an applet that responds to user selections in a **UIList** object. Figure 4.15 shows the applet running in Applet Viewer, after the user has selected an item from the list. (Note that the **MessageCanvas** class referred to in Listing 4.10 is exactly the same as the **MessageCanvas** class in Listing 4.5, so it is not shown here.)

**Listing 4.10  The source code for ListEventApplet.**

```
///////////////////////////////////////////////
// ListEventApplet.java
//
// An AFC applet that shows how to capture list
// selections.
///////////////////////////////////////////////

import com.ms.ui.*;
import com.ms.ui.event.*;
import com.ms.fx.*;

public class ListEventApplet extends AwtUIApplet
{
    public ListEventApplet()
    {
        super(new AppletImplementation());
    }
}
```

```
class AppletImplementation extends UIApplet
    implements IUIActionListener
{
    UIList list;
    MessageCanvas canvas;

    public void init()
    {
        UIGridLayout layout = new UIGridLayout(2,1);
        setLayout(layout);

        list = new UIList();
        list.add("List Item 1");
        list.add("List Item 2");
        list.add("List Item 3");
        list.add("List Item 4");
        list.addActionListener(this);

        UIPanel panel = new UIPanel();
        UIFlowLayout panelLayout = new UIFlowLayout();
        panel.setLayout(panelLayout);
        panel.add(list);
        list.requestFocus();
        add(panel);

        canvas = new MessageCanvas("", 24, 70, 60);
        add(canvas);

        setValid(true);
    }

    public void actionPerformed(UIActionEvent event)
    {
        String str = (String)event.getActionCommand();
        canvas.showMessage(str);
    }
}
```

## Managing Multiple List Selections

List controls are versatile creatures. Normally, the user can select a single item. However, you can set up the component to allow multiple selections as well. In the previous section, you learned how a program responds to a single-selection list. There, the program responded to action events to capture the user's selection. In a multiple-selection list, the program responds to item commands to gather a collection of selections as each selection occurs.

The first step is to create the list with its multiple-selection attribute set, like this:

```
UIList list = new UIList(UIList.MULTISELECT);
```

Then, register the list's container as an item listener for the list:

```
list.addItemListener(this);
```

Now, each time the user selects an item in the list, the component calls the container's **itemStateChanged()** method, which the container must have defined to implement the **IUIItemListener** interface. In **itemStateChanged()**, the program calls the event object's **getItemSelectable()** method to obtain a reference to the list component. Then, the program gets the indexes of the selected items by calling the list's **getSelectedIndices()** method, which returns an integer array of item indexes, like this:

```
UIList comp = (UIList)event.getItemSelectable();
int indexes[] = comp.getSelectedIndices();
```

Listing 4.11 shows the source code for an applet that demonstrates the techniques just discussed. When you run the applet in Applet Viewer, a window appears with a list near the top and a canvas component at the bottom. Each time you select an item, the indexes of all selected items appear in the canvas, as shown in Figure 4.16. (Note that the **MessageCanvas** class referred to in Listing 4.11 is exactly the same as the **MessageCanvas** class in Listing 4.5 and so is not shown here.)

**Figure 4.16**

*MultipleListApplet, running in Applet Viewer.*

## Listing 4.11   The source code for MultipleListApplet.

```
/////////////////////////////////////////////////
// MultipleListApplet.java
//
// An AFC applet that shows how to handle
// multiple list selections.
/////////////////////////////////////////////////

import com.ms.ui.*;
import com.ms.ui.event.*;
import com.ms.fx.*;

public class MultipleListApplet extends AwtUIApplet
{
    public MultipleListApplet()
    {
        super(new AppletImplementation());
    }
}

class AppletImplementation extends UIApplet
    implements IUIItemListener
{
    UIList list;
    MessageCanvas canvas;

    public void init()
    {
        UIGridLayout layout = new UIGridLayout(2,1);
        setLayout(layout);

        UIList list = new UIList(UIList.MULTISELECT);
        list.add("List Item 1");
        list.add("List Item 2");
        list.add("List Item 3");
        list.add("List Item 4");
        list.addItemListener(this);

        UIPanel panel = new UIPanel();
        UIFlowLayout panelLayout = new UIFlowLayout();
        panel.setLayout(panelLayout);
        panel.add(list);
        list.requestFocus();
        add(panel);

        canvas = new MessageCanvas("", 24, 70, 60);
        add(canvas);
```

```
          setValid(true);
     }

     public void itemStateChanged(UIItemEvent event)
     {
          UIList comp = (UIList)event.getItemSelectable();
          int indexes[] = comp.getSelectedIndices();
          if (indexes != null)
          {
               String str = new String();
               for (int x=0; x<indexes.length; ++x)
                    str = str + "  " + String.valueOf(indexes[x]+1);

               canvas.showMessage(str);
          }
          else
               canvas.showMessage("");
     }
}
```

##  Responding To Choice Events

Creating a choice object and loading it with items is a piece of cake. However, when you try to write the program code that will respond to the user's selections, you're in for a surprise. If you use the delegation event model, the control doesn't seem to function, never calling the functions that implement the **IUIActionListener** and **IUIItemListener** interfaces. This problem is a result of the fact that a choice component contains several other components, one of which is a **UIMenuList** object.

It's the menu list that responds to events, so the choice component's container must register with the menu list if it needs to respond to selections in the choice component. To do this, create your choice component, and then call the choice component's **getMenu()** method to get a reference to the menu list.

```
UIMenuList menu = choice.getMenu();
```

Once you have the menu list reference, register the choice component's container as an action listener with the menu:

```
menu.addActionListener(this);
```

Listing 4.12 shows the source code for an applet that demonstrates how to respond to choice selections. When you run the applet in Applet Viewer, you see the window

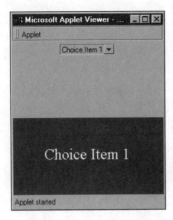

**Figure 4.17**

*ChoiceEventApplet, running in Applet Viewer.*

shown in Figure 4.17. Select an item from the choice component, and your selection appears in the canvas. (Note that the **MessageCanvas** class referred to in Listing 4.12 is the same as the **MessageCanvas** class in Listing 4.5 and so is not shown here.)

**Listing 4.12  The source code for ChoiceEventApplet.**

```
/////////////////////////////////////////////////
// ChoiceEventApplet.java
//
// An AFC applet that responds to choice item
// selections.
/////////////////////////////////////////////////

import com.ms.ui.*;
import java.awt.*;
import com.ms.fx.*;
import com.ms.ui.event.*;

public class ChoiceEventApplet extends AwtUIApplet
{
    public ChoiceEventApplet()
    {
        super(new AppletImplementation());
    }
}

class AppletImplementation extends UIApplet
    implements IUIActionListener
{
```

```
UIChoice choice;
MessageCanvas canvas;

public void init()
{
    UIGridLayout layout = new UIGridLayout(2,1);
    setLayout(layout);

    choice = new UIChoice();
    choice.addString("Choice Item 1");
    choice.addString("Choice Item 2");
    choice.addString("Choice Item 3");
    choice.addSelectedIndex(0);

    UIMenuList menu = choice.getMenu();
    menu.addActionListener(this);

    UIPanel panel = new UIPanel();
    UIFlowLayout panelLayout = new UIFlowLayout();
    panel.setLayout(panelLayout);
    panel.add(choice);
    add(panel);

    canvas = new MessageCanvas("Choice Item 1",
        24, 50, 65);
    add(canvas);

    choice.requestFocus();
    setValid(true);
}

public void actionPerformed(UIActionEvent event)
{
    String str = event.getActionCommand();
    canvas.showMessage(str);
}
}
```

## Adding And Removing Choice Items

When you initialize a choice component at program startup, you're not stuck with it.
You can add or remove items based on the user's interactions with the choice component or with other components in the program. To add an item to the choice
component, just call the component's **add()** or **addString()** methods as you did to
initialize the choice object.

However, if your program tries to remove items by calling the choice component's **remove()** method with an index, the program won't work. To remove items by index, you first need to get a reference to the choice object's menu list. Then, you can then call **remove()** through the menu object to remove an item by index.

Listing 4.13 is a short applet that demonstrates how to add or remove items in a choice object in response to a user's actions. When you run the applet, and display the selections in its choice component, you'll see Add Choice Item and Remove Choice Item commands. Select the former to add an item to the list (Figure 4.18), and select the latter to remove a newly added item from the list. You can't remove the initial items from the list. (Note that the **MessageCanvas** class referred to in Listing 4.13 is exactly the same as the **MessageCanvas** class in Listing 4.5 and so is not shown here.)

## Listing 4.13  The source code for ChoiceItemApplet.

```
///////////////////////////////////////////////////
// ChoiceItemApplet.java
//
// An AFC applet that responds to choice item
// selections by adding or removing menu items.
///////////////////////////////////////////////////

import com.ms.ui.*;
import java.awt.*;
import com.ms.fx.*;

public class ChoiceItemApplet extends AwtUIApplet
{
    public ChoiceItemApplet()
    {
        super(new AppletImplementation());
    }
}

class AppletImplementation extends UIApplet
{
    UIChoice choice;
    MessageCanvas canvas;

    public void init()
    {
```

```
        UIGridLayout layout = new UIGridLayout(2,1);
        setLayout(layout);

        choice = new UIChoice();
        choice.addString("Add Choice Item");
        choice.addString("Remove Choice Item");
        choice.addString("Choice Item 1");
        choice.addString("Choice Item 2");
        choice.addString("Choice Item 3");
        choice.addSelectedIndex(2);

        UIPanel panel = new UIPanel();
        UIFlowLayout panelLayout = new UIFlowLayout();
        panel.setLayout(panelLayout);
        panel.add(choice);
        add(panel);

        canvas = new MessageCanvas("Choice Item 1",
            24, 15, 60);
        add(canvas);

        choice.requestFocus();
        setValid(true);
    }

    public boolean action(Event event, Object arg)
    {
        if (event.target == choice)
        {
            String str = choice.getValueText();
            canvas.showMessage(str);

            if (str == "Add Choice Item")
                choice.addString("NEW CHOICE ITEM");
            else if (str == "Remove Choice Item")
            {
                UIMenuList menu = choice.getMenu();
                menu.remove(5);
            }
            return true;
        }
        return false;
    }
}
```

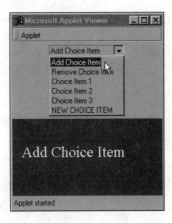

**Figure 4.18**

*ChoiceItemApplet, running in Applet Viewer.*

## Handling A Group Box That Contains Different Component Types

In previous programs in this book, you've seen group boxes (as well as check boxes and radio boxes) used to organize similar types of components. For example, you've used a radio box to group three radio buttons together. There's no reason, however, that you can't include more than one type of component in a group box. You might, for instance, want to create a group box that contains both check buttons and push buttons.

You can add these different component types easily enough, just by calling the group box's **add()** method. Nothing special there. But how do you respond to the events from the different components in the group box? If you're using the delegation event model, just register the container with each component, implementing the appropriate listener interfaces. If two components happen to rely on the same listener interface, that's no problem. You can sort them out in the method that responds to the event.

Listing 4.14 is an applet that places three different types of components in a group box, and then responds to the components through the **IUIActionListener** and **IUIItemListener** interfaces. Run the applet and click any of the components in the group box. The name of the selected component appears in the applet's canvas component, as shown in Figure 4.19. (Note that the **MessageCanvas** class referred to in Listing 4.14 is exactly the same as the **MessageCanvas** class in Listing 4.5, so it is not shown here.)

**Figure 4.19**

*GroupEventApplet, running in Applet Viewer.*

**Listing 4.14   The source code for GroupEventApplet.**
```
/////////////////////////////////////////////////
// GroupEventApplet.java
//
// An AFC applet that responds to multiple
// components in a group box.
/////////////////////////////////////////////////

import com.ms.ui.*;
import com.ms.fx.*;
import com.ms.ui.event.*;

public class GroupEventApplet extends AwtUIApplet
{
    public GroupEventApplet()
    {
        super(new AppletImplementation());
    }
}

class AppletImplementation extends UIApplet
    implements IUIActionListener, IUIItemListener
{
    UIPushButton pushButton;
    UICheckButton checkButton;
    UIChoice choice;
    MessageCanvas canvas;
```

```
public void init()
{
    UIGridLayout layout = new UIGridLayout(2,1);
    setLayout(layout);

    UIGroup group = new UIGroup("Sample Group");
    UIText text = new UIText(" ");
    group.add(text);
    pushButton = new UIPushButton("Push Button",
        UIPushButton.RAISED);
    group.add(pushButton);
    text = new UIText(" ");
    group.add(text);
    checkButton = new UICheckButton("Check Button");
    group.add(checkButton);
    text = new UIText(" ");
    group.add(text);

    choice = new UIChoice();
    choice.addString("Choice Item 1");
    choice.addString("Choice Item 2");
    choice.addString("Choice Item 3");
    choice.addSelectedIndex(0);
    group.add(choice);

    UIPanel panel = new UIPanel();
    UIFlowLayout panelLayout = new UIFlowLayout();
    panel.setLayout(panelLayout);
    panel.add(group);
    add(panel);

    canvas = new MessageCanvas("", 24, 70, 75);
    add(canvas);

    pushButton.addActionListener(this);
    checkButton.addItemListener(this);
    UIMenuList menu = choice.getMenu();
    menu.addActionListener(this);

    setValid(true);
}

public void actionPerformed(UIActionEvent event)
{
    String str = event.getActionCommand();
        canvas.showMessage(str);
    if (str == "Push Button");
        canvas.showMessage(str);
}
```

```
    public void itemStateChanged(UIItemEvent event)
    {
        IUIComponent comp = event.getItemSelectable();
        if (comp == checkButton)
            canvas.showMessage("Check Button");
    }
}
```

## Customizing A Group Box's Layout

In this chapter, you probably gave little thought to the way in which components are laid
out in a group box. In programs so far, components in group boxes were organized in a
vertical stack. This is the result of the group box's default **UIVerticalFlowLayout** layout
manager. You can, however, use any type of layout manager you want. To do so, create
the group box component, and then call its **setLayout()** to change the layout manager, as
in the following example:

```
UIGroup group = new UIGroup("Sample Group");
group.setLayout(new UIFlowLayout());
```

Listing 4.15 presents a short applet that displays a group box with a **UIFlowLayout**
layout manager. In Figure 4.20, you can see that the components are now arranged
horizontally, rather than vertically.

**Figure 4.20**

*GroupLayoutApplet, running in Applet Viewer.*

**Listing 4.15   The source code for GroupLayoutApplet.**

```
/////////////////////////////////////////////////
// GroupLayoutApplet.java
//
// An AFC applet that provides a new layout
// manager for a group box.
/////////////////////////////////////////////////

import com.ms.ui.*;
import com.ms.fx.*;
import com.ms.ui.event.*;

public class GroupLayoutApplet extends AwtUIApplet
{
    public GroupLayoutApplet()
    {
        super(new AppletImplementation());
    }
}

class AppletImplementation extends UIApplet
{
    UIPushButton pushButton;
    UICheckButton checkButton;
    UIChoice choice;

    public void init()
    {
        UIFlowLayout layout = new UIFlowLayout();
        setLayout(layout);

        UIGroup group = new UIGroup("Sample Group");
        group.setLayout(new UIFlowLayout());

        UIText text = new UIText(" ");
        group.add(text);
        pushButton = new UIPushButton("Push Button",
            UIPushButton.RAISED);
        group.add(pushButton);
        text = new UIText(" ");
        group.add(text);
        checkButton = new UICheckButton("Check Button");
        group.add(checkButton);
        text = new UIText(" ");
        group.add(text);
```

```
        choice = new UIChoice();
        choice.addString("Choice Item 1");
        choice.addString("Choice Item 2");
        choice.addString("Choice Item 3");
        choice.addSelectedIndex(0);
        group.add(choice);

        add(group);
        setValid(true);
    }
}
```

# Progress Bar, Scroll, Slider, And Spinner Components

*You can't say that civilizations don't advance…for in every war they kill you a new way.*
*—Will Rogers,*
*The Autobiography of Will Rogers*

# Notes...

# Chapter 5

Back when Will Rogers made his observations on the advancement of civilization, the idea of desktop computers was as inconceivable as men walking on the moon. Still, here we are, doing everything from balancing checkbooks to downloading files from the other side of the world on computers the size of bread boxes (not to mention walking on the moon). However, each new advancement in computer technology finds ways to make programming—like Will Rogers's wars—a little more dangerous. Just when a programmer has figured out a new technology, along comes the latest Big Thing, loaded with a whole new set of land mines.

Java is a good example. The Java language changes so quickly that it seems a new version comes out once a week. (Is it Friday yet? Good, let's download Java 1.4.45329, cycle 354, build 32859.) Third-party Java libraries appear and disappear almost as fast. Such is progress. These days it's almost impossible to keep up with all advancements in a single field of computing, let alone to keep up with the entire science of computing. AFC is a case in point. Even as your humble author writes these words, he wonders whether AFC will have changed by the time this book sees print.

Yep, that's progress. Luckily, the measurement of progress isn't always the new ways we've discovered to wage war. Sometimes measuring progress is as simple as checking the version number on the latest AFC release. Sometimes, in fact, it's even as easy as watching a progress bar in a window tracking the completion of a file being saved. Which, of course, brings us once again to AFC's controls, not the least of which is the progress bar. In this chapter, you will learn not only about the progress bar, but also about components that enable applications either to display or to retrieve values from the user. These components include scrollers, sliders, and spinners.

# The **UIProgress** Class

Despite the amazing speeds at which today's computers run, at times the user must wait for a long process to complete. When a program must perform some time-consuming task, it's important to give the user visual feedback. Otherwise, the user may think the system has locked up or is otherwise not responding to input.

One way to provide visual feedback is with a progress bar, which looks much like a horizontal thermometer. As the process represented by the progress bar proceeds, the progress bar fills slowly, from left to right, with colored blocks. The filled portion of the progress bar represents the completed portion of the task. That is, when the progress bar is half filled with blocks, the task is half-complete.

In AFC, the **UIProgress** class represents a progress bar component. **UIProgress** extends the **UIStatus** class, which, as you'll learn in Chapter 6, represents a status bar in a window. **UIStatus** traces its AFC ancestry from **UISingleContainer** up through **UIStateContainer** and **UIContainer** to **UIComponent**. Because **UIProgress** has no Java AWT counterpart, it has no standard Java class in its ancestry. **UIProgress** inherits methods from all of its superclasses, but it also defines its own small set of methods, as shown in Table 5.1.

**Table 5.1  Methods of the UIProgress class.**

| Method | Description |
|---|---|
| getPos() | Gets the progress control's position |
| getRange() | Gets the progress control's range |
| getRoleCode() | Gets the progress bar's role code, which is **ROLE_SYSTEM_PROGRESSBAR** |
| paint() | Paints the progress control |
| setPos() | Sets the progress control's position |
| setRange() | Sets the progress control's range |
| update() | Draws the progress control by calling **paint()** |

As with any component, you create a progress bar component by calling the class's constructor:

```
UIProgress progress = new UIProgress(range, position);
```

Here, the constructor's two arguments are the progress bar's range (represented by the maximum value) and the progress bar's current position (the amount of bar that's filled in). The position is relative to the range. For example, a progress bar with a range of 100 and a position of 50 would be half filled.

AFC overloads the **UIProgress** constructor, giving you several ways to create the component. Calling the constructor with no arguments results in a default progress bar with a range of 100 and a position of 0 (zero):

```
UIProgress progress = new UIProgress();
```

After creating the progress bar in this way, you can change its default attributes by calling progress bar methods, as follows:

```
progress.setRange(500);
progress.setPos(100);
```

You also can specify just the range when creating the progress bar component:

```
UIProgress progress = new UIProgress(500);
```

In this case, AFC uses the default value of zero for the component's position.

Listing 5.1 presents a short applet that creates and displays a half-filled progress bar. Figure 5.1 shows the applet running in Applet Viewer.

### Listing 5.1   The source code for ProgressApplet.

```
//////////////////////////////////////////////////
// ProgressApplet.java
//
// An AFC applet that creates and displays a
// progress bar component.
//////////////////////////////////////////////////

import com.ms.ui.*;

public class ProgressApplet extends AwtUIApplet
{
```

```
    public ProgressApplet()
    {
        super(new AppletImplementation());
    }
}

class AppletImplementation extends UIApplet
{
    UIProgress progress;

    public void init()
    {
        UIGridLayout layout = new UIGridLayout(3,1);
        setLayout(layout);

        progress = new UIProgress(100, 50);
        add(progress);

        setValid(true);
    }
}
```

## The **UIScroll** Class

Many AFC components rely on the capability to scroll. The **UIScroll** class supplies
this capability and is the superclass for components such as scroll bars and sliders.
**UIScroll** components appear as a scroll track, containing a scroll box (or "thumb,"
as it's often called) that the user can manipulate. The user drags the scroll thumb to

**Figure 5.1**

*ProgressApplet with its menu displayed.*

different positions or clicks inside the scroll track, before or after the scroll thumb, to move the box. Each position represents a value in a range.

**UIScroll** extends the **UIPanel** class, which traces its superclasses through **UIState-Container** and **UIContainer** to **UIComponent**. Although **UIScroll** inherits methods from all its superclasses, it defines its own large set, as shown in Table 5.2.

**Table 5.2   Methods of the UIScroll class.**

| Method | Description |
| --- | --- |
| action() | Responds to action events |
| add() | Adds a component to the control's layout at a given index |
| addAdjustmentListener() | Registers an adjustment listener with this component |
| getLayoutComponent() | Gets the component at a layout index |
| getMinimumSize() | Gets the scroller's minimum size |
| getPosition() | Gets the scroll-box position |
| getPreferredSize() | Gets the scroller's preferred size |
| getRoleCode() | Gets the scroller's role code, which is **ROLE_SYSTEM_SCROLLBAR** |
| getScrollLine() | Gets the number of scroll positions in a line |
| getScrollMax() | Gets the scroller's maximum selectable position |
| getScrollMin() | Gets the scroller's minimum selectable position |
| getScrollPage() | Gets the number of scroll positions in a page |
| getScrollPos() | Gets the scroll-box position |
| getStyle() | Gets the slider's styles |
| getXPosition() | Gets the scroll box's horizontal position |
| getYPosition() | Gets the scroll box's vertical position |
| isKeyable() | Returns **true** if the scroller can receive keyboard input |

*(continued)*

**Table 5.2  Methods of the UIScroll class (continued).**

| Method | Description |
|---|---|
| isScrollable() | Returns **true** if the control is scrollable |
| layout() | Lays out the scroller |
| mouseDrag() | Manages scroll-box dragging |
| processAdjustmentEvent() | Handles adjustment events |
| processEvent() | Handles events |
| removeAdjustmentListener() | Removes adjustment listeners from the listener list |
| scrollEnd() | Positions the scroll box at its maximum value |
| scrollHome() | Positions the scroll box at its minimum value |
| scrollLineDown() | Moves the scroll box up one line |
| scrollLineUp() | Moves scroll box down one line |
| scrollPageDown() | Moves scroll box up one page |
| scrollPageUp() | Moves scroll box down one page |
| setPosition() | Sets the scroll box's position |
| setScrollInfo() | Sets the scroller's attributes |
| setScrollLine() | Sets the number of scroll positions in a line |
| setScrollMax() | Sets the scroller's maximum value |
| setScrollMin() | Sets the scroller's minimum value |
| setScrollPage() | Sets the number of scroll positions in a page |
| setScrollPos() | Sets the scroller's current position |
| setScrollRange() | Sets the scroller's minimum and maximum values |
| setStyle() | Sets the scroller's styles |
| setXPosition() | Sets the scroller's horizontal position |
| setYPosition() | Sets the scroller's vertical position |

Although AFC uses **UIScroll** as a superclass for other more specific types of scrolling components, you can create and use **UIScroll** components in your Java programs. To do this, call the class's constructor, by using the following syntax:

```
UIScroll scroller = new UIScroll(style, min, max, page, line, position);
```

The constructor's arguments are described as follows:

- **style**—The component's style flags, which can be one or more of **VERTICAL**, **NOHIDE**, **NOSHOW**, **NONPROPORTIONAL**, **NOKEY**, or zero

- **min**—The scroller's minimum value

- **max**—The scroller's maximum value

- **page**—The number of scroll units in a page

- **line**—The number of scroll units in a line

- **position**—The scroller's current position

A style flag of zero gives you the default horizontal scroller. AFC overloads the **UIScroll** constructor so that you can create the component in various ways. Calling the constructor with no arguments results in a default horizontal scroller with a range of zero to 100. You also can call the constructor supplying only the scroller's style, as in the following:

```
UIScroll scroller = new UIScroll(UIScroll.VERTICAL | UIScroll.NONPROPORTIONAL);
```

In Listing 5.2, you see a short applet that creates and displays a scroller component. Figure 5.2 shows the applet running in Applet Viewer. Figure 5.3 shows the applet with a vertical scroller.

### Listing 5.2   The source code for ScrollApplet.

```
///////////////////////////////////////////////
// ScrollApplet.java
//
// An AFC applet that creates and displays a
// scroller component.
///////////////////////////////////////////////

import com.ms.ui.*;

public class ScrollApplet extends AwtUIApplet
{
```

```
    public ScrollApplet()
    {
        super(new AppletImplementation());
    }
}

class AppletImplementation extends UIApplet
{
    UIScroll scroller;

    public void init()
    {
        UIGridLayout layout = new UIGridLayout(2,1);
        setLayout(layout);

        scroller = new UIScroll(0, 0, 109, 10, 1, 25);
        add(scroller);

        setValid(true);
    }
}
```

# The **UIScrollBar** Class

A scroll bar, represented by AFC's **UIScrollBar** class, is a scroller component that contains the track and scroll thumb of a **UIScroll** object, but it also has two additional arrow controls. The arrow controls, which are positioned at each end of the scroll bar, enable the user to increment the scroller more precisely, a line at a time.

**Figure 5.2**

*ScrollApplet, running in Applet Viewer.*

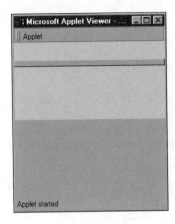

## Figure 5.3

*ScrollApplet with a vertical scroller.*

Although applications most often use scroll bars to scroll the contents of containers, you can use them to select values from a given range.

As you can guess, **UIScrollBar** extends **UIScroll** and so continues up the AFC hierarchy from **UIPanel**, **UIStateContainer**, and **UIContainer** to **UIComponent**. **UIScrollBar** inherits methods from all these superclasses, as well as defines its own small set of methods, as shown in Table 5.3. All of these methods except **getInsets()**, however, override methods defined in the **UIScroll** class.

**Table 5.3   Methods of the UIScrollBar class.**

| Method | Description |
|---|---|
| add() | Adds a component at a layout index |
| getInsets() | Gets the scroll bar's insets |
| getLayoutComponent() | Gets the component at a layout index |
| getMinimumSize() | Gets the scroll bar's minimum size |
| getPreferredSize() | Gets the scroll bar's preferred size |
| layout() | Lays out the scroll bar |
| setStyle() | Sets the scroll bar's styles |

To create a scroll-bar component, call the class's constructor:

```
UIScrollBar scroller =
    new UIScrollBar(style, min, max, page, line, position);
```

The constructor's arguments are described as follows:

- **style**—The component's style flags, which can be one or more of **VERTICAL, NOHIDE, NOSHOW, NONPROPORTIONAL, NOKEY,** or zero

- **min**—The scroller's minimum value

- **max**—The scroller's maximum value

- **page**—The number of scroll units in a page

- **line**—The number of scroll units in a line

- **position**—The scroller's current position

A style flag of zero gets you the default horizontal scroller. AFC overloads the **UIScrollBar** constructor so that you can create the component in various ways. Calling the constructor with no arguments results in a default, horizontal scroller with a range of zero to 100. You also can call the constructor by supplying only the scroller's style:

```
UIScrollBar scroller = new UIScrollBar(UIScroll.VERTICAL |
UIScroll.NONPROPORTIONAL);
```

Listing 5.3 presents a short applet that creates and displays a scroll-bar component. Figure 5.4 shows the applet running in Applet Viewer. Figure 5.5 shows the applet with a vertical scroll bar.

**Listing 5.3   The source code for ScrollBarApplet.**

```
/////////////////////////////////////////////////
// ScrollBarApplet.java
//
// An AFC applet that creates and displays a
// scroll bar component.
/////////////////////////////////////////////////

import com.ms.ui.*;

public class ScrollBarApplet extends AwtUIApplet
{
```

```
        public ScrollBarApplet()
        {
            super(new AppletImplementation());
        }
}

class AppletImplementation extends UIApplet
{
        UIScrollBar scrollBar;

        public void init()
        {
            UIBorderLayout layout = new UIBorderLayout();
            setLayout(layout);

            scrollBar = new UIScrollBar(0, 0, 109, 10, 1, 25);
            add(scrollBar, "North");

            setValid(true);
        }
}
```

## The **UIThumb** And **UIScrollThumb** Classes

AFC uses the **UIThumb** and **UIScrollThumb** classes to create various scroller-support components; the most obvious component is the scroll thumb used in a **UIScroll** or **UIScrollBar** component. **UIScrollThumb** extends **UIThumb**, which counts **UISingleContainer**, **UIStateContainer**, **UIContainer**, and **UIComponent**

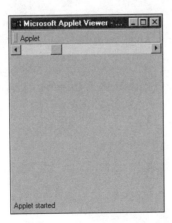

**Figure 5.4**

*ScrollBarApplet, running in Applet Viewer.*

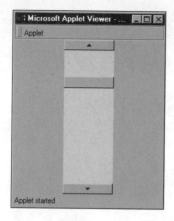

**Figure 5.5**

*ScrollBarApplet with a vertical scroll bar.*

as its superclasses. You probably will not have much use for the **UIThumb** and **UIScrollThumb** support classes in your own programs—unless you start building custom controls.

## The **UISlider** Class

In previous sections of this chapter, you learned to use scrollers and scroll bars as controls for getting values from the user. Chances are that you won't use scrollers this way, however, because AFC features controls better designed for this task. The slider is the first of these controls, which is a fancier version of a scroll bar. Unlike a scroll bar, however, a slider looks like a real-world control; you may have similar controls on your stereo system, for example.

In AFC, the **UISlider** class represents a slider control. Not surprisingly, given its similarity to a scroll bar, **UISlider** extends **UIScroll** class (which itself has **UIPanel**, **UIStateContainer**, **UIContainer**, and **UIComponent** as superclasses). **UISlider** inherits methods from all of these superclasses, but also defines its own methods. Table 5.4 lists these methods and their descriptions.

To create a slider component, call the class's constructor by using the following syntax:

```
UISlider slider =
    new UISlider(style, min, max, page, line, pos, spacing);
```

**Table 5.4  Methods of the UISlider class.**

| Method | Description |
|---|---|
| add() | Adds or replaces a slider component |
| clearSelection() | Clears the current selection |
| getInsets() | Gets the slider's insets |
| getLayoutComponent() | Gets the layout of a slider component |
| getMinimumSize() | Gets the slider control's minimum size |
| getPreferredSize() | Gets the slider control's preferred size |
| getSelectionEnd() | Gets the current selection's ending value |
| getSelectionStart() | Gets the current selection's starting value |
| getStyle() | Gets the slider control's styles |
| getTickSpacing() | Gets the slider control's tick-mark spacing |
| layout() | Lays out the slider control |
| removeAll() | Removes all components from the slider |
| setSelection() | Sets the slider's current selection |
| setSelectionEnd() | Sets the slider's selection ending point |
| setSelectionStart() | Sets the slider's selection starting point |
| setSliderInfo() | Sets the slider's attributes |
| setStyle() | Sets the slider's styles |
| setTickSpacing() | Sets the slider's tick spacing |

The constructor's arguments are described as follows:

- **style**—The component's style flags, which can be one or more of **VERTICAL**, **POINTSABOVE**, **POINTSBELOW**, **TICKSABOVE**, **TICKSBELOW**, and zero

- **min**—The slider's minimum value

- **max**—The slider's maximum value

- **page**—The number of scroll units in a page

- **line**—The number of scroll units in a line

- **position**—The slider's current position

- **spacing**—The spacing of the slider's tick marks

A style flag of zero produces the default horizontal slider. AFC overloads the **UISlider** constructor so that you can create the component in various ways. Calling the constructor with no arguments results in a default, horizontal slider with a range of zero to 10. You also can call the constructor supplying only the scroller's style:

```
UISlider slider = new UISlider(UISlider.TICKSABOVE);
```

Listing 5.4 presents a short applet that creates and displays a slider component. Figure 5.6 shows the applet running in Applet Viewer. Figure 5.7 shows the applet with a vertical slider.

### Listing 5.4   The source code for SliderApplet.

```
///////////////////////////////////////////////////
// SliderApplet.java
//
// An AFC applet that creates and displays a
// slider component.
///////////////////////////////////////////////////

import com.ms.ui.*;

public class SliderApplet extends AwtUIApplet
{
    public SliderApplet()
    {
        super(new AppletImplementation());
    }
}

class AppletImplementation extends UIApplet
{
    UISlider slider;

    public void init()
    {
```

```
UIBorderLayout layout = new UIBorderLayout();
setLayout(layout);

slider = new UISlider(UISlider.TICKSABOVE |
    UISlider.TICKSBELOW, 0, 100, 10, 1, 25, 10);
add(slider, "North");

setValid(true);
    }
}
```

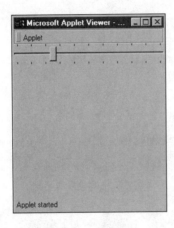

**Figure 5.6**

*SliderApplet, running in Applet Viewer.*

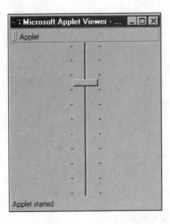

**Figure 5.7**

*SliderApplet with a vertical slider.*

# The **UISpinner** Class

A *spinner* is yet another type of control that an application can use to get a value from the user. Unlike a slider, however, a spinner has no real-world analogue. Rather, a spinner is like a scroll bar, but without the bar. That is, a spinner comprises two arrow buttons that enable the user to set the control's current value. A spinner has a minimum and maximum value, just like scrollers and sliders. A spinner differs from scrollers and sliders in its capability to automatically wrap around from the maximum value to the minimum, or vice versa.

The **UISpinner** class represents spinner controls in AFC. **UISpinner** extends **UIScroll**, so it inherits methods from a long line of AFC classes, including **UIScroll**, **UIPanel**, **UIStateContainer**, **UIContainer**, and **UIComponent**. Table 5.5 lists and briefly describes **UISpinner**'s own methods.

**Table 5.5  Methods of the UISpinner class.**

| Method | Description |
|---|---|
| add() | Adds or replaces a spinner component |
| getLayoutComponent() | Gets a component at a layout index |
| getMinimumSize() | Gets the spinner's minimum size |
| getPreferredSize() | Gets the spinner's preferred size |
| getRoleCode() | Gets the spinner's role code, which is **ROLE_SYSTEM_SCROLLBAR** |
| getScrollPos() | Gets the spinner's position |
| layout() | Lays out the spinner component |
| scrollLineDown() | Sets the spinner position down one unit |
| scrollLineUp() | Sets the spinner position up one unit |
| scrollPageDown() | Sets the spinner down one page |
| scrollPageUp() | Sets the spinner up one page |
| setScrollInfo() | Sets the spinner's attributes |
| setStyle() | Sets the spinner's style |

To create a spinner component, call the class's constructor, as in the following:

```
UISpinner spinner =
    new UISpinner(style, min, max, page, line, pos);
```

The constructor's arguments are described as follows:

- **style**—The component's style flags, which can be one or more of **RAISED**, **VERTICAL**, and **CIRCULAR**

- **min**—The spinner's minimum value

- **max**—The spinner's maximum value

- **page**—The number of scroll units in a page

- **line**—The number of scroll units in a line

- **position**—The spinner's current position

AFC overloads the **UISpinner** constructor, so that you can create the component in various ways. Calling the constructor with no arguments results in a default spinner with raised buttons and with a range of zero to 100. You also can call the constructor supplying only the spinner's style:

```
UISpinner spinner = new UISpinner(UISpinner.CIRCULAR);
```

Listing 5.5 presents a short applet that creates and displays a spinner component. Figure 5.8 shows the applet running in Applet Viewer.

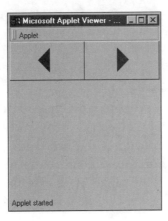

**Figure 5.8**

*SpinnerApplet, running in Applet Viewer.*

**Listing 5.5   The source code for SpinnerApplet.**

```
///////////////////////////////////////////////////
// SpinnerApplet.java
//
// An AFC applet that creates and displays a
// spinner component.
///////////////////////////////////////////////////

import com.ms.ui.*;

public class SpinnerApplet extends AwtUIApplet
{
    public SpinnerApplet()
    {
        super(new AppletImplementation());
    }
}

class AppletImplementation extends UIApplet
{
    UISpinner spinner;

    public void init()
    {
        UIGridLayout layout = new UIGridLayout(2,1);
        setLayout(layout);

        spinner = new UISpinner(UISpinner.RAISED,
            0, 10, 1, 1, 0);
        add(spinner);

        setValid(true);
    }
}
```

# The **UISpinnerEdit** Class

**UISpinnerEdit** is the last class covered in this chapter. It is a component that consists of a spinner and an edit control. The edit control serves double duty. First, it displays the spinner's current value, providing the user with visual feedback. Second, the user can type a value directly into the edit control, rather than have to use the arrows to cycle to the desired value. This capability is especially useful when the spinner's range is large.

Of course, **UISpinnerEdit** extends the **UISpinner** class, and so have **UISpinner**, **UIScroll**, **UIPanel**, **UIStateContainer**, **UIContainer**, and **UIComponent** as superclasses.

Besides its inherited methods, **UISpinnerEdit** defines **getEditStyle()** and **setEditStyle()** methods for managing the component's edit control.

To create a spinner component, call the class's constructor:

```
UISpinnerEdit spinner =
    new UISpinnerEdit(style, editStyle, min, max, page, line, pos);
```

The constructor's arguments are described as follows:

- **style**—The component's style flags, which can be one or more of **RAISED**, **VERTICAL**, and **CIRCULAR**

- **editStyle**—The edit control's style flags, which can be **BORDER**, along with one of **LEFT** (left-aligned text), **RIGHT** (right-aligned text), or **CENTER** (center-aligned text)

- **min**—The spinner's minimum value

- **max**—The spinner's maximum value

- **page**—The number of scroll units in a page

- **line**—The number of scroll units in a line

- **pos**—The spinner's current position

As with **UISpinner**, AFC overloads the **UISpinnerEdit** constructor, so that you can create the component in various ways. Calling the constructor with no arguments results in a default spinner with raised buttons and with a range of zero to 100. You also can call the constructor supplying only the spinner's and edit component's styles:

```
UISpinner spinner = new UISpinner(UISpinnerEdit.CIRCULAR,
    UISpinnerEdit.BORDER | UISpinnerEdit.CENTER);
```

Listing 5.6 presents a short applet that creates and displays a spinner-edit component. Figure 5.9 shows the applet running in Applet Viewer.

### Listing 5.6  The source code for SpinnerEditApplet.
```
/////////////////////////////////////////////////
// SpinnerEditApplet.java
//
// An AFC applet that creates and displays a
// spinner-edit component.
/////////////////////////////////////////////////
```

```
import com.ms.ui.*;

public class SpinnerEditApplet extends AwtUIApplet
{
    public SpinnerEditApplet()
    {
        super(new AppletImplementation());
    }
}

class AppletImplementation extends UIApplet
{
    UISpinnerEdit spinner;

    public void init()
    {
        UIFlowLayout layout = new UIFlowLayout();
        setLayout(layout);

        spinner = new UISpinnerEdit(UISpinner.RAISED,
            UISpinnerEdit.BORDER | UISpinnerEdit.CENTER,
            0, 10, 1, 1, 0);
        add(spinner);

        setValid(true);
    }
}
```

## Figure 5.9

*SpinnerEditApplet, running in Applet Viewer.*

# Practical Guide To

# Using Progress Bar, Scroll, Slider, And Spinner Components

- Managing A Progress Bar
- Responding To Scroll Events
- Customizing Scroller Components
- Responding To Scroll-Bar Events
- Responding To Slider Events
- Managing Slider Range Selections
- Responding To Spinner Events

## Managing A Progress Bar

As you already know, a progress bar represents the status of an ongoing task, such as saving a large file or processing a database. The progress bar usually starts off empty, which represents that none of the task is yet complete. As the task proceeds, the progress bar fills with color until, at the end of the task, the progress bar is completely filled. Getting the progress bar to fill is as easy as periodically calling the control's **setPos()** method with larger and larger numbers.

For example, suppose your Java program needs to process 10 files. You might set the progress bar's range to 100 to represent a percentage. Then, each time the application processes a file, it increases the progress bar's position by 10. After processing the 10 files, the progress bar will be filled. A progress bar with a range of 10 works exactly the same way if you increase its position by ones rather than by tens.

Listing 5.7 shows the source code for an applet that uses a button to simulate an ongoing process. Each time you click the button, the progress bar fills a little more with color. Additionally, the lower canvas shows the progress bar's current setting. When the bar fills, it empties and starts over. Figure 5.10 shows the applet running in Applet Viewer.

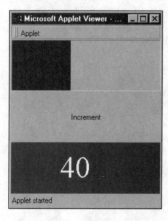

**Figure 5.10**

*ProgressApplet2, running in Applet Viewer.*

## Listing 5.7   The source code for ProgressApplet2.

```
/////////////////////////////////////////////////
// ProgressApplet2.java
//
// An AFC applet that demonstrates updating a
// progress bar component.
/////////////////////////////////////////////////

import com.ms.ui.*;
import com.ms.fx.*;
import com.ms.ui.event.*;

public class ProgressApplet2 extends AwtUIApplet
{
    public ProgressApplet2()
    {
        super(new AppletImplementation());
    }
}

class AppletImplementation extends UIApplet
    implements IUIActionListener
{
    UIProgress progress;
    MessageCanvas canvas;
    UIPushButton button;
    int progressPos;

    public void init()
    {
        UIGridLayout layout = new UIGridLayout(3,1);
        setLayout(layout);

        progress = new UIProgress(100, 0);
        add(progress);

        button = new UIPushButton("Increment");
        button.addActionListener(this);
        add(button);

        canvas = new MessageCanvas("", 48, 80, 55);
        add(canvas);

        progressPos = 0;

        setValid(true);
    }
```

```java
    public void actionPerformed(UIActionEvent event)
    {
        String str = event.getActionCommand();

        if (str == "Increment")
        {
            progressPos += 10;
            if (progressPos > 100)
                progressPos = 0;
            progress.setPos(progressPos);
            str = String.valueOf(progressPos);
            canvas.showMessage(str);
        }
    }
}


class MessageCanvas extends UICanvas
{
    String displayString;
    int pointSize;
    int col, row;

    public MessageCanvas(String msg, int points, int x, int y)
    {
        displayString = msg;
        pointSize = points;
        col = x;
        row = y;
        setBackground(FxColor.blue);
    }

    public void paint(FxGraphics graphics)
    {
        FxFont font =
            new FxFont("TimesRoman", FxFont.PLAIN, pointSize);
        graphics.setFont(font);
        graphics.setColor(FxColor.white);
        graphics.drawString(displayString, col, row);
    }

    public void showMessage(String str)
    {
        displayString = str;
        repaint();
    }
}
```

# Responding To Scroll Events

As always with Java, how your applications respond to scrollers depends on whether you're using the propagation event model (Java 1.0) or the delegation event model (Java 1.1). For the most part, using the delegation event model is easiest. To do this, the container class must implement the **IUIAdjustmentListener** interface. Then, you call the scroller's **addAdjustmentListener()** method to add the container to the scroller's listener list. Finally, you add the **adjustmentValueChanged()** method to the container. The scroller calls this method for each adjustment listener in its list. The method receives a **UIAdjustmentEvent** object as its single parameter. You get the scroller's new value by calling the event object's **getValue()** method.

Listing 5.8 presents the source code for ScrollEventApplet, which is an applet that demonstrates responding to a scroller component by using the delegation event model. (The **MessageCanvas** class referenced in the applet is exactly the same as the **MessageCanvas** class shown in Listing 5.7 and so is not shown here.) The applet contains a scroller component and a canvas. The canvas displays the scroller's current value, which you can change by dragging the scroller's thumb or by clicking in the scroller's track. Figure 5.11 shows ScrollEventApplet, running in Applet Viewer.

### Listing 5.8  The source code for ScrollEventApplet.

```
///////////////////////////////////////////////
// ScrollEventApplet.java
//
// An AFC applet that demonstrates how to respond
// to events generated by a scroller component.
///////////////////////////////////////////////

import com.ms.ui.*;
import com.ms.fx.*;
import com.ms.ui.event.*;

public class ScrollEventApplet extends AwtUIApplet
{
    public ScrollEventApplet()
    {
        super(new AppletImplementation());
    }
}

class AppletImplementation extends UIApplet
    implements IUIAdjustmentListener
```

```
{
    UIScroll scroller;
    MessageCanvas canvas;

    public void init()
    {
        UIGridLayout layout = new UIGridLayout(2,1);
        setLayout(layout);

        scroller = new UIScroll(0, 0, 109, 10, 1, 25);
        scroller.addAdjustmentListener(this);
        add(scroller);

        canvas = new MessageCanvas("25", 72, 70, 90);
        add(canvas);

        setValid(true);
    }

    public void adjustmentValueChanged(UIAdjustmentEvent event)
    {
        int newValue = event.getValue();
        String str = String.valueOf(newValue);
        canvas.showMessage(str);
    }
}
```

## Figure 5.11

*ScrollEventApplet, running in Applet Viewer.*

Responding to the scroller by using the propagation event model is easier in some ways and harder in others. On the easy side, you don't have to implement any interfaces or register components as event listeners; you only need to add the **handleEvent()** method to the container's class. However, in the **handleEvent()** method, you need to watch for every type of event that may be generated by the scroller. In the case of a **UIScroll** component, these events are **SCROLL_PAGE_UP**, **SCROLL_PAGE_DOWN**, and **SCROLL_ABSOLUTE**.

Listing 5.9 presents a version of ScrollEventApplet (known as ScrollEventApplet2) that uses the propagation event model to track the applet's scroller component. The applet looks and acts just like the previous version. (The **MessageCanvas** class referenced in the applet is exactly the same as the **MessageCanvas** class shown in Listing 5.7 and so is not shown here.)

## Listing 5.9   The source code for ScrollEventApplet2.

```
/////////////////////////////////////////////////////
// ScrollEventApplet2.java
//
// An AFC applet that demonstrates how to respond
// to scroll events using the propagation event
// model.
/////////////////////////////////////////////////////

import com.ms.ui.*;
import com.ms.fx.*;
import java.awt.*;

public class ScrollEventApplet2 extends AwtUIApplet
{
    public ScrollEventApplet2()
    {
        super(new AppletImplementation());
    }
}

class AppletImplementation extends UIApplet
{
    UIScroll scroller;
    MessageCanvas canvas;

    public void init()
    {
        UIGridLayout layout = new UIGridLayout(2,1);
        setLayout(layout);
```

```
        scroller = new UIScroll(0, 0, 109, 10, 1, 25);
        add(scroller);

        canvas = new MessageCanvas("25", 72, 70, 90);
        add(canvas);

        setValid(true);
    }

    public boolean handleEvent(Event event)
    {
        switch (event.id)
        {
            case Event.SCROLL_PAGE_UP:
            case Event.SCROLL_PAGE_DOWN:
            case Event.SCROLL_ABSOLUTE:
                int pos = scroller.getScrollPos();
                String str = String.valueOf(pos);
                canvas.showMessage(str);
                return true;
        }
        return false;
    }
}
```

## Customizing Scroller Components

A scroller is actually several components that work together. For example, a **UIScroll** control contains two repeat buttons and one scroll thumb. The repeat buttons represent the scroller's track on either side of the thumb. You can modify or even replace the components that make up the control using methods of the class.

If you want to modify an existing component, you must first get a reference to the component. You can get this reference by calling the scroller's **getLayoutComponent()** method with an appropriate index. The valid indexes for a **UIScroll** object are **THUMB** (gets the thumb component), **PAGE_UP** (gets the left track's repeat button), and **PAGE_DOWN** (gets the right track's repeat button).

Listing 5.10 presents an applet that creates and displays a scroller component with a red thumb. (The **MessageCanvas** class referenced in the applet is exactly the same as the **MessageCanvas** class shown in Listing 5.7 and so is not shown here.)

## Listing 5.10  The source code for ScrollButtonApplet.

```
///////////////////////////////////////////////
// ScrollButtonApplet.java
//
// An AFC applet that demonstrates how to modify
// scroller components.
///////////////////////////////////////////////

import com.ms.ui.*;
import com.ms.fx.*;
import com.ms.ui.event.*;

public class ScrollButtonApplet extends AwtUIApplet
{
    public ScrollButtonApplet()
    {
        super(new AppletImplementation());
    }
}

class AppletImplementation extends UIApplet
    implements IUIAdjustmentListener
{
    UIScroll scroller;
    MessageCanvas canvas;

    public void init()
    {
        UIGridLayout layout = new UIGridLayout(2,1);
        setLayout(layout);

        scroller = new UIScroll(0, 0, 109, 10, 1, 25);
        scroller.addAdjustmentListener(this);

        UIScrollThumb thumb =(UIScrollThumb)
            scroller.getLayoutComponent(UIScroll.THUMB);
        thumb.setBackground(new FxColor(255,0,0));

        add(scroller);

        canvas = new MessageCanvas("25", 72, 70, 90);
        add(canvas);

        setValid(true);
    }
```

```
    public void adjustmentValueChanged(UIAdjustmentEvent event)
    {
        int newValue = event.getValue();
        String str = String.valueOf(newValue);
        canvas.showMessage(str);
    }
}
```

You can do a lot more, however, than just change a component's attributes. You can actually replace the components that make up the scroller with your own components. The trick is to call the scroller's **add()** method with the index of the component you want to replace and with a reference to the new component. Just as with **getLayoutComponent()**, the valid indexes for a **UIScroll** object are **THUMB**, **PAGE_UP**, and **PAGE_DOWN**.

In Listing 5.11, you see an applet that creates and displays a scroller control that replaces all the scroller's components with push buttons. (The **MessageCanvas** class referenced in the applet is exactly the same as the **MessageCanvas** class shown in Listing 5.7 and so is not shown here.) Figure 5.12 shows the applet running in Applet Viewer. The buttons that represent the scroller's track (left and right) were replaced with push buttons that pop up when the mouse passes over them. The scroller's thumb was replaced with a raised push button.

When you drag the DRAG ME button, the buttons in the track change size to accommodate the control's new state. Figure 5.13, for example, shows the custom scroller

**Figure 5.12**

*ScrollButtonApplet2, running in Applet Viewer.*

**Figure 5.13**

*ScrollButtonApplet2, with the thumb almost fully to the right.*

with the thumb button dragged almost completely to the right. The left track button has expanded, while the right track button is barely visible.

Besides dragging the thumb button, you can change the scroller's value by clicking either the DOWN or UP buttons. When you do, the scroll thumb moves in the appropriate direction and the canvas displays the new value. If you examine Listing 5.11, however, you see that, because the applet replaced the scroller's components with new buttons, the applet must respond to the buttons on its own. That's why the program implements the **IUIActionListener** interface, represented by the **actionPerformed()** method, which responds to the scroller's DOWN and UP buttons.

**Listing 5.11   The source code for ScrollButtonApplet2.**

```
/////////////////////////////////////////////////
// ScrollButtonApplet2.java
//
// An AFC applet that demonstrates how to replace
// scroller components.
/////////////////////////////////////////////////

import com.ms.ui.*;
import com.ms.fx.*;
import com.ms.ui.event.*;

public class ScrollButtonApplet2 extends AwtUIApplet
{
    public ScrollButtonApplet2()
    {
        super(new AppletImplementation());
```

```
        }
    }

class AppletImplementation extends UIApplet
    implements IUIAdjustmentListener, IUIActionListener
{
    UIScroll scroller;
    MessageCanvas canvas;

    public void init()
    {
        UIGridLayout layout = new UIGridLayout(2,1);
        setLayout(layout);

        scroller = new UIScroll(0, 0, 109, 10, 1, 25);
        scroller.addAdjustmentListener(this);

        UIPushButton upButton = new UIPushButton("DOWN");
        upButton.addActionListener(this);
        scroller.add(UIScroll.PAGE_UP, upButton);

        UIPushButton downButton = new UIPushButton("UP");
        downButton.addActionListener(this);
        scroller.add(UIScroll.PAGE_DOWN, downButton);

        UIPushButton dragButton = new UIPushButton("DRAG ME",
            UIPushButton.RAISED);
        scroller.add(UIScroll.THUMB, dragButton);

        add(scroller);

        canvas = new MessageCanvas("25", 72, 70, 90);
        add(canvas);

        setValid(true);
    }

    public void adjustmentValueChanged(UIAdjustmentEvent event)
    {
        int newValue = event.getValue();
        String str = String.valueOf(newValue);
        canvas.showMessage(str);
    }

    public void actionPerformed(UIActionEvent event)
    {
        int page = scroller.getScrollPage();
        int pos = scroller.getScrollPos();
        String str = event.getActionCommand();
```

```
        if (str == "UP")
            scroller.setScrollPos(pos+page);
        else if (str == "DOWN")
            scroller.setScrollPos(pos-page);

        pos = scroller.getScrollPos();
        str = String.valueOf(pos);
        canvas.showMessage(str);
    }
}
```

## Responding To Scroll-Bar Events

Scroll bars, represented by the **UIScrollBar** class, are merely **UIScroll** controls with arrow buttons. The arrow buttons enable the user to change the scroller's value line by line, without having to drag the scroll thumb. So, when using the delegation event model, responding to scroll-bar events works just as it works for a **UIScroll** control, as shown in Listing 5.12. (The **MessageCanvas** class referenced in the applet is exactly the same as the **MessageCanvas** class shown in Listing 5.7 and so is not shown here.)

When you run the applet, drag the scroll bar's thumb, click within the scroll bar's track, or click the arrow buttons to change the value of the scroll bar. Dragging the thumb generates absolute scroll events, while clicking within the track generates page-up or page-down scroll events. The arrow buttons generate line-up or line-down events. But, no matter which events the scroll bar generates, the **adjustmentValueChanged()** method, which implements the **IUIAdjustmentListener** interface, handles the event. Figure 5.14 shows the applet, running in Applet Viewer.

**Figure 5.14**

*ScrollBarEventApplet, running in Applet Viewer.*

## Listing 5.12  The source code for ScrollBarEventApplet.

```java
///////////////////////////////////////////////
// ScrollBarEventApplet.java
//
// An AFC applet that demonstrates how to respond
// to events generated by a scroll bar.
///////////////////////////////////////////////

import com.ms.ui.*;
import com.ms.fx.*;
import com.ms.ui.event.*;

public class ScrollBarEventApplet extends AwtUIApplet
{
    public ScrollBarEventApplet()
    {
        super(new AppletImplementation());
    }
}

class AppletImplementation extends UIApplet
    implements IUIAdjustmentListener
{
    UIScrollBar scrollBar;
    MessageCanvas canvas;

    public void init()
    {
        UIBorderLayout layout = new UIBorderLayout();
        setLayout(layout);

        scrollBar = new UIScrollBar(0, 0, 109, 10, 1, 25);
        scrollBar.addAdjustmentListener(this);
        add(scrollBar, "North");

        canvas = new MessageCanvas("25", 72, 70, 120);
        add(canvas, "Center");

        setValid(true);
    }

    public void adjustmentValueChanged(UIAdjustmentEvent event)
    {
        int newValue = event.getValue();
        String str = String.valueOf(newValue);
        canvas.showMessage(str);
    }
}
```

When you're using the propagation event model with a scroll-bar component, the applet must watch for five types of events, as compared with the three events needed with a **UIScroll** component. These scroll events are as follows:

- **SCROLL_LINE_UP**—Generated by clicking the left or top arrow button

- **SCROLL_LINE_DOWN**—Generated by clicking the right or bottom arrow button

- **SCROLL_PAGE_UP**—Generated by clicking the left or top track

- **SCROLL_PAGE_DOWN**—Generated by clicking the right or bottom track

- **SCROLL_ABSOLUTE**—Generated by dragging the scroll thumb

Listing 5.13 is a version of ScrollBarEventApplet (called ScrollBarEventApplet2) that uses the propagation event model to track the applet's scroller component. The applet looks and acts just like the previous version. (The **MessageCanvas** class referenced in the applet is exactly the same as the **MessageCanvas** class shown in Listing 5.7 and so is not shown here.) Notice how the **handleEvent()** method now watches for all five types of scroll events. In a full-fledged program, you probably need to use the **switch** statement to call a different method for each event type, updating the application's data as appropriate for the type of event.

### Listing 5.13  The source code for ScrollBarEventApplet2.

```
/////////////////////////////////////////////////
// ScrollBarEventApplet2.java
//
// An AFC applet that demonstrates how to respond
// to events generated by a scroll bar by using the
// propagation event model.
/////////////////////////////////////////////////

import com.ms.ui.*;
import com.ms.fx.*;
import java.awt.*;

public class ScrollBarEventApplet2 extends AwtUIApplet
{
    public ScrollBarEventApplet2()
    {
        super(new AppletImplementation());
    }
}
```

```
class AppletImplementation extends UIApplet
{
    UIScrollBar scrollBar;
    MessageCanvas canvas;

    public void init()
    {
        UIBorderLayout layout = new UIBorderLayout();
        setLayout(layout);

        scrollBar = new UIScrollBar(0, 0, 109, 10, 1, 25);
        add(scrollBar, "North");

        canvas = new MessageCanvas("25", 72, 70, 120);
        add(canvas, "Center");

        setValid(true);
    }

    public boolean handleEvent(Event event)
    {
        switch (event.id)
        {
            case Event.SCROLL_LINE_UP:
            case Event.SCROLL_LINE_DOWN:
            case Event.SCROLL_PAGE_UP:
            case Event.SCROLL_PAGE_DOWN:
            case Event.SCROLL_ABSOLUTE:
                int pos = scrollBar.getScrollPos();
                String str = String.valueOf(pos);
                canvas.showMessage(str);
                return true;
        }
        return false;
    }
}
```

## Responding To Slider Events

A slider is just a fancy scroller, so it generates the same kinds of events that a scroller generates. If you're using the delegation event model, implement the **IUIAdjustment-Listener** interface to capture and respond to slider events. Listing 5.14 presents a short applet that demonstrates how similar slider event handling is to scroller event handling. (The **MessageCanvas** class referenced in the applet is exactly the same as the **MessageCanvas** class shown in Listing 5.7 and so is not shown here.)

**Figure 5.15**

*SliderEventApplet, running in Applet Viewer.*

When you run the applet, drag the slider or click within the slider's track to change the displayed value. Dragging the thumb generates absolute scroll events, while clicking within the track generates page-up or page-down scroll events. The **adjustmentValueChanged()** method, which implements the **IUIAdjustmentListener** interface, handles the events. Figure 5.15 shows the applet while it runs in Applet Viewer.

**Listing 5.14   The source code for SliderEventApplet.**

```
/////////////////////////////////////////////////
// SliderEventApplet.java
//
// An AFC applet that demonstrates how to respond
// to events generated by a slider component.
/////////////////////////////////////////////////

import com.ms.ui.*;
import com.ms.fx.*;
import com.ms.ui.event.*;

public class SliderEventApplet extends AwtUIApplet
{
    public SliderEventApplet()
    {
        super(new AppletImplementation());
    }
}
```

```
class AppletImplementation extends UIApplet
    implements IUIAdjustmentListener
{
    UISlider slider;
    MessageCanvas canvas;

    public void init()
    {
        UIBorderLayout layout = new UIBorderLayout();
        setLayout(layout);

        slider = new UISlider(UISlider.TICKSABOVE |
            UISlider.TICKSBELOW, 0, 100, 10, 1, 25, 10);
        slider.addAdjustmentListener(this);
        add(slider, "North");

        canvas = new MessageCanvas("25", 72, 70, 120);
        add(canvas, "Center");

        setValid(true);
    }

    public void adjustmentValueChanged(UIAdjustmentEvent event)
    {
        int newValue = event.getValue();
        String str = String.valueOf(newValue);
        canvas.showMessage(str);
    }
}
```

In Listing 5.15, you see a version of SliderEventApplet (named SliderEventApplet2)
that uses the propagation event model to track the applet's slider component. The
applet looks and acts just like the previous version. (The **MessageCanvas** class
referenced in the applet is exactly the same as the **MessageCanvas** class shown in
Listing 5.7 and so is not shown here.)

### Listing 5.15   The source code for SliderEventApplet2.
```
/////////////////////////////////////////////////
// SliderEventApplet2.java
//
// An AFC applet that demonstrates how to respond
// to events generated by a slider component by
// using the propagation event model.
/////////////////////////////////////////////////
```

```java
import com.ms.ui.*;
import com.ms.fx.*;
import java.awt.*;

public class SliderEventApplet2 extends AwtUIApplet
{
    public SliderEventApplet2()
    {
        super(new AppletImplementation());
    }
}

class AppletImplementation extends UIApplet
{
    UISlider slider;
    MessageCanvas canvas;

    public void init()
    {
        UIBorderLayout layout = new UIBorderLayout();
        setLayout(layout);

        slider = new UISlider(UISlider.TICKSABOVE |
            UISlider.TICKSBELOW, 0, 100, 10, 1, 25, 10);
        add(slider, "North");

        canvas = new MessageCanvas("25", 72, 70, 120);
        add(canvas, "Center");

        setValid(true);
    }

    public boolean handleEvent(Event event)
    {
        switch (event.id)
        {
            case Event.SCROLL_PAGE_UP:
            case Event.SCROLL_PAGE_DOWN:
            case Event.SCROLL_ABSOLUTE:
                int pos = slider.getScrollPos();
                String str = String.valueOf(pos);
                canvas.showMessage(str);
                return true;
        }
        return false;
    }
}
```

## Managing Slider Range Selections

Although sliders are most often used to select a single value from a range of values, the control can also be used to select a subrange of values from its total range. For example, suppose you have a slider with a range of zero to 100. You then can enable the user to select a subrange—for example, 25 through 75—of the slider's total range.

Unfortunately, handling subranges with sliders isn't as straightforward as you might expect. For some strange reason, slider controls—even those used in C++ Windows programs—provide no built-in method for enabling the user to select a subrange. These controls enable the application to set only the range, which means that you must write the code needed to extend this capability to the user.

There are several ways of adding user-range-selection capabilities to your Java program. In one sample program, Microsoft uses three sliders to implement range selection, as shown in Figure 5.16. (The HTML document that runs this sample is C:\SDK-Java.20\Samples\AFC\Scrolls\Classes\afcsamp.htm in your Microsoft Java SDK 2.0 installation.) In the applet's UISlider box, the left slider selects the subrange

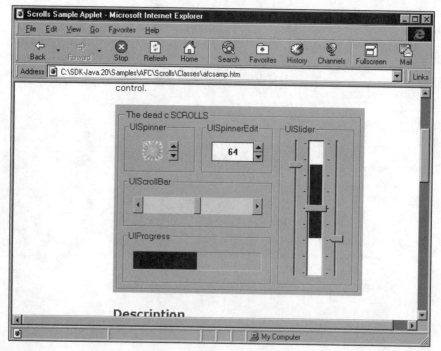

**Figure 5.16**

*Microsoft's sample applet, with slider subrange selection.*

start, the right slider selects the subrange end, and the center slider selects single values. This example is snazzy, but complex.

You can implement range selections in another way—by using buttons along with the slider. This approach is used in the SliderSelApplet sample applet, presented in Listing 5.16. When you run the applet in Applet Viewer, you see the window shown in Figure 5.17. Set the slider to the starting value in the subrange, and click the Start button. Then, set the slider to the ending value in the subrange, and click the End button. The slider updates itself to show the selection, as shown in Figure 5.18. To remove the current selection, click the Clear button.

**Figure 5.17**

*SliderSelApplet, running in Applet Viewer.*

**Figure 5.18**

*SliderSelApplet with a subrange selected.*

Notice that the button event handler in Listing 5.16 provides logic for managing cases where the subrange start value ends up larger than the ending value. In this case, the program reverses the start and end values to create a valid selection. If the program tried to set such a selection without reversing the values, the subrange selection wouldn't work. In other words, the start value must always be lower than the end value.

Notice also, in the line that creates the slider, the addition of the **RANGESELECT** style flag. Including this style flag not only enables the application to call slider selection methods (which would be ignored without the **RANGESELECT** style flag), it also changes the slider's appearance to include a wide slider channel that can display the currently selected subrange.

### Listing 5.16   The source code for SliderSelApplet.

```
/////////////////////////////////////////////////////
// SliderSelApplet.java
//
// An AFC applet that demonstrates how to handle
// range selection with a slider.
/////////////////////////////////////////////////////

import com.ms.ui.*;
import com.ms.fx.*;
import com.ms.ui.event.*;

public class SliderSelApplet extends AwtUIApplet
{
    public SliderSelApplet()
    {
        super(new AppletImplementation());
    }
}

class AppletImplementation extends UIApplet
    implements IUIAdjustmentListener, IUIActionListener
{
    UISlider slider;
    UIPushButton startButton;
    UIPushButton endButton;
    UIPushButton clearButton;
    MessageCanvas canvas;
    int selectionStart;
    int selectionEnd;

    public void init()
    {
```

```
        UIBorderLayout layout = new UIBorderLayout();
        setLayout(layout);

        slider = new UISlider(UISlider.TICKSABOVE |
            UISlider.TICKSBELOW | UISlider.RANGESELECT,
            0, 100, 10, 1, 25, 10);
        slider.addAdjustmentListener(this);
        add(slider, "North");

        canvas = new MessageCanvas("25", 72, 70, 120);
        add(canvas, "Center");

        UIPanel buttonPanel = new UIPanel();
        UIGridLayout panelLayout = new UIGridLayout(1,3);
        buttonPanel.setLayout(panelLayout);

        startButton =
            new UIPushButton("Start", UIPushButton.RAISED);
        startButton.addActionListener(this);
        buttonPanel.add(startButton);

        endButton =
            new UIPushButton("End", UIPushButton.RAISED);
        endButton.addActionListener(this);
        buttonPanel.add(endButton);

        clearButton =
            new UIPushButton("Clear", UIPushButton.RAISED);
        clearButton.addActionListener(this);
        buttonPanel.add(clearButton);

        add(buttonPanel, "South");

        selectionStart = -1;
        selectionEnd = -1;

        setValid(true);
}

public void adjustmentValueChanged(UIAdjustmentEvent event)
{
    int newValue = event.getValue();
    String str = String.valueOf(newValue);
    canvas.showMessage(str);
}

public void actionPerformed(UIActionEvent event)
{
    String str = event.getActionCommand();
```

```
            if (str == "Start")
            {
                selectionStart = slider.getScrollPos();
                if ((selectionEnd != -1) &&
                    (selectionStart > selectionEnd))
                {
                    int temp = selectionEnd;
                    selectionEnd = selectionStart;
                    selectionStart = temp;
                    slider.setSelectionEnd(selectionEnd);
                }
                slider.setSelectionStart(selectionStart);
            }
            else if (str == "End")
            {
                selectionEnd = slider.getScrollPos();
                if ((selectionStart != -1) &&
                    (selectionStart > selectionEnd))
                {
                    int temp = selectionStart;
                    selectionStart = selectionEnd;
                    selectionEnd = temp;
                    slider.setSelectionStart(selectionStart);
                }
                slider.setSelectionEnd(selectionEnd);
            }
            else if (str == "Clear")
            {
                slider.clearSelection();
                selectionStart = -1;
                selectionEnd = -1;
            }
        }
    }
```

## Responding To Spinner Events

A spinner doesn't look much like a scroll control, but it generates the same kind
of adjustment events that your program can handle by implementing the **IUI-
AdjustmentListener** Interface. Listing 5.17 presents a short applet that demonstrates
how similar spinner event handling is to scroller event handling. (The **MessageCanvas**
class referenced in the applet is exactly the same as the **MessageCanvas** class shown
in Listing 5.7 and so is not shown here.)

When you run the applet, click the spinner's arrows to change the displayed value.
Listing 5.18 shows the **handleEvent()** method that you might add to the applet to

## Figure 5.19

*SpinnerEventApplet, running in Applet Viewer.*

accommodate the propagation event model. Figure 5.19 shows the applet, running in Applet Viewer.

### Listing 5.17   The source code for SpinnerEventApplet.

```
/////////////////////////////////////////////
// SpinnerEventApplet.java
//
// An AFC applet that demonstrates how to respond
// to events generated by a spinner component.
/////////////////////////////////////////////

import com.ms.ui.*;
import com.ms.fx.*;
import com.ms.ui.event.*;

public class SpinnerEventApplet extends AwtUIApplet
{
    public SpinnerEventApplet()
    {
        super(new AppletImplementation());
    }
}

class AppletImplementation extends UIApplet
    implements IUIAdjustmentListener
{
    UISpinner spinner;
    MessageCanvas canvas;
```

```
public void init()
{
    UIGridLayout layout = new UIGridLayout(2,1);
    setLayout(layout);

    spinner = new UISpinner(UISpinner.RAISED |
        UISpinner.CIRCULAR, 0, 10, 1, 1, 0);
    spinner.addAdjustmentListener(this);
    add(spinner);

    canvas = new MessageCanvas("0", 72, 90, 90);
    add(canvas);

    setValid(true);
}

public void adjustmentValueChanged(UIAdjustmentEvent event)
{
    int newValue = event.getValue();
    String str = String.valueOf(newValue);
    canvas.showMessage(str);
}
}
```

**Listing 5.18  The handleEvent() method.**
```
public boolean handleEvent(Event event)
{
    switch (event.id)
    {
        case Event.SCROLL_LINE_UP:
        case Event.SCROLL_LINE_DOWN:
            int pos = spinner.getScrollPos();
            String str = String.valueOf(pos);
            canvas.showMessage(str);
            return true;
    }
    return false;
}
```

**UISpinnerEdit** components are a whole other ball of wax when it comes to handling events. Although you can manage the spinner portion of the control just like any other spinner (by implementing the **IUIAdjustmentListener** interface), you also need to consider the attached edit control. If the user decides to type the desired value directly into the edit control, your program will need to handle text listener events, as well as adjustment listener events. (If you need a refresher on the edit control events, please refer back to Chapter 4.)

Listing 5.19 is the source code for SpinnerEditEventApplet, which is an applet that demonstrates responding to a spinner-edit component using the delegation event model. (The **MessageCanvas** class referenced in the applet is exactly the same as the **MessageCanvas** class shown in Listing 5.7 and so is not shown here.) The applet contains a spinner-edit component and a canvas. The canvas displays the spinner's current value, which you can change by clicking the spinner's arrows or by typing directly into the edit control. Figure 5.20 shows SpinnerEditEventApplet running, in Applet Viewer.

### Listing 5.19  The source code for SpinnerEditEventApplet.

```
//////////////////////////////////////////////////
// SpinnerEditEventApplet.java
//
// An AFC applet that demonstrates how to respond
// to events generated by a spinner-edit control.
//////////////////////////////////////////////////

import com.ms.ui.*;
import com.ms.fx.*;
import com.ms.ui.event.*;

public class SpinnerEditEventApplet extends AwtUIApplet
{
    public SpinnerEditEventApplet()
    {
        super(new AppletImplementation());
    }
}

class AppletImplementation extends UIApplet
    implements IUIAdjustmentListener, IUITextListener
{
    UISpinnerEdit spinner;
    UIEdit edit;
    MessageCanvas canvas;

    public void init()
    {
        UIGridLayout layout = new UIGridLayout(3,1);
        setLayout(layout);

        spinner = new UISpinnerEdit(UISpinnerEdit.RAISED |
            UISpinnerEdit.CIRCULAR, UISpinnerEdit.BORDER,
            0, 1000, 1, 1, 500);
        spinner.addAdjustmentListener(this);
        add(spinner);
```

```
        edit = (UIEdit)spinner.getLayoutComponent
            (UISpinnerEdit.BUDDY);
        FxFont font =
            new FxFont("TimesRoman", FxFont.BOLD, 64);
        edit.setFont(font);
        edit.addTextListener(this);

        UIPanel panel = new UIPanel();
        add(panel);

        canvas = new MessageCanvas("500", 72, 50, 65);
        add(canvas);

        setValid(true);
    }

    public void adjustmentValueChanged(UIAdjustmentEvent event)
    {
        int newValue = event.getValue();
        String str = String.valueOf(newValue);
        canvas.showMessage(str);
    }

    public void textValueChanged(UITextEvent e)
    {
        String str = edit.getValueText();
        canvas.showMessage(str);
    }
}
```

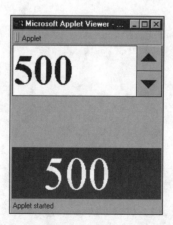

**Figure 5.20**

*SpinnerEditEventApplet, running in Applet Viewer.*

# Chapter 6

# Band Boxes And Status Bars

*A tart temper never mellows with age, and a sharp tongue is the only edged tool that grows keener with constant use.*
—*Washington Irving,*
*Rip Van Winkle*

# Notes...

# Chapter

# 6

I don't know about you, but when I'm learning to program a new set of libraries, I hope that the kids stay away. Otherwise, the little folk will not only overhear some delightfully expressive new words, but they may also find out about that sharp tongue that Washington Irving mentioned. Luckily, everyone in the house knows that Dad can be a bit of a bear when error messages keep popping up on the screen. In fact, the more the compiler whines, the emptier the house gets. Sometimes, I swear I can actually see the dust settling in the family's wake.

Hopefully, you won't have these kinds of problems as you learn to use AFC. I've dug into the libraries on your behalf, saving you from the cursing, the sharp tongue, and the monitor pounding. In this chapter, for example, you'll get painless lessons in how to add toolbars and status bars to your AFC programs. Although these two components are relatively easy to use, knowing a couple of tricks makes them more useful.

## The **UIBandBox** Class

Most modern applications have a *toolbar*, an area usually near the top of the window that contains buttons and other controls for selecting frequently used menu commands. Until recently, toolbars were just simple rows of components. Now, however, toolbars often contain several sets of controls that the user can slide horizontally on and off the toolbar, enabling the user not only to customize the toolbar as he needs, but also to provide access to many more commands than would fit in a single toolbar. This type of toolbar is called a *band box*.

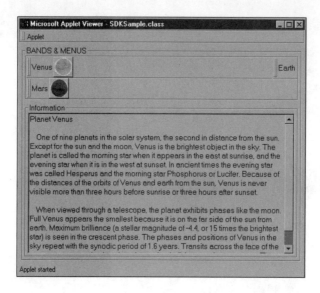

**Figure 6.1**

*BandsnMenus, running in Applet Viewer.*

Figure 6.1 shows a sample program called BandsnMenus, from the Microsoft Java SDK 2.0, running in Applet Viewer. Under the BANDS & MENUS label, you can see two band boxes. The first band box contains two bands labeled Venus and Earth, and the second band box contains one band labeled Mars. Each band contains not only buttons, but also a band thumb (the thing that looks like two 3D vertical lines), which is the control the user can drag to slide the bands horizontally on and off the band box.

In BandsnMenus, the user can slide only the Earth band. The leftmost bands in a band box are stationary. When the applet first runs, the Earth band lays far to the right of the first band box—it's so far to the right that you can't even see its buttons. To make the Earth band's buttons accessible, drag the band's thumb to the left, which brings the entire band into view (Figure 6.2). Another way to display the band is to click it. This action causes the band to slide as far as it can to the left.

In AFC, the **UIBandBox** class represents a band-box component. **UIBandBox** extends the **UIMenuList** class, which, as you learned in Chapter 3, represents a collection of menu commands. **UIMenuList** traces its AFC ancestry from **UIList** up through **UISelector**, **UIPanel**, **UIStateContainer**, and **UIContainer** to **UIComponent**. Because **UIBandBox** has no Java AWT counterpart, it has no standard Java class in its ancestry. **UIBandBox** inherits methods from all of its superclasses, but it also defines its own set of methods, as shown in Table 6.1.

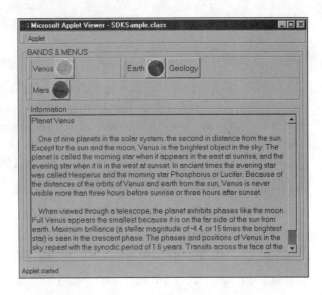

**Figure 6.2**

*The Earth band is now completely visible.*

**Table 6.1  Methods of the UIBandBox class.**

| Method | Description |
| --- | --- |
| dragBand() | Enables the user to resizes the band |
| getBreak() | Returns **true** if the band's break style is set |
| getDragBreak() | Returns **true** if the band's drag break style is set |
| getRoleCode() | Returns the band's role code, which is **ROLE_SYSTEM_TOOLBAR** |
| mouseDown() | Sets the control for dragging if the mouse button is pressed over a band component |
| mouseDrag() | Handles mouse dragging over band components |
| mouseUp() | Handles mouse-button releases |
| paint() | Draws the band box |

To create a band-box component, call the class's constructor:

```
UIBandBox bandbox = new UIBandBox();
```

As you can see, the constructor takes no arguments. However, a band box that contains no bands is about as useful as a towel at the bottom of the ocean. To create a useful band box, you must add bands and buttons, which means that you have to know about the **UIBand** class.

# The **UIBand** Class

As mentioned previously, a band box has multiple toolbars that the user can slide on and off of the band box. Each of these toolbars is actually a band component. To create a complete band box, then, you perform the following steps:

1.  Create buttons that represent the commands the user can select from the band box.

2.  Create a band for each group of buttons you'll have in the band box.

3.  Add the buttons to the bands.

4.  Add the bands to the band box.

In AFC, the **UIBand** class represents a band component. **UIBand**, like **UIBandBox**, extends the **UIMenuList** class. As you know, **UIMenuList** traces its AFC ancestry from **UIList** up through **UISelector**, **UIPanel**, **UIStateContainer**, and **UIContainer** to **UIComponent**. Because **UIBand** has no Java AWT counterpart, it has no standard Java class in its ancestry. Still, **UIBand** inherits methods from all of its superclasses and also defines its own set of methods, as shown in Table 6.2.

**Table 6.2  Methods of the UIBand class.**

| Method | Description |
| --- | --- |
| getBreak() | Returns **true** if the component's break style is set |
| getDragBreak() | Returns **true** if the component's drag break style is set |
| getInsets() | Gets the component's insets |
| getMinimumSize() | Determines the component's minimum size |

*(continued)*

**Table 6.2 Methods of the UIBand class *(continued)*.**

| Method | Description |
| --- | --- |
| getRestoredWidth() | Gets the component's restore width |
| getRoleCode() | Gets the band's role code, which is **ROLE_SYSTEM_TOOLBAR** |
| getStyle() | Gets the band's current style |
| handleEvent() | Handles the band's events |
| layout() | Lays out the band's components |
| setBreak() | Toggles the band's break style |
| setDragBreak() | Toggles the band's drag break style |
| setRestoredWidth() | Sets the component's restore width |
| setStyle() | Sets the band control's styles |

To create a band component, call the class's constructor:

```
UIBand band = new UIBand("Band's Name");
```

The constructor takes a single argument, which is the band name that will appear in the band box. You also can create a band component by giving a style, as well as a name, as in the following:

```
UIBand band = new UIBand("Band Name", UIBand.BREAK);
```

The **UIBand** class defines two creation styles: **BREAK** and **DRAGBREAK**. The **BREAK** style indicates that the band component should start a new row in the band box, whereas the **DRAGBREAK** style specifies that the band component should start a new row because no room remains in the current row. Normally, you use only the **BREAK** style. AFC uses the **DRAGBREAK** style internally, when it positions bands in their band boxes.

Listing 6.1 presents a short applet that creates and displays a band-box component. Figure 6.3 shows the applet running in Applet Viewer. Figure 6.4 shows the applet after the user drags the third band's buttons into view.

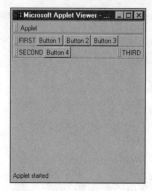

**Figure 6.3**

*BandBoxApplet, running in Applet Viewer.*

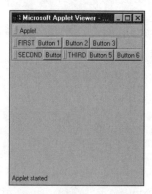

**Figure 6.4**

*BandBoxApplet with its third band component revealed.*

## Listing 6.1   The source code for BandBoxApplet.

```
///////////////////////////////////////////////
// BandBoxApplet.java
//
// An AFC applet that demonstrates how to create
// a band-box component.
///////////////////////////////////////////////

import com.ms.ui.*;

public class BandBoxApplet extends AwtUIApplet
{
```

```
    public BandBoxApplet()
    {
        super(new AppletImplementation());
    }
}


class AppletImplementation extends UIApplet
{
    public void init()
    {
        UIBorderLayout layout = new UIBorderLayout();
        setLayout(layout);

        UIBandBox bandbox = new UIBandBox();
        UIBand band1 = new UIBand("FIRST");
        UIBand band2 = new UIBand("SECOND", UIBand.BREAK);
        UIBand band3 = new UIBand("THIRD");

        UIPushButton button1 =
            new UIPushButton("Button 1", UIPushButton.RAISED);
        UIPushButton button2 =
            new UIPushButton("Button 2", UIPushButton.RAISED);
        UIPushButton button3 =
            new UIPushButton("Button 3", UIPushButton.RAISED);
        UIPushButton button4 =
            new UIPushButton("Button 4", UIPushButton.RAISED);
        UIPushButton button5 =
            new UIPushButton("Button 5", UIPushButton.RAISED);
        UIPushButton button6 =
            new UIPushButton("Button 6", UIPushButton.RAISED);

        band1.add(button1);
        band1.add(button2);
        band1.add(button3);
        band2.add(button4);
        band3.add(button5);
        band3.add(button6);

        bandbox.add(band1);
        bandbox.add(band2);
        bandbox.add(band3);

        add(bandbox, "North");

        setValid(true);
    }
}
```

# The **UIBandThumb** Class

As you may have guessed, a band component's thumb actually is a component, which AFC defines in the **UIBandThumb** class. **UIBandThumb** extends **UIBand**, which boasts **UISingleContainer**, **UIStateContainer**, **UIContainer**, and **UIComponent** as superclasses. Normally, you don't have to bother with the **UIBandThumb** class because AFC uses it internally to construct band components. Outside of its inherited methods, **UIBandThumb** defines only the **getInsets()** and **paint()** methods, both of which override methods inherited from the **UIContainer** class.

# The **UIStatus** Class

Almost as ubiquitous in modern applications as the toolbar, the status bar provides a place for a program to present messages to the user. These messages may represent the status of an ongoing operation, command hints, the status of the keyboard, or other types of information. A toolbar usually appears at the top of an application's window; the status bar usually appears at the bottom of the same window.

In AFC, the **UIStatus** class represents a status-bar component. **UIStatus** extends the **UISingleContainer** class, which traces its AFC ancestry from **UIStateContainer** and **UIContainer** to **UIComponent**. Because **UIStatus** has no Java AWT counterpart, it has no standard Java class in its ancestry. Like all classes, **UIStatus** inherits methods from all of its superclasses, but defines only its own **getRoleCode()** and **isKeyable()** methods, both of which override **UIComponent** methods.

To do create a status-bar component, call the class's constructor:

```
UIStatus statusbar = new UIStatus();
```

As you can see, the constructor takes no arguments. The **UIStatus** class, however, overloads its constructor, providing you with several ways to create the component. Specifically, you also can supply a text string to the constructor, or supply a text string and a style, as shown in the following syntax:

```
UIStatus statusbar = new UIStatus("Status bar text");
UIStatus statusbar = new UIStatus("Status bar text", UIStatic.RIGHT);
```

The styles, which specify text alignments, are defined in the **UIStatic** class, which you learn more about in Chapter 10. Listing 6.2 presents a short applet that creates

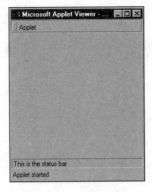

## Figure 6.5

*StatusBarApplet, running in Applet Viewer.*

and displays a status-bar component. Figure 6.5 shows the applet running in Applet Viewer. Notice that applications and applets usually display status bars in the "South" position of a border layout. This positioning places the status bar at the bottom of the window, where users expect to find it.

### Listing 6.2  The source code for StatusBarApplet.

```
///////////////////////////////////////////////
// StatusBarApplet.java
//
// An AFC applet that demonstrates how to create
// a status-bar component.
///////////////////////////////////////////////

import com.ms.ui.*;

public class StatusBarApplet extends AwtUIApplet
{
    public StatusBarApplet()
    {
        super(new AppletImplementation());
    }
}

class AppletImplementation extends UIApplet
{
    public void init()
    {
```

```
        UIBorderLayout layout = new UIBorderLayout();
        setLayout(layout);

        UIStatus statusbar = new UIStatus();
        statusbar.setName("This is the status bar");

        add(statusbar, "South");

        setValid(true);
    }
}
```

# Practical Guide To

## Using Band-Box And Status-Bar Components

- Responding To Band-Box Events
- Placing Components In A Band Box
- Creating A Menu Bar From A Band Box
- Creating A Complex Status Bar

## Responding To Band-Box Events

A band box doesn't do you much good if your application doesn't respond to the commands that the user selects. However, no one way exists to respond to band-box selections, because the type of events generated depend on the type of components in the band box. Traditionally, a toolbar, and by extension a band box, contains buttons that represent frequently used menu commands. In an application with a band box that contains buttons, you would respond to the events generated by the buttons.

If you're using the delegation event model, you must implement the **IUIAction-Listener** interface for the buttons, which means writing an **actionPerformed()** method. Using this interface also means calling each button's **addActionListener()** method to register the applet with the button. Listing 6.3 presents an applet that creates a band box with three bands. The bands contain only buttons, so the applet implements the **IUIActionListener** interface.

Figure 6.6 shows the applet running in Applet Viewer. When the applet first appears, you can see the buttons on the COLORS band, but the FRUIT and TOOLS bands sit all the way to the right, obscuring their buttons. Figure 6.7 shows the applet after the user drags the FRUIT band into view and selects the Grapes button, and Figure 6.8 shows the applet with the TOOLS band exposed.

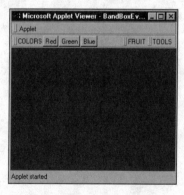

**Figure 6.6**

*BandBoxEventApplet, running in Applet Viewer.*

**Figure 6.7**

*BandBoxEventApplet displaying its FRUIT band.*

**Figure 6.8**

*BandBoxEventApplet displaying its TOOLS band.*

### Listing 6.3 The source code for BandBoxEventApplet.

```
/////////////////////////////////////////////////
// BandBoxEventApplet.java
//
// An AFC applet that demonstrates how to handle
// events from a band box.
/////////////////////////////////////////////////

import com.ms.ui.*;
import com.ms.fx.*;
import com.ms.ui.event.*;
```

```java
public class BandBoxEventApplet extends AwtUIApplet
{
    public BandBoxEventApplet()
    {
        super(new AppletImplementation());
    }
}

class AppletImplementation extends UIApplet
    implements IUIActionListener
{
    MessageCanvas canvas;

    public void init()
    {
        UIBorderLayout layout = new UIBorderLayout();
        setLayout(layout);

        UIBandBox bandbox = new UIBandBox();
        UIBand colorBand = new UIBand("COLORS");
        UIBand fruitBand = new UIBand("FRUIT");
        UIBand toolBand = new UIBand("TOOLS");

        UIPushButton redButton =
            new UIPushButton("Red", UIPushButton.RAISED);
        UIPushButton greenButton =
            new UIPushButton("Green", UIPushButton.RAISED);
        UIPushButton blueButton =
            new UIPushButton("Blue", UIPushButton.RAISED);
        UIPushButton appleButton =
            new UIPushButton("Apple", UIPushButton.RAISED);
        UIPushButton orangeButton =
            new UIPushButton("Orange", UIPushButton.RAISED);
        UIPushButton grapesButton =
            new UIPushButton("Grapes", UIPushButton.RAISED);
        UIPushButton hammerButton =
            new UIPushButton("Hammer", UIPushButton.RAISED);
        UIPushButton sawButton =
            new UIPushButton("Saw", UIPushButton.RAISED);
        UIPushButton wrenchButton =
            new UIPushButton("Wrench", UIPushButton.RAISED);

        redButton.addActionListener(this);
        greenButton.addActionListener(this);
        blueButton.addActionListener(this);
```

```
        appleButton.addActionListener(this);
        orangeButton.addActionListener(this);
        grapesButton.addActionListener(this);
        hammerButton.addActionListener(this);
        sawButton.addActionListener(this);
        wrenchButton.addActionListener(this);

        colorBand.add(redButton);
        colorBand.add(greenButton);
        colorBand.add(blueButton);
        fruitBand.add(appleButton);
        fruitBand.add(orangeButton);
        fruitBand.add(grapesButton);
        toolBand.add(hammerButton);
        toolBand.add(sawButton);
        toolBand.add(wrenchButton);

        bandbox.add(colorBand);
        bandbox.add(fruitBand);
        bandbox.add(toolBand);

        add(bandbox, "North");

        canvas = new MessageCanvas(" ", 48, 65, 110);
        add(canvas, "Center");

        setValid(true);
    }

    public void actionPerformed(UIActionEvent event)
    {
        String str = event.getActionCommand();
        canvas.showMessage(str);
    }
}

class MessageCanvas extends UICanvas
{
    String displayString;
    int pointSize;
    int col, row;

    public MessageCanvas(String msg, int points, int x, int y)
    {
```

```
        displayString = msg;
        pointSize = points;
        col = x;
        row = y;
        setBackground(FxColor.blue);
    }

    public void paint(FxGraphics graphics)
    {
        FxFont font =
            new FxFont("TimesRoman", FxFont.PLAIN, pointSize);
        graphics.setFont(font);
        graphics.setColor(FxColor.white);
        graphics.drawString(displayString, col, row);
    }

    public void showMessage(String str)
    {
        displayString = str;
        repaint();
    }
}
```

When using the propagation event model, you can capture button events in the applet's **action()** method. Listing 6.4 shows the source code for a version of BandBoxEventApplet that uses the propagation event model. This version of the program must import the **java.awt.*** package for the **Event** class. In addition, BandBoxEventApplet2 contains no **IUIActionListener** interface implementation. Instead, the program implements the **action()** method. The **MessageCanvas** class referenced in the listing is exactly the same as the **MessageCanvas** class shown in Listing 6.3, so it isn't shown here.

## Listing 6.4 The source code for BandBoxEventApplet2.

```
/////////////////////////////////////////////////
// BandBoxEventApplet2.java
//
// An AFC applet that demonstrates how to handle
// events from a band box by using the
// propagation event model.
/////////////////////////////////////////////////

import com.ms.ui.*;
import com.ms.fx.*;
import java.awt.*;
```

```java
public class BandBoxEventApplet2 extends AwtUIApplet
{
    public BandBoxEventApplet2()
    {
        super(new AppletImplementation());
    }
}

class AppletImplementation extends UIApplet
{
    MessageCanvas canvas;

    public void init()
    {
        UIBorderLayout layout = new UIBorderLayout();
        setLayout(layout);

        UIBandBox bandbox = new UIBandBox();
        UIBand colorBand = new UIBand("COLORS");
        UIBand fruitBand = new UIBand("FRUIT");
        UIBand toolBand = new UIBand("TOOLS");

        UIPushButton redButton =
            new UIPushButton("Red", UIPushButton.RAISED);
        UIPushButton greenButton =
            new UIPushButton("Green", UIPushButton.RAISED);
        UIPushButton blueButton =
            new UIPushButton("Blue", UIPushButton.RAISED);
        UIPushButton appleButton =
            new UIPushButton("Apple", UIPushButton.RAISED);
        UIPushButton orangeButton =
            new UIPushButton("Orange", UIPushButton.RAISED);
        UIPushButton grapesButton =
            new UIPushButton("Grapes", UIPushButton.RAISED);
        UIPushButton hammerButton =
            new UIPushButton("Hammer", UIPushButton.RAISED);
        UIPushButton sawButton =
            new UIPushButton("Saw", UIPushButton.RAISED);
        UIPushButton wrenchButton =
            new UIPushButton("Wrench", UIPushButton.RAISED);

        colorBand.add(redButton);
        colorBand.add(greenButton);
        colorBand.add(blueButton);
        fruitBand.add(appleButton);
        fruitBand.add(orangeButton);
```

```
        fruitBand.add(grapesButton);
        toolBand.add(hammerButton);
        toolBand.add(sawButton);
        toolBand.add(wrenchButton);

        bandbox.add(colorBand);
        bandbox.add(fruitBand);
        bandbox.add(toolBand);

        add(bandbox, "North");

        canvas = new MessageCanvas(" ", 48, 65, 110);
        add(canvas, "Center");

        setValid(true);
    }

    public boolean action(Event event, Object arg)
    {
        if (arg instanceof UIPushButton)
        {
            String str = ((UIPushButton)arg).getName();
            canvas.showMessage(str);
            return true;
        }

        return false;
    }
}
```

## Placing Components In A Band Box

Although band boxes usually contain buttons, they can also hold other types of components. These components often include menu buttons, choice controls, and maybe even controls such as check boxes. Because you can add almost any type of component you want to a band box, you should be able to create the perfect band box for your application. However, remember that you need to supply event code for each component type you add.

To give you a quick idea of how versatile a band box can be, the applet shown in Listing 6.5 displays a band box that contains a menu button, choice control, and check box. The applet contains no event-handling code, but handling events for the various components was covered earlier in Chapter 3 and Chapter 4. Figure 6.9 shows **BandCompApplet** running in Applet Viewer.

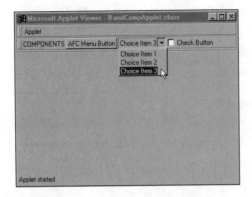

## Figure 6.9

*BandCompApplet running in Applet Viewer.*

## Listing 6.5   The source code for BandCompApplet.

```
/////////////////////////////////////////////////
// BandCompApplet.java
//
// An AFC applet that demonstrates how to add
// different types of components to a band box.
/////////////////////////////////////////////////

import com.ms.ui.*;

public class BandCompApplet extends AwtUIApplet
{
    public BandCompApplet()
    {
        super(new AppletImplementation());
    }
}

class AppletImplementation extends UIApplet
{
    MessageCanvas canvas;

    public void init()
    {
        UIBorderLayout layout = new UIBorderLayout();
        setLayout(layout);

        UIBandBox bandbox = new UIBandBox();
        UIBand band = new UIBand("COMPONENTS");
```

```
UIMenuList menuList = new UIMenuList();
menuList.add("Menu Item 1");
menuList.add("Menu Item 2");
menuList.add("Menu Item 3");
menuList.add("Menu Item 4");
menuList.add("Menu Item 5");
UIMenuButton menuButton =
    new UIMenuButton("AFC Menu Button", menuList);

UIChoice choice = new UIChoice();
choice.addString("Choice Item 1");
choice.addString("Choice Item 2");
choice.addString("Choice Item 3");
choice.addSelectedIndex(0);

UICheckButton button = new UICheckButton("Check Button");

band.add(menuButton);
band.add(choice);
band.add(button);
bandbox.add(band);
add(bandbox, "North");

setValid(true);
    }
}
```

## Creating A Menu Bar From A Band Box

Although band boxes often provide buttons that mirror an application's menu commands, you also can use band boxes to create a menu bar in an applet. This programming technique requires that you create and add menu buttons to the band box, rather than regular pushbuttons, and that you give the band box no text label.

Listing 6.6, for example, presents the source code for MenuBarApplet, which uses a band box to create a menu bar. Figure 6.10 shows the applet when it first appears in Applet Viewer. You can see that it has four menus, Colors, Fruit, Tools, and Animals. Each of the menus is a flat menu button. When the user passes the mouse over a menu, its associated button pops up. If the user clicks the button, the menu, of course, appears. Figure 6.11 shows the Colors menu (which contains a submenu) exposed, after the user selected the Animals menu's Kangaroo command.

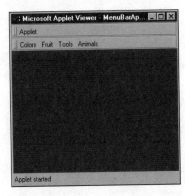

**Figure 6.10**

*MenuBarApplet, running in Applet Viewer.*

**Figure 6.11**

*MenuBarApplet, showing off its Colors menu.*

**Listing 6.6   The source code for MenuBarApplet.**

```
/////////////////////////////////////////////////
// MenuBarApplet.java
//
// An AFC applet that demonstrates how to create
// a menu bar from a band-box component.
/////////////////////////////////////////////////

import com.ms.ui.*;
import com.ms.fx.*;
import com.ms.ui.event.*;

public class MenuBarApplet extends AwtUIApplet
{
```

```
    public MenuBarApplet()
    {
        super(new AppletImplementation());
    }
}


class AppletImplementation extends UIApplet
    implements IUIActionListener
{
    MessageCanvas canvas;

    public void init()
    {
        UIBorderLayout layout = new UIBorderLayout();
        setLayout(layout);

        UIBandBox menuBar = new UIBandBox();
        UIBand menus = new UIBand("");

        UIMenuList subColorMenuList = new UIMenuList();
        subColorMenuList.add("Yellow");
        subColorMenuList.add("Purple");
        subColorMenuList.add("Orange");
        UIMenuItem menuItem =
            new UIMenuItem("Other Colors", subColorMenuList);

        UIMenuList colorMenuList = new UIMenuList();
        colorMenuList.add("Red");
        colorMenuList.add("Green");
        colorMenuList.add("Blue");
        colorMenuList.add(menuItem);

        UIMenuList fruitMenuList = new UIMenuList();
        fruitMenuList.add("Apple");
        fruitMenuList.add("Orange");
        fruitMenuList.add("Grapes");

        UIMenuList toolsMenuList = new UIMenuList();
        toolsMenuList.add("Hammer");
        toolsMenuList.add("Saw");
        toolsMenuList.add("Wrench");

        UIMenuList animalsMenuList = new UIMenuList();
        animalsMenuList.add("Tiger");
        animalsMenuList.add("Kangaroo");
        animalsMenuList.add("Elephant");
```

```
    colorMenuList.addActionListener(this);
    fruitMenuList.addActionListener(this);
    toolsMenuList.addActionListener(this);
    animalsMenuList.addActionListener(this);

    UIMenuButton colorMenuButton =
        new UIMenuButton("Colors", 0, colorMenuList);
    UIMenuButton fruitMenuButton =
        new UIMenuButton("Fruit", 0, fruitMenuList);
    UIMenuButton toolsMenuButton =
        new UIMenuButton("Tools", 0, toolsMenuList);
    UIMenuButton animalsMenuButton =
        new UIMenuButton("Animals", 0, animalsMenuList);

    menus.add(colorMenuButton);
    menus.add(fruitMenuButton);
    menus.add(toolsMenuButton);
    menus.add(animalsMenuButton);
    menuBar.add(menus);
    add(menuBar, "North");

    canvas = new MessageCanvas(" ", 48, 65, 110);
    add(canvas, "Center");

    setValid(true);
    }

    public void actionPerformed(UIActionEvent event)
    {
        String str = event.getActionCommand();
        canvas.showMessage(str);
    }
}
```

## Creating A Complex Status Bar

In its typical state, an AFC status bar contains only a line of text that can be aligned in several ways. In many Windows applications, however, status bars are much more complex, containing separate panes for displaying information and sometimes even containing areas that respond to user mouse clicks.

At first glance, you may think that AFC cannot produce complex status bars. However, with a little thought, you can see how you might add several types of components to a status bar. The **UIStatus** class enables you to construct a status bar that contains either a line of text or a component. Having a single display component like this doesn't make for an exciting toolbar. However, what if that one component acts as a container for other components?

Now you're getting somewhere. You can create a status bar that contains a panel component. The panel component, in turn, can hold the row of components that you want to display in the status bar. The user can't see the panel, so the status bar seems to be hosting the components directly.

Listing 6.7 presents the source code for an applet named ComplexStatusBarApplet. Figure 6.12 shows the applet when it first appears in Applet Viewer. As you can see, the status bar displays a line of text and two buttons. In your own applets, you can use the buttons as panes to separate information in the status bar. In this case, you wouldn't respond to any mouse clicks on the buttons.

However, sometimes a status bar displays a program status item that can be conveniently changed from the status bar. In this case, you can respond to the user's clicks. As an example, ComplexStatusBarApplet changes the applet's **col** and **row** variables when the user clicks on the status-bar buttons. As they do in a good status bar, the buttons update themselves to show the new status of the **col** and **row** variables. Moreover, the status bar's text message also changes to indicate the action the user selects.

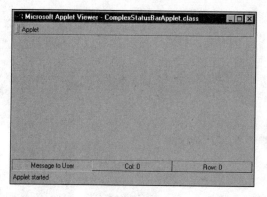

**Figure 6.12**

*ComplexStatusBarApplet running in Applet Viewer.*

## Listing 6.7    The source code for ComplexStatusBarApplet.

```
///////////////////////////////////////////////
// ComplexStatusBarApplet.java
//
// An AFC applet that demonstrates how to create
// and manage more complex status bars.
///////////////////////////////////////////////

import com.ms.ui.*;
import com.ms.fx.*;
import com.ms.ui.event.*;

public class ComplexStatusBarApplet extends AwtUIApplet
{
    public ComplexStatusBarApplet()
    {
        super(new AppletImplementation());
    }
}

class AppletImplementation extends UIApplet
    implements IUIActionListener
{
    int col = 0;
    int row = 0;
    StatusPanel panel;

    public void init()
    {
        UIBorderLayout layout = new UIBorderLayout();
        setLayout(layout);

        panel = new StatusPanel(this);
        UIStatus statusbar = new UIStatus(panel);

        add(statusbar, "South");

        setValid(true);
    }

    public void actionPerformed(UIActionEvent event)
    {
        IUIComponent comp = event.getActionItem();
        if (comp instanceof UIPushButton)
        {
```

```
                String str = event.getActionCommand();
                char c = str.charAt(0);
                if (c == 'C')
                {
                    ++col;
                    String colStr = "Col: " + String.valueOf(col);
                    panel.setColButtonName(colStr);
                    panel.setStatusName("Col Incremented");
                }
                else if (c == 'R')
                {
                    ++row;
                    String rowStr = "Row: " + String.valueOf(row);
                    panel.setRowButtonName(rowStr);
                    panel.setStatusName("Row Incremented");
                }
            }
        }
    }

    class StatusPanel extends UIPanel
    {
        UIText statusText;
        UIPushButton colButton;
        UIPushButton rowButton;

        public StatusPanel(AppletImplementation applet)
        {
            UIGridLayout layout = new UIGridLayout(1, 3);
            setLayout(layout);
            statusText = new UIText("Message to User");
            add(statusText);
            colButton = new UIPushButton("Col: 0", UIPushButton.RAISED);
            colButton.addActionListener(applet);
            add(colButton);
            rowButton = new UIPushButton("Row: 0", UIPushButton.RAISED);
            rowButton.addActionListener(applet);
            add(rowButton);
        }

        public void setColButtonName(String str)
        {
            colButton.setName(str);
        }
```

```
    public void setRowButtonName(String str)
    {
        rowButton.setName(str);
    }

    public void setStatusName(String str)
    {
        statusText.setName(str);
    }
}
```

Listing 6.7's version of ComplexStatusBarApplet uses the delegation event model to respond to the status bar's buttons. If you prefer the propagation event model, you'll find some interesting code in Listing 6.8, which shows the **action()** method you need to implement for the propagation event model.

**Listing 6.8  The source code for ComplexStatusBarApplet's action() method.**

```
public boolean action(Event event, Object arg)
{
    if (arg instanceof UIPushButton)
    {
        String str = ((UIPushButton)arg).getName();
        char c = str.charAt(0);
        if (c == 'C')
        {
            ++col;
            String colStr = "Col: " + String.valueOf(col);
            panel.setColButtonName(colStr);
            panel.setStatusName("Col Incremented");
            return true;
        }
        else if (c == 'R')
        {
            ++row;
            String rowStr = "Row: " + String.valueOf(row);
            panel.setRowButtonName(rowStr);
            panel.setStatusName("Row Incremented");
            return true;
        }
    }

    return false;
}
```

# Windows, Dialog Boxes, And Message Boxes

*It is impossible for me to envisage a picture as being other than a window, and why my first concern is then to know what it looks out on.*
*—André Breton,*
*Surrealism and Painting*

# Notes...

# Chapter 7

Windows are everywhere in most modern computer operating systems. In many ways, a window provides a look into the innards of your computer, displaying the data that hides in the computer's memory. Whether the computer is in there, looking back at you…well…we'll leave that mystery to the philosophers. The fact is, however, that Java, and the third-party libraries built for Java, wouldn't last long in the marketplace if they didn't support, in one way or another, the concept of a window. As you learned in Chapter 2, AFC's **UIFrame** class provides a window element for standalone Java applications, whereas AFC applets (like their Java counterparts) reside in a container's window. That container usually is a Web browser or a test application such as Applet Viewer.

Both Java and AFC, however, enable you to create other types of windows in your programs. These windows include basic windows and dialog boxes. AFC also supports message boxes, which are special-purpose dialog boxes. In this chapter, you'll learn to create AFC windows, as well as see how Java AWT windows and AFC windows compare.

## The **UIWindow** Class

Both Java's AWT and Microsoft's AFC provide window classes for creating a basic window, and a basic window is exactly what you get: no title bar, menu, or even a border. Both the AWT and AFC windows are merely a rectangle drawn in the background color. Think of these windows as blank containers that can hold other components, but that can't be moved or resized by the user.

In AFC, the **UIWindow** class represents a basic window. Although Java has a window class, called appropriately enough **Window**, AFC's **UIWindow** class has no connection to Java. Instead, **UIWindow** extends **UIRoot**, which traces its ancestry back through **UIPanel**, **UIStateContainer**, and **UIContainer** to **UIComponent**. **UIWindow** inherits methods from all these classes, as well as defines a set of it own, shown in Table 7.1.

To create a window component, call the **UIWindow** class's constructor:

```
UIWindow window = new UIWindow(frame);
```

### Table 7.1  Methods of the **UIWindow** class.

| Method | Description |
| --- | --- |
| addWindowListener() | Registers an object with the window as a window listener |
| dispose() | Destroys the window |
| hide() | Hides the window. Obsolete: Should call **setVisible()** instead |
| navigate() | Moves to a new component in the given direction |
| pack() | Packs the window's components |
| processEvent() | Processes the given event |
| processWindowEvent() | Processes action events |
| removeWindowListener() | Removes an object from the window's window listener list |
| reshape() | Sets the window's bounding rectangle. Obsolete: Should call **setBounds()** instead |
| resize() | Resizes the window. Obsolete: Should call **setSize()** instead |
| setBounds() | Sets the window's bounding rectangle |
| setCursor() | Sets the window's cursor |

*(continued)*

Table 7.1  Methods of the **UIWindow** class *(continued)*.

| Method | Description |
|---|---|
| setFont() | Sets the window's font |
| setLocation() | Sets the window's location |
| setSize() | Sets the window's size |
| setVisible() | Shows or hides the window |
| show() | Shows the window. Obsolete: Should call **setVisible()** instead |

As you can see, the constructor takes a single argument, which is a reference to a frame window. Because a **UIWindow** component must have a frame window as a parent component, you cannot create a window in an applet (unless you first create a frame window in the applet). However, AFC overloads the **UIWindow** class's constructor, enabling you to create window components in several ways. The class's four constructors look like the following example:

```
public UIWindow(UIFrame frame);
public UIWindow(Frame frame);
public UIWindow(UIFrame frame, int edge);
public UIWindow(Frame frame, int edge);
```

These constructor signatures show that you can create a **UIWindow** component with an AFC **UIFrame** or AWT **Frame** parent. Moreover, you can specify an edge style in a second argument. The possible values for this second argument are defined in the **IFxGraphicsConstants** interface, as shown below:

```
0 (No edge style)
IFxGraphicsConstants.BDR_FLAT
IFxGraphicsConstants.BDR_INNER
IFxGraphicsConstants.BDR_OUTER
IFxGraphicsConstants.BDR_RAISED
IFxGraphicsConstants.BDR_RAISEDINNER
IFxGraphicsConstants.BDR_RAISEDOUTER
IFxGraphicsConstants.BDR_SUNKEN
IFxGraphicsConstants.BDR_SUNKENINNER
IFxGraphicsConstants.BDR_SUNKENOUTER
IFxGraphicsConstants.EDGE_BUMP
IFxGraphicsConstants.EDGE_ETCHED
IFxGraphicsConstants.EDGE_RAISED
IFxGraphicsConstants.EDGE_SUNKEN
```

Listing 7.1 reveals an AFC standalone application that creates a **UIWindow** component. When you run the application, you see two windows on the screen. The window with the title bar is the application's main frame window. The blank, plain window (in the lower right corner) is the **UIWindow** component. Figure 7.1 shows the basic window with no edge style, whereas Figure 7.2 shows the basic window after you add the **IFxGraphics Constants.BDR_RAISED** edge style to the constructor, as in the following:

```
UIWindow window = new UIWindow(this,
    IFxGraphicsConstants.BDR_RAISED);
```

Notice the calls to the window object's **setSize()** and **setVisible()** methods. If you fail to call these methods, no window appears on the screen.

**Figure 7.1**

*The WindowApp application, showing a* **UIWindow** *component with no edge style.*

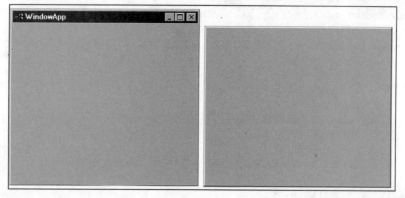

**Figure 7.2**

*The WindowApp application, showing a* **UIWindow** *component with a raised edge style.*

## Listing 7.1  The source code for WindowApp.

```
//////////////////////////////////////////////////
// WindowApp.java
//
// An AFC standalone application that creates and
// displays a basic window.
//////////////////////////////////////////////////

import java.awt.*;
import com.ms.ui.*;
import com.ms.fx.*;

public class WindowApp
{
    public static void main(String args[])
    {
        MyFrame frame = new MyFrame("WindowApp");
        frame.setSize(300, 250);
        frame.setVisible(true);
    }
}

class MyFrame extends UIFrame
{
    public MyFrame(String title)
    {
        super(title);

        UIWindow window = new UIWindow(this,
            IFxGraphicsConstants.BDR_RAISED);
        window.setSize(300, 250);
        window.setLocation(400, 250);
        window.setVisible(true);

        setValid(true);
    }

    public boolean handleEvent(Event event)
    {
        switch (event.id)
        {
            case Event.WINDOW_DESTROY:
                System.exit(0);
                return true;

            default:
                return super.handleEvent(event);
        }
    }
}
```

# The **UIDialog** Class

As mentioned previously, the **UIWindow** class provides the basic window from which AFC creates other types of window components, not the least of which is the frame window. Another of these types of window components is the dialog box, a special window that enables a user and an application to exchange information. Most dialog boxes contain edit boxes into which a user can type information and buttons the user can click to issue commands. Other types of controls, such as radio buttons and option buttons, also often appear in dialog boxes.

In AFC, the **UIDialog** class represents a dialog-box window. Although Java has a dialog-box class (named **Dialog**), AFC's **UIDialog** class has no connection to Java. Instead, **UIDialog** extends **UIWindow**, whose AFC ancestry you traced in the previous section. You can call any of **UIWindow**'s methods through a **UIDialog** object, but the **UIDialog** class also defines its own methods, as shown in Table 7.2.

**Table 7.2  Methods of the UIDialog class.**

| Method | Description |
| --- | --- |
| adjustLayoutSize() | Adjusts a component's layout size |
| dispose() | Destroys the dialog box |
| getPosition() | Gets the dialog box's position |
| getTitle() | Gets the dialog box's title |
| handleEvent() | Handles the dialog box's events |
| isAutoPack() | Returns **true** if the window's components will be packed |
| isModal() | Returns **true** if the dialog box is modal |
| keyDown() | Handles key-press events |
| keyUp() | Handles key-release events |
| position() | Moves the dialog box to the position set by **setPosition()** |
| setAutoPack() | Sets the dialog box's automatic packing |
| setModal() | Sets the dialog box's modal state |

*(continued)*

Table 7.2  Methods of the **UIDialog** class *(continued)*.

| Method | Description |
|---|---|
| setName() | Sets the dialog box's name and title |
| setPosition() | Sets the position of the dialog window, based on the specified point |
| setResizable() | Sets the dialog box's resizable state |
| setTitle() | Sets the dialog box's title |
| show() | Shows the applet |

To create a dialog-box component, call the **UIDialog** class's constructor:

```
UIDialog dialog = new UIDialog(this, "Test Dialog");
```

As you can see, the constructor takes two arguments, a reference to a frame window and a text string to use as the dialog box's title. Because a **UIDialog** component must have a frame window as a parent component, you cannot create a dialog in an applet (unless you create a frame window in the applet first). However, AFC overloads the **UIDialog** class's constructor, enabling you to create dialog-box components in several ways. The class's four constructors look like the following:

```
public UIDialog(UIFrame parent);
public UIDialog(UIFrame parent, boolean modal);
public UIDialog(UIFrame parent, String title);
public UIDialog(UIFrame parent, String title, boolean modal);
```

These constructor signatures show that you can create a **UIDialog** component only with an AFC **UIFrame** parent window and not, as with **UIWindow**, with an AWT frame window. You can specify, however, a title string, as well as the dialog box's modal state. (A *modeless* dialog box enables the user to switch between the parent window and the dialog box. A *modal* dialog box takes over the application, forcing the user to dismiss the dialog box before being allowed to go back to the application's main window.)

Listing 7.2 shows an AFC standalone application that creates a **UIDialog** component. When you run the application, you see the two windows shown in Figure 7.3. The topmost window is the dialog box.

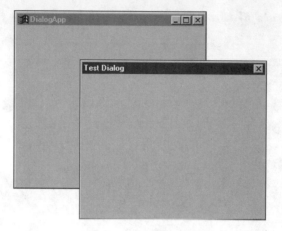

## Figure 7.3

*The DialogApp application shows off its dialog box.*

### Listing 7.2   The source code for DialogApp.

```
/////////////////////////////////////////////////
// DialogApp.java
//
// An AFC standalone application that creates and
// displays a dialog-box window.
/////////////////////////////////////////////////

import java.awt.*;
import com.ms.ui.*;
import com.ms.fx.*;

public class DialogApp
{
    public static void main(String args[])
    {
        MyFrame frame = new MyFrame("DialogApp");
        frame.setSize(300, 250);
        frame.setVisible(true);
    }
}

class MyFrame extends UIFrame
{
    public MyFrame(String title)
    {
        super(title);

        UIDialog dialog = new UIDialog(this, "Test Dialog");
        dialog.setSize(300, 250);
```

```
        dialog.setLocation(50, 50);
        dialog.setVisible(true);

        setValid(true);
    }

    public boolean handleEvent(Event event)
    {
        switch (event.id)
        {
            case Event.WINDOW_DESTROY:
                System.exit(0);
                return true;

            default:
                return super.handleEvent(event);
        }
    }
}
```

# The **UIMessageBox** Class

The last type of window you'll explore in this chapter is the message box. A *message box* is just a special purpose dialog box that gives the user quick messages and obtains quick responses to simple questions, such as "Do you really want to quit?" AFC defines many standard types of message boxes that you can select by specifying certain arguments when constructing the message box. You can choose between four standard images, as well as many predefined button arrangements.

In AFC, the **UIMessageBox** class represents a message-box window. Java's AWT has no message-box class, and **UIMessageBox** has no connection to Java. Instead, **UIMessageBox** extends **UIDialog**, whose AFC ancestry goes from **UIWindow** through **UIRoot**, **UIPanel**, **UIStateContainer**, and **UIContainer** to **UIComponent**. **UIMessageBox** inherits methods from all these classes, as well as defines a set of its own, shown in Table 7.3.

To create a message-box component, call the **UIMessageBox** class's constructor:

```
UIMessageBox messageBox = new UIMessageBox(this, "Message Box",
    "This is a message box.", UIMessageBox.INFORMATION, UIButtonBar.OK );
```

As you can see, this form of the constructor takes five arguments, which are described as follows, in the order they appear in the constructor's arguments:

- The parent frame window

- The message box's title

**Table 7.3  Methods of the UIMessageBox class.**

| Method | Description |
|---|---|
| action() | Responds to button presses in the message box |
| addNotify() | Called when the graphics context first becomes available |
| doModal() | Displays the message box |
| doModalIndex() | Displays a modal message box, getting the index of the pressed button |
| getButtonAlignment() | Gets the message box's button alignment |
| getButtons() | Gets the message box's buttons as a the **UIButtonBar** object |
| getDefaultButton() | Gets the index of the **UIButtonBar** object used for the message box's default button |
| getFrame() | Gets the message box's parent window |
| getImage() | Gets the message box's image |
| getInsets() | Gets the message box's insets |
| getPreferredSize() | Gets the component's preferred dimensions |
| getText() | Gets the message box's text |
| getTimeout() | Gets the message box's display time |
| insets() | Gets the message box's insets |
| keyDown() | Responds to message-box key presses |
| keyUp() | Responds to message-box key releases |
| preferredSize() | Calculates the message box's minimum size |
| setButtonAlignment() | Sets the message box's button alignment |
| setButtons() | Sets the message box's buttons |
| setDefaultButton() | Sets the message box's default button |
| setImage() | Sets the message box's image |

*(continued)*

## Table 7.3  Methods of the **UIMessageBox** class *(continued)*.

| Method | Description |
|---|---|
| setText() | Sets the message box's text |
| setTimeout() | Sets the message box's timer |
| timeTriggered() | Sends the message box a window destroy event |

- The message box's message
- The type of image to display
- The type of button bar to display

Because, like **UIWindow** and **UIDialog**, a **UIMessageBox** component must have a frame window as a parent component, you cannot create a dialog in an applet (unless you create a frame window in the applet first). AFC overloads the **UIMessageBox** class's constructor, enabling you to create message-box components in several ways. The class's four constructors look like the following examples:

```
public UIMessageBox(UIFrame frame);
public UIMessageBox(UIFrame frame, String Title,
    String Text, int image, int buttonSet);
public UIMessageBox(UIFrame frame, String Title,
    String Text, Image image, UIButtonBar buttons);
public UIMessageBox(UIFrame frame, String Title,
    String Text, Image Image, UIButtonBar Buttons,
    int Alignment, int Default );
```

Using these constructors, you can create an empty message box, a message box with your own custom button bar and image, a message box that aligns buttons in various ways, and more. AFC defines four values you can use to select a standard image, as shown in the following lines:

```
UIMessageBox.EXCLAMATION
UIMessageBox.INFORMATION
UIMessageBox.QUESTION
UIMessageBox.STOP
```

AFC also defines a set of standard button bars that you can use for the message box's buttons. These standard button sets are defined in the **UIButtonBar** class, as follows (the name of the style indicates what buttons are included in the button bar):

```
UIButtonBar.OK
UIButtonBar.OKCANCEL
UIButtonBar.OKCANCELAPPLY
UIButtonBar.RETRYCANCEL
UIButtonBar.YESNO
UIButtonBar.YESNOCANCEL
```

Listing 7.3 presents an AFC standalone application that creates a **UIMessageBox** component in response to a button click. When you run the application and click the button, you see the two windows shown in Figure 7.4. Figures 7.5 through 7.7 show some other types of message boxes you can create with the standard images and button bars.

**Figure 7.4**

*The MessageBoxApp application, displaying its message box.*

**Figure 7.5**

*A message box, using the EXCLAMATION image and the OKCANCEL button bar.*

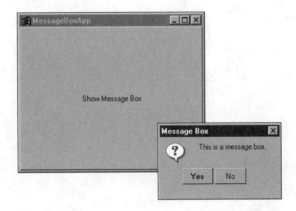

**Figure 7.6**

A message box, using the QUESTION image and the YESNO button bar.

**Figure 7.7**

A message box, using the STOP image and the RETRYCANCEL button bar.

### Listing 7.3   The source code for MessageBoxApp.

```
/////////////////////////////////////////////////
// MessageBoxApp.java
//
// An AFC standalone application that creates and
// displays a message-box window.
/////////////////////////////////////////////////

import java.awt.*;
import com.ms.ui.*;
import com.ms.fx.*;
```

```java
public class MessageBoxApp
{
    public static void main(String args[])
    {
        MyFrame frame = new MyFrame("MessageBoxApp");
        frame.setSize(300, 250);
        frame.setVisible(true);
    }
}

class MyFrame extends UIFrame
{
    public MyFrame(String title)
    {
        super(title);

        UIPushButton button =
            new UIPushButton("Show Message Box",
            UIPushButton.RAISED);
        add(button, "Center");

        setValid(true);
    }

    public boolean handleEvent(Event event)
    {
        switch (event.id)
        {
            case Event.ACTION_EVENT:
                UIMessageBox messageBox =
                    new UIMessageBox(this, "Message Box",
                    "This is a message box.",
                    UIMessageBox.INFORMATION, UIButtonBar.OK );
                messageBox.doModal();
                return true;

            case Event.WINDOW_DESTROY:
                System.exit(0);
                return true;

            default:
                return super.handleEvent(event);
        }
    }
}
```

# Practical Guide To

# Using Window, Dialog-Box, And Message-Box Components

- Creating Custom Components From A Window
- Creating And Managing A Dialog Box
- Creating A Message Box In An Applet
- Creating A Timed Message Box
- Creating And Managing A Custom Message Box

## Creating Custom Components From A Window

AFC uses **UIWindow** mostly as a base class for more specific kinds of windows, including the frame window, dialog box, and message box. You probably won't find many uses for this very basic window component. However, because a window is a component that can stand on its own—that is, it doesn't have to be placed inside another container—you can do some tricky things with the class.

Listing 7.4, for example, presents an AFC application that displays a custom button made from a **UIWindow** component. This button component seems to float freely on the screen, without being anchored inside a container, as shown in Figure 7.8. If you look at the **ButtonWindow** class, though, you'll see that the button is actually contained in a **UIWindow** component. Because a **UIWindow** component uses a **UIBorderLayout** layout manager by default, the button fills the window when it's placed in the center position.

### Listing 7.4 The source code for CustWindowApp.

```
/////////////////////////////////////////////////
// CustWindowApp.java
//
// An AFC standalone application that creates and
// displays a custom window component.
/////////////////////////////////////////////////

import java.awt.*;
import com.ms.ui.*;
import com.ms.fx.*;
import com.ms.ui.event.*;

public class CustWindowApp
{
    public static void main(String args[])
    {
        MyFrame frame = new MyFrame("WindowApp");
        frame.setSize(300, 250);
        frame.setVisible(true);
    }
}

class MyFrame extends UIFrame
{
    public MyFrame(String title)
    {
        super(title);
```

```
        ButtonWindow window = new ButtonWindow(this,
            IFxGraphicsConstants.BDR_RAISED);
        window.setSize(300, 250);
        window.setLocation(200, 150);
        window.setVisible(true);

        setValid(true);
    }

    public boolean handleEvent(Event event)
    {
        switch (event.id)
        {
            case Event.WINDOW_DESTROY:
                System.exit(0);
                return true;

            default:
                return super.handleEvent(event);
        }
    }
}

class ButtonWindow extends UIWindow
    implements IUIActionListener
{
    ButtonWindow(UIFrame frame, int edge)
    {
        super(frame, edge);
        UIPushButton button =
            new UIPushButton("Close Window",
            UIPushButton.RAISED);
        button.addActionListener(this);
        add(button, "Center");
    }

    public void actionPerformed(UIActionEvent event)
    {
        String str = event.getActionCommand();
        if (str == "Close Window")
            dispose();
    }
}
```

The CustWindowApp application contains three classes: the main application class, the frame window class, and the button window class. The main application class

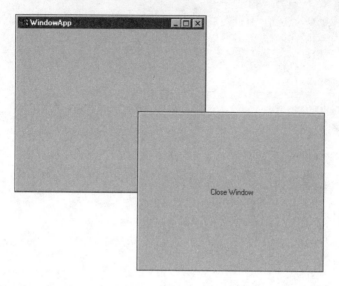

**Figure 7.8**

*CustWindowApp, displaying its custom button component.*

merely supplies a **main()** method, at which program execution begins. The **main()** method creates and displays the frame window, whereas the frame window class's constructor creates and displays the button window.

The **ButtonWindow** class uses the delegation event model to respond to the user's button clicks. If you prefer the propagation event model, you might write the **ButtonWindow** class, as shown in Listing 7.5. Don't forget to import the **java.awt.Event** package when using the propagation event model.

**Listing 7.5   Using the propagation event model in the ButtonWindow class.**

```
class ButtonWindow extends UIWindow
{
    UIPushButton button;

    ButtonWindow(UIFrame frame, int edge)
    {
        super(frame, edge);
        button = new UIPushButton("Close Window",
            UIPushButton.RAISED);
        add(button, "Center");
    }
```

```
    public boolean action(Event event, Object arg)
    {
        if (arg == button)
        {
            dispose();
            return true;
        }
        return false;
    }
}
```

## Creating And Managing A Dialog Box

Previously in this chapter, you saw how to create a dialog-box component from the **UIDialog** class. The dialog box you created, however, contained only a title bar and no other components—not a particularly impressive dialog box. To create a useful dialog box, you must place components into the dialog box's window and then respond to these components as the user manipulates them. Usually, you'll add components such as edit boxes and check boxes for getting information from the user, and then add at least an OK and Cancel button to enable the user to exit the dialog box, after which your program can extract the information the user entered.

As you'll discover, however, getting a dialog box to work under Java takes some work. Just creating an attractive component layout for the dialog box can be a frustrating task. (Why is it that, when it comes to designing component layouts, Java seems to fight you every step of the way?) Then, you have to find a way to exchange information between the application's frame window and the dialog box, another task that requires some finagling.

Listing 7.6 presents an AFC application that displays a dialog box created from the **UIDialog** class. When you run the application, you see the window shown in Figure 7.9. Click the button at the top of the window to display the dialog box. When the dialog box appears (Figure 7.10), type your first name (or any other text string) into the edit box. If you then click the dialog's Cancel button or close the dialog with its close button, your entry is ignored. Clicking the OK button, however, dismisses the dialog box and causes your entry to appear in the application's main window, as shown in Figure 7.11.

**Figure 7.9**

*FullDialogApp when it first runs.*

**Figure 7.10**

*FullDialogApp, showing off its dialog box.*

**Figure 7.11**

*FullDialogApp, displaying the text entered into the dialog box's edit box.*

## Listing 7.6   The source code for FullDialogApp.

```java
/////////////////////////////////////////////////
// FullDialogApp.java
//
// An AFC standalone application that creates and
// displays a full-featured dialog-box window.
/////////////////////////////////////////////////

import java.awt.*;
import com.ms.ui.*;
import com.ms.fx.*;

public class FullDialogApp
{
    public static void main(String args[])
    {
        MyFrame frame = new MyFrame("FullDialogApp");
        frame.setSize(300, 250);
        frame.setValid(true);
        frame.setVisible(true);
    }
}

class MyFrame extends UIFrame
{
    MessageCanvas canvas;

    public MyFrame(String title)
    {
        super(title);
        UIPushButton button =
            new UIPushButton("Show Dialog",
            UIPushButton.RAISED);
        add(button, "North");
        canvas = new MessageCanvas("", 72, 20, 110);
        add(canvas, "Center");
    }

    public boolean handleEvent(Event event)
    {
        switch (event.id)
        {
            case Event.ACTION_EVENT:
                FullDialog dialog =
                    new FullDialog(this, "Test Dialog");
                dialog.setSize(200, 100);
                dialog.setLocation(50, 50);
                dialog.setVisible(true);
                return true;
```

```
                 case Event.WINDOW_DESTROY:
                     System.exit(0);
                     return true;

                 default:
                     return super.handleEvent(event);
        }
    }

    public void dialogClosed(String editStr)
    {
        canvas.showMessage(editStr);
    }
}

class FullDialog extends UIDialog
{
    MyFrame parentWnd;
    UIPushButton okButton;
    UIPushButton cancelButton;
    UIEdit edit;

    FullDialog(UIFrame parent, String title)
    {
        super(parent, title);
        parentWnd = (MyFrame)parent;
        UIGridLayout layout = new UIGridLayout(3, 1);
        setLayout(layout);

        UIPanel topPanel = new UIPanel();
        UIGridLayout topLayout = new UIGridLayout(1, 2);
        topPanel.setLayout(topLayout);
        UIText label =
            new UIText("Enter name here:");
        edit = new UIEdit();
        edit.setBordered(true);
        edit.setSingleLine(true);
        topPanel.add(label);
        topPanel.add(edit);

        UIPanel middlePanel = new UIPanel();

        UIPanel bottomPanel = new UIPanel();
        UIGridLayout bottomLayout = new UIGridLayout(1, 2);
        bottomPanel.setLayout(bottomLayout);
        okButton =
            new UIPushButton("OK", UIPushButton.RAISED);
```

```
        cancelButton =
            new UIPushButton("Cancel", UIPushButton.RAISED);
        bottomPanel.add(okButton);
        bottomPanel.add(cancelButton);

        add(topPanel);
        add(middlePanel);
        add(bottomPanel);

        setValid(true);
    }

    public boolean handleEvent(Event event)
    {
        switch (event.id)
        {
            case Event.ACTION_EVENT:
                handleActionEvent(event);
                return true;

            case Event.WINDOW_DESTROY:
                dispose();
                return true;

            default:
                return super.handleEvent(event);
        }
    }

    public void handleActionEvent(Event event)
    {
        if (event.arg instanceof UIPushButton)
        {
            String str =
                ((UIPushButton)event.arg).getName();
            if (str == "Cancel")
                dispose();
            else if (str == "OK")
            {
                str = edit.getValueText();
                parentWnd.dialogClosed(str);
                dispose();
            }
        }
    }
}
```

```
class MessageCanvas extends UICanvas
{
    String displayString;
    int pointSize;
    int col, row;

    public MessageCanvas(String msg, int points, int x, int y)
    {
        displayString = msg;
        pointSize = points;
        col = x;
        row = y;
        setBackground(FxColor.blue);
    }

    public void paint(FxGraphics graphics)
    {
        FxFont font =
            new FxFont("TimesRoman", FxFont.PLAIN, pointSize);
        graphics.setFont(font);
        graphics.setColor(FxColor.white);
        graphics.drawString(displayString, col, row);
    }

    public void showMessage(String str)
    {
        displayString = str;
        repaint();
    }
}
```

As you can see, FullDialogApp is a fairly lengthy program for an application that does so little. The program must handle every detail of managing a dialog box; it gets no help from Java or AFC. The program contains four classes:

- **FullDialogApp**—The main application class, which creates only the frame window

- **MyFrame**—The application's frame window class, which creates its own display, as well as creates and shows the dialog box

- **FullDialog**—The dialog-box class

- **MessageCanvas**—A custom canvas component that displays a text string

When the user clicks the Show Dialog button, the frame window handles the generated action event in the **handleEvent()** function. There, the program creates and displays the dialog box. When the user dismisses the dialog box with the OK button, the dialog-box object calls the frame window's **dialogClosed()** method, which receives the text string the user entered into the dialog's edit box. The **dialogClosed()** method just passes the string on to the **MessageCanvas** object to be displayed.

If you examine the **FullDialog** class, you'll see that the dialog box builds its component layout using several panels. When the user clicks either the OK or the Cancel button, the dialog box's **handleEvent()** method receives the message, but routes the message to the class's **handleActionEvent()** method. In **handleAction-Event()**, the program checks to see which button the user clicked. If the user clicked the Cancel button, the dialog dismisses itself by calling its **dispose()** method. If the user clicked OK, the program gets the contents of the edit box and passes it to the frame window by calling the frame window's **dialogClosed()** method. It is the **dialogClosed()** method that enables the frame window and the dialog box to communicate.

## Creating A Message Box In An Applet

Earlier in this chapter, you learned that a message box must have a frame window as a parent, which means that applets can't display message boxes. Or can they? Although message boxes weren't designed to display from applets, a little trick overcomes this design bugaboo. There's nothing stopping you from creating a frame window in your applet and using it as a parent for a message box.

But, you say, you don't want a big ol' frame window popping up at the same time your message box appears? No problem. When you create the frame window, don't call its **setVisible()** method. Not calling **setVisible()** leaves the frame window invisible, but it will still be a suitable parent for a message box. After you create the invisible frame window, you can go ahead and create the message box, giving the invisible frame window as the message box's parent window.

Listing 7.7 presents an AFC program that displays a message box from an applet. When you run the applet in Applet Viewer, you see the window shown in Figure 7.12. Click the button to display the message box, shown in Figure 7.13.

**Figure 7.12**

*MessageBoxApplet when it first runs.*

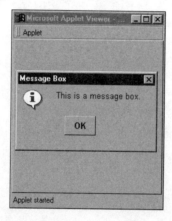

**Figure 7.13**

*MessageBoxApplet, showing off its message box.*

**Listing 7.7   The source code for MessageBoxApplet.**

```
/////////////////////////////////////////////////
// MessageBoxApplet.java
//
// An AFC applet that demonstrates how to create
// and display a message box in an applet.
/////////////////////////////////////////////////

import com.ms.ui.*;
import com.ms.ui.event.*;
```

```
public class MessageBoxApplet extends AwtUIApplet
{
    public MessageBoxApplet()
    {
        super(new AppletImplementation());
    }
}

class AppletImplementation extends UIApplet
    implements IUIActionListener
{
    public void init()
    {
        UIPushButton button = new UIPushButton("Show Message Box",
            UIPushButton.RAISED);
        button.addActionListener(this);
        add(button, "Center");

        setValid(true);
    }

    public void actionPerformed(UIActionEvent event)
    {
        UIFrame frame = new UIFrame();
        UIMessageBox messageBox =
            new UIMessageBox(frame, "Message Box",
            "This is a message box.",
            UIMessageBox.INFORMATION, UIButtonBar.OK );
        messageBox.doModal();
    }
}
```

## Creating A Timed Message Box

AFC gives its message boxes a feature that even Windows message boxes don't have—a timeout attribute. When you create an AFC message box, you can set a timer that automatically closes the message box when the time runs out. Performing this message box magic is as easy as calling the message box's **setTimeout()** method.

Listing 7.8 presents an AFC standalone application named TimedMsgBoxApp that displays a timed message box. Run the application and then click the Show Message Box button to display the message box (Figure 7.14). You can dismiss the message box by clicking its OK button or by waiting five seconds, after which the message box closes.

Notice that TimedMsgBoxApp implements both the **IUIActionListener** and the **IUIWindowListener** interfaces, which means the application uses the delegation event

**Figure 7.14**

*TimedMsgBoxApp and its message box.*

model for responding to the button, as well as for responding to window messages. This is the first time in this book that a program has implemented the **IUIWindowListener** interface. As you can see in Listing 7.8, one problem with handling window messages in this way is that you must implement all seven of the **IUIWindowListener** interface's methods, even if you only need one. This is a lot of baggage just to close a window. Listing 7.9 shows the **handleEvent()** method that you might write if you wanted to use the propagation event model instead. If you liked, you could handle the button clicks in an **action()** method instead of in **handleEvent()**.

**Listing 7.8   The source code for TimedMsgBoxApp.**

```
/////////////////////////////////////////////////
// TimedMsgBoxApp.java
//
// An AFC standalone application that creates and
// displays a timed message-box window.
/////////////////////////////////////////////////

import java.awt.*;
import com.ms.ui.*;
import com.ms.ui.event.*;
import com.ms.fx.*;

public class TimedMsgBoxApp
{
    public static void main(String args[])
    {
        MsgBoxFrame frame = new MsgBoxFrame("MessageBoxApp");
        frame.setSize(300, 250);
```

```
            frame.setVisible(true);
        }
    }

    class MsgBoxFrame extends UIFrame
        implements IUIActionListener, IUIWindowListener
    {
        public MsgBoxFrame(String title)
        {
            super(title);

            UIPushButton button =
                new UIPushButton("Show Message Box",
                UIPushButton.RAISED);
            button.addActionListener(this);
            add(button, "Center");

            addWindowListener(this);

            setValid(true);
        }

        public void actionPerformed(UIActionEvent event)
        {
            UIMessageBox messageBox =
                new UIMessageBox(this, "Message Box",
                "This is a timed message box.",
                UIMessageBox.INFORMATION, UIButtonBar.OK );
            messageBox.setTimeout(5000);
            messageBox.doModal();
        }

        public void windowActivated(UIWindowEvent e)
        {
        }

        public void windowClosed(UIWindowEvent e)
        {
        }

        public void windowClosing(UIWindowEvent e)
        {
            System.exit(0);
        }

        public void windowDeactivated(UIWindowEvent e)
        {
        }
```

```
    public void windowDeiconified(UIWindowEvent e)
    {
    }

    public void windowIconified(UIWindowEvent e)
    {
    }

    public void windowOpened(UIWindowEvent e)
    {
    }
}
```

**Listing 7.9  The source code for the handleEvent() method.**
```
public boolean handleEvent(Event event)
{
    switch (event.id)
    {
        case Event.ACTION_EVENT:
            UIMessageBox messageBox =
                new UIMessageBox(this, "Message Box",
                "This is a timed message box.",
                UIMessageBox.INFORMATION, UIButtonBar.OK );
            messageBox.setTimeout(5000);
            messageBox.doModal();
            return true;

        case Event.WINDOW_DESTROY:
            System.exit(0);
            return true;

        default:
            return super.handleEvent(event);
    }
}
```

## Creating And Managing A Custom Message Box

Although AFC defines a complete set of images and button bars for creating message boxes, you occasionally may want to supply your own image and button bar. Luckily, the **UIMessageBox** class includes a perfect constructor for these occasions, taking a reference to an image and a reference to a button bar as two of its arguments. To create a custom message box, load your image, create your button bar (see Chapter 6 for more information on creating button bars), and hand them to the **UIMessageBox** constructor.

Listing 7.10 presents an AFC applet named CustMsgBoxApplet that creates and displays a custom message box. Run the application and then click the Show Message Box button to display the message box (Figure 7.15). Notice how, in the **actionPerformed()** method, the program calls **doModalIndex()** to display the message box. This method not only displays the message box, it also returns the index of the button the user used to dismiss the message box. The button indexes match the order in which the buttons are arranged in the button bar component. That is, the first button has an index of zero, the second an index of 1, and so on. In the sample program, when the user clicks a button, the main window displays the user's choice, as shown in Figure 7.16.

**Figure 7.15**

*CustMsgBoxApplet and its message box.*

**Figure 7.16**

*CustMsgBoxApplet, displaying the user's button selection.*

**Listing 7.10  The source code for CustMsgBoxApplet.**

```java
///////////////////////////////////////////////
// CustMsgBoxApplet.java
//
// An AFC applet that demonstrates how to create
// and display a custom message box.
///////////////////////////////////////////////

import java.awt.*;
import java.net.*;
import com.ms.ui.*;
import com.ms.fx.*;
import com.ms.ui.event.*;

public class CustMsgBoxApplet extends AwtUIApplet
{
    public CustMsgBoxApplet()
    {
        super(new AppletImplementation());
    }
}

class AppletImplementation extends UIApplet
    implements IUIActionListener
{
    MessageCanvas canvas;

    public void init()
    {
        UIPushButton button = new UIPushButton("Show Message Box",
            UIPushButton.RAISED);
        button.addActionListener(this);
        add(button, "North");

        canvas = new MessageCanvas("", 56, 20, 110);
        add(canvas, "Center");

        setValid(true);
    }

    public void actionPerformed(UIActionEvent event)
    {
        String str = event.getActionCommand();
        if (str == "Show Message Box")
        {
            UIFrame frame = new UIFrame();
            URL codeBase = getCodeBase();
```

```
            Image image = getImage(codeBase, "image1.gif");
            UIButtonBar buttonBar =
                new UIButtonBar("Button 1,Button 2",
            UIButtonBar.RAISED);

            UIMessageBox messageBox =
                new UIMessageBox(frame, "Message Box",
                "This is a message box.", image, buttonBar);
            int index = messageBox.doModalIndex();
            if (index == 0)
                canvas.showMessage("Button 1");
            else if (index == 1)
                canvas.showMessage("Button 2");
        }
    }
}


class MessageCanvas extends UICanvas
{
    String displayString;
    int pointSize;
    int col, row;

    public MessageCanvas(String msg, int points, int x, int y)
    {
        displayString = msg;
        pointSize = points;
        col = x;
        row = y;
        setBackground(FxColor.blue);
    }

    public void paint(FxGraphics graphics)
    {
        FxFont font =
            new FxFont("TimesRoman", FxFont.PLAIN, pointSize);
        graphics.setFont(font);
        graphics.setColor(FxColor.white);
        graphics.drawString(displayString, col, row);
    }

    public void showMessage(String str)
    {
        displayString = str;
        repaint();
    }

}
```

# Property Sheets And Wizards

*An idea is always a generalization, and generalization is a property of thinking. To generalize means to think.*
—*Georg Hegel,*
*The Philosophy of Right*

# Notes...

*Chapter*

# 8

Every object in the known universe has properties—even, as Georg Hegel pointed out, intangible objects such as ideas. In object-oriented programming, object properties have an important role in determining the way in which objects in a program look and act. Even the Windows system has innumerable properties that determine how the operating system interacts with the many other objects under its control. For example, you can set Windows' display properties to control how the desktop looks on your monitor, including the resolution and the color depth.

Because properties are so important to today's applications, Windows provides a special dialog box named a *property sheet* to make it easy for users to find and change properties. These property sheets are everywhere in Windows 95 and are found in most applications that run under Windows 95. Unfortunately, because Java is a system-neutral programming language, it doesn't support property sheets. Microsoft fixed this lack by endowing AFC with classes that enable you to add property sheets to your Java applets and applications. These classes are **UIPropertyDialog** and **UIPropertyPage**.

Similar to property sheets, but performing a different function, are wizards, which guide a user step by step through a complex process. Windows 98, for example, uses a wizard to help users set up Internet connections. Java, as you may have guessed, also doesn't support wizards. So, Microsoft made wizards a part of AFC, by including the **UIWizard** and **UIWizardStep** classes, with which you can add wizards to your AFC applets and applications.

# The **UIPropertyDialog** Class

A property sheet is really little more than a fancy dialog box. Before Microsoft came up with the name "property sheet", these windows were named *tabbed dialog boxes* because of the tabbed pages contained in the dialog box. Figure 8.1, for example, shows Windows 95's Display Properties property sheet. In the figure, you can see the tabbed pages that organize the properties contained in the dialog box. The Background properties, for example, enable the user to set background patterns or wallpaper for the Windows desktop. By clicking the Settings tab in the property sheet, the user can view and change the system's video settings. Figure 8.2 shows the Settings page, displaying the screen resolution and color depth.

You can create property sheets for your AFC applets and applications by creating objects of the **UIPropertyDialog** and **UIPropertyPage** classes. **UIPropertyDialog** is a special type of dialog box derived from **UIDialog**, which itself has a long AFC ancestry, including **UIWindow**, **UIRoot**, **UIPanel**, **UIStateContainer**, **UIContainer,** and **UIComponent**. Besides the methods **UIPropertyDialog** inherits from its superclasses, **UIPropertyDialog** also defines many of its own methods, as shown in Table 8.1.

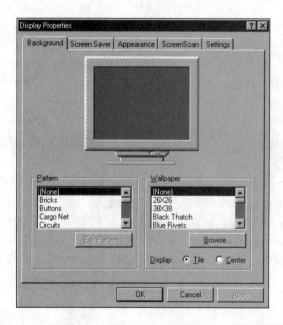

## Figure 8.1

*The Display Properties property sheet, displaying background settings.*

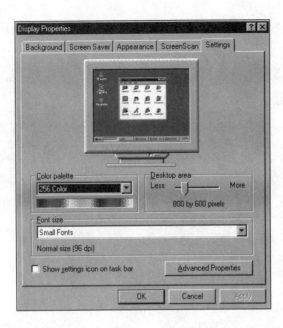

**Figure 8.2**

*The Settings Properties property sheet, displaying video settings.*

**Table 8.1  Methods of the UIPropertyDialog class.**

| Method | Description |
| --- | --- |
| action() | Handles button clicks |
| addNotify() | Called when the graphics context is first available |
| addPage() | Adds a property page to the property sheet |
| display() | Displays the property sheet |
| doApplyAction() | Handles clicks on the property sheet's Apply button |
| doCancelAction() | Handles clicks on the property sheet's Cancel button |
| doOKAction() | Handles clicks on the property sheet's OK button |
| getButtonAlignment() | Gets the property sheet's button alignment |
| getInsets() | Gets the property sheet's insets |

*(continued)*

**Table 8.1  Methods of the UIPropertyDialog class (continued).**

| Method | Description |
|---|---|
| getPageDimension() | Gets the property sheet's page dimensions |
| getPageSize() | Gets the property sheet's page size |
| insets() | Gets the property sheet's insets |
| isApplyable() | Returns **true** if any options in the property sheet can be applied |
| setApplyable() | Sets the state of the property sheet's Apply button |
| setButtonAlignment() | Sets the property sheet's button alignment |
| setPageSize() | Sets the property sheet's page size |

Creating and manipulating a complete property sheet is a fairly complex process. However, to create an empty **UIPropertyDialog** object, you just call the class's constructor, like this example:

```
UIPropertyDialog propDialog = new UIPropertyDialog(frame,
    "Property Sheet", true, UIPropertyDialog.SMALL);
```

As you can see, the constructor takes the following four arguments:

- The parent frame window

- The property sheet's title

- A Boolean value indicating whether the property sheet will be a modal dialog box

- The size of the property sheet's pages

The fourth argument controls the size of the property sheet. You can specify one of three values: **UIPropertyDialog.SMALL**, **UIPropertyDialog.MEDIUM**, and **UIPropertyDialog.LARGE**. The size you use depends on how much space you need for each page's contents. To give you an idea of how these size values affect the property sheet, Figure 8.3 shows a property sheet with a single small page, and Figure 8.4 shows a property sheet with a single large page.

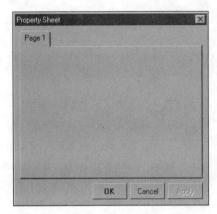

**Figure 8.3**

*A property sheet with a small page.*

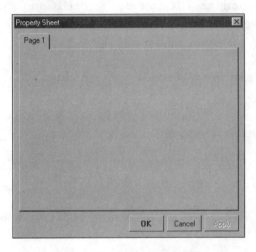

**Figure 8.4**

*A property sheet with a large page.*

The **UIPropertyDialog** class overloads its constructor with a version that takes only three arguments, like this:

```
UIPropertyDialog propDialog = new UIPropertyDialog(frame,
    "Property Sheet", true);
```

Here, the constructor call leaves off the page size argument, which is automatically set to **MEDIUM**.

If you try to create and display a property sheet without adding pages to it, the property sheet doesn't appear on the screen. Before you can create and display a functional property sheet, you must know about the **UIPropertyPage** class, which represents each property-sheet page.

## The **UIPropertyPage** Class

Each tabbed page in an AFC property sheet is represented by an object of the **UIPropertyPage** class. To create a working property sheet, you must create the **UIPropertyDialog** object and then add one or more **UIPropertyPage** objects to it. Because it makes sense to create a property sheet only with two or more pages, you should never create a one-page property sheet, even though it's possible.

The **UIPropertyPage** class extends AFC's **UIPanel** class, which means **UIPropertyPage** also counts **UIStateContainer**, **UIContainer**, and **UIComponent** among its super-classes. Besides the methods it inherits from these superclasses, **UIPropertyPage** also defines a set of its own methods, shown in Table 8.2.

**Table 8.2   Methods of the UIPropertyPage class.**

| Method | Description |
|---|---|
| **addAt()** | Adds a component to the property page |
| **addContent()** | Called to add components when the property page is first displayed |
| **doApplyAction()** | Handles clicks on the property page's Apply button |
| **doConstruct()** | Called to construct components when the property page is first displayed |
| **doNotVisible()** | Called to update the property page when it's hidden |
| **doVisible()** | Called to update the property page when it's shown |
| **getInsets()** | Gets the property page's insets |
| **getSheet()** | Gets the property page's property sheet |
| **isApplyable()** | Returns **true** if any of the property page's options are applyable |
| **isConstructed()** | Returns **true** if the components on the property page have been constructed |

*(continued)*

Table 8.2   Methods of the **UIPropertyPage** class *(continued).*

| Method | Description |
|---|---|
| isContentAdded() | Returns **true** if a component was added to a visible property page |
| setApplyable() | Sets the state of the property page's Apply button |
| setConstructed() | Sets the state of the property page's components |
| setContentAdded() | Sets the property page's content state |
| setSheet() | Sets the property page's container to the given property sheet |
| setVisible() | Displays or hides the property page |

Because **UIPropertyPage** is an *abstract class* (that is, it's not fully implemented), to create a property-page object, you first must create a class for your property page. To do so, you extend the **UIPropertyPage** class and provide the **addContent()** method, as shown in Listing 8.1, which is the source code for an applet that creates and displays a simple, one-page property sheet. When you run BasicPropSheetApplet, the property sheet shown in Figure 8.5 appears.

Notice in Listing 8.1 the steps required to display a property sheet in an applet. First, you create a frame-window object to act as the property sheet's parent window:

```
UIFrame frame = new UIFrame();
```

**Figure 8.5**

BasicPropSheetApplet's property sheet.

Then, you create the **UIPropertyDialog** object:

```
UIPropertyDialog propSheet =
    new UIPropertyDialog(frame,
    "Property Sheet", true, UIPropertyDialog.SMALL);
```

With the property-sheet object created, you create one or more property pages from classes extended from **UIPropertyPage**:

```
MyPropPage propPage = new MyPropPage(propSheet);
```

You add the property pages to the property sheet by calling the property sheet's **addPage()** method:

```
propSheet.addPage("Property Page", propPage);
```

Finally, you display the property sheet by calling its **display()** method:

```
propSheet.display();
```

Note that BasicPropSheetApplet demonstrates only the basic techniques required to create and display a property sheet. You still need to know how to add components to the property sheet, as well as how to respond to the buttons that AFC includes in the property sheet. You'll discover these other programming techniques in this chapter's Practical Guide.

### Listing 8.1   Source code for BasicPropSheetApplet.

```
/////////////////////////////////////////////////
// BasicPropSheetApplet.java
//
// An AFC applet that demonstrates how to create
// and display a property sheet with a single
// empty property page.
/////////////////////////////////////////////////

import com.ms.ui.*;

public class BasicPropSheetApplet extends AwtUIApplet
{
    public BasicPropSheetApplet()
    {
        super(new AppletImplementation());
    }
}
```

```
class AppletImplementation extends UIApplet
{
    public void init()
    {
        UIFrame frame = new UIFrame();
        UIPropertyDialog propSheet =
            new UIPropertyDialog(frame,
            "Property Sheet", true, UIPropertyDialog.SMALL);
        MyPropPage propPage = new MyPropPage(propSheet);
        propSheet.addPage("Property Page", propPage);
        propSheet.display();

        setValid(true);
    }
}

class MyPropPage extends UIPropertyPage
{
    public MyPropPage(UIPropertyDialog ps)
    {
        super(ps);
    }

    public boolean addContent()
    {
        // Add the page's components here.

        return true;
    }
}
```

# The **UIWizard** Class

A *wizard* is a special dialog box (or, actually, a series of dialog boxes) that guides the user through the completion of a complex task. The Windows 95 operating system, as well as many Microsoft applications, uses wizards to make software more user-friendly. You can use Microsoft Word's Résumé Wizard (see Figure 8.6), for example, to create a basic résumé step by step. Many other software publishers add wizards to their products. Wizards are such a great way to provide help for a software package's user that Microsoft included classes for creating wizards in AFC. These classes are **UIWizard** and **UIWizardStep**.

Creating a wizard is much like creating a property sheet; you create a container object that holds a series of pages. The big difference between a property sheet and

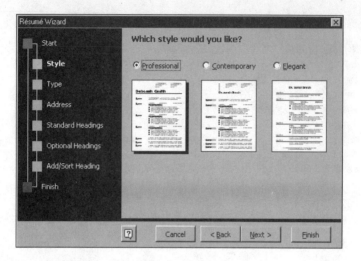

**Figure 8.6**

*Microsoft Word's Résumé Wizard.*

a wizard is that, in a wizard, the pages have no tabs and can be viewed only in sequence, which forces users to complete a series of steps. Users can move forward or backward through the steps, but they cannot jump directly to any particular page as they can in a property sheet.

In AFC, the **UIWizard** class represents a wizard dialog box. This dialog box is the container that holds the various pages that represent the steps in the task to be completed. You probably won't be surprised to learn that **UIWizard** extends **UIDialog**, which means it traces its AFC ancestry up through **UIWindow**, **UIRoot**, **UIPanel**, **UIStateContainer**, **UIContainer**, and **UIComponent**. **UIWizard** inherits methods from this respectable list of superclasses, but it also defines a set of its own, shown in Table 8.3.

Creating and manipulating a complete wizard is a fairly complex process. However, creating an empty **UIWizard** object is just a matter of calling the class's constructor, like the following example:

```
UIWizard wizard = new UIWizard(frame, "Basic Wizard");
```

As you can see, the constructor takes two arguments, which are a reference to the parent frame window and the wizard's title.

**Table 8.3  Methods of the UIWizard class.**

| Method | Description |
|---|---|
| action() | Handles button presses in the wizard |
| addNotify() | Called to create the wizard's buttons when the graphics context becomes available |
| addStep() | Adds a page to the wizard |
| doBackAction() | Handles clicks on the wizard's Back button |
| doCancelAction() | Handles clicks on the wizard's Cancel button |
| doFinishAction() | Handles clicks on the wizard's Finish button |
| doModal() | Displays the wizard and manages the wizard's interaction with the user |
| doNextAction() | Handles clicks on the wizard's Next button |
| getBeingShown() | Gets the wizard step page about to be displayed |
| getButtonAlignment() | Gets the wizard's button alignment |
| getFirstStep() | Gets the wizard's first step page |
| getInsets() | Gets the wizard's insets |
| getNextStep() | Gets the wizard's next step page |
| getPreviousStep() | Gets the wizard's previous step page |
| getVisibleStep() | Gets the currently displayed step page |
| isFinishStep() | Returns **true** if the currently displayed step page is a finish page |
| isLastStep() | Returns **true** if the currently displayed step page is the last wizard page |
| setButtonAlignment() | Sets the wizard's button alignment |
| setForcedBounds() | Sets the dimensions of a wizard component |
| setVisibleStep() | Makes the given step page visible in the wizard |

# The **UIWizardStep** Class

Each step in the wizard is represented by an object of the **UIWizardStep** class in the same way each page of a property sheet is represented by a **UIPropertyPage** object. That is, you need to create a **UIWizardStep** object for each step required to guide the user through the completion of the task represented by the wizard.

Unlike **UIPropertyPage**, which extends the **UIPanel** class, the **UIWizardStep** class has no AFC superclasses, being a class unto itself. Despite this lack of AFC or Java ancestry, **UIWizard** defines a surprisingly small number of methods, which are listed in Table 8.4 along with their descriptions.

Creating a **UIWizardStep** object is as simple as calling the class's constructor, as shown in the following line:

```
UIWizardStep wizardStep = new UIWizardStep(graphic, comp);
```

The constructor's two arguments are:

- A **UIGraphic** object that contains the step's image

- The component that contains the step's content

**Table 8.4  Methods of the UIWizardStep class.**

| Method | Description |
|---|---|
| getContent() | Gets the wizard step's content component |
| getImage() | Gets the wizard step's image |
| getNextStep() | Gets the next step page |
| getWizard() | Gets the wizard step's **UIWizard** object |
| isFinishStep() | Returns **true** if the step page should enable the Finish button |
| isLastStep() | Returns **true** if the step is the last step in the series |
| nextStep() | Gets the next step page |
| previousStep() | Gets the previous step page |
| setNextStep() | Sets the next step page |
| setWizard() | Sets the page's wizard |

Usually, the component is a panel containing other components that enable the user to enter the information required by the step.

Listing 8.2 is the source code for an applet that creates and displays a simple, one-step wizard. When you run BasicWizardApplet, the wizard shown in Figure 8.7 appears.

In Listing 8.2, notice the steps required to display a wizard in an applet. First, you create a frame-window object to act as the property sheet's parent window:

```
UIFrame frame = new UIFrame();
```

Then, you create the **UIWizard** object:

```
UIWizard wizard = new UIWizard(frame, "Basic Wizard");
```

With the wizard object created, you create one or more step pages, as follows:

```
UIPanel panel = new UIPanel();
UIWizardStep wizardStep = new UIWizardStep(null, panel);
```

You add the steps to the wizard by calling the wizard's **addStep()** method:

```
wizard.addStep(wizardStep);
```

Finally, you display the wizard by calling its **doModal()** method:

```
Object button = wizard.doModal();
```

**Figure 8.7**

*BasicWizardApplet's wizard.*

The **doModal()** function returns a reference to the button the user pressed to exit the wizard.

Note that BasicWizardApplet demonstrates only the basic techniques required to create and display a wizard. You still need to know how to add components to the wizard, as well as how to respond to the buttons that AFC includes in the wizard. You'll discover these other programming techniques in this chapter's Practical Guide.

**Listing 8.2  Source code for BasicWizardApplet.**

```
///////////////////////////////////////////////////
// BasicWizardApplet.java
//
// An AFC applet that demonstrates how to create
// and display a basic, one-step wizard in an
// applet.
///////////////////////////////////////////////////

import com.ms.ui.*;
import java.awt.*;

public class BasicWizardApplet extends AwtUIApplet
{
    public BasicWizardApplet()
    {
        super(new AppletImplementation());
    }
}

class AppletImplementation extends UIApplet
{
    public void init()
    {
        UIFrame frame = new UIFrame();
        UIWizard wizard =
            new UIWizard(frame, "Basic Wizard");

        UIPanel panel = new UIPanel();
        UIWizardStep wizardStep =
            new UIWizardStep(null, panel);
        wizard.addStep(wizardStep);
        Object button = wizard.doModal();

        setValid(true);
    }
}
```

# Practical Guide To

- Creating And Managing A Property Sheet
- Creating And Managing A Wizard

# Using Property Sheets And Wizards

## Creating And Managing A Property Sheet

Previously in this chapter, you learned to create and display a basic property sheet. However, because this program displays an empty property sheet—and doesn't provide a means for interacting with the user—it's about as useful as sunglasses in a cave. To create a useful property sheet, you first must determine the properties you want the user to manipulate, as well as decide how you want to organize these properties onto different pages. In any case, every property sheet should have at least two pages. If you need only a single page, you might as well create a conventional dialog box.

After determining how you want to organize your property pages, you must decide what flavors of components are best suited for representing each property in its page. A set of mutually exclusive properties (for example, fonts for displaying a line of text) can be represented by a group of radio buttons, a list, a menu button, or some type of component that forces the user to select a single value for the property.

When you've selected the components you want to use to represent the properties, you're ready to start programming. You already know how to create the property sheet and add a page to it. What you haven't learned yet is how to add components to each page and how to interact with the user, setting the properties the user has selected.

When you write your property-page class (remember: **UIPropertyPage** is an abstract class) extending **UIPropertyPage**, you must implement the **addContent()** method. In **addContent()**, you supply the components that enable the user to set properties. You can add to the page any of the AFC components you learned about in this book, including buttons, edit boxes, lists, and more. To add a component, you call the **addAt()** method, like this:

```
addAt(comp, xPos, yPos, size);
```

Here, the **addAt()** method takes four arguments, which are described as follows:

- **comp**—The component to add to the page
- **xPos**—The component's X position
- **yPos**—The component's Y position
- **size**—The component's size as a **Dimension** object

There is also a second version of **addAt()** that takes only three arguments, leaving off the component's size.

Listing 8.3 presents a simple property-page class whose **addContent()** method adds a single edit component to a property page. Figure 8.8 shows what the resultant property page looks like.

### Listing 8.3  Adding content to a property page.

```
class MyPropPage extends UIPropertyPage
{
    public MyPropPage(UIPropertyDialog ps)
    {
        super(ps);
    }

    public boolean addContent()
    {
        UIEdit edit = new UIEdit();
        edit.setBordered(true);
        edit.setSingleLine(true);
        addAt(edit, 20, 20, new Dimension(180, 20));

        return true;
    }
}
```

You also need to know another thing to complete a property sheet—how to respond to the buttons supplied by AFC. Every property sheet has three buttons: OK, Cancel,

**Figure 8.8**

*The property page created by Listing 8.3.*

and Apply. The OK and Cancel buttons should work as they do in any dialog box (OK indicating that the contents of the dialog box should be extracted and processed, and Cancel meaning any changes should be ignored). The Apply button should work like the OK button, but with a little twist. When the user clicks the Apply button, the changes made to the contents of the property sheet should be processed— but without dismissing the property sheet from the screen. This enables the user to try out different properties and see the result, without being forced to continually redisplay the property sheet.

To enable you to implement button responses in your program, the **UIPropertyPage** class includes the **doApplyAction()**, **doOKAction()**, and **doCancelAction()** methods, which AFC calls in response to Apply, OK, and Cancel button clicks, respectively. Simply override these methods in your custom property-page class and handle the buttons as needed in your program. You'll probably need to manage only the Apply and OK buttons, letting AFC deal with Cancel by closing the property sheet. Listing 8.4 presents a complete skeleton class for a property page.

### Listing 8.4   A complete skeleton property-page class.

```
class MyPropPage extends UIPropertyPage
{
    public MyPropPage(UIPropertyDialog ps)
    {
        super(ps);
    }

    public boolean addContent()
    {
        // Add components here.

        return true;
    }

    public boolean doApplyAction()
    {
        // Handle the Apply button here.

        return true;
    }

    public boolean doOKAction()
    {
        // Handle the OK button here.
```

```
        return true;
    }

    public boolean doCancelAction()
    {
        // Handle the Cancel button here.

        return true;
    }
}
```

Now you can apply what you learned about property sheets by experimenting with a complete example program. Listing 8.5 presents the source code for an AFC applet named PropertySheetApplet. When you run the applet in Applet Viewer, you see the window shown in Figure 8.9. The button at the top of the applet enables you to display the property sheet. The text string displayed below the button represents the currently set properties, which include the text size and color.

Click the Properties button to display the property sheet. As you see in Figure 8.10, the property sheet has two pages, one for setting the text size and one for setting the text color. Clicking on a tab selects the associated page. Change the text size to 16 points and click the Apply button. The text in the applet's window immediately changes size, but the property sheet remains on the screen (Figure 8.11). Now, go to the Text Colors page, select green, and click OK. The property sheet vanishes from the screen, and the text in the applet's display area changes to green.

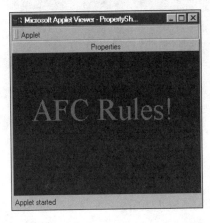

**Figure 8.9**

*PropertySheetApplet running in Applet Viewer.*

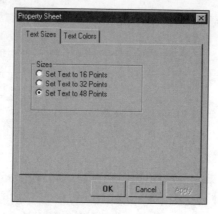

**Figure 8.10**

*PropertySheetApplet's property sheet.*

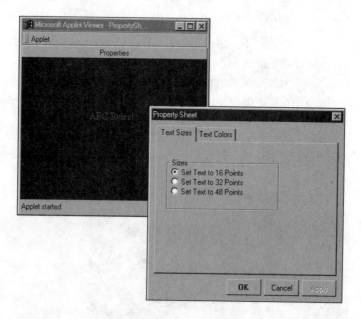

**Figure 8.11**

*PropertySheetApplet with 16-point text.*

Notice a couple of things about Listing 8.5: The property-page classes implement the **IUIItemListener** interface, so that, whenever the user clicks a button in a property page, AFC calls the class's **itemStateChanged()** method. In **itemStateChanged()**, the program calls the page's **setApplyable()** method, which enables the page's Apply button. Normally, the Apply button is disabled until the user changes a property in some valid way. Notice also how each property page maintains a link to the applet's **TextCanvas** object, so that the property sheet can directly change the text string's size and color properties.

### Listing 8.5 Source code for PropertySheetApplet.

```
/////////////////////////////////////////////////
// PropertySheetApplet.java
//
// An AFC applet that demonstrates how to create
// and display a property sheet in an applet.
/////////////////////////////////////////////////

import com.ms.ui.*;
import com.ms.fx.*;
import com.ms.ui.event.*;
import java.awt.*;

public class PropertySheetApplet extends AwtUIApplet
{
    public PropertySheetApplet()
    {
        super(new AppletImplementation());
    }
}

class AppletImplementation extends UIApplet
    implements IUIActionListener
{
    TextPropSheet propSheet;
    TextCanvas canvas;

    public void init()
    {
        UIPushButton button =
            new UIPushButton("Properties",
            UIPushButton.RAISED);
        button.addActionListener(this);
        add(button, "North");

        canvas = new TextCanvas();
        add(canvas, "Center");

        setValid(true);
    }
```

```
        public void actionPerformed(UIActionEvent event)
        {
            UIFrame frame = new UIFrame();
            propSheet = new TextPropSheet(frame, canvas);
            propSheet.display();
        }
}


class TextPropSheet extends UIPropertyDialog
{
    public TextPropSheet(UIFrame frame, TextCanvas canvas)
    {
        super(frame, "Property Sheet", true, UIPropertyDialog.SMALL);
        TextPropPage textPage = new TextPropPage(this, canvas);
        addPage("Text Sizes", textPage);
        ColorPropPage colorPage = new ColorPropPage(this, canvas);
        addPage("Text Colors", colorPage);
    }
}


class TextPropPage extends UIPropertyPage
    implements IUIItemListener
{
    TextCanvas canvas;
    UIRadioButton button1;
    UIRadioButton button2;
    UIRadioButton button3;

    public TextPropPage(UIPropertyDialog ps, TextCanvas canvas)
    {
        super(ps);
        this.canvas = canvas;
    }

    public boolean addContent()
    {
        UIRadioGroup group = new UIRadioGroup("Sizes");

        button1 = new UIRadioButton("Set Text to 16 Points");
        button1.addItemListener(this);
        group.add(button1);

        button2 = new UIRadioButton("Set Text to 32 Points");
        button2.addItemListener(this);
        group.add(button2);

        button3 = new UIRadioButton("Set Text to 48 Points");
        button3.addItemListener(this);
        group.add(button3);
```

```
        checkButton();
        addAt(group, 6, 10, new Dimension(120, 50));

        return true;
    }

    public void itemStateChanged(UIItemEvent event)
    {
        setApplyable(true);
    }

    public boolean doApplyAction()
    {
        setPointSize();
        return true;
    }

    public boolean doOKAction()
    {
        setPointSize();
        return true;
    }

    public void setPointSize()
    {
        if (button1.isChecked())
            canvas.setPointSize(16);
        else if (button2.isChecked())
            canvas.setPointSize(32);
        else if (button3.isChecked())
            canvas.setPointSize(48);
    }

    public void checkButton()
    {
        int points = canvas.getPointSize();
        if (points == 16)
            button1.setChecked(true);
        else if (points == 32)
            button2.setChecked(true);
        else if (points == 48)
            button3.setChecked(true);
    }
}

class ColorPropPage extends UIPropertyPage
    implements IUIItemListener
```

```
{
    TextCanvas canvas;
    UIRadioButton button1;
    UIRadioButton button2;
    UIRadioButton button3;

    public ColorPropPage(UIPropertyDialog ps, TextCanvas canvas)
    {
        super(ps);
        this.canvas = canvas;
    }

    public boolean addContent()
    {
        UIRadioGroup group = new UIRadioGroup("Colors");

        button1 = new UIRadioButton("Set Color to Red");
        button1.addItemListener(this);
        group.add(button1);

        button2 = new UIRadioButton("Set Color to Green");
        button2.addItemListener(this);
        group.add(button2);

        button3 = new UIRadioButton("Set Color to Blue");

        button3.addItemListener(this);
        group.add(button3);

        checkButton();
        addAt(group, 6, 10, new Dimension(120, 50));

        return true;
    }

    public void itemStateChanged(UIItemEvent event)
    {
        setApplyable(true);
    }

    public boolean doApplyAction()
    {
        setColor();
        return true;
    }
```

```java
    public boolean doOKAction()
    {
        setColor();
        return true;
    }

    public void setColor()
    {
        if (button1.isChecked())
            canvas.setColor(FxColor.red);
        else if (button2.isChecked())
            canvas.setColor(FxColor.green);
        else if (button3.isChecked())
            canvas.setColor(FxColor.blue);
    }

    public void checkButton()
    {
        Color color = canvas.getColor();
        if (color == FxColor.red)
            button1.setChecked(true);
        else if (color == FxColor.green)
            button2.setChecked(true);
        else if (color == FxColor.blue)
            button3.setChecked(true);
    }
}

class TextCanvas extends UICanvas
{
    int pointSize;
    Color color;
    int col, row;

    public TextCanvas()
    {
        pointSize = 48;
        color = FxColor.red;
        col = 30;
        row = 105;
        setBackground(FxColor.black);
    }

    public void paint(FxGraphics graphics)
    {
```

```
            FxFont font =
                new FxFont("TimesRoman", FxFont.PLAIN, pointSize);
            graphics.setFont(font);
            graphics.setColor(color);
            graphics.drawString("AFC Rules!", col, row);
        }

        public void setPointSize(int points)
        {
            pointSize = points;
            if (pointSize == 16)
            {
                col = 110;
                row = 95;
            }
            else if (pointSize == 32)
            {
                col = 70;
                row = 100;
            }
            else if (pointSize == 48)
            {
                col = 30;
                row = 105;
            }

            repaint();
        }

        public void setColor(Color color)
        {
            this.color = color;
            repaint();
        }

        public int getPointSize()
        {
            return pointSize;
        }

        public Color getColor()
        {
            return color;
        }
    }
```

## Creating And Managing A Wizard

Previously in this chapter, you learned to create and display a basic wizard. However, to create a useful wizard, you first must plan the steps that the user must perform to complete the task represented by the wizard, as well as decide how you want to organize these steps onto different pages. Usually, a wizard has at least two pages.

After determining how you want to organize your wizard steps, you must decide what types of components are best suited for receiving the information the user must enter for each step of the task. For example, you might use an edit box to hold a file name and a set of option buttons for selecting task options.

After you select the components you want to use, you're ready to start programming your wizard. You already know how to create the wizard dialog box and add a page to it. You haven't yet learned, however, how to add components to each page and how to interact with the user, gathering the information entered into the wizard's pages.

Each wizard page requires two objects: an image for the page and the component to display in the page. If you don't want to display an image in the page, the **UIWizardStep** constructor's first argument can be **null**. Otherwise, it should be a **UIGraphic** object. The wizard step's component, given as the constructor's second argument, usually is a custom panel object that contains all the components needed for the page.

If you want the wizard step to have an enabled Finish button, you must return **true** from the wizard-step class's **isFinishStep()** method. This, of course, requires that you create a custom class that extends **UIWizardStep**. Listing 8.6 shows a simple wizard page class that overrides **isFinishStep()**.

**Listing 8.6   Overriding the isFinishStep() method in a custom wizard-page class.**

```
class MyWizardStep extends UIWizardStep
{
    MyWizardStep(UIGraphic image, Panel panel)
    {
        super(image, panel);
    }

    public boolean isFinishStep()
    {
        return true;
    }
}
```

To complete a wizard, you also need to know how to respond to the buttons supplied by AFC. Every wizard page has four buttons: Back, Next, Finish, and Cancel. The Back and Next buttons enable the user to navigate from one step to another and are handled automatically by AFC. The Finish and Cancel buttons should work just as OK and Cancel buttons work in a dialog box, with Finish indicating that the contents of the wizard should be extracted and processed and with Cancel meaning any changes should be ignored. The Finish and Cancel buttons both dismiss the dialog box. You can tell which button the user used to exit the wizard by examining the return value from the wizard's **doModal**() function, which displays the wizard. That code would look something like the following example:

```
Object button = wizard.doModal();
if (button != null)
{
    // User clicked the Finish button.
}
else
{
    // User clicked the Cancel button.
}
```

Now you can apply what you learned about wizards by experimenting with a complete example program. Listing 8.7 presents the source code for an AFC applet named WizardApplet. When you run the applet in Applet Viewer, you see the window shown in Figure 8.12. The button at the top of the applet enables you to display the wizard.

**Figure 8.12**

*WizardApplet running in Applet Viewer.*

The text string displayed below the button represents the currently set properties for the text, which include the text string, text size, and text color.

Click the Show Wizard button to display the wizard. As you can see in Figure 8.13, the first wizard step requests that you enter the string to display. Enter text into the text box, and then click the Next button to display the next step in the progression.

The second step requests a point size for the text, enabling you to choose one of three options (Figure 8.14). Select a text size and click the Next button to display the final step.

Finally, the wizard's third step requests a text color (Figure 8.15). Again, you can choose one of three options. After you make your selection, click the Finish button. The program then extracts the information from the wizard and changes its display to fit your selections.

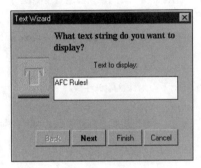

**Figure 8.13**

*The wizard's first step.*

**Figure 8.14**

*The wizard's second step.*

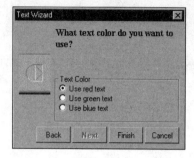

## Figure 8.15

*The wizard's final step.*

Three important items to notice about WizardApplet are the three custom panel classes, **Step1Panel**, **Step2Panel**, and **Step3Panel**. Each panel contains components that the wizard displays on the matching wizard step. For example, a **Step1Panel** object is the component displayed in the first wizard step page. This panel contains the text prompt for the page, as well as the edit box into which the user types a response.

### Listing 8.7  Source code for WizardApplet.

```
/////////////////////////////////////////////////
// WizardApplet.java
//
// An AFC applet that demonstrates how to create
// and display a wizard dialog in an applet.
/////////////////////////////////////////////////

import com.ms.ui.*;
import com.ms.fx.*;
import com.ms.ui.event.*;
import java.awt.*;

public class WizardApplet extends AwtUIApplet
{
    public WizardApplet()
    {
        super(new AppletImplementation());
    }
}

class AppletImplementation extends UIApplet
    implements IUIActionListener
{
```

```java
WizardCanvas canvas;
Image images[];
Step1Panel panel1;
Step2Panel panel2;
Step3Panel panel3;

public void init()
{
    UIPushButton button =
        new UIPushButton("Show Wizard",
        UIPushButton.RAISED);
    button.addActionListener(this);
    add(button, "North");

    images = new Image[3];
    images[0] = getImage(getCodeBase(), "step1.gif");
    images[1] = getImage(getCodeBase(), "step2.gif");
    images[2] = getImage(getCodeBase(), "step3.gif");

    canvas = new WizardCanvas();
    add(canvas, "Center");

    setValid(true);
}

public void actionPerformed(UIActionEvent event)
{
    UIFrame frame = new UIFrame();
    UIWizard wizard =
        new UIWizard(frame, "Text Wizard");

    panel1 = new Step1Panel(canvas);
    UIGraphic image = new UIGraphic(images[0]);
    WizStep1 wizardStep1 = new WizStep1(image, panel1);
    wizard.addStep(wizardStep1);

    panel2 = new Step2Panel(canvas);
    image = new UIGraphic(images[1]);
    WizStep2 wizardStep2 = new WizStep2(image, panel2);
    wizard.addStep(wizardStep2);

    panel3 = new Step3Panel(canvas);
    image = new UIGraphic(images[2]);
    WizStep3 wizardStep3 = new WizStep3(image, panel3);
    wizard.addStep(wizardStep3);

    Object button = wizard.doModal();
    if (button != null)
    {
```

```
            String msg = panel1.edit.getValueText();
            int points = getPoints();
            Color color = getColor();
            canvas.setTextOptions(msg, points, color);
        }
    }

    public int getPoints()
    {
        int points = 16;

        if (panel2.button2.isChecked())
            points = 32;
        else if (panel2.button3.isChecked())
            points = 48;

        return points;
    }

    public Color getColor()
    {
        Color color = FxColor.red;

        if (panel3.button2.isChecked())
            color = FxColor.green;
        else if (panel3.button3.isChecked())
            color = FxColor.blue;

        return color;
    }
}

class WizStep1 extends UIWizardStep
{
    WizStep1(UIGraphic image, Step1Panel panel)
    {
        super(image, panel);
    }

    public boolean isFinishStep()
    {
        return true;
    }
}

class WizStep2 extends UIWizardStep
{
```

```
    WizStep2(UIGraphic image, Step2Panel panel)
    {
        super(image, panel);
    }

    public boolean isFinishStep()
    {
        return true;
    }
}

class WizStep3 extends UIWizardStep
{
    WizStep3(UIGraphic image, Step3Panel panel)
    {
        super(image, panel, true);
    }

    public boolean isFinishStep()
    {
        return true;
    }

    public boolean isLastStep()
    {
        return true;
    }
}

class Step1Panel extends UIPanel
{
    UIEdit edit;

    public Step1Panel(WizardCanvas canvas)
    {
        UIGridLayout layout = new UIGridLayout(4, 0);
        setLayout(layout);

        String str = "What text string do you";
        str = str + " want to display?";
        UIDrawText msg = new UIDrawText(str);
        msg.setWordWrap(IFxTextConstants.wwKeepWordIntact);
        Font font = new Font("TimesRoman", Font.BOLD, 14);
        msg.setFont(font);

        UIText caption = new UIText("Text to display:");
        String textMsg = canvas.getTextMsg();
        edit = new UIEdit(textMsg);
        edit.setBordered(true);
```

```
            add(msg);
            add(caption);
            add(edit);
        }
    }

class Step2Panel extends UIPanel
{
    UIRadioButton button1;
    UIRadioButton button2;
    UIRadioButton button3;

    public Step2Panel(WizardCanvas canvas)
    {
        UIGridLayout layout = new UIGridLayout(2, 0);
        setLayout(layout);

        String str = "What text point-size";
        str = str + " do you want to use?";
        UIDrawText msg = new UIDrawText(str);
        msg.setWordWrap(IFxTextConstants.wwKeepWordIntact);
        Font font = new Font("TimesRoman", Font.BOLD, 14);
        msg.setFont(font);

        UIRadioGroup group = new UIRadioGroup("Point Size");

        button1 =
            new UIRadioButton("Use 16-point text");
        group.add(button1);

        button2 =
            new UIRadioButton("Use 32-point text");
        group.add(button2);

        button3 =
            new UIRadioButton("Use 48-point text");
        group.add(button3);

        int points = canvas.getTextPoints();
        if (points == 16)
            button1.setChecked(true);
        else if (points == 32)
            button2.setChecked(true);
        else if (points == 48)
            button3.setChecked(true);

        add(msg);
        add(group);
```

```
        }
    }

    class Step3Panel extends UIPanel
    {
        UIRadioButton button1;
        UIRadioButton button2;
        UIRadioButton button3;

        public Step3Panel(WizardCanvas canvas)
        {
            UIGridLayout layout = new UIGridLayout(2, 0);
            setLayout(layout);

            String str = "What text color";
            str = str + " do you want to use?";
            UIDrawText msg = new UIDrawText(str);
            msg.setWordWrap(IFxTextConstants.wwKeepWordIntact);
            Font font = new Font("TimesRoman", Font.BOLD, 14);
            msg.setFont(font);

            UIRadioGroup group = new UIRadioGroup("Text Color");

            button1 =
                new UIRadioButton("Use red text");
            group.add(button1);

            button2 =
                new UIRadioButton("Use green text");
            group.add(button2);

            button3 =
                new UIRadioButton("Use blue text");
            group.add(button3);

            Color color = canvas.getTextColor();
            if (color == FxColor.red)
                button1.setChecked(true);
            else if (color == FxColor.green)
                button2.setChecked(true);
            else if (color == FxColor.blue)
                button3.setChecked(true);

            add(msg);
            add(group);
        }
    }
```

```
class WizardCanvas extends UICanvas
{
    int points;
    Color color;
    String msg;

    public WizardCanvas()
    {
        points = 48;
        color = FxColor.red;
        msg = "AFC Rules!";
        setBackground(FxColor.black);
    }

    public void paint(FxGraphics graphics)
    {
        FxFont font =
            new FxFont("TimesRoman", FxFont.PLAIN, points);
        graphics.setFont(font);
        graphics.setColor(color);
        graphics.drawString(msg, 30, 100);
    }

    public void setTextOptions(String msg, int points, Color color)
    {
        this.msg = msg;
        this.points = points;
        this.color = color;
        repaint();
    }

    public String getTextMsg()
    {
        return msg;
    }

    public int getTextPoints()
    {
        return points;
    }

    public Color getTextColor()
    {
        return color;
    }
}
```

# Chapter 9

# Layout Managers

*Design in art, is a recognition of the relation between various things, various elements in the creative flux. You can't invent a design. You recognise it, in the fourth dimension. That is, with your blood and your bones, as well as with your eyes.*
—D.H. Lawrence,
*Phoenix: The Posthumous Papers of D.H. Lawrence*

# Notes…

# Chapter 9

Designing good component layouts for Java applets and applications can be a meticulous process. Java's AWT provides many layout managers to help you accomplish this task. However, if you're anything like I am, despite good planning and a reasonably good grasp of layout managers, your layouts often come out much differently than you expect. You're far from alone. One of the highest hurdles Java programmers have to leap is learning to produce component layouts.

AFC makes this task a little easier by supplying not only its own versions of AWT layout managers, but also a bunch of new ones, including **UIBarLayout**, **UIFixedFlowLayout**, **UIRowLayout**, and **UISplitLayout**. Although some AFC custom layouts—which AFC uses internally to create things such as lists, property sheets, and wizards—have limited value to the programmer, a few provide special advantages that enable you to design more creative and attractive component layouts.

In this chapter, you first take a general look at AFC's layout-manager classes. Then, in the Practical Guide, you discover some tricks for creating complex layouts without resorting to the more unwieldy layout managers such as **UIGridBagLayout**. The tricks you learn here will go a long way toward getting you over that aforementioned hurdle.

# The **UILayoutManager** Class

The granddaddy of all AFC layout managers is the **UILayoutManager** class. That is, all of AFC's layout manager classes have **UILayoutManager** as a superclass, extending and refining that class's general functionality with a specific layout manager's features. Some of AFC's layout-manager classes override functions in the **UILayoutManager** class, while others define additional new methods. Because **UILayoutManager** is an abstract class—declaring methods that must be implemented in extended classes—you cannot create a **UILayoutManager** object.

**UILayoutManager** is a granddaddy in more ways than one. It is an absolute base class, having no other class as a superclass; **UILayoutManager** inherits no methods from other classes. Instead, it defines its own set of classes, as shown in Table 9.1 Although many of the AFC layout-manager classes build upon the functionality of Java AWT layout managers, the AFC layout managers have no direct connection with AWT classes.

**Table 9.1  Methods of the UILayoutManager class.**

| Method | Description |
| --- | --- |
| addLayoutComponent() | Adds a specified component to the layout |
| adjustLayoutSize() | Adjust the layout size of a component |
| getComponent() | Gets the component at the given index |
| getComponentIndex() | Gets a components layout index |
| getHgap() | Gets the horizontal spacing between the layout's components |
| getMinimumSize() | Calculates the layout's minimum dimensions |
| getPreferredSize() | Calculates the layout's preferred dimensions |
| getVgap() | Gets the vertical spacing between the layout's components |
| isHeightRelative() | Returns **true** if the layout uses the container's height to lay out its components |
| isOverlapping() | Returns **true** if the layout manager's components overlap |

*(continued)*

**Table 9.1  Methods of the UILayoutManager class (continued).**

| Method | Description |
|---|---|
| isWidthRelative() | Returns **true** if the layout manager uses the container's width to lay out its components |
| layout() | Lays out the components |
| navigate() | Navigates from one component to another |
| paintContainer() | Draws the container |
| removeLayoutComponent() | Removes a component from the container |
| setHgap() | Sets the components' horizontal spacing |
| setVgap() | Sets the components' vertical spacing |

# The UIBarLayout Class

Although many of the AFC layout-manager classes resemble and improve upon AWT layout managers, many of these layout managers are unique to AFC. The **UIBarLayout** class is one example. Java's AWT has no layout manager that resembles **UIBarLayout**, which AFC uses to organize components in its band box components.

As you learned in Chapter 6, a band box is similar to a toolbar, except that a band box can contain sliding bands of components. The **UIBarLayout** layout manager enables the band-box component to organize the controls placed in bands. Simply, a **UIBarLayout** layout manager enables you to organize a group of components into a horizontal row, with the first component in the row stretching to fill the space not used by the remaining components.

Because **UIBarLayout** extends **UILayoutManager**, it inherits all of that class's methods. However, **UIBarLayout** implements its own versions of the **UILayoutManager** functions, as shown in Table 9.2. As you can see in the table, **UIBarLayout** defines no methods that aren't declared in **UILayoutManager**.

To create a **UIBarLayout** object, use the **new** operator to call the class's constructor, as in the following:

```
UIBarLayout layout = new UIBarLayout();
```

## Table 9.2  Methods of the **UIBarLayout** class.

| Method | Description |
| --- | --- |
| getMinimumSize() | Calculates the layout's minimum dimensions |
| getPreferredSize() | Calculates the layout's preferred dimensions |
| isOverlapping() | Returns **true** if the layout manager's components overlap |
| layout() | Lays out the components |
| navigate() | Navigates from one component to another |
| removeLayoutComponent() | Removes a component from the container |

Like all layout managers, after you create the **UIBarLayout** object, you give it to the container by calling the container's **setLayout()** method:

```
setLayout(layout);
```

The **UIBarLayout** class overloads it constructor, giving you two ways to create the layout object. You call the second constructor as shown in the following example:

```
UIBarLayout layout = new UIBarLayout(10, 10);
```

Here, the constructor's two arguments are the vertical and horizontal gaps between components in the layout. You can set these gap values by calling the layout manager's **setHgap()** and **setVgap()** methods:

```
UIBarLayout layout = new UIBarLayout();
layout.setHgap(15);
layout.setVgap(50);
```

Listing 9.1 presents the source code for an applet that arranges five buttons by using a **UIBarLayout** layout manager. When you first run the applet in Applet Viewer, you see the window shown in Figure 9.1. Note that in the figure, the layout manager arranges five buttons across the top of the applet, but wraps the fifth button around to a second line. If you resize the applet horizontally, you see that the fifth button moves back to the first line. Moreover, as you make the applet larger, the first button stretches to take up the slack, as shown in Figure 9.2.

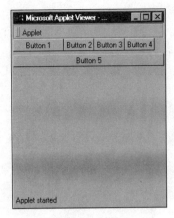

**Figure 9.1**

*BarLayoutApplet, running in Applet Viewer.*

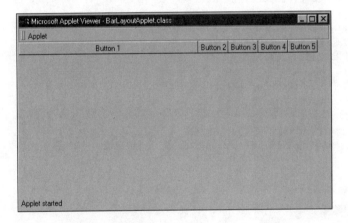

**Figure 9.2**

*BarLayoutApplet, after being resized.*

### Listing 9.1   Source code for BarLayoutApplet.

```
////////////////////////////////////////////////
// BarLayoutApplet.java
//
// An AFC applet that demonstrates how to use
// the UIBarLayout layout manager.
////////////////////////////////////////////////

import com.ms.ui.*;
```

```
public class BarLayoutApplet extends AwtUIApplet
{
    public BarLayoutApplet()
    {
        super(new AppletImplementation());
    }
}

class AppletImplementation extends UIApplet
{
    public void init()
    {
        UIBarLayout layout = new UIBarLayout();
        setLayout(layout);
        UIPushButton button = new UIPushButton("Button 1",
            UIPushButton.RAISED);
        add(button);
        button = new UIPushButton("Button 2",
            UIPushButton.RAISED);
        add(button);
        button = new UIPushButton("Button 3",
            UIPushButton.RAISED);
        add(button);
        button = new UIPushButton("Button 4",
            UIPushButton.RAISED);
        add(button);
        button = new UIPushButton("Button 5",
            UIPushButton.RAISED);
        add(button);

        setValid(true);
    }
}
```

# The **UIBorderLayout** Class

**UIBorderLayout** has a slightly different name than its AWT counterpart, but you should recognize this type of layout manager from your previous Java programming. Specifically, **UIBorderLayout** is the AFC version of the AWT **BorderLayout** layout manager. As such, **UIBorderLayout** provides all the same functionality of AWT's **BorderLayout** class, but enables AFC components, such as panels, to take advantage of the layout. (A **UIPanel** object, for example, must have an AFC layout manager.)

The **UIBorderLayout** layout manager, just like its AWT counterpart, enables you to position components by using directional constraints. These constraints are **North**,

**East**, **South**, **West**, and **Center**. But **UIBorderLayout** does AWT one better by also defining additional names for the conventional border layout constraints. Those new names are **TOP**, **RIGHT**, **BOTTOM**, **LEFT**, and **CENTER**. You can use either set of constraints when adding components to a border layout.

Because **UIBorderLayout** extends **UILayoutManager**, it inherits all of this class's methods. However, **UIBorderLayout** implements many of its own versions of the **UILayoutManager** functions, as shown in Table 9.3. As you can see in the table, **UIBorderLayout** defines no methods that aren't declared in **UILayoutManager**.

To create a **UIBorderLayout** object, use the **new** operator to call the class's constructor, as in the following:

```
UIBorderLayout layout = new UIBorderLayout();
```

Like all layout managers, after you create the **UIBorderLayout** object, you give it to the container by calling the container's **setLayout()** method:

```
setLayout(layout);
```

The **UIBorderLayout** class overloads it constructor, giving you two ways to create the layout object. You call the second constructor, as shown in the following example:

```
UIBorderLayout layout = new UIBorderLayout(10, 10);
```

**Table 9.3  Methods of the UIBorderLayout class.**

| Method | Description |
|---|---|
| addLayoutComponent() | Adds a specified component to the layout |
| adjustLayoutSize() | Adjusts the layout size of a component |
| getMinimumSize() | Calculates the layout's minimum dimensions |
| getPreferredSize() | Calculates the layout's preferred dimensions |
| isOverlapping() | Returns **true** if the layout manager's components overlap |
| layout() | Lays out the components |
| navigate() | Navigates from one component to another |
| removeLayoutComponent() | Removes a component from the container |

Here, the constructor's two arguments are the vertical and horizontal gaps between components in the layout.

Listing 9.2 presents the source code for an applet that arranges five buttons by using a **UIBorderLayout** layout manager. When you first run the applet in Applet Viewer, you see the window shown in Figure 9.3. Notice how the layout manager positions the five buttons according to their constraints, given as the **add()** method's second argument. Notice also that the **add()** method for an AFC program places the constraints as the second argument rather than the first, as in a conventional Java AWT program.

### Listing 9.2   Source code for BorderLayoutApplet.

```
/////////////////////////////////////////////////
// BorderLayoutApplet.java
//
// An AFC applet that demonstrates how to use
// the UIBorderLayout layout manager.
/////////////////////////////////////////////////

import com.ms.ui.*;

public class BorderLayoutApplet extends AwtUIApplet
{
    public BorderLayoutApplet()
    {
        super(new AppletImplementation());
    }
}

class AppletImplementation extends UIApplet
{
    public void init()
    {
        UIBorderLayout layout = new UIBorderLayout();
        setLayout(layout);
        UIPushButton button = new UIPushButton("Button 1",
            UIPushButton.RAISED);
        add(button, "North");
        button = new UIPushButton("Button 2",
            UIPushButton.RAISED);
        add(button, "East");
        button = new UIPushButton("Button 3",
            UIPushButton.RAISED);
        add(button, "South");
        button = new UIPushButton("Button 4",
            UIPushButton.RAISED);
```

```
        add(button, "West");
        button = new UIPushButton("Button 5",
            UIPushButton.RAISED);
        add(button, "Center");

        setValid(true);
    }
}
```

# The **UICardLayout** Class

In Chapter 8, you saw how AFC implements tabbed dialog boxes, also known as property sheets. The **UICardLayout** layout manager, which is an AFC version of AWT's **CardLayout** class, enables you to create property sheet-like layouts by using a stack of panels or other components. This layout manager gets its name from a deck of cards, where only one card is visible at a time, with the remaining cards hidden beneath the visible one.

Because **UICardLayout** extends **UILayoutManager**, it inherits all of this class's methods. However, **UICardLayout** implements many of its own versions of the **UILayout-Manager** functions, as shown in Table 9.4, as well as adds several methods of its own. Specifically, **UICardLayout** adds the methods **first()**, **last()**, **next()**, and **previous()** to enable programs to manipulate which "card" is currently visible.

To create a **UICardLayout** object, use the **new** operator to call the class's constructor, as in the following:

```
UICardLayout layout = new UICardLayout();
```

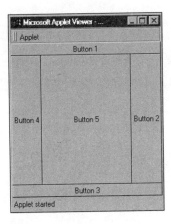

## Figure 9.3

*BorderLayoutApplet, running in Applet Viewer.*

## Table 9.4   Methods of the **UICardLayout** class.

| Method | Description |
| --- | --- |
| addLayoutComponent() | Adds a specified component to the layout |
| first() | Displays the container's first card |
| getMinimumSize() | Calculates the layout's minimum dimensions |
| getPreferredSize() | Calculates the layout's preferred dimensions |
| isOverlapping() | Returns **true** if the layout manager's components overlap |
| last() | Displays the container's last card |
| layout() | Lays out the components |
| navigate() | Navigates from one component to another |
| next() | Displays the container's next card |
| previous() | Displays the container's previous card |
| show() | Displays the given card |

Like all layout managers, after you create the **UICardLayout** object, you give it to the container by calling the container's **setLayout()** method:

```
setLayout(layout);
```

The **UICardLayout** class overloads it constructor, giving you two ways to create the layout object. You call the second constructor, as shown in the following example:

```
UICardLayout layout = new UICardLayout(10, 10);
```

Here, the constructor's two arguments are the vertical and horizontal gaps between components in the layout.

Creating a card layout requires that you take the following steps:

1.   Create a **UICardLayout** object and set it as the current layout manager

2.   Create the components that will act as the cards (or pages) in the layout

3.  Add the card components to the container in the order they should appear

4.  Call the layout manager's methods to display the required card

Listing 9.3 presents the source code for an applet that arranges three panels by using a **UICardLayout** layout manager. When you first run the applet in Applet Viewer, you see the window shown in Figure 9.4. Click the Next Card button to cycle through the three panels, each of which has a text label. Figure 9.5, for example, shows the applet after the user clicks the Next Card button once.

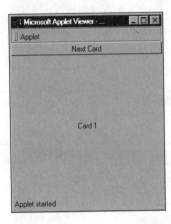

**Figure 9.4**

*CardLayoutApplet, running in Applet Viewer.*

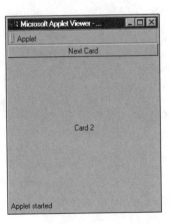

**Figure 9.5**

*CardLayoutApplet, showing its second card.*

## Listing 9.3 Source code for CardLayoutApplet.

```java
/////////////////////////////////////////////////
// CardLayoutApplet.java
//
// An AFC applet that demonstrates how to use
// the UICardLayout layout manager.
/////////////////////////////////////////////////

import com.ms.ui.*;
import java.awt.*;

public class CardLayoutApplet extends AwtUIApplet
{
    public CardLayoutApplet()
    {
        super(new AppletImplementation());
    }
}

class AppletImplementation extends UIApplet
{
    UIPanel mainPanel;
    UICardLayout cardLayout;

    public void init()
    {
        UIBorderLayout layout = new UIBorderLayout();
        setLayout(layout);

        UIPushButton button = new UIPushButton("Next Card",
            UIPushButton.RAISED);
        add(button, UIBorderLayout.TOP);

        mainPanel = new UIPanel();
        cardLayout = new UICardLayout();
        mainPanel.setLayout(cardLayout);
        Card1 card1 = new Card1();
        mainPanel.add(card1);
        Card2 card2 = new Card2();
        mainPanel.add(card2);
        Card3 card3 = new Card3();
        mainPanel.add(card3);
        add(mainPanel, UIBorderLayout.CENTER);

        setValid(true);
    }
```

```
        public boolean action(Event event, Object obj)
        {
            cardLayout.next(mainPanel);
            return true;
        }
}

class Card1 extends UIPanel
{
    Card1()
    {
        UIBorderLayout layout = new UIBorderLayout();
        setLayout(layout);
        UIText text = new UIText("Card 1");
        add(text, UIBorderLayout.CENTER);
    }
}

class Card2 extends UIPanel
{
    Card2()
    {
        UIBorderLayout layout = new UIBorderLayout();
        setLayout(layout);
        UIText text = new UIText("Card 2");
        add(text);
    }
}

class Card3 extends UIPanel
{
    Card3()
    {
        UIBorderLayout layout = new UIBorderLayout();
        setLayout(layout);
        UIText text = new UIText("Card 3");
        add(text);
    }
}
```

# The **UIFlowLayout** Class

The most common layout manager is the flow layout. In a flow layout, each component in the layout gets added horizontally one after the other, wrapping around to the next row when space gets scarce. In conventional, non-AFC Java programs, the flow-layout manager, represented by the **FlowLayout** class, is the default layout manager for most components. So that you can use flow-layout managers in your AFC programs, AFC offers the **UIFlowLayout** class.

Because **UIFlowLayout** extends **UILayoutManager**, it inherits all of that class's methods. However, **UIFlowLayout** implements many of its own versions of the **UILayoutManager** functions, as shown in Table 9.5, as well as adds several new methods. Specifically, **UICardLayout** adds the methods **getAlignment()**, **isWrap()**, **setAlignment()**, and **setWrap()**.

To create a **UIFlowLayout** object, use the **new** operator to call the class's constructor, like this:

```
UIFlowLayout layout = new UIFlowLayout();
```

Like all layout managers, once you've created the **UIFlowLayout** object, you give it to the container by calling the container's **setLayout()** method:

```
setLayout(layout);
```

The **UIFlowLayout** class overloads its constructor, giving you three ways to create the layout object. You already saw one way to create a **UIFlowLayout** object. Another way is to supply an alignment—which can be **LEFT**, **CENTER**, or **RIGHT**—to the constructor, as in the following:

```
UIFlowLayout layout = new UIFlowLayout(UIFlowLayout.CENTER);
```

**Table 9.5   Methods of the UIFlowLayout class.**

| Method | Description |
|---|---|
| getAlignment() | Gets the layout's currently set alignment |
| getMinimumSize() | Calculates the layout's minimum dimensions |
| getPreferredSize() | Calculates the layout's preferred dimensions |
| isHeightRelative() | Returns **true** if the layout uses the container's height to lay out its components |
| isOverlapping() | Returns **true** if the layout manager's components overlap |
| isWidthRelative() | Returns **true** if the layout manager uses the container's width to lay out its components |

*(continued)*

Table 9.5   Methods of the **UIFlowLayout** class *(continued).*

| Method | Description |
|---|---|
| isWrap() | Returns **true** if the layout's component-wrapping attribute is set |
| layout() | Lays out the components |
| navigate() | Navigates from one component to another |
| setAlignment() | Sets the layout's current alignment |
| setWrap() | Sets the layout's component-wrapping attribute |

You can also supply three arguments when calling the constructor, including not only the alignment, but also the horizontal and vertical gap between components:

```
UIFlowLayout layout = new UIFlowLayout(UIFlowLayout.CENTER, 20, 50);
```

Listing 9.4 presents the source code for an applet that arranges five buttons by using a **UIFlowLayout** layout manager. When you first run the applet in Applet Viewer, you see the window shown in Figure 9.6. To see how the layout manager wraps components around to the next line, resize the applet horizontally, as shown in Figure 9.7. Then, all the components fit on a single row.

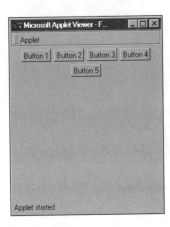

## Figure 9.6

*FlowLayoutApplet, running in Applet Viewer.*

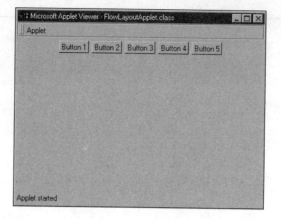

**Figure 9.7**

*FlowLayoutApplet after being enlarged.*

## Listing 9.4   Source code for FlowLayoutApplet.

```
///////////////////////////////////////////////
// FlowLayoutApplet.java
//
// An AFC applet that demonstrates how to use
// the UIFlowLayout layout manager.
///////////////////////////////////////////////

import com.ms.ui.*;

public class FlowLayoutApplet extends AwtUIApplet
{
    public FlowLayoutApplet()
    {
        super(new AppletImplementation());
    }
}

class AppletImplementation extends UIApplet
{
    public void init()
    {
        UIFlowLayout layout = new UIFlowLayout();
        setLayout(layout);
        UIPushButton button = new UIPushButton("Button 1",
            UIPushButton.RAISED);
        add(button);
        button = new UIPushButton("Button 2",
            UIPushButton.RAISED);
        add(button);
```

```
    button = new UIPushButton("Button 3",
        UIPushButton.RAISED);
    add(button);
    button = new UIPushButton("Button 4",
        UIPushButton.RAISED);
    add(button);
    button = new UIPushButton("Button 5",
        UIPushButton.RAISED);
    add(button);

    setValid(true);
    }
}
```

# The **UIFixedFlowLayout** Class

**UIFixedFlowLayout** is another of AFC's layout managers that has no AWT counterpart. **UIFixedFlowLayout** works much like **UIFlowLayout,** except all components stay at fixed sizes, and the components don't wrap to another line when they run out of space. Instead, unless the applet is resized to fit the components in the layout, they just run off the right edge of the applet.

To see the difference fixed-component widths make, look at Figure 9.8, which shows four buttons and an edit control, displayed in a flow-layout manager. Notice how the edit box (between Button 1 and Button 3) is so narrow it's almost invisible. Now, look at Figure 9.9, which shows the results of the same controls being laid out with a fixed flow-layout manager. Now, the edit box is the same fixed width as the buttons.

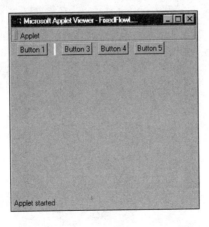

**Figure 9.8**

*Components laid out in a flow layout.*

**Figure 9.9**

*The same components from Figure 9.8 laid out in a fixed flow layout.*

Because **UIFixedFlowLayout** extends **UILayoutManager**, it inherits all of that class's methods. However, **UIFixedFlowLayout** implements many of its own versions of the **UILayoutManager** functions, as shown in Table 9.6, as well as adds the **computeUnit-Dimension()** method.

**Table 9.6  Methods of the UIFixedFlowLayout class.**

| Method | Description |
| --- | --- |
| computeUnitDimension() | Gets the biggest component's maximum size |
| getAlignment() | Gets the layout's currently set alignment |
| getMinimumSize() | Calculates the layout's minimum dimensions |
| getPreferredSize() | Calculates the layout's preferred dimensions |
| isOverlapping() | Returns **true** if the layout manager's components overlap |
| isWidthRelative() | Returns **true** if the layout manager uses the container's width to lay out its components |
| layout() | Lays out the components |
| navigate() | Navigates from one component to another |
| setAlignment() | Sets the layout's current alignment |

To create a **UIFixedFlowLayout** object, use the **new** operator to call the class's constructor, as in the following:

```
UIFixedFlowLayout layout = new UIFixedFlowLayout();
```

Like all layout managers, after you create the **UIFixedFlowLayout** object, you give it to the container by calling the container's **setLayout()** method:

```
setLayout(layout);
```

The **UIFixedFlowLayout** class overloads its constructor, giving you three ways to create the layout object. You already saw one way to create a **UIFixedFlowLayout** object. Another way is to supply horizontal and vertical gap values, as in the following:

```
UIFixedFlowLayout layout = new UIFixedFlowLayout(10, 10);
```

You can also supply three arguments when calling the constructor, including not only the horizontal and vertical gap between components, but also an alignment flag, which can be **LEFT**, **CENTER**, or **RIGHT**, as follows:

```
UIFlowLayout layout = new UIFlowLayout(20, 50, UIFixedFlowLayout.CENTER);
```

Listing 9.5 presents the source code for an applet that arranges five buttons by using a **UIFixedFlowLayout** layout manager. When you first run the applet in Applet Viewer, you see the window shown in Figure 9.10. Notice how the layout manager doesn't wrap components around to a new row, as usually happens with a regular flow-layout manager.

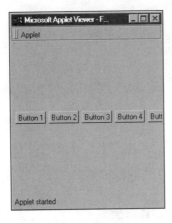

**Figure 9.10**

FixedFlowLayoutApplet, running in Applet Viewer.

**Listing 9.5   Source code for FixedFlowLayoutApplet.**

```
//////////////////////////////////////////////////
// FixedFlowLayoutApplet.java
//
// An AFC applet that demonstrates how to use
// the UIFixedFlowLayout layout manager.
//////////////////////////////////////////////////

import com.ms.ui.*;

public class FixedFlowLayoutApplet extends AwtUIApplet
{
    public FixedFlowLayoutApplet()
    {
        super(new AppletImplementation());
    }
}

class AppletImplementation extends UIApplet
{
    public void init()
    {
        UIFixedFlowLayout layout = new UIFixedFlowLayout();
        setLayout(layout);
        UIPushButton button = new UIPushButton("Button 1",
            UIPushButton.RAISED);
        add(button);
        button = new UIPushButton("Button 2",
            UIPushButton.RAISED);
        add(button);
        button = new UIPushButton("Button 3",
            UIPushButton.RAISED);
        add(button);
        button = new UIPushButton("Button 4",
            UIPushButton.RAISED);
        add(button);
        button = new UIPushButton("Button 5",
            UIPushButton.RAISED);
        add(button);

        setValid(true);
    }
}
```

# The **UIGridLayout** Class

**UIGridLayout** is the AFC version of the AWT's **GridLayout** layout-manager class. Just like its AWT counterpart, **UIGridLayout** enables programs to arrange components into a grid of cells. The number of columns and rows in the grid depends on values passed to the class's constructor.

Because **UIGridLayout** extends **UILayoutManager**, it inherits all of this class's methods. However, **UIGridLayout** implements many of its own versions of the **UILayoutManager** functions, as shown in Table 9.7, as well as adds the **continueInvalidate()** method.

To create a **UIGridLayout** object, use the **new** operator to call the class's constructor, as in the following:

```
UIGridLayout layout = new UIGridLayout(3, 2);
```

Here, the constructor's two arguments are the number of rows and number of columns, respectively, in the grid.

Like all layout managers, after you create the **UIGridLayout** object, you give it to the container by calling the container's **setLayout()** method:

```
setLayout(layout);
```

The **UIGridLayout** class overloads its constructor, giving you two ways to create the layout object. You already saw one way to create a **UIGridLayout** object. Another way is to supply horizontal and vertical gap values in addition to the number of rows and columns, as in the following example:

```
UIFixedFlowLayout layout = new UIFixedFlowLayout(3, 2, 10, 10);
```

Listing 9.6 presents the source code for an applet that arranges five buttons by using a **UIGridLayout** layout manager. When you run the applet in Applet Viewer, you see the

**Table 9.7 Methods of the UIGridLayout class.**

| Method | Description |
|---|---|
| continueInvalidate() | Determines whether the container needs to be invalidated |
| getMinimumSize() | Calculates the layout's minimum dimensions |
| getPreferredSize() | Calculates the layout's preferred dimensions |
| isOverlapping() | Returns **true** if the layout manager's components overlap |
| layout() | Lays out the components |
| navigate() | Navigates from one component to another |

window shown in Figure 9.11. Notice how the layout manager arranges the buttons into the grid in the order in which they were added to the layout. Notice also that, although the grid layout has three rows and two columns, one cell is left empty for lack of a sixth button. Finally, like many layout managers, **UIGridLayout** resizes the layout when the applet is resized, as shown in Figure 9.12.

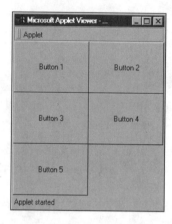

**Figure 9.11**

*GridLayoutApplet, running in Applet Viewer.*

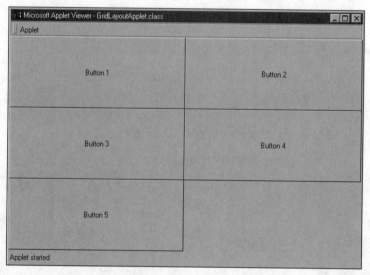

**Figure 9.12**

*GridLayoutApplet after being resized.*

**Listing 9.6  Source code for GridLayoutApplet.**

```java
///////////////////////////////////////////////
// GridLayoutApplet.java
//
// An AFC applet that demonstrates how to use
// the UIGridLayout layout manager.
///////////////////////////////////////////////

import com.ms.ui.*;

public class GridLayoutApplet extends AwtUIApplet
{
    public GridLayoutApplet()
    {
        super(new AppletImplementation());
    }
}

class AppletImplementation extends UIApplet
{
    public void init()
    {
        UIGridLayout layout = new UIGridLayout(3, 2);
        setLayout(layout);
        UIPushButton button = new UIPushButton("Button 1",
            UIPushButton.RAISED);
        add(button);
        button = new UIPushButton("Button 2",
            UIPushButton.RAISED);
        add(button);
        button = new UIPushButton("Button 3",
            UIPushButton.RAISED);
        add(button);
        button = new UIPushButton("Button 4",
            UIPushButton.RAISED);
        add(button);
        button = new UIPushButton("Button 5",
            UIPushButton.RAISED);
        add(button);

        setValid(true);
    }
}
```

# The **UIGridBagLayout** Class

When programming with Java's AWT classes, the **GridBagLayout** layout manager enables you to create sophisticated grid layouts. However, this layout manager is not only intricate and unwieldy, it's also poorly documented. Worse, the AFC version of this layout, named **UIGridBagLayout**, is both poorly documented and seems to be unusable. **GridBagLayout** layouts that work fine under Java's AWT crash consistently when converted to **UIGridBagLayout**. (Suspiciously, not one of Microsoft's sample AFC programs even tries to implement a **UIGridBagLayout**.) Because you can accomplish the same types of layouts by using one or more of the other layout manager, this author's advice is to stay away from grid bag layouts completely.

Still, for completeness, this section takes a quick look at the **UIGridBagLayout** class, which, of course, extends **UILayoutManager** and so inherits all this class's methods. **UIGridBagLayout** also defines a few methods of its own for managing grid bag constraints, which are the values that determine how a layout looks. Table 9.8 shows the methods defined in the **UIGridBagLayout** class.

To help you draw your own conclusions about the usability of AFC's **UIGridBagLayout** class, first look at Listing 9.7, which is the source code for a traditional Java AWT applet, using a grid bag layout to organize three buttons into a grid. This program represents a very simple grid bag layout, one that AFC's **UIGridBagLayout** class should handle in its sleep (assuming that Java classes sleep). Figure 9.13 shows the applet running under Applet Viewer.

**Table 9.8   Methods of the UIGridBagLayout class.**

| Method | Description |
| --- | --- |
| addLayoutComponent() | Adds a specified component to the layout |
| getAlignment() | Gets the layout's currently set alignment |
| getConstraints() | Gets a copy of the component's constraints |
| getMinimumSize() | Calculates the layout's minimum dimensions |
| getPreferredSize() | Calculates the layout's preferred dimensions |
| layout() | Lays out the components |
| lookupConstraints() | Gets a component's constraints |
| setAlignment() | Sets the layout's current alignment |
| setConstraints() | Sets a component's constraints for the specified component |

**Figure 9.13**

*GridBagLayoutApplet, running in Applet Viewer.*

## Listing 9.7  Source code for GridBagLayoutApplet.

```java
/////////////////////////////////////////////////
// GridBagLayoutApplet.java
//
// An AWT applet that demonstrates how to use
// the GridBagLayout layout manager.
/////////////////////////////////////////////////

import java.applet.*;
import java.awt.*;

public class GridBagLayoutApplet extends Applet
{
    public void init()
    {
        GridBagLayout layout = new GridBagLayout();
        setLayout(layout);

        GridBagConstraints constraints = new GridBagConstraints();
        constraints.fill = GridBagConstraints.BOTH;

        constraints.gridwidth = GridBagConstraints.RELATIVE;
        Button button = new Button("Button 1");
        layout.setConstraints(button, constraints);
        add(button);

        constraints.gridwidth = GridBagConstraints.REMAINDER;
        button = new Button("Button 2");
        layout.setConstraints(button, constraints);
```

```
        add(button);

        constraints.gridwidth = GridBagConstraints.REMAINDER;
        button = new Button("Button 3");
        layout.setConstraints(button, constraints);
        add(button);
    }
}
```

Listing 9.8 is a direct translation of Listing 9.7 into AFC. All that was done to the program was moving the **init()** method to the **AppletImplementation** class and changing the AWT classes used in the program to AFC classes (for example, changing **GridBagLayout** to **UIGridBagLayout**). Unfortunately, the AFC version crashes faster than you can say "Whoops!"

### Listing 9.8   Source code for the AFC version of GridBagLayoutApplet.

```
/////////////////////////////////////////////////
// GridBagLayoutApplet.java
//
// An AFC applet that demonstrates how to use
// the UIGridBagLayout layout manager.
/////////////////////////////////////////////////

import com.ms.ui.*;

public class GridBagLayoutApplet extends AwtUIApplet
{
    public GridBagLayoutApplet()
    {
        super(new AppletImplementation());
    }
}

class AppletImplementation extends UIApplet
{
    public void init()
    {
        UIGridBagLayout layout = new UIGridBagLayout();
        setLayout(layout);

        UIGridBagConstraints constraints = new UIGridBagConstraints();
        constraints.fill = UIGridBagConstraints.BOTH;
        constraints.gridwidth = UIGridBagConstraints.RELATIVE;
        UIPushButton button = new UIPushButton("Button 1");
        layout.setConstraints(button, constraints);
        add(button);
```

```
            constraints.gridwidth = UIGridBagConstraints.REMAINDER;
            button = new UIPushButton("Button 2");
            layout.setConstraints(button, constraints);
            add(button);

            constraints.gridwidth = UIGridBagConstraints.REMAINDER;
            button = new UIPushButton("Button 3");
            layout.setConstraints(button, constraints);
            add(button);

            setValid(true);
      }
}
```

# The **UIRowLayout** Class

Another AFC layout manager with no AWT counterpart, **UIRowLayout**, enables you to organize a set of components into a single row in much the same way you might organize components into a grid layout with a single row. The difference here, however, is that you can manipulate the positions of components in the rows, even after they're displayed on the screen. For example, you can move the first component in the row into the third position with a single method call.

Because **UIRowLayout** extends **UILayoutManager**, it inherits all of this class's methods. However, **UIRowLayout** implements many of its own versions of the **UILayoutManager** functions, as shown in Table 9.9, and also adds the **getOrder Index()**, **getWidth()**, **getWidths()**, **moveColumn()**, and **setWidths()** methods.

To create a **UIRowLayout** object, use the **new** operator to call the class's constructor, as in the following:

```
UIRowLayout layout = new UIRowLayout(5);
```

Here, the constructor's single argument is the number of columns in the row.

Like all layout managers, after you create the **UIRowLayout** object, you give it to the container by calling the container's **setLayout()** method:

```
setLayout(layout);
```

The **UIRowLayout** class overloads its constructor, giving you four ways to create the layout object. You already saw one way to create a **UIRowLayout** object, by supplying only the number of columns. The remaining three constructors' signatures look like the following:

```
public UIRowLayout(IUIComponent header, int columns);
public UIRowLayout(IUIComponent header, int columns, int widths);
public UIRowLayout(IUIComponent header, int columns, int widths[]);
```

Using these constructors, you can create row layouts that have columns of various widths. The first argument in all cases is the layout's header component, which is used as a reference for other component indexes. The second constructor in the preceding lines uses **widths** as the width of all columns, whereas the third constructor uses the array **widths[]** to specify a different width for each column.

Listing 9.9 presents the source code for an applet that arranges five buttons by using a **UIRowLayout** layout manager. When you run the applet in Applet Viewer, you see the window shown in Figure 9.14. Notice that the default widths of the components are determined by the width of the container. When you enlarge the container horizontally, as shown in Figure 9.15, the layout remains the same size. The layout will, however, expand vertically.

**Table 9.9  Methods of the UIRowLayout class.**

| Method | Description |
| --- | --- |
| getComponent() | Gets the component at the given index |
| getMinimumSize() | Calculates the layout's minimum dimensions |
| getOrderIndex() | Gets the position of a column |
| getPreferredSize() | Calculates the layout's preferred dimensions |
| getWidth() | Gets a column's current width |
| getWidths() | Gets all columns' current widths |
| isOverlapping() | Returns **true** if the layout manager's components overlap |
| isWidthRelative() | Returns **true** if the layout manager uses the container's width to lay out its components |
| layout() | Lays out the components |
| moveColumn() | Moves a column |
| navigate() | Navigates from one component to another |
| setWidths() | Sets all columns' widths |

**Figure 9.14**

*RowLayoutApplet, running in Applet Viewer.*

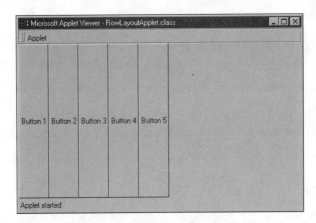

**Figure 9.15**

*RowLayoutApplet after being enlarged horizontally.*

### Listing 9.9   Source code for RowLayoutApplet.

```
/////////////////////////////////////////////////
// RowLayoutApplet.java
//
// An AFC applet that demonstrates how to use
// the UIRowLayout layout manager.
/////////////////////////////////////////////////

import com.ms.ui.*;
```

```
public class RowLayoutApplet extends AwtUIApplet
{
    public RowLayoutApplet()
    {
        super(new AppletImplementation());
    }
}

class AppletImplementation extends UIApplet
{
    public void init()
    {
        UIRowLayout layout = new UIRowLayout(5);
        setLayout(layout);
        UIPushButton button = new UIPushButton("Button 1",
            UIPushButton.RAISED);
        add(button);
        button = new UIPushButton("Button 2",
            UIPushButton.RAISED);
        add(button);
        button = new UIPushButton("Button 3",
            UIPushButton.RAISED);
        add(button);
        button = new UIPushButton("Button 4",
            UIPushButton.RAISED);
        add(button);
        button = new UIPushButton("Button 5",
            UIPushButton.RAISED);
        add(button);

        setValid(true);
    }
}
```

# The **UISplitLayout** Class

The **UISplitLayout** class represents another layout manager unique to AFC. That is, there is no AWT counterpart. You can use the **UISplitLayout** class whenever you want to divide the layout into two sections, either horizontally or vertically.

Like all the layout-manager classes, **UISplitLayout** extends **UILayoutManager**, and so it inherits all of this class's methods. However, **UISplitLayout** implements many of its own versions of the **UILayoutManager** functions, as shown in Table 9.10. The class also defines the **getPos()** and **setPos()** methods, which aren't defined in the **UILayoutManager** superclass.

**Table 9.10  Methods of the UISplitLayout class.**

| Method | Description |
|---|---|
| addLayoutComponent() | Adds a specified component to the layout |
| adjustLayoutSize() | Adjusts the layout size of a component |
| getComponent() | Gets the component at the given index |
| getMinimumSize() | Calculates the layout's minimum dimensions |
| getPos() | Gets the split position |
| getPreferredSize() | Calculates the layout's preferred dimensions |
| isOverlapping() | Returns **true** if the layout manager's components overlap |
| layout() | Lays out the components |
| navigate() | Navigates from one component to another |
| removeLayoutComponent() | Removes a component from the container |
| setPos() | Sets the split position |

To create a **UISplitLayout** object, use the **new** operator to call the class's constructor, like this:

```
UISplitLayout layout = new UISplitLayout();
```

Like all layout managers, after you create the **UISplitLayout** object, you give it to the container by calling the container's **setLayout()** method, as in the following example:

```
setLayout(layout);
```

The **UISplitLayout** class overloads its constructor, giving you three ways to create the layout object. You already saw one way to create a **UISplitLayout** object. You can also supply a style flag to the constructor. This style flag, which can be **0** (zero) or **HORIZONTAL**, determines which way the layout area is split. Here's an example:

```
UISplitLayout layout = new UISplitLayout(UISplitLayout.HORIZONTAL);
```

You can also specify a split position in addition to the flag, as in the following:

```
UISplitLayout layout = new UISplitLayout(UISplitLayout.HORIZONTAL, 20);
```

Listing 9.10 presents the source code for an applet that arranges two buttons by using a **UISplitLayout** layout manager. When you run the applet in Applet Viewer, you see the window shown in Figure 9.16. Figure 9.17 shows the applet with a horizontal split.

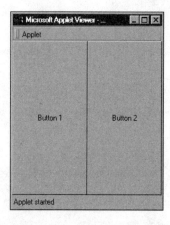

**Figure 9.16**

*SplitLayoutApplet, running in Applet Viewer.*

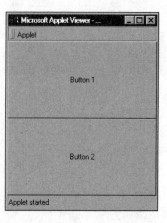

**Figure 9.17**

*SplitLayoutApplet with a horizontal split.*

**Listing 9.10   Source code for SplitLayoutApplet.**

```java
/////////////////////////////////////////////////
// SplitLayoutApplet.java
//
// An AFC applet that demonstrates how to use
// the UISplitLayout layout manager.
/////////////////////////////////////////////////

import com.ms.ui.*;

public class SplitLayoutApplet extends AwtUIApplet
{
    public SplitLayoutApplet()
    {
        super(new AppletImplementation());
    }
}

class AppletImplementation extends UIApplet
{
    public void init()
    {
        UISplitLayout layout = new UISplitLayout();
        setLayout(layout);
        UIPushButton button = new UIPushButton("Button 1",
            UIPushButton.RAISED);
        add(button, "nw");
        button = new UIPushButton("Button 2",
            UIPushButton.RAISED);
        add(button, "se");

        setValid(true);
    }
}
```

# The **UIVerticalFlowLayout** Class

The **UIVerticalFlowLayout** layout manager is much like the regular flow-layout manager, except it flows components vertically onto the layout rather than horizontally. AFC uses **UIVerticalFlowLayout** to create components such as **UIList**, which must manage one or more vertical columns of components.

Like all the layout-manager classes, **UIVerticalFlowLayout** extends **UILayoutManager**, and so it inherits all of this class's methods. However, **UIVerticalFlowLayout** implements many of its own versions of the **UILayoutManager** functions, as shown in Table 9.11. The class also defines the **setStyle()** method, which is not defined in the **UILayoutManager** superclass.

To create a **UIVerticalFlowLayout** object, use the **new** operator to call the class's constructor, as in the following syntax:

```
UIVerticalFlowLayout layout = new UIVerticalFlowLayout();
```

The **UIVerticalFlowLayout** class overloads its constructor, giving you three ways to create the layout object. You already saw one way to create a **UIVerticalFlowLayout** object. You can also supply a style flag to the constructor. This style flag can be **0** (zero) for the default style or either or both of **MULTICOLUMN** and **FILL**. Here's an example:

```
UIVerticalFlowLayout layout =
    new UIVerticalFlowLayout(UIVerticalFlowLayout.FILL);
```

**Table 9.11    Methods of the UIVerticalFlowLayout class.**

| Method | Description |
|---|---|
| adjustLayoutSize() | Adjusts the layout size of a component |
| getMinimumSize() | Calculates the layout's minimum dimensions |
| getPreferredSize() | Calculates the layout's preferred dimensions |
| isHeightRelative() | Returns **true** if the layout uses the container's height to lay out its components |
| isOverlapping() | Returns **true** if the layout manager's components overlap |
| isWidthRelative() | Returns **true** if the layout manager uses the container's width to lay out its components |
| layout() | Lays out the components |
| navigate() | Navigates from one component to another |
| setStyle() | Sets the layout manager's style (**0** (zero), **MULTICOLUMN**, **FILL**) |

You can also specify a horizontal-gap value in addition to the flag, as in the following:

```
UIVerticalFlowLayout layout =
    new UIVerticalFlowLayout(UIVerticalFlowLayout.FILL, 10);
```

Listing 9.11 presents the source code for an applet that arranges five buttons by using a **UIVerticalFlowLayout** layout manager. When you run the applet in Applet Viewer, you see the window shown in Figure 9.18. Figure 9.19 shows the layout with the **FILL** style.

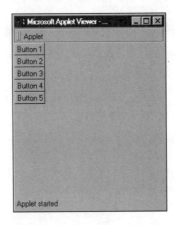

**Figure 9.18**

*VerticalFlowLayoutApplet, running in Applet Viewer.*

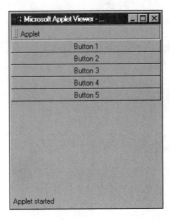

**Figure 9.19**

*VerticalFlowLayoutApplet with the **FILL** style.*

**Listing 9.11   Source code for VerticalFlowLayoutApplet.**

```java
//////////////////////////////////////////////////
// VerticalFlowLayoutApplet.java
//
// An AFC applet that demonstrates how to use
// the UIVerticalFlowLayout layout manager.
//////////////////////////////////////////////////

import com.ms.ui.*;

public class VerticalFlowLayoutApplet extends AwtUIApplet
{
    public VerticalFlowLayoutApplet()
    {
        super(new AppletImplementation());
    }
}

class AppletImplementation extends UIApplet
{
    public void init()
    {
        UIVerticalFlowLayout layout =
            new UIVerticalFlowLayout();
        setLayout(layout);

        UIPushButton button = new UIPushButton("Button 1",
            UIPushButton.RAISED);
        add(button);
        button = new UIPushButton("Button 2",
            UIPushButton.RAISED);
        add(button);
        button = new UIPushButton("Button 3",
            UIPushButton.RAISED);
        add(button);
        button = new UIPushButton("Button 4",
            UIPushButton.RAISED);
        add(button);
        button = new UIPushButton("Button 5",
            UIPushButton.RAISED);
        add(button);

        setValid(true);
    }
}
```

# The **UITabLayout**, **UITabListLayout**, And **UITreeLayout** Classes

The **UITabLayout**, **UITabListLayout**, and **UITreeLayout** classes are of limited value to an AFC programmer because they are used internally by AFC to create property sheets and tree components. All of these classes extend **UILayoutManager**, but they also define their own methods. Tables 9.12 through 9.14 shows the methods defined by these classes.

**Table 9.12   Methods of the UITabLayout class.**

| Method | Description |
| --- | --- |
| getMinimumSize() | Calculates the layout's minimum dimensions |
| getPreferredSize() | Calculates the layout's preferred dimensions |
| layout() | Lays out the components |
| navigate() | Navigates from one component to another |

**Table 9.13   Methods of the UITabListLayout class.**

| Method | Description |
| --- | --- |
| getMinimumSize() | Calculates the layout's minimum dimensions |
| getPreferredSize() | Calculates the layout's preferred dimensions |
| isWidthRelative() | Returns **true** if the layout manager uses the container's width to lay out its components |
| layout() | Lays out the components |
| navigate() | Navigates from one component to another |

## Table 9.14 Methods of the **UITreeLayout** class.

| Method | Description |
| --- | --- |
| adjustLayoutSize() | Adjusts the layout size of a component |
| drawLine() | Draws a line |
| getMinimumSize() | Calculates the layout's minimum dimensions |
| getPreferredSize() | Calculates the layout's preferred dimensions |
| isHeightRelative() | Returns **true** if the layout uses the container's height to lay out its components |
| isOverlapping() | Returns **true** if the layout manager's components overlap |
| isWidthRelative() | Returns **true** if the layout manager uses the container's width to lay out its components |
| layout() | Lays out the components |
| paintContainer() | Draws the container |

# Practical Guide To

# Using Layout Managers

- Filling An Applet With A Component
- Creating Windows-Like Layouts
- Creating Dynamic Controls With Layouts
- Creating Pages Of Components
- Creating Simple Component Grids
- Creating Complex Component Grids

## Filling An Applet With A Component

**UIBorderLayout** is one of the most useful layout managers. One reason is that any component placed in the layout's center position expands to fill all remaining area in the layout. Effectively, this means you can use **UIBorderLayout** when you want to fill an applet's entire display area with a component. Just create the component you want displayed and call **add(comp, "Center")**, where **comp** is the component to add. For example, Listing 9.12 presents an applet that displays one large button that fills the entire applet. Figure 9.20 shows the applet running in Applet Viewer.

**Listing 9.12   Source code for BigButtonApplet.**

```
////////////////////////////////////////////////
// BigButtonApplet.java
//
// An AFC applet that demonstrates how to use
// the UIBorderLayout layout manager to create
// an applet with a single component that fills
// the applet's display area.
////////////////////////////////////////////////

import com.ms.ui.*;

public class BigButtonApplet extends AwtUIApplet
{
    public BigButtonApplet()
    {
        super(new AppletImplementation());
    }
}

class AppletImplementation extends UIApplet
{
    public void init()
    {
        UIBorderLayout layout = new UIBorderLayout();
        setLayout(layout);

        UIPushButton button =
            new UIPushButton("One Big Button!",
            UIPushButton.RAISED);
        add(button, "Center");

        setValid(true);
    }
}
```

**Figure 9.20**

*BigButtonApplet, running in Applet Viewer.*

## Creating Windows-Like Layouts

Another reason the **UIBorderLayout** layout manager is handy is the way in which you can use it to simulate the layout of most Windows applications. That is, by creating a panel of components for the "North" position in the layout, a status bar for the "South" position, and a "full-screen" component for the "Center" position, you can create a reasonably familiar Windows-style layout for the user. Listing 9.13, for example, shows how easy it is to create a mini word processor with just a few components positioned judiciously in a border-layout manager. Figure 9.21 shows the applet

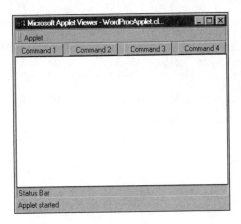

**Figure 9.21**

*WordProcApplet, running in Applet Viewer.*

running in Applet Viewer. Note that none of the applet's buttons is operational, and they are included only to demonstrate the layout techniques.

## Listing 9.13  Source code for WordProcApplet.

```
///////////////////////////////////////////////////
// WordProcApplet.java
//
// An AFC applet that demonstrates how to use the
// UIBorderLayout layout manager to create an applet
// with a toolbar, status bar, and text-editing
// pane.
///////////////////////////////////////////////////

import com.ms.ui.*;

public class WordProcApplet extends AwtUIApplet
{
    public WordProcApplet()
    {
        super(new AppletImplementation());
    }
}

class AppletImplementation extends UIApplet
{
    public void init()
    {
        UIBorderLayout layout = new UIBorderLayout();
        setLayout(layout);

        ButtonPanel buttonPanel = new ButtonPanel();
        add(buttonPanel, "North");

        UIEdit edit = new UIEdit();
        edit.setBordered(true);
        edit.setSingleLine(false);
        edit.setWordWrap(UIEdit.wwKeepWordIntact);
        add(edit, "Center");

        UIStatus status = new UIStatus("Status Bar");
        add(status, "South");

        setValid(true);
    }
}
```

```
class ButtonPanel extends UIPanel
{
    ButtonPanel()
    {
        UIGridLayout layout = new UIGridLayout(1, 3);
        layout.setHgap(10);
        setLayout(layout);
        UIPushButton button =
            new UIPushButton("Command 1", UIPushButton.RAISED);
        add(button);
        button = new UIPushButton("Command 2",
            UIPushButton.RAISED);
        add(button);
        button = new UIPushButton("Command 3",
            UIPushButton.RAISED);
        add(button);
        button = new UIPushButton("Command 4",
            UIPushButton.RAISED);
        add(button);
    }
}
```

## Creating Dynamic Controls With Layouts

Card layouts, like border layouts, give you a great deal of layout power with a minimum of effort. In its simplest form, a card layout enables you to create a component that changes with use. You could use a card layout, for example, to create a button that changes each time it's clicked. To do so, you could actually have several buttons, each representing a "card" in the layout. (Of course, you can also accomplish this trick by changing a button's attributes each time it's clicked, rather than cycling through several buttons, as is demonstrated here. There are many ways to accomplish the same outcome by using Java and AFC.)

Listing 9.14, for example, shows how such a button applet may work. The program creates four buttons, adding them to a card layout. When the user clicks a button, the next card in the series comes into view, which makes it appear as though the button's label has changed. This example is trivial, but it shows how this layout technique works. Figure 9.22 shows the applet running under Applet Viewer.

Notice how, in Listing 9.14, the applet responds to button clicks in the **action-Performed()** method, by calling the layout manager's **next()** method. The **next()** method causes the applet to display the next card in the series. When the last card is already displayed, the display wraps around back to the first card.

**Figure 9.22**

*ButtonCardApplet, running in Applet Viewer.*

### Listing 9.14   Source code for ButtonCardApplet.

```
///////////////////////////////////////////////////
// ButtonCardApplet.java
//
// An AFC applet that demonstrates how to use
// the UICardLayout layout manager to create
// a control that changes in response to the
// user.
///////////////////////////////////////////////////

import com.ms.ui.*;
import com.ms.ui.event.*;

public class ButtonCardApplet extends AwtUIApplet
{
    public ButtonCardApplet()
    {
        super(new AppletImplementation());
    }
}

class AppletImplementation extends UIApplet
    implements IUIActionListener
{
    UICardLayout cardLayout;

    public void init()
    {
```

```
        cardLayout = new UICardLayout();
        setLayout(cardLayout);

        UIPushButton button = new UIPushButton("Click Me!",
            UIPushButton.RAISED);
        button.addActionListener(this);
        add(button);
        button = new UIPushButton("That's One Click",
            UIPushButton.RAISED);
        button.addActionListener(this);
        add(button);
        button = new UIPushButton("That's Two Clicks",
            UIPushButton.RAISED);
        button.addActionListener(this);
        add(button, UIBorderLayout.TOP);
        button = new UIPushButton("You're Still Clicking?",
            UIPushButton.RAISED);
        button.addActionListener(this);
        add(button);

        setValid(true);
    }

    public void actionPerformed(UIActionEvent event)
    {
        cardLayout.next(this);
    }
}
```

## Creating Pages Of Components

A more sophisticated use for a card layout is to create several sets, or pages, of components that the user can access in much the same way as the user accesses a property sheet. For example, you can create a set of buttons that enables the user to browse through each page of components or even jump directly to a particular page. Unfortunately, AFC's **UICardLayout** class doesn't seem to work completely as advertised. Calling the **previous()** method yields unpredictable results that you will need to work around in your applets. (Suspiciously, as with the defective **UIGridBagLayout** class, none of Microsoft's AFC sample applets employs a card layout.)

Listing 9.15 shows the source code for an AFC applet, named PageCardApplet, that enables the user to browse through three pages of components. In this case, each page contains only a text label. In an actual application, you complete the **Page1**, **Page2**, and **Page3** panel classes by creating more sophisticated component layouts, much as you do for a property sheet.

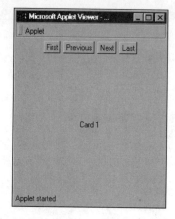

**Figure 9.23**

*PageCardApplet, running in Applet Viewer.*

When you run the applet in Applet Viewer, you see the window show in Figure 9.23.
Go ahead and click the First, Next, or Last buttons to cycle through the pages. When
you click the First button, the first page appears; when you click the Last button, the
last page appears; and when you click the Next button, the next page (relative to the
currently displayed page) appears. (For now, leave the Previous button alone.)

**Listing 9.15   Source code for PageCardApplet.**

```
/////////////////////////////////////////////////
// PageCardApplet.java
//
// An AFC applet that demonstrates how to use
// the UICardLayout layout manager to display
// and manipulate pages of components.
/////////////////////////////////////////////////

import com.ms.ui.*;
import java.awt.*;

public class PageCardApplet extends AwtUIApplet
{
    public PageCardApplet()
    {
        super(new AppletImplementation());
    }
}

class AppletImplementation extends UIApplet
{
```

```
    public void init()
    {
        UIBorderLayout layout = new UIBorderLayout();
        setLayout(layout);

        MainPanel mainPanel = new MainPanel();
        add(mainPanel, "Center");

        ButtonPanel buttonPanel = new ButtonPanel(mainPanel);
        add(buttonPanel, "North");

        setValid(true);
    }
}

class ButtonPanel extends UIPanel
{
    MainPanel mainPanel;

    public ButtonPanel(MainPanel mainPanel)
    {
        this.mainPanel = mainPanel;

        UIGridLayout layout = new UIGridLayout(1, 4);
        UIPushButton firstButton =
            new UIPushButton("First", UIPushButton.RAISED);
        add(firstButton);

        UIPushButton prevButton =
            new UIPushButton("Previous", UIPushButton.RAISED);
        add(prevButton);

        UIPushButton nextButton =
            new UIPushButton("Next", UIPushButton.RAISED);
        add(nextButton);

        UIPushButton lastButton =
            new UIPushButton("Last", UIPushButton.RAISED);
        add(lastButton);
    }

    public boolean action(Event event, Object arg)
    {
        mainPanel.handleCard(arg);
        return true;
    }
}
```

```
class MainPanel extends UIPanel
{
    UICardLayout cardLayout;

    public MainPanel()
    {
        cardLayout = new UICardLayout();
        setLayout(cardLayout);
        Card1 card1 = new Card1();
        add(card1);
        Card2 card2 = new Card2();
        add(card2);
        Card3 card3 = new Card3();
        add(card3);
    }

    public void handleCard(Object arg)
    {
        String label = ((UIPushButton)arg).getName();
        if (label == "First")
            cardLayout.first(this);
        else if (label == "Previous")
            cardLayout.previous(this);
        else if (label == "Next")
            cardLayout.next(this);
        else if (label == "Last")
            cardLayout.last(this);
    }
}

class Card1 extends UIPanel
{
    Card1()
    {
        UIBorderLayout layout = new UIBorderLayout();
        setLayout(layout);
        UIText text = new UIText("Card 1");
        add(text, UIBorderLayout.CENTER);
    }
}

class Card2 extends UIPanel
{
    Card2()
    {
        UIBorderLayout layout = new UIBorderLayout();
        setLayout(layout);
```

```
            UIText text = new UIText("Card 2");
            add(text);
        }
    }

    class Card3 extends UIPanel
    {
        Card3()
        {
            UIBorderLayout layout = new UIBorderLayout();
            setLayout(layout);
            UIText text = new UIText("Card 3");
            add(text);
        }
    }
}
```

When you're convinced that the applet works, experiment with the Previous button, which calls the layout manager's **previous()** method. The **previous()** method should work like the opposite of the **next()** method, showing the previous page (relative to the currently displayed page). However, you'll soon see how unpredictable this method is, sometimes displaying the wrong page and sometimes displaying no page at all.

If you want to see how the **previous()** method should work, look at the applet shown in Listing 9.16. This listing is a direct translation from the AFC version of PageCardApplet to a conventional AWT applet. The applet's display looks almost the same, except each page's label is not centered in the applet. In this applet, all the card layout methods work properly.

## Listing 9.16  Source code for the AWT version of PageCardApplet.

```
///////////////////////////////////////////////////
// PageCardApplet.java
//
// An AWT applet that demonstrates how to use
// the CardLayout layout manager to display
// and manipulate pages of components.
///////////////////////////////////////////////////

import java.applet.*;
import java.awt.*;

public class PageCardApplet extends Applet
{
    public void init()
    {
```

```
        BorderLayout layout = new BorderLayout();
        setLayout(layout);

        MainPanel mainPanel = new MainPanel();
        add(mainPanel, "Center");

        ButtonPanel buttonPanel = new ButtonPanel(mainPanel);
        add(buttonPanel, "North");
    }
}

class ButtonPanel extends Panel
{
    MainPanel mainPanel;

    public ButtonPanel(MainPanel mainPanel)
    {
        this.mainPanel = mainPanel;

        GridLayout layout = new GridLayout(1, 4);
        Button firstButton = new Button("First");
        add(firstButton);

        Button prevButton = new Button("Previous");
        add(prevButton);

        Button nextButton = new Button("Next");
        add(nextButton);

        Button lastButton = new Button("Last");
        add(lastButton);
    }

    public boolean action(Event event, Object arg)
    {
        mainPanel.handleCard(arg);
        return true;
    }
}

class MainPanel extends Panel
{
    CardLayout cardLayout;

    public MainPanel()
    {
        cardLayout = new CardLayout();
        setLayout(cardLayout);
```

```
        Card1 card1 = new Card1();
        add(card1);
        Card2 card2 = new Card2();
        add(card2);
        Card3 card3 = new Card3();
        add(card3);
    }

    public void handleCard(Object arg)
    {
        if (arg == "First")
            cardLayout.first(this);
        else if (arg == "Previous")
            cardLayout.previous(this);
        else if (arg == "Next")
            cardLayout.next(this);
        else if (arg == "Last")
            cardLayout.last(this);
    }
}

class Card1 extends Panel
{
    Card1()
    {
        BorderLayout layout = new BorderLayout();
        setLayout(layout);
        Label text = new Label("Card 1");
        add(text, "Center");
    }
}

class Card2 extends Panel
{
    Card2()
    {
        BorderLayout layout = new BorderLayout();
        setLayout(layout);
        Label text = new Label("Card 2");
        add(text, "Center");
    }
}

class Card3 extends Panel
{
    Card3()
    {
```

```
        BorderLayout layout = new BorderLayout();
        setLayout(layout);
        Label text = new Label("Card 3");
        add(text, "Center");
    }
}
```

## Creating Simple Component Grids

Previously, I mentioned that grid-bag layouts were often more unwieldy than they're worth. The truth is that you can create most grid-bag-type layouts by using other layout techniques. The simplest of these layouts is a simple grid layout, which is much like a grid-bag layout without all the constraints. Using a few panels and a **UIGridLayout**, you can produce attractive displays relatively easily.

Listing 9.17, for example, is an applet named SimpleGridApplet that organizes four groups of radio buttons into a four-by-four grid. When you run the applet in Applet Viewer, you see the window shown in Figure 9.24. This applet demonstrates a couple of handy layout techniques. First, as with many of the programs you've seen so far, SimpleGridApplet defines custom panel classes—**Panel1**, **Panel2**, **Panel3**, and **Panel4**—that contain the components that need to be displayed in the main layout. When you define custom panel classes in this way, you can give each panel any type of layout manager you like, enabling you to put together truly creative displays.

Second, notice how each of the custom panel classes defines a **getInsets()** method. This method tells AFC how much space to put between the inside edge of the panel

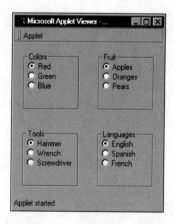

### Figure 9.24

*SimpleGridApplet running in Applet Viewer.*

and the outside edge of the radio group box. By getting the insets just right, you can easily center the group boxes inside their panels—a neat trick that can save a lot of headaches and experimentation.

## Listing 9.17   Source code for SimpleGridApplet.

```
/////////////////////////////////////////////////
// SimpleGridApplet.java
//
// An AFC applet that demonstrates how to use
// the UIGridLayout layout manager to organize
// groups of components into a simple grid.
/////////////////////////////////////////////////

import com.ms.ui.*;
import java.awt.Insets;

public class SimpleGridApplet extends AwtUIApplet
{
    public SimpleGridApplet()
    {
        super(new AppletImplementation());
    }
}

class AppletImplementation extends UIApplet
{
    public void init()
    {
        UIGridLayout layout = new UIGridLayout(2, 2);
        setLayout(layout);

        Panel1 panel1 = new Panel1();
        add(panel1);
        Panel2 panel2 = new Panel2();
        add(panel2);
        Panel3 panel3 = new Panel3();
        add(panel3);
        Panel4 panel4 = new Panel4();
        add(panel4);

        setValid(true);
    }
}

class Panel1 extends UIPanel
{
```

```java
    public Panel1()
    {
        UIBorderLayout layout = new UIBorderLayout();
        setLayout(layout);

        UIRadioGroup group = new UIRadioGroup("Colors");

        UIRadioButton button = new UIRadioButton("Red");
        button.setChecked(true);
        group.add(button);
        button = new UIRadioButton("Green");
        group.add(button);
        button = new UIRadioButton("Blue");
        group.add(button);

        add(group, "Center");
    }

    public Insets getInsets()
    {
        return new Insets(15, 15, 15, 15);
    }
}

class Panel2 extends UIPanel
{
    public Panel2()
    {
        UIBorderLayout layout = new UIBorderLayout();
        setLayout(layout);

        UIRadioGroup group = new UIRadioGroup("Fruit");

        UIRadioButton button = new UIRadioButton("Apples");
        button.setChecked(true);
        group.add(button);
        button = new UIRadioButton("Oranges");
        group.add(button);
        button = new UIRadioButton("Pears");
        group.add(button);

        add(group, "Center");
    }

    public Insets getInsets()
    {
```

```
            return new Insets(15, 15, 15, 15);
        }
}

class Panel3 extends UIPanel
{
    public Panel3()
    {
        UIBorderLayout layout = new UIBorderLayout();
        setLayout(layout);

        UIRadioGroup group = new UIRadioGroup("Tools");

        UIRadioButton button = new UIRadioButton("Hammer");
        button.setChecked(true);
        group.add(button);
        button = new UIRadioButton("Wrench");
        group.add(button);
        button = new UIRadioButton("Screwdriver");
        group.add(button);

        add(group, "Center");
    }

    public Insets getInsets()
    {
        return new Insets(15, 15, 15, 15);
    }
}

class Panel4 extends UIPanel
{
    public Panel4()
    {
        UIBorderLayout layout = new UIBorderLayout();
        setLayout(layout);

        UIRadioGroup group = new UIRadioGroup("Languages");

        UIRadioButton button = new UIRadioButton("English");
        button.setChecked(true);
        group.add(button);
        button = new UIRadioButton("Spanish");
        group.add(button);
        button = new UIRadioButton("French");
        group.add(button);
```

```
        add(group, "Center");
    }

    public Insets getInsets()
    {
        return new Insets(15, 15, 15, 15);
    }
}
```

## Creating Complex Component Grids

One of the big advantages of grid-bag layouts is their ability to create complex grids containing cells of differing sizes. While a regular grid layout can neatly organize components, each cell in the grid must be the same size. You might think that the only way to create a complex grid is to give up and struggle with grid-bag layouts. Not under AFC! AFC provides the **UISplitLayout** class, which, with a little clever manipulation and some help from panels and grid layouts, can create almost any kind of grid you can imagine.

To prove this claim, take a look at Listing 9.18, which shows the source code for an applet named ComplexGridApplet. When you run the applet under Applet Viewer, you see the window shown in Figure 9.25. Can you figure out how the layout works? In the listing, you should notice several programming techniques that are the keys to this snazzy layout:

- The layout uses nested panels, most of which incorporate split layout managers to divide a panel into two sections, either horizontally or vertically.

- A couple of the split layout managers divide their containers into different-sized cells by specifying a location for the split.

- Many of the custom panel classes define the **getInsets()** method to better arrange the child components inside the panel.

- Many of the lower-level panel classes (**Panel1**, **Panel2**, and **Panel3**) use border layouts so that their main component (a radio group) can fill the panel within the constraints supplied by the **getInsets()** method.

- The **ButtonPanel** class uses a simple grid layout to organize four buttons in a row. By calling the layout's **setHgap()** method, the layout places a little space between each button.

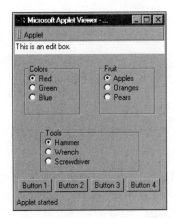

**Figure 9.25**

*ComplexGridApplet running in Applet Viewer.*

## Listing 9.18   Source code for ComplexGridApplet.

```
/////////////////////////////////////////////////
// ComplexGridApplet.java
//
// An AFC applet that demonstrates how to use
// the UISplitLayout layout manager to organize
// groups of components into a complex grid.
/////////////////////////////////////////////////

import com.ms.ui.*;
import java.awt.Insets;

public class ComplexGridApplet extends AwtUIApplet
{
    public ComplexGridApplet()
    {
        super(new AppletImplementation());
    }
}

class AppletImplementation extends UIApplet
{
    public void init()
    {
        UISplitLayout layout =
            new UISplitLayout(UISplitLayout.HORIZONTAL, 20);
        setLayout(layout);
```

```
            UIEdit edit = new UIEdit();
            edit.setValueText("This is an edit box.");
            add(edit, "nw");

            MainPanel mainPanel = new MainPanel();
            add(mainPanel, "se");

            setValid(true);
        }
}

class MainPanel extends UIPanel
{
    public MainPanel()
    {
        UISplitLayout layout =
            new UISplitLayout(UISplitLayout.HORIZONTAL);
        setLayout(layout);

        SecondLevelPanel1 panel1 = new SecondLevelPanel1();
        add(panel1, "nw");

        SecondLevelPanel2 panel2 = new SecondLevelPanel2();
        add(panel2, "se");
    }
}

class SecondLevelPanel1 extends UIPanel
{
    public SecondLevelPanel1()
    {
        UISplitLayout layout = new UISplitLayout();
        setLayout(layout);

        Panel1 panel1 = new Panel1();
        add(panel1, "nw");
        Panel2 panel2 = new Panel2();
        add(panel2, "se");
    }
}

class SecondLevelPanel2 extends UIPanel
{
    public SecondLevelPanel2()
    {
```

```
        UISplitLayout layout =
            new UISplitLayout(UISplitLayout.HORIZONTAL, 80);
        setLayout(layout);

        Panel3 panel3 = new Panel3();
        add(panel3, "nw");
        ButtonPanel panel4 = new ButtonPanel();
        add(panel4, "se");
    }

    public Insets getInsets()
    {
        return new Insets(5, 5, 5, 5);
    }
}

class Panel1 extends UIPanel
{
    public Panel1()
    {
        UIBorderLayout layout = new UIBorderLayout();
        setLayout(layout);

        UIRadioGroup group = new UIRadioGroup("Colors");

        UIRadioButton button = new UIRadioButton("Red");
        button.setChecked(true);
        group.add(button);
        button = new UIRadioButton("Green");
        group.add(button);
        button = new UIRadioButton("Blue");
        group.add(button);

        add(group, "Center");
    }

    public Insets getInsets()
    {
        return new Insets(15, 15, 15, 15);
    }
}

class Panel2 extends UIPanel
{
    public Panel2()
    {
        UIBorderLayout layout = new UIBorderLayout();
        setLayout(layout);
```

```
            UIRadioGroup group = new UIRadioGroup("Fruit");

            UIRadioButton button = new UIRadioButton("Apples");
            button.setChecked(true);
            group.add(button);
            button = new UIRadioButton("Oranges");
            group.add(button);
            button = new UIRadioButton("Pears");
            group.add(button);

            add(group, "Center");
        }

        public Insets getInsets()
        {
            return new Insets(15, 15, 15, 15);
        }
}

class Panel3 extends UIPanel
{
        public Panel3()
        {
            UIBorderLayout layout = new UIBorderLayout();
            setLayout(layout);

            UIRadioGroup group = new UIRadioGroup("Tools");

            UIRadioButton button = new UIRadioButton("Hammer");
            button.setChecked(true);
            group.add(button);
            button = new UIRadioButton("Wrench");
            group.add(button);
            button = new UIRadioButton("Screwdriver");
            group.add(button);

            add(group, "Center");
        }

        public Insets getInsets()
        {
            return new Insets(0, 35, 10, 35);
        }
}

class ButtonPanel extends UIPanel
{
```

```
public ButtonPanel()
{
    UIGridLayout layout = new UIGridLayout(1, 4);
    layout.setHgap(5);
    setLayout(layout);

    UIPushButton button =
        new UIPushButton("Button 1", UIPushButton.RAISED);
    add(button);

    button = new UIPushButton("Button 2",
        UIPushButton.RAISED);
    add(button);

    button = new UIPushButton("Button 3",
        UIPushButton.RAISED);
    add(button);

    button = new UIPushButton("Button 4",
        UIPushButton.RAISED);
    add(button);
}
}
```

# Line, Graphic, Item, And Marquee Components

*Art—the one achievement of Man which has made the long trip up from all fours seem well advised.*
*—James Thurber, Forum and Century*

# Notes...

*Chapter*

# 10

Windows and many other modern operating systems rely on graphics like Mozart relied on notes. The art of creating a graphical application—even a small-scale Java applet—requires a great deal of thought as to the layout and the graphical components that represent the user interface. Although most people consider programming to be a science, there's little question that application design is an art.

AFC helps you produce this modern form of art by providing classes from which you can build your user interface, much of which is graphical. Along with the many graphical components included with AFC, you can call upon the **UILine**, **UIGraphic**, and **UIItem** classes to spiff up everything from a lowly button to a complex component layout. As an extra bonus, the **UIMarquee** class gives you a way to take static components and move them across the screen. In this chapter, you learn to incorporate these objects into your AFC programs.

## The **UILine** Class

If you've browsed through many of Microsoft's AFC sample applications, you may have noticed that 3D lines are used to separate panels in some displays. These 3D lines are objects of the **UILine** class. You, too, can add lines such as these to your Java program just by creating **UILine** objects. As one of AFC's smaller classes, there's not a lot to say about **UILine**, except that its superclass is **UICanvas**, which means it inherits methods from **UICanvas**, **UIStateComponent**, and **UIComponent**. **UILine** also defines a few of its own methods, shown in Table 10.1.

To create a 3D line, use the **new** operator to create an object of the **UILine** class, and then add the object to the applet's or application's layout:

```
UILine 3DLine = new UILine();
add(3DLine);
```

Listing 10.1 presents a small applet that displays a **UILine** object. Figure 10.1 shows the applet running in Applet Viewer. You can see the 3D line near the top of the applet window, but you need to look closely because it tends to blend in with the menu bar.

### Listing 10.1   Source code for LineApplet.

```
/////////////////////////////////////////////////
// LineApplet.java
//
// An AFC applet that demonstrates how to create
// and display a UILine component.
/////////////////////////////////////////////////

import com.ms.ui.*;

public class LineApplet extends AwtUIApplet
{
    public LineApplet()
    {
        super(new AppletImplementation());
    }
}

class AppletImplementation extends UIApplet
{
    public void init()
    {
        UIBorderLayout layout = new UIBorderLayout(2, 2);
        setLayout(layout);

        UILine line = new UILine();
        add(line, "Center");

        setValid(true);
    }
}
```

**Table 10.1    Methods of the UILine class.**

| Method | Description |
|---|---|
| getMinimumSize() | Gets the line's the minimum size |
| getPreferredSize() | Gets the line's the preferred size |
| getRoleCode() | Gets the line's **ROLE_SYSTEM** code, which is **ROLE_SYSTEM_TOOLBAR** |
| paint() | Draws the line |

**Figure 10.1**

*LineApplet, running in Applet Viewer.*

## The **UIStatic** Class

Almost all programs use some form of static object, whether it's a line of text used as a label, an icon for a button, or any other type of graphical object that is meant as a visual element, not to be edited by the user. Java's AWT features classes for text labels and images. AFC includes a few of its own unique static objects that display graphics, text, and graphics and text together. These static objects, which all extend AFC's **UIStatic** class, are **UIGraphic**, **UIText**, and **UIItem**.

The **UIStatic** class extends **UICanvas** and so, like **UILine**, inherits methods from **UICanvas**, **UIStateComponent**, and **UIComponent**. **UIStatic** also defines a few methods of its own, which are shown in Table 10.2.

**Table 10.2  Methods of the UIStatic class.**

| Method | Description |
|---|---|
| calcString() | Gets the dimensions of a text string |
| drawString() | Draws a text string |
| getContentBounds() | Gets the bounding rectangle of the control's contents |
| isKeyable() | Returns true if the control can accept keyboard input |
| paint() | Draws the control |
| setFlags() | Sets the control's alignment and style |
| setHot() | Sets the control's hot-tracked state |

Because **UIStatic** is an abstract class, you cannot create **UIStatic** objects. Instead, you must create objects of classes that extend **UIStatic**. In previous chapters, you had experience with one of these classes, **UIText**, which represents simply a line of text, much like AWT's **Label** class. In this chapter, you also will examine the **UIGraphic** and **UIItem** classes.

## The **UIGraphic** Class

When you need to display an image, you can call upon the **UIGraphic** class. In fact, under AFC you can use the **UIGraphic** class to add images to buttons, menus, and other kinds of components, as well as to display graphics in an applet or application's main display area. **UIGraphic** extends **UIStatic** and so inherits methods from **UIStatic**, **UICanvas**, **UIStateComponent**, and **UIComponent**. **UIGraphic** also defines a set of it own methods, which you can see in Table 10.3.

To create a **UIGraphic** object, you must first have loaded an image, which you do just as you would in a typical Java applet:

```
Image image = getImage(getCodeBase(), "image.gif");
```

After you load the image, you can create the **UIGraphic** object by calling the class's constructor through the **new** operator, like this:

```
UIGraphic graphic = new UIGraphic(image);
```

## Table 10.3  Methods of the **UIGraphic** class.

| Method | Description |
|---|---|
| getImage() | Gets the image associated with the control |
| getPreferredSize() | Gets the control's preferred size |
| getRoleCode() | Retrieves the **ROLE_SYSTEM** code, which is **ROLE_SYSTEM_GRAPHIC** |
| imageUpdate() | Draws the control as the image is loaded |
| paint() | Draws the image |
| setImage() | Sets the image associated with the control |

You can then use the **UIGraphic** object as needed in your program.

The **UIGraphic** class overloads its constructor, giving you three ways to create a **UIGraphic** object. You already saw one version of the constructor. The second version enables you to create the object without an image, calling the **setImage()** method to set the control's image, like this:

```
Image image = getImage(getCodeBase(), "image.gif");
UIGraphic graphic = new UIGraphic();
graphic.setImage(image);
```

Finally, you can create a **UIGraphic** object by supplying both an image and a style flag to the constructor, as in the following:

```
Image image = getImage(getCodeBase(), "image.gif");
UIGraphic graphic = new UIGraphic(image, UIStatic.CENTERED);
```

The **UIStatic** class defines the style flags that you can use. You will learn about these flags in this chapter's Practical Guide. For now, Listing 10.2 presents a small applet that creates a **UIGraphic** object from an image and displays the object in the applet's window. Figure 10.2 shows the applet running in Applet Viewer.

### Listing 10.2  Source code for GraphicApplet.

```
/////////////////////////////////////////////////
// GraphicApplet.java
//
// An AFC applet that demonstrates how to create
```

```
// and display UIGraphic objects.
/////////////////////////////////////////////////

import com.ms.ui.*;
import java.awt.*;

public class GraphicApplet extends AwtUIApplet
{
    public GraphicApplet()
    {
        super(new AppletImplementation());
    }
}

class AppletImplementation extends UIApplet
{
    public void init()
    {
        UIBorderLayout layout = new UIBorderLayout();
        setLayout(layout);

        Image image1 = getImage(getCodeBase(), "image1.gif");
        UIGraphic graphic = new UIGraphic(image1);
        add(graphic, "Center");

        setValid(true);
    }
}
```

**Figure 10.2**

*GraphicApplet, running in Applet Viewer.*

# The **UIItem** Class

The **UIItem** class gives you a way to attach a text string to a graphic. This kind of visual element appears often in modern operating systems and applications. An example is the icons and text that represent files in Windows Explorer, as shown in Figure 10.3. AFC's **UIItem** class enables you to create graphics/text components that can be placed almost anywhere any other components can appear, including within buttons, menus, and panels. **UIGraphic** extends **UIStatic** and so inherits methods from **UIStatic**, **UICanvas**, **UIStateComponent**, and **UIComponent**. It also defines a set of it own methods, which you can see in Table 10.4.

To create a **UIItem** object, you must first have loaded an image, which you do just as you do in a typical Java applet, as follows:

```
Image image = getImage(getCodeBase(), "image.gif");
```

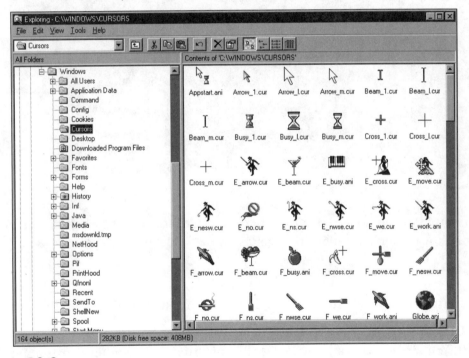

## Figure 10.3

*The Windows operating system often uses combinations of graphics and text to represent objects on the screen.*

## Table 10.4 Methods of the **UIItem** class.

| Method | Description |
|---|---|
| getGap() | Gets the size of the space between the item's image and text |
| getImage() | Gets the image associated with the control |
| getImagePos() | Gets the relative position of the control's image |
| getPreferredSize() | Gets the control's the preferred size |
| getRoleCode() | Gets the **ROLE_SYSTEM** code, which is **ROLE_SYSTEM_GRAPHIC** code |
| imageUpdate() | Draws the control's image as it's loaded |
| paint() | Draws the control's image and text |
| setFocused() | Sets the control's focus state |
| setGap() | Sets the size of the space between the item's image and text |
| setHot() | Sets the control's hot-tracked state |
| setImage() | Sets the image associated with the control |
| setImagePos() | Sets the relative position of the control's image |
| setName() | Sets the control's text |
| setSelected() | Sets the control's selected state |

After you load the image, you can create the **UIItem** object by calling the class's constructor through the **new** operator, as in the following example:

```
UIItem item = new UIItem(image, "Item Text");
```

The constructor's two arguments are the image and text to display in the control.

The **UIItem** class overloads its constructor, giving you four ways to create a **UIItem** object. You already saw one version of the constructor. The other constructors' signatures look the following examples:

```
public UIItem();
public UIItem(Image image, String text, int style);
public UIItem(Image image, String text, int style, int imagePos);
```

The arguments used in the preceding signatures are described as follows:

- *image*—The image to display

- *text*—The text to display

- *style*—One or more of the style flags defined by **UIStatic**

- *imagePos*—The relative position of the image; can be **ONLEFT**, **ABOVE**, or **FIRSTLINE**

If you use the constructor that specifies no arguments, you must call the **UIItem** object's **setImage()** and **setName()** methods to give the control its image and text, as in the following:

```
Image image = getImage(getCodeBase(), "image.gif");
UIItem item = new UIItem();
item.setImage(image);
item.setName("Item Text");
```

The **UIStatic** class defines the flags that you can use for the **style** argument. You'll learn about these flags in this chapter's Practical Guide.

Listing 10.3 presents a small applet that creates a **UIItem** object from an image and displays the object in the applet's window. Figure 10.4 shows the applet running in Applet Viewer.

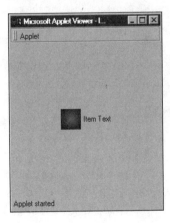

**Figure 10.4**

*ItemApplet, running in Applet Viewer.*

**Listing 10.3  Source code for ItemApplet.**

```
///////////////////////////////////////////////////
// ItemApplet.java
//
// An AFC applet that demonstrates how to create
// and display UIItem objects.
///////////////////////////////////////////////////

import com.ms.ui.*;
import java.awt.*;

public class ItemApplet extends AwtUIApplet
{
    public ItemApplet()
    {
        super(new AppletImplementation());
    }
}

class AppletImplementation extends UIApplet
{
    public void init()
    {
        UIBorderLayout layout = new UIBorderLayout();
        setLayout(layout);

        Image image = getImage(getCodeBase(), "sunburst.gif");
        UIItem item = new UIItem(image, "Item Text");
        add(item, "Center");

        setValid(true);
    }
}
```

# The **UIMarquee** Class

The **UIMarquee** class doesn't represent a visible control like the other classes explored in this chapter. Nevertheless, it adds graphical pizzazz to your AFC applets and applications by scrolling components within a display. **UIMarquee** extends the **UIViewer** class, which you can examine in Chapter 11. By extending the **UIViewer** class, **UIMarquee** inherits methods from **UIViewer**, **UIPanel**, **UIStateContainer**, **UIContainer**, and **UIComponent**. **UIMarquee** also defines methods of its own, as listed in Table 10.5.

Table 10.5   Methods of the **UIMarquee** class.

| Method | Description |
|--------|-------------|
| addNotify() | Performs control initialization |
| ensureVisible() | Ensures that a specified area is visible |
| getRoleCode() | Gets the **ROLE_SYSTEM** code, which is **ROLE_SYSTEM_ANIMATION** |
| getStateCode() | Gets the control's state |
| setContent() | Sets the control's content |
| timeTriggered() | Scrolls the marquee's content |

Getting components to scroll in an AFC applet is a snap with **UIMarquee**. Just create the **UIMarquee** object and add it to the layout, as in the following:

```
UIMarquee marquee = new UIMarquee(comp);
add(marquee);
```

The constructor's single argument is the component to scroll.

The **UIMarquee** class overloads its constructor, giving you four ways to create a **UIMarquee** object. You already saw one version of the constructor. The other constructors' signatures look like the following:

```
public UIMarquee();
public UIMarquee(IUIComponent comp, int rate);
public UIMarquee(IUIComponent comp, int rate, int dx, int dy);
```

The arguments used in the preceding signatures are described as follows:

- *comp*—The component to scroll
- *rate*—The scrolling rate in milliseconds
- *dx*—Horizontal scroll amount
- *dy*—Vertical scroll amount

If you use the constructor that specifies no arguments, you must call the **UIMarquee** object's **setContent()** to give the control its child component, as follows:

```
UIMarquee marquee = new UIMarquee();
marquee.setContent(comp);
```

Listing 10.4 presents a small applet that creates a **UIMarquee** object with an image and displays the object in the applet's window. Figure 10.5 shows the applet running in Applet Viewer (though, of course, you can't see the scrolling action in the figure).

### Listing 10.4   Source code for MarqueeApplet.

```
///////////////////////////////////////////////////
// MarqueeApplet.java
//
// An AFC applet that demonstrates how to create
// and display UIMarquee objects.
///////////////////////////////////////////////////

import com.ms.ui.*;
import java.awt.*;

public class MarqueeApplet extends AwtUIApplet
{
    public MarqueeApplet()
    {
        super(new AppletImplementation());
    }
}

class AppletImplementation extends UIApplet
{
    public void init()
    {
        UIBorderLayout layout = new UIBorderLayout();
        setLayout(layout);

        Image image = getImage(getCodeBase(), "image1.gif");
        UIGraphic graphic = new UIGraphic(image);
        UIMarquee marquee = new UIMarquee(graphic);
        add(marquee, "Center");

        setValid(true);
    }
}
```

**Figure 10.5**

*MarqueeApplet, running in Applet Viewer.*

# Practical Guide To

# Line, Graphic, Item, And Marquee Components

- Using A 3D Line As A Panel Separator
- Aligning A Graphic Object
- Changing Graphic Content On The Fly
- Setting An Item's Relative Alignment
- Setting A Marquee's Scrolling Speed
- Creating A Changing Marquee Message
- Changing A Marquee's Scroll Direction

# Using A 3D Line As A Panel Separator

For the most part, **UILine** is useful to AFC as an internal class used by other component classes to create their displays. About the only use for **UILine** is to…well…draw a line. If you need to draw a 3D separator in one of your layouts, you may want to call upon **UILine**'s meager services. You may want to draw a 3D line, for example, between two panels containing other components. Listing 10.5 presents one way you can accomplish this task.

### Listing 10.5  Source code for LineDividerApplet.

```
/////////////////////////////////////////////////
// LineDividerApplet.java
//
// An AFC applet that demonstrates how to use
// a UILine component as a layout divider.
/////////////////////////////////////////////////

import com.ms.ui.*;
import java.awt.Insets;

public class LineDividerApplet extends AwtUIApplet
{
    public LineDividerApplet()
    {
        super(new AppletImplementation());
    }
}

class AppletImplementation extends UIApplet
{
    public void init()
    {
        UIGridLayout layout = new UIGridLayout(3, 1);
        setLayout(layout);

        Panel1 panel1 = new Panel1();
        add(panel1);
        Panel2 panel2 = new Panel2();
        add(panel2);
        Panel3 panel3 = new Panel3();
        add(panel3);

        setValid(true);
    }
}
```

```
class Panel1 extends UIPanel
{
    public Panel1()
    {
        UIBorderLayout layout = new UIBorderLayout();
        setLayout(layout);

        UIText text = new UIText("This is the top panel");
        add(text, "Center");
    }
}

class Panel2 extends UIPanel
{
    public Panel2()
    {
        UIBorderLayout layout = new UIBorderLayout();
        setLayout(layout);

        UILine line = new UILine();
        add(line, "Center");
    }

    public Insets getInsets()
    {
        return new Insets(35, 0, 0, 0);
    }
}

class Panel3 extends UIPanel
{
    public Panel3()
    {
        UIBorderLayout layout = new UIBorderLayout();
        setLayout(layout);

        UIText text = new UIText("This is the bottom panel");
        add(text, "Center");
    }
}
```

Figure 10.6 shows the applet running in Applet Viewer. Notice how the 3D line acts as a border between the upper and lower panels. As you can see from the listing, the applet uses a grid layout with one column of three cells. The program positions a panel object in the upper and lower panels, and then places the **UILine** component in the center panel. Getting the line's vertical position just right is a little tricky,

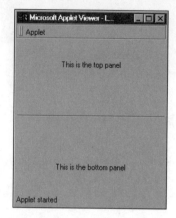

**Figure 10.6**

*LineDividerApplet, running in Applet Viewer.*

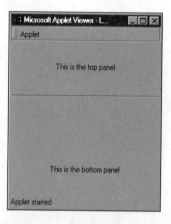

**Figure 10.7**

*LineDividerApplet, without specifying the center panel's insets.*

requiring that the panel define a **getInsets()** method that forces the line down from the top of the panel. Figure 10.7 shows what the applet looks like without specifying the panel's insets. As you can see here, the line component gets positioned at the top rather than in the middle of the panel.

## Aligning A Graphic Object

Often, when you create and display a **UIGraphic** object, the default center alignment works just fine. However, you have a great deal of control over where the graphic appears in its container. If the default doesn't work for you, you can call the class's **setFlags()** method to specify a new position. The **UIStatic** class defines the position flags you can use, which are **LEFT**, **RIGHT**, **TOP**, **BOTTOM**, **TOPLEFT**, **TOPRIGHT**, **BOTTOMLEFT**, **BOTTOMRIGHT**, **HCENTER**, **VCENTER**, and **CENTERED**.

You can tell what a flag does by its name. However, to see the position styles in action, run the applet presented in Listing 10.6.

### Listing 10.6   Source code for GraphicAlignApplet.

```
/////////////////////////////////////////////////
// GraphicAlignApplet.java
//
// An AFC applet that demonstrates how to create
// and display UIGraphic objects with different
// alignments.
/////////////////////////////////////////////////

import com.ms.ui.*;
import com.ms.ui.event.*;
import java.awt.*;

public class GraphicAlignApplet extends AwtUIApplet
{
    public GraphicAlignApplet()
    {
        super(new AppletImplementation());
    }
}

class AppletImplementation extends UIApplet
    implements IUIActionListener
{
    int flagNum;
    UIGraphic graphic;

    public void init()
    {
        UIBorderLayout layout = new UIBorderLayout();
        setLayout(layout);

        UIPushButton button = new UIPushButton("Change Position",
            UIPushButton.RAISED);
        button.addActionListener(this);
        add(button, "North");

        Image image1 = getImage(getCodeBase(), "image1.gif");
        graphic = new UIGraphic(image1, UIStatic.CENTERED);
```

```
        add(graphic, "Center");

        flagNum = 0;
        setValid(true);
    }

    public void actionPerformed(UIActionEvent event)
    {
        int flags = 0;

        ++flagNum;
        if (flagNum == 9)
            flagNum = 0;

        switch(flagNum)
        {
            case 0:
                flags = UIStatic.CENTERED;
                break;
            case 1:
                flags = UIStatic.TOPLEFT;
                break;
            case 2:
                flags = UIStatic.TOP | UIStatic.HCENTER;
                break;
            case 3:
                flags = UIStatic.TOPRIGHT;
                break;
            case 4:
                flags = UIStatic.RIGHT | UIStatic.VCENTER;
                break;
            case 5:
                flags = UIStatic.BOTTOMRIGHT;
                break;
            case 6:
                flags = UIStatic.BOTTOM | UIStatic.HCENTER;
                break;
            case 7:
                flags = UIStatic.BOTTOMLEFT;
                break;
            case 8:
                flags = UIStatic.LEFT | UIStatic.VCENTER;
                break;
        }

        graphic.setFlags(flags);
    }
}
```

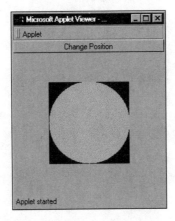

**Figure 10.8**

*GraphicAlignApplet, running in Applet Viewer.*

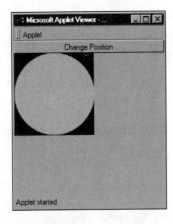

**Figure 10.9**

*GraphicAlignApplet with **TOPLEFT** alignment.*

When you run the applet in Applet Viewer, you see the window shown in Figure 10.8. By clicking the Change Position button, you can move the graphic around the window. Figure 10.9, for example, shows the applet in its **TOPLEFT** position.

 ## Changing Graphic Content On The Fly

You may recall that you can create a **UIGraphic** object without specifying an image. When you do, you must call the **UIGraphic** object's **setImage()** method to give the

**Figure 10.10**

*GraphicChangeApplet, running in Applet Viewer.*

object its image. Actually, you can call **setImage()** at any time in your program, after which the graphic will update itself with the newly set image. In this way, you can make the image respond to user interaction.

Listing 10.7 presents a small applet that demonstrates one way you can change a graphical image in response to user input.

When you run the applet in Applet Viewer, you see the window shown in Figure 10.10. When you click the Change Graphic button, a new image appears in the window. In all, the applet will cycle through three different images. The applet loads all three images in its **init()** method, so that they're all ready to go when the user clicks the button.

**Listing 10.7   Source code for GraphicChangeApplet.**

```
/////////////////////////////////////////////////
// GraphicChangeApplet.java
//
// An AFC applet that demonstrates changing
// a UIGraphic object's image on the fly.
/////////////////////////////////////////////////

import com.ms.ui.*;
import com.ms.ui.event.*;
import java.awt.*;

public class GraphicChangeApplet extends AwtUIApplet
{
```

```
    public GraphicChangeApplet()
    {
        super(new AppletImplementation());
    }
}

class AppletImplementation extends UIApplet
    implements IUIActionListener
{
    Image image1;
    Image image2;
    Image image3;
    UIGraphic graphic;
    int imageNum;

    public void init()
    {
        UIBorderLayout layout = new UIBorderLayout();
        setLayout(layout);

        image1 = getImage(getCodeBase(), "image1.gif");
        image2 = getImage(getCodeBase(), "image2.gif");
        image3 = getImage(getCodeBase(), "image3.gif");
        graphic = new UIGraphic(image1);
        add(graphic, "Center");

        UIPushButton button = new UIPushButton("Change Graphic",
            UIPushButton.RAISED);
        button.addActionListener(this);
        add(button, "North");

        imageNum = 0;
        setValid(true);
    }

    public void actionPerformed(UIActionEvent event)
    {
        ++imageNum;
        if (imageNum == 3)
            imageNum = 0;

        switch(imageNum)
        {
            case 0:
                graphic.setImage(image1);
                break;
```

```
        case 1:
            graphic.setImage(image2);
            break;
        case 2:
            graphic.setImage(image3);
            break;
        }
    }
}
```

## Setting An Item's Relative Alignment

Previously, you saw how to set the alignment of a graphic object within its container. You can also use this kind of alignment with a **UIItem** object. However, **UIItem** objects also enable you to align the item's image relative to the text. You do this alignment by calling the **UIItem** object's **setImagePos()** method. You can set the relative alignment so that the image is to the left of the text, above the text, or on the "first line," which means that the applet positions the image and test on the same baseline.

Listing 10.8 presents an applet that demonstrates the different relative alignments.

When you run the applet under Applet Viewer, you see the window shown in Figure 10.11. As it first appears, the **UIItem**'s relative alignment is set to **LEFT**. Click the Change Position button to cycle the **UIItem** object through its three relative image alignments. Figure 10.12, for example, shows the alignment set to **ABOVE**, whereas Figure 10.13 shows the **FIRSTLINE** alignment.

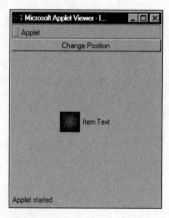

**Figure 10.11**

*ItemAlignApplet, running in Applet Viewer.*

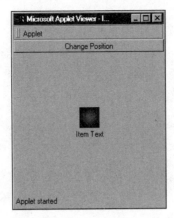

**Figure 10.12**

*ItemAlignApplet, set to **ABOVE** alignment.*

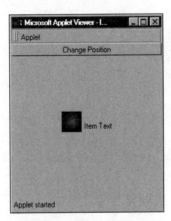

**Figure 10.13**

*ItemAlignApplet, set to **FIRSTLINE** alignment.*

## Listing 10.8 Source code for ItemAlignApplet.

```
/////////////////////////////////////////////////
// ItemAlignApplet.java
//
// An AFC applet that demonstrates how to create
// and display UIItem objects with different
// alignments.
/////////////////////////////////////////////////

import com.ms.ui.*;
import com.ms.ui.event.*;
import java.awt.*;
```

```java
public class ItemAlignApplet extends AwtUIApplet
{
    public ItemAlignApplet()
    {
        super(new AppletImplementation());
    }
}

class AppletImplementation extends UIApplet
    implements IUIActionListener
{
    int flagNum;
    UIItem item;

    public void init()
    {
        UIBorderLayout layout = new UIBorderLayout();
        setLayout(layout);

        UIPushButton button = new UIPushButton("Change Position",
            UIPushButton.RAISED);
        button.addActionListener(this);
        add(button, "North");

        Image image = getImage(getCodeBase(), "sunburst.gif");
        item = new UIItem(image, "Item Text", UIStatic.CENTERED);
        add(item, "Center");

        flagNum = 0;
        setValid(true);
    }

    public void actionPerformed(UIActionEvent event)
    {
        int flags = 0;

        ++flagNum;
        if (flagNum == 3)
            flagNum = 0;

        switch(flagNum)
        {
            case 0:
                flags = UIItem.ONLEFT;
                break;
```

```
            case 1:
                flags = UIItem.ABOVE;
                break;
            case 2:
                flags = UIItem.FIRSTLINE;
                break;
        }

        item.setImagePos(flags);
    }
}
```

## Setting A Marquee's Scrolling Speed

If you create a **UIMarquee** object without specifying a scrolling speed, you get a default speed of 75 milliseconds. Often, the default speed works fine. However, you may have times when you need to change the scrolling speed to suit some special purpose. You can accomplish this task easily by specifying a scrolling speed when you create the **UIMarquee** object. In fact, because each marquee object has its own scrolling speed, you can have different marquees running concurrently but with different speeds.

Listing 10.9 presents an applet that demonstrates this AFC technique. When you run the applet in Applet Viewer, you see a window with four different marquee objects (a line of text and three images), scrolling at different speeds. (Hmmm. Makes me want to write a horse-race applet.) Figure 10.14 shows the running applet.

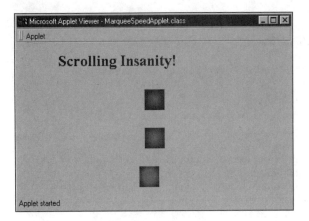

**Figure 10.14**

*MarqueeSpeedApplet, running in Applet Viewer.*

Notice in the **init()** method how the applet creates the four marquee objects by specifying four different speeds. Just adding the four marquee objects to the applet's grid layout is all that's needed to get them going. That's a great deal of animation that's practically free!

### Listing 10.9   Source code for MarqueeSpeedApplet.

```
/////////////////////////////////////////////////
// MarqueeSpeedApplet.java
//
// An AFC applet that demonstrates several
// UIMarquee objects, all scrolling at different
// speeds.
/////////////////////////////////////////////////

import com.ms.ui.*;
import com.ms.fx.FxFont;
import java.awt.*;

public class MarqueeSpeedApplet extends AwtUIApplet
{
    public MarqueeSpeedApplet()
    {
        super(new AppletImplementation());
    }
}

class AppletImplementation extends UIApplet
{
    public void init()
    {
        UIGridLayout layout = new UIGridLayout(4, 1);
        setLayout(layout);

        UIText text = new UIText("Scrolling Insanity!");
        FxFont font = new FxFont("TimesRoman", FxFont.BOLD, 24);
        text.setFont(font);
        UIMarquee marquee1 = new UIMarquee(text, 75);
        add(marquee1);

        Image image1 = getImage(getCodeBase(), "sunburst1.gif");
        UIGraphic graphic1 = new UIGraphic(image1);
        UIMarquee marquee2 = new UIMarquee(graphic1, 100);
        add(marquee2);
```

```
        Image image2 = getImage(getCodeBase(), "sunburst2.gif");
        UIGraphic graphic2 = new UIGraphic(image2);
        UIMarquee marquee3 = new UIMarquee(graphic2, 150);
        add(marquee3);

        Image image3 = getImage(getCodeBase(), "sunburst3.gif");
        UIGraphic graphic3 = new UIGraphic(image3);
        UIMarquee marquee4 = new UIMarquee(graphic3, 200);
        add(marquee4);

        setValid(true);
    }
}
```

## Creating A Changing Marquee Message

Scrolling messages can be pretty snazzy. However, you can improve on the scroll-ing-message idea by changing the message as it scrolls. Using this technique, whenever a message scrolls off the screen, a new message appears from the other side. You can change the message's content as often as you want to create messages of any length.

To pull off this handy trick, you have to create a timer thread to control when the marquee's message content should change. Listing 10.10 presents an applet that demonstrates one way you can get a timer going. This applet uses a few classes defined in Microsoft's **com.ms.util** package, which comes with the Microsoft SDK for Java. To start a timer, you create an object of the **Timer** class, specifying the compo-nent to receive the timer messages, the length of time in milliseconds between timer messages, and a flag specifying whether the timer should trigger either one event or continuous events.

To receive the timer events, the applet implements the **TimerListener** interface, which declares the **timeTriggered()** method. By adding the **timeTriggered()** method to the applet, the applet receives the timer messages. With Listing 10.10, the program receives timer events every five seconds. In the **timeTriggered()** method, the program calls the marquee object's **setContent()** method to change to the next message.

When you run the applet in Applet Viewer, you see the window shown in Figure 10.15. Figure 10.16 shows the applet after the message has changed the first time.

**Figure 10.15**

*MarqueeChangeApplet, running in Applet Viewer.*

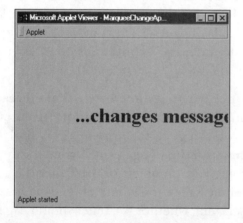

**Figure 10.16**

*MarqueeChangeApplet, showing its second message.*

**Listing 10.10   Source code for MarqueeChangeApplet.**

```
/////////////////////////////////////////////////
// MarqueeChangeApplet.java
//
// An AFC applet that demonstrates how to create
// and display UIMarquee objects with changing
// text.
/////////////////////////////////////////////////

import com.ms.fx.FxFont;
import com.ms.ui.*;
```

```
import com.ms.util.Timer;
import com.ms.util.TimerEvent;
import com.ms.util.TimerListener;

public class MarqueeChangeApplet extends AwtUIApplet
{
    public MarqueeChangeApplet()
    {
        super(new AppletImplementation());
    }
}

class AppletImplementation extends UIApplet
    implements TimerListener
{
    UIText text1;
    UIText text2;
    UIText text3;
    UIMarquee marquee;
    int msgNum;

    public void init()
    {
        UIBorderLayout layout = new UIBorderLayout();
        setLayout(layout);

        text1 = new UIText("This scrolling text...");
        text2 = new UIText("...changes messages...");
        text3 = new UIText("...every five seconds.");
        FxFont font = new FxFont("TimesRoman", FxFont.BOLD, 32);
        text1.setFont(font);
        text2.setFont(font);
        text3.setFont(font);
        marquee = new UIMarquee(text1);
        add(marquee, "Center");

        Timer timer = new Timer(this, 5000, true);
        timer.start();

        msgNum = 0;

        setValid(true);
    }

    public void timeTriggered(TimerEvent te)
    {
```

```
        ++msgNum;
        if (msgNum == 3)
            msgNum = 0;

        if (msgNum == 0)
            marquee.setContent(text1);
        else if (msgNum == 1)
            marquee.setContent(text2);
        else
            marquee.setContent(text3);
    }
}
```

## Changing A Marquee's Scroll Direction

All the marquee objects you've seen so far in this chapter have scrolled horizontally from right to left. Most people expect to see a text message scroll in this direction because it suits the way we read. However, if you use marquee objects frequently, you may find yourself wishing that you could change the direction the marquee component scrolls. Unfortunately, if you examine the **UIMarquee** class, you see that it has no method for setting the scroll direction. Still you can easily set the scroll direction at the time you create the marquee object, by providing horizontal and vertical scroll increments as arguments to the class's constructor.

For example, Listing 10.11 presents the source code for an applet that creates and displays three marquee objects. One of the marquee objects scrolls vertically, one scrolls from left to right, and one scrolls diagonally. Although running the code will better demonstrate the action, Figure 10.17 shows the applet running in Applet Viewer.

To see how to set the scrolling directions, look at the applet's **init()** method where the program creates the marquee objects. The program creates the first marquee object by specifying 0 (zero) for the horizontal scroll increment and 10 for the vertical. These settings cause the text to scroll vertically. The second marquee object has a horizontal increment of -10 and a vertical increment of 0 (zero). This setting causes the text to scroll horizontally from left to right rather than from right to left. Finally, the third marquee component has a horizontal increment of 10 and a vertical increment of 10. Scrolling in both directions causes the text to scroll diagonally.

Note that both the speed in milliseconds and the scroll increments determine the scrolling speed. For example, a marquee set to 75 milliseconds and a horizontal scroll increment of 10 scrolls faster than a marquee set to 75 milliseconds with a

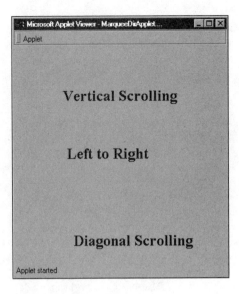

**Figure 10.17**

*MarqueeDirApplet, running in Applet Viewer.*

horizontal scroll increment of 5. Collectively, the higher the millisecond setting, the slower the scroll, whereas the higher the increment setting (horizontal or vertical), the faster the scroll.

**Listing 10.11   Source code for MarqueeDirApplet.**

```
//////////////////////////////////////////////////
// MarqueeDirApplet.java
//
// An AFC applet that demonstrates how to specify
// a scrolling direction for UIMarquee objects.
//////////////////////////////////////////////////

import com.ms.ui.*;
import com.ms.fx.FxFont;
import java.awt.*;

public class MarqueeDirApplet extends AwtUIApplet
{
    public MarqueeDirApplet()
    {
        super(new AppletImplementation());
    }
}
```

```
class AppletImplementation extends UIApplet
{
    public void init()
    {
        UIGridLayout layout = new UIGridLayout(3, 1);
        setLayout(layout);

        UIText text1 = new UIText("Vertical Scrolling");
        FxFont font = new FxFont("TimesRoman", FxFont.BOLD, 24);
        text1.setFont(font);
        UIMarquee marquee1 = new UIMarquee(text1, 75, 0, 10);
        add(marquee1);

        UIText text2 = new UIText("Left to Right");
        text2.setFont(font);
        UIMarquee marquee2 = new UIMarquee(text2, 75, -10, 0);
        add(marquee2);

        UIText text3 = new UIText("Diagonal Scrolling");
        text3.setFont(font);
        UIMarquee marquee3 = new UIMarquee(text3, 75, 10, 10);
        add(marquee3);

        setValid(true);
    }
}
```

# Chapter 11

# Viewer Components

*There are many paths to the top of the mountain, but the view is always the same.*
—*Chinese proverb*

# Notes…

*Chapter*

# 11

You can display data in a program in as many ways as there are types of data to display—probably even more. Still, most kinds of information look best when organized in some special way. For example, a list of objects and the objects' attributes may look best in a table, yet a large image may best be displayed in a small container with scroll bars. Everything depends on how the user must interpret and manipulate the data to be displayed.

To help you display your data, AFC features a set of viewer classes that can do anything from simply display a component on the screen to animate the component or organize a set of components into columns with headings. These handy viewer classes are **UIViewer**, **UIScrollViewer**, **UISplitViewer**, **UIColumnViewer**, and **UITabViewer**. In this chapter, you examine the classes and also learn how to use them in your own AFC projects.

## The **UIViewer** Class

Because applets and applications often need special ways to display data, AFC offers a set of view classes; the most basic is **UIViewer**. You may remember from the Chapter 10 that **UIViewer** is the superclass for **UIMarquee**. In its basic form, a **UIViewer** object enables you to display a component anywhere within a container's display area. The class includes member functions that move the component, as well as implements the **TimerListener** interface so that the class can manage timer events.

435

The **UIViewer** class, like most other viewer classes, extends **UIPanel**, and so can count **UIStateContainer**, **UIContainer**, and **UIComponent** as its ancestors. **UIViewer**, of course, inherits methods from all its superclasses, but it also defines a large set of its own methods, as shown in Table 11.1.

**Table 11.1   Methods of the UIViewer class.**

| Method | Description |
| --- | --- |
| ensureVisible() | Ensures a given area is visible |
| getContent() | Gets the viewer's content component |
| getPosition() | Gets the control's scroll position |
| getRoleCode() | Gets this control's **ROLE_SYSTEM** code, which is **ROLE_SYSTEM_PANE** |
| getXPosition() | Gets the control's horizontal scroll position |
| getYPosition() | Gets the control's vertical scroll position |
| isKeyable() | Returns **true** if the viewer can receive keyboard input |
| isOverlapping() | Returns **true** if the layout manager overlaps child components |
| layout() | Lays out viewer's content |
| mouseDown() | Handles a mouse-down event |
| mouseDrag() | Handles a mouse-drag event |
| mouseUp() | Handles a mouse-up event |
| requestFocus() | Requests the focus for viewer's component |
| setContent() | Sets the viewer's content component |
| setPosition() | Sets the viewer control's scroll position |
| setXPosition() | Sets the viewer control's horizontal scroll position |
| setYPosition() | Sets the viewer control's vertical scroll position |
| timeTriggered() | Handles timer events |

There isn't much to creating and displaying a **UIViewer** object. First, create the component that the viewer will hold, and then use the **new** operator to create the **UIViewer** object, as in the following:

```
UIText text = new UIText("Text In A Viewer");
UIViewer viewer = new UIViewer(text);
```

You then add the viewer to your program's layout, just as you add any other component. If you want, you can call the **UIViewer** object's **setPosition()** method to specify where the viewer's child component will appear within its container:

```
viewer.setPosition(xPos, xPos);
```

Here, **xPos** and **yPos** are the child component's X and Y coordinates.

A second **UIViewer** constructor adds the starting positions as arguments, like the following:

```
UIViewer viewer = new UIViewer(text, xPos, yPos);
```

Listing 11.1 presents a short applet that demonstrates a simple **UIViewer** component. Figure 11.1 shows the applet running in Applet Viewer. Notice how the applet positions the text line as specified by the call to **setPosition()**. Without the call to **setPosition()**, the text string would appear in the center of the viewer.

**Figure 11.1**

*ViewerApplet, running in Applet Viewer.*

**Listing 11.1  Source code for ViewerApplet.**

```
///////////////////////////////////////////////////
// ViewerApplet.java
//
// An AFC applet that demonstrates how to create
// and display a viewer component.
///////////////////////////////////////////////////

import com.ms.ui.*;

public class ViewerApplet extends AwtUIApplet
{
    public ViewerApplet()
    {
        super(new AppletImplementation());
    }
}

class AppletImplementation extends UIApplet
{
    public void init()
    {
        UIBorderLayout layout = new UIBorderLayout();
        setLayout(layout);

        UIText text = new UIText("Text In A Viewer");
        UIViewer viewer = new UIViewer(text);
        viewer.setPosition(50, 50);
        add(viewer, "Center");

        setValid(true);
    }
}
```

# The **UIScrollViewer** Class

Although the **UIViewer** class provides a display area that can display a child component at any location, the **UIScrollViewer** class enables you to display large objects or sets of data that require scroll bars. For example, you can create an applet that can display complete images up to 100 by 100 pixels, but you can also display larger images by adding scroll bars that enable users to see the parts of the image that fall outside the display area.

Rather than calling methods to position the child component in the viewer—as you do with **UIViewer**—with **UIScrollViewer** you instead call **setPosition()** to set the viewer's scroll position, which determines what part of the child component is visible inside the viewer. More often, however, you will let the **UIScrollViewer** class set the scroll bars, and then let the user position the scroll bars as needed.

The **UIScrollViewer** class extends **UIPanel**, and so counts **UIStateContainer**, **UIContainer**, and **UIComponent** among its ancestors. **UIScrollViewer** inherits methods from all its superclasses, but it also defines a large set of its own methods, as shown in Table 11.2.

**Table 11.2  Methods of the UIScrollViewer class.**

| Method | Description |
| --- | --- |
| add() | Adds a component to the viewer |
| addNotify() | Calls **addNotify()** for each of the viewer's components |
| ensureVisible() | Ensures that a given area is visible |
| getContent() | Gets the control's content component |
| getHLine() | Gets the number of pixels in a horizontal scroll line |
| getLayoutComponent() | Gets the component at a given constraint |
| getLine() | Gets the number of pixels in the horizontal and vertical scroll lines |
| getMinimumSize() | Gets the viewer's minimum size |
| getPosition() | Gets the viewer's scroll position |
| getPreferredSize() | Gets the viewer's preferred size |
| getRoleCode() | Gets the viewer's **ROLE_SYSTEM** code, which is **ROLE_SYSTEM_PANE** |
| getVLine() | Gets the number of pixels in a vertical scroll line |
| getXPosition() | Gets the viewer's horizontal scroll position |
| getYPosition() | Gets the viewer's vertical scroll position |
| handleEvent() | Handles the viewer's scroll events |

*(continued)*

**Table 11.2   Methods of the UIScrollViewer class (continued).**

| Method | Description |
|---|---|
| isKeyable() | Returns **true** if the viewer can receive keyboard input |
| keyDown() | Scrolls the viewer in response to key presses |
| layout() | Lays out the viewer |
| remove() | Removes a component from the viewer's layout |
| replace() | Replaces a component in the viewer's layout |
| requestFocus() | Requests the focus for the viewer's component |
| setContent() | Sets the viewer's content component |
| setHLine() | Sets the number of pixels in a horizontal scroll line |
| setLine() | Sets the number of pixels in the horizontal and vertical scroll lines |
| setPosition() | Sets the viewer's scroll position |
| setScrollStyle() | Sets the viewer's scroll bar style |
| setVLine() | Sets the number of pixels in a vertical scroll line |
| setXPosition() | Sets the viewer's horizontal scroll position |
| setYPosition() | Sets the viewer's vertical scroll position |

To create and display a **UIScrollViewer** object, first create the component that the viewer will hold, and then use the **new** operator to create the **UIScrollViewer** object, as in the following:

```
UIGraphic graphic = new UIGraphic(image);
UIScrollViewer viewer = new UIScrollViewer(graphic);
```

You then add the viewer to your program's layout, just as you add any other component. If you want, you can call the **UIScrollViewer** object's **setPosition()** method to specify where the viewer's scroll bars will be positioned:

```
viewer.setPosition(xPos, xPos);
```

Here, **xPos** and **yPos** are, respectively, the viewer's horizontal and vertical scroll positions.

**UIScrollViewer** overloads its constructor, providing a whopping seven separate ways to create a **UIScrollViewer** object. You already saw one form of the constructor. Following are the signatures of the remaining constructors:

```
public UIScrollViewer();
public UIScrollViewer(IUIComponent comp, int style);
public UIScrollViewer(IUIComponent comp, int hLine, int vLine);
public UIScrollViewer(IUIComponent comp, int hLine, int vLine,
    int style);
public UIScrollViewer(IUIComponent comp, int hLine, int vLine,
    int style, int scrollStyle);
public UIScrollViewer(IUIComponent comp, int hLine, int vLine,
    int style, int hstyle, int vstyle);
```

The arguments that you use with these constructors are described as follows:

- *comp*—The viewer's child component

- *style*—Style flags that position the scrollers; can be a combination of **SCROLL_TOP**, **SCROLL_LEFT**, **HEADER_BOTTOM**, and **HEADER_RIGHT**

- *hLine*—The horizontal scrolling increment

- *vLine*—The vertical scrolling increment

- *scrollStyle*—Scroll bar styles; can be **UIScroll.NOHIDE**, **UIScroll.NOSHOW**, or **UIScroll.NONPROPORTIONAL**

- *hStyle*—The horizontal scroll bar's style; can be same values as **scrollStyle**

- *vStyle*—The vertical scroll bar's style; can be same values as **scrollStyle**

Listing 11.2 presents a short applet that demonstrates a simple **UIScrollViewer** component. Figure 11.2 shows the applet running in Applet Viewer. When the applet first appears, its window is too small to display the entire image, so scroll bars appear. If you enlarge the applet, as shown in Figure 11.3, the scroll bars vanish.

**Figure 11.2**

*ScrollViewerApplet, running in Applet Viewer.*

**Figure 11.3**

*ScrollViewerApplet, enlarged to display the entire image.*

### Listing 11.2   Source code for ScrollViewerApplet.

```
///////////////////////////////////////////////
// ScrollViewerApplet.java
//
// An AFC applet that demonstrates how to create
// and display a scroll viewer component.
///////////////////////////////////////////////
```

```
import java.awt.Image;
import com.ms.ui.*;

public class ScrollViewerApplet extends AwtUIApplet
{
    public ScrollViewerApplet()
    {
        super(new AppletImplementation());
    }
}

class AppletImplementation extends UIApplet
{
    public void init()
    {
        UIBorderLayout layout = new UIBorderLayout();
        setLayout(layout);

        Image image = getImage(getCodeBase(), "mountain.gif");
        UIGraphic graphic = new UIGraphic(image);
        UIScrollViewer viewer = new UIScrollViewer(graphic);
        add(viewer, "Center");

        setValid(true);
    }
}
```

# The **UISplitViewer** Class

In Chapter 9, you learned about the **UISplitLayout** class, which enables you to divide layouts into two horizontal or vertical areas. AFC also provides a viewer class, named **UISplitViewer**, which does much the same thing, but throws scroll bars and a user-movable split bar into the bargain.

The **UISplitViewer** class extends **UIPanel**, and so counts **UIStateContainer**, **UIContainer**, and **UIComponent** among its ancestors. **UISplitViewer** inherits methods from all its superclasses, but it also defines a set of its own methods, as shown in Table 11.3.

To create and display a **UISplitViewer** object. First, create the components that the viewer will hold, and then use the **new** operator to create the **UISplitViewer** object, as in the following:

```
UIGraphic graphic1 = new UIGraphic(image1);
UIGraphic graphic2 = new UIGraphic(image2);
UISplitViewer viewer =
    new UISplitViewer(graphic1, graphic2, 0, -50, true);
```

## Table 11.3 Methods of the UISplitViewer class.

| Method | Description |
|---|---|
| getComponent() | Gets a component from the viewer |
| getFloater() | Gets the viewer's floating component |
| getPos() | Gets the viewer's split position |
| getStyle() | Gets the viewer's style |
| mouseDown() | Handles mouse-down events |
| mouseDrag() | Handles mouse-drag events |
| mouseUp() | Handles mouse-up events |
| setPos() | Sets the viewer's split position |

Here, the constructor's arguments are as follows:

- The first child component
- The second child component
- The viewer's style
- The first child component's size
- A flag specifying whether the viewer should have scroll bars

You then add the viewer to your program's layout, just as you add any other component.

**UISplitViewer** overloads its constructor, providing five separate ways to create a **UISplitViewer** object. You already saw one form of the constructor. Following are the signatures of the remaining constructors:

```
public UISplitViewer();
public UISplitViewer(IUIComponent nw, IUIComponent se);
public UISplitViewer(IUIComponent nw, IUIComponent se,
    int style);
public UISplitViewer(IUIComponent nw, IUIComponent se,
    int style, int size);
public UISplitViewer(IUIComponent nw, IUIComponent se,
    int style, int size, boolean addScroll);
```

The arguments that you use with these constructors are described as follows:

- *nw*—The first child component
- *se*—The second child component
- *style*—The viewer's style; can be **0** (zero) or **HORIZONTAL**
- *size*—The size of the first child component; negative numbers are translated as a percentage; positive numbers are translated as absolute sizes
- *addScroll*—The viewer's scroll bar flag; a value of **true** displays scroll bars if needed

Listing 11.3 presents a short applet that demonstrates a simple **UISplitViewer** component. Figure 11.4 shows the applet running in Applet Viewer. When the applet first appears, its window is too small to display the two images, so scroll bars appear. If you enlarge the applet a bit, as shown in Figure 11.5, the horizontal scroll bar on the first child component vanishes, but the scroll bars in the second pane remain. If you continue to enlarge the applet, the second set of scroll bars also vanishes, as shown in Figure 11.6. Finally, you can change the sizes of the panes by dragging the split bar. Figure 11.7 shows the split bar dragged to the left, causing the first child component's scroll bar to reappear.

Note that by providing the **HORIZONTAL** style when creating the split viewer, you can create a viewer that splits its areas horizontally rather than vertically. The following lines demonstrate the programming, and Figure 11.8 shows the result:

```
Image image1 = getImage(getCodeBase(), "image1.gif");
UIGraphic graphic1 = new UIGraphic(image1);
Image image2 = getImage(getCodeBase(), "desertsun.gif");
UIGraphic graphic2 = new UIGraphic(image2);
UISplitViewer viewer =
    new UISplitViewer(graphic1, graphic2,
    UISplitViewer.HORIZONTAL, -50, true);
```

**Listing 11.3  Source code for SplitViewerApplet.**
```
/////////////////////////////////////////////////
// SplitViewerApplet.java
//
// An AFC applet that demonstrates how to create
// and display a split viewer component.
/////////////////////////////////////////////////
```

```
import java.awt.Image;
import com.ms.ui.*;

public class SplitViewerApplet extends AwtUIApplet
{
    public SplitViewerApplet()
    {
        super(new AppletImplementation());
    }
}


class AppletImplementation extends UIApplet
{
    public void init()
    {
        UIBorderLayout layout = new UIBorderLayout();
        setLayout(layout);

        Image image1 = getImage(getCodeBase(), "image1.gif");
        UIGraphic graphic1 = new UIGraphic(image1);
        Image image2 = getImage(getCodeBase(), "desertsun.gif");
        UIGraphic graphic2 = new UIGraphic(image2);
        UISplitViewer viewer =
            new UISplitViewer(graphic1, graphic2, 0, -50, true);

        add(viewer, "Center");

        setValid(true);
    }
}
```

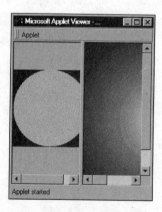

**Figure 11.4**

*SplitViewerApplet, running in Applet Viewer.*

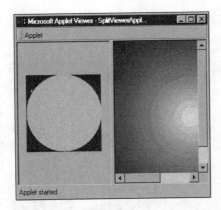

**Figure 11.5**

*SplitViewerApplet, enlarged to display the entire first image.*

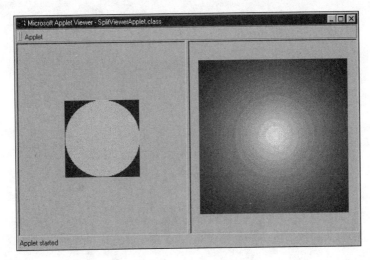

**Figure 11.6**

*SplitViewerApplet, enlarged to display both entire images.*

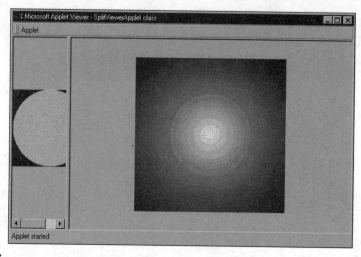

**Figure 11.7**

*SplitViewerApplet, with its split bar dragged to the left.*

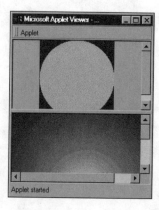

**Figure 11.8**

*SplitViewerApplet with a horizontal split.*

# The **UIColumnViewer** Class

Many varieties of data are best represented as a table. When writing straight Java applets or applications, creating such tables can be a frustrating task. AFC, however, features the **UIColumnViewer** class that makes it easy to display virtually any information in table form. This table includes not only columns of data, but also column headers the help identify the data in the table.

Unlike the other viewer classes, **UIColumnViewer** extends **UIScrollViewer** rather than **UIPanel**. Still, because **UIScrollViewer** extends **UIPanel**, **UIColumnViewer** inherits methods from **UIPanel**, **UIStateContainer**, **UIContainer**, and **UIComponent**, and also from **UIScrollViewer**. **UIColumnViewer** also defines a set of its own methods, as shown in Table 11.4.

To create and display a **UIColumnViewer** object, first create an array of **UIColumnHeader** objects to represent the column heads, like the following:

```
UIColumnHeader headings[] =
{
    new UIColumnHeader("Column 1"),
    new UIColumnHeader("Column 2"),
    new UIColumnHeader("Column 3"),
};
```

**Table 11.4   Methods of the UIColumnViewer class.**

| Method | Description |
| --- | --- |
| action() | Handles action events for the viewer |
| add() | Adds an array of objects to the viewer |
| addActionListener() | Registers an action listener component with the viewer |
| addItemListener() | Registers an item listener component with the viewer |
| getOrderIndex() | Gets a column's order |
| getWidth() | Gets a column's width |
| getWidths() | Gets all columns' widths |
| moveColumn() | Moves a column |
| processActionEvent() | Dispatches action events |
| processEvent() | Handles viewer events |
| processItemEvent() | Handles viewer item events |
| removeActionListener() | Removes an action listener from the viewer's listener list |

*(continued)*

**Table 11.4  Methods of the UIColumnViewer class (continued).**

| Method | Description |
|---|---|
| removeItemListener() | Removes an item listener from the viewer's listener list |
| setColumns() | Sets the viewer's columns |
| setWidth() | Sets a column's width |
| setWidths() | Sets all column widths |

A **UIColumnHeader** object can hold any kind of component, not just text. Text column heads, however, are the most common.

After creating the column heads, create string arrays (or arrays of other types of objects) to represent the data you'll display in the table, as in the following:

```
String rowData1[] =
    {"Entry 1", "Subentry 1", "Subentry 2"};
String rowData2[] =
    {"Entry 2", "Subentry 3", "Subentry 4"};
String rowData3[] =
    {"Entry 3", "Subentry 5", "Subentry 6"};
```

Here, each array of strings represents one row of data in the table.

Next, use the data arrays you just created as the content for **UIRow** objects:

```
UIRow row1 = new UIRow(rowData1);
UIRow row2 = new UIRow(rowData2);
UIRow row3 = new UIRow(rowData3);
```

You now use the **UIRow** objects for a **UIList** component's content:

```
UIList list = new UIList();
list.add(row1);
list.add(row2);
list.add(row3);
```

Finally, you use the **UIColumnHeader** array and the **UIList** component as arguments in a call to the **UIColumnViewer** constructor:

```
UIColumnViewer colViewer =
    new UIColumnViewer(headings, list);
```

Listing 11.4 brings together all the previous steps in a short program named ColumnViewerApplet. Figure 11.9 shows the applet running in Applet Viewer. Although the program calls **setWidths()** to set the column widths, the user can change the width of any column by using his mouse to drag the line between two columns. Figure 11.10, for example, shows the applet after the user enlarges the first column.

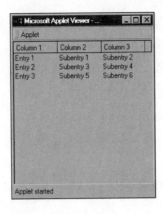

**Figure 11.9**

*ColumnViewerApplet, running in Applet Viewer.*

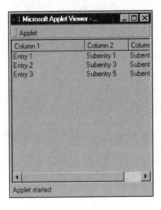

**Figure 11.10**

*ColumnViewerApplet, with its first column expanded.*

**Listing 11.4 Source code for ColumnViewerApplet.**

```java
//////////////////////////////////////////////////
// ColumnViewerApplet.java
//
// An AFC applet that demonstrates how to create
// a column viewer component.
//////////////////////////////////////////////////

import com.ms.ui.*;
import com.ms.ui.event.*;
import com.ms.fx.*;

public class ColumnViewerApplet extends AwtUIApplet
{
    public ColumnViewerApplet()
    {
        super(new AppletImplementation());
    }
}

class AppletImplementation extends UIApplet
{
    public void init()
    {
        UIBorderLayout layout = new UIBorderLayout();
        setLayout(layout);

        UIColumnHeader headings[] =
        {
            new UIColumnHeader("Column 1"),
            new UIColumnHeader("Column 2"),
            new UIColumnHeader("Column 3"),
        };

        String rowData1[] =
            {"Entry 1", "Subentry 1", "Subentry 2"};
        String rowData2[] =
            {"Entry 2", "Subentry 3", "Subentry 4"};
        String rowData3[] =
            {"Entry 3", "Subentry 5", "Subentry 6"};

        UIRow row1 = new UIRow(rowData1);
        UIRow row2 = new UIRow(rowData2);
        UIRow row3 = new UIRow(rowData3);
```

```
        UIList list = new UIList();
        list.add(row1);
        list.add(row2);
        list.add(row3);

        UIColumnViewer colViewer =
            new UIColumnViewer(headings, list);
        colViewer.setWidths(75);

        add(colViewer);

        setValid(true);
    }
}
```

# The **UITabViewer** Class

In Chapter 8, you learned about property sheets and how you can create them with AFC. The AFC class **UITabViewer** represents a similar type of display, containing tabbed pages, but no buttons. You can use the **UITabViewer** class when you want to organize groups of components into tabbed pages, but don't need the added benefits of creating a property sheet.

The **UITabViewer** class extends **UIPanel**, and so counts **UIStateContainer**, **UIContainer**, and **UIComponent** among its ancestors. **UITabViewer** inherits methods from all its superclasses, but it also defines a set of its own, as shown in Table 11.5.

**Table 11.5  Methods of the UITabViewer class.**

| Method | Description |
| --- | --- |
| **add()** | Adds a tab to the viewer |
| **addItemListener()** | Registers an item listener component with the viewer |
| **addNotify()** | Initializes the viewer |
| **addTab()** | Adds a tab to the viewer |
| **getInsets()** | Gets the viewer's insets |
| **getSelectedIndex()** | Gets the selected tab's index |
| **getSelectedItem()** | Gets the selected tab component |

*(continued)*

**Table 11.5 Methods of the UITabViewer class** *(continued).*

| Method | Description |
|---|---|
| handleEvent() | Handles events for the viewer |
| paint() | Draws the viewer |
| postEvent() | Posts an event to the viewer |
| processEvent() | Handles a given event |
| processItemEvent() | Handles item events |
| removeItemListener() | Removes an item listener from the viewer's listener list |
| removeTab() | Removes a tab from the viewer |
| requestFocus() | Requests the focus for the viewer's content component |
| setSelectedIndex() | Selects a tab, given the tab's index |
| setSelectedItem() | Selects a tab, given the tab's component |

While not as complicated as creating a **UIColumnViewer** object, creating and initializing a **UITabViewer** object requires a few steps. First, create the **UITabViewer** object:

```
UITabViewer viewer = new UITabViewer();
```

Next, create the components that will appear in each page of the viewer:

```
UIText text1 = new UIText("Page 1");
UIText text2 = new UIText("Page 2");
UIText text3 = new UIText("Page 3");
```

Then, add the components to the viewer:

```
viewer.add("Tab 1", text1);
viewer.add("Tab 2", text2);
viewer.add("Tab 3", text3);
```

Here, the **add()** method's two arguments are the text to display on the page's tab and component to display in the page.

Finally, add the viewer to the container's layout:

```
add(viewer, "Center");
```

Listing 11.5 brings together all the previous steps in a short program named TabViewerApplet. Figure 11.11 shows the applet running in Applet Viewer. To switch between pages, just click a tab. Figure 11.12, for example, shows the applet after the user clicks the Tab 3 tab.

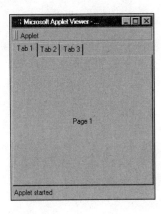

**Figure 11.11**

*TabViewerApplet, running in Applet Viewer.*

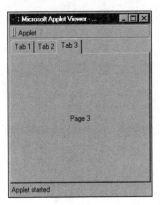

**Figure 11.12**

*TabViewerApplet, showing its third page.*

## Listing 11.5   Source code for TabViewerApplet.

```
/////////////////////////////////////////////////
// TabViewerApplet.java
//
// An AFC applet that demonstrates how to create
// and display a tab viewer component.
/////////////////////////////////////////////////

import com.ms.ui.*;

public class TabViewerApplet extends AwtUIApplet
{
    public TabViewerApplet()
    {
        super(new AppletImplementation());
    }
}

class AppletImplementation extends UIApplet
{
    public void init()
    {
        UIBorderLayout layout = new UIBorderLayout();
        setLayout(layout);

        UITabViewer viewer = new UITabViewer();

        UIText text1 = new UIText("Page 1");
        UIText text2 = new UIText("Page 2");
        UIText text3 = new UIText("Page 3");

        viewer.add("Tab 1", text1);
        viewer.add("Tab 2", text2);
        viewer.add("Tab 3", text3);

        add(viewer, "Center");

        setValid(true);
    }
}
```

# Practical Guide To

# Viewer Components

- Using A Viewer To Create Simple Animation
- Creating Your Own Viewer Class
- Displaying Flip-Style Animation
- Responding To Column Viewer Selections
- Laying Out Components In Tab Viewer Pages

## Using A Viewer To Create Simple Animation

You may remember the **UIMarquee** class that you explored in Chapter 10. A marquee object enables your applet or application to display automatically scrolling components. For example, in Chapter 10, you learned to create scrolling banners. Because **UIMarquee** extends **UIViewer**, you shouldn't be too amazed to learn that you can use the **UIViewer** class to create your own animated viewers.

The keys to this bit of AFC magic are the **Timer**, **TimerListener**, and **TimerEvent** classes, which are defined as part of the full Microsoft SDK for Java 2.0. If you implement a timer in your applet, you can respond to the timer events by changing the position of a **UIViewer**'s content component. **UIViewer** provides the **setPosition()**, **setXPosition()**, and **setYPosition()** methods to handle the component movement tasks.

Listing 11.6 presents an applet that scrolls an image back and forth across the applet's display area—sort of a two-way marquee. Figure 11.13 shows the applet running in Applet Viewer, although, of course, you can't see the animation in the figure. (For more information on using the **Timer**, **TimerListener**, and **TimerEvent** classes, see Chapter 10.)

### Listing 11.6   Source code for MotionViewerApplet.

```
/////////////////////////////////////////////////////
// MotionViewerApplet.java
//
// An AFC applet that demonstrates how to create
// and manipulate a viewer control.
/////////////////////////////////////////////////////

import com.ms.ui.*;
import java.awt.*;
import com.ms.util.Timer;
import com.ms.util.TimerEvent;
import com.ms.util.TimerListener;

public class MotionViewerApplet extends AwtUIApplet
{
    public MotionViewerApplet()
    {
        super(new AppletImplementation());
    }
}

class AppletImplementation extends UIApplet
    implements TimerListener
{
```

```
UIViewer viewer;
int increment;

public void init()
{
    UIBorderLayout layout = new UIBorderLayout();
    setLayout(layout);

    Image image = getImage(getCodeBase(), "image.gif");
    UIGraphic graphic = new UIGraphic(image);
    viewer = new UIViewer(graphic);
    add(viewer, "Center");

    Timer timer = new Timer(this, 100, true);
    timer.start();

    increment = 5;

    setValid(true);
}

public void timeTriggered(TimerEvent te)
{
    int xPos = viewer.getXPosition();
    xPos += increment;
    if ((xPos < -150) || (xPos > 150))
        increment = -increment;
    viewer.setXPosition(xPos);
}
}
```

## Figure 11.13

*MotionViewerApplet, running in Applet Viewer.*

## Creating Your Own Viewer Class

Because Java is an object-oriented language, nothing stops you from extending AFC classes to refine the way in which they work. In fact, you already extend AFC classes all the time. For example, you always extend **AwtUIApplet** to create your own AFC applet class. You also extend **UIApplet** to create your own applet-implementation class. To create your own viewer class, you may consider extending the **UIViewer** class.

For example, take the MotionViewerApplet (refer to Listing 11.6). Rather than using the **UIViewer** class in the applet, you can convert the applet to use a new class named **MotionViewer** that extends **UIViewer** and takes care of all the details of scrolling a component. Listing 11.7 is just such an applet. When you run the applet in Applet Viewer, you see the window shown in Figure 11.14. Click the Speed or Increment buttons to change the animation's speed or increment, respectively, on the fly.

Notice that the **MotionViewer** class isn't declared as implementing the **TimerListener** interface, yet it still defines a **timeTriggered()** method, which responds to timer messages. **MotionViewer** doesn't need to declare itself as implementing the **TimerListener** interface because **UIViewer**, from which **MotionViewer** is derived, already does. **MotionViewer** simply overrides **UIViewer**'s **timeTriggered()** method and so receives timer events.

Notice also how the main applet can create a **MotionViewer** object by simply passing the viewer's content component as the **MotionViewer** constructor's single argument. The main applet can control the speed of the animation by calling the **MotionViewer**

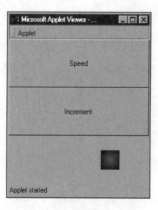

**Figure 11.14**

*MotionViewerApplet2, running in Applet Viewer.*

object's **setSpeed()** and **setIncrement()** methods; however, the applet doesn't have
to call these methods. Just creating the viewer and adding it to the layout is all it
takes to get the animation going.

### Listing 11.7  Source code for MotionViewerApplet2.

```
/////////////////////////////////////////////////
// MotionViewerApplet2.java
//
// An AFC applet that demonstrates how to create
// a custom viewer component.
/////////////////////////////////////////////////

import java.awt.*;
import com.ms.ui.*;
import com.ms.ui.event.*;
import com.ms.util.Timer;
import com.ms.util.TimerEvent;

public class MotionViewerApplet2 extends AwtUIApplet
{
    public MotionViewerApplet2()
    {
        super(new AppletImplementation());
    }
}

class AppletImplementation extends UIApplet
    implements IUIActionListener
{
    int speed;
    int increment;
    UIPushButton spdButton;
    UIPushButton incButton;
    MotionViewer viewer;

    public void init()
    {
        UIGridLayout layout = new UIGridLayout(3, 1);
        setLayout(layout);

        spdButton = new UIPushButton("Speed",
            UIPushButton.RAISED);
        spdButton.addActionListener(this);
        incButton = new UIPushButton("Increment",
            UIPushButton.RAISED);
        incButton.addActionListener(this);
```

```
            Image image = getImage(getCodeBase(), "sunburst1.gif");
            UIGraphic graphic = new UIGraphic(image);
            viewer = new MotionViewer(graphic);

            add(spdButton);
            add(incButton);
            add(viewer);

            speed = 100;
            increment = 5;

            setValid(true);
        }

    public void actionPerformed(UIActionEvent event)
    {
        String label = event.getActionCommand();
        if (label == "Speed")
        {
            speed -= 10;
            if (speed < 10)
                speed = 10;
            viewer.setSpeed(speed);
        }
        else if (label == "Increment")
        {
            increment += 5;
            if (increment > 35)
                increment = 35;
            viewer.setIncrement(increment);
        }
    }
}

class MotionViewer extends UIViewer
{
    IUIComponent comp;
    int speed;
    int increment;
    Timer timer;

    public MotionViewer(IUIComponent comp)
    {
        super(comp);
        this.comp = comp;
        speed = 100;
        increment = 5;
```

```
        timer = new Timer(this, 100, true);
        timer.start();
    }

    public void timeTriggered(TimerEvent te)
    {
        int xPos = getXPosition();
        xPos += increment;
        if ((xPos < -150) || (xPos > 150))
            increment = -increment;
        setXPosition(xPos);
    }

    public int getSpeed()
    {
        return speed;
    }

    public void setSpeed(int speed)
    {
        this.speed = speed;
        timer.stop();
        timer = new Timer(this, speed, true);
        timer.start();
    }

    public int getIncrement()
    {
        return increment;
    }

    public void setIncrement(int increment)
    {
        this.increment = increment;
    }
}
```

 ## Displaying Flip-Style Animation

The original MotionViewerApplet animated an image by constantly changing the image's position, making it move across the display. Another type of animation you can perform with a **UIViewer** object is flip-style animation, where you constantly flip between different images. You can perform this type of animation easily enough by setting up a timer and calling the **UIViewer** object's **setContent()** method in your **timeTriggered()** method.

Listing 11.8, for example, is an applet that displays flip-style animation. When you run the applet in Applet Viewer, you see the window shown in Figure 11.15. As you watch the applet, the image displayed in the viewer constantly changes in response to the arriving timer messages.

## Listing 11.8  Source code for MotionViewerApplet3.

```
///////////////////////////////////////////////
// MotionViewerApplet3.java
//
// An AFC applet that demonstrates how to create
// animation with a viewer control.
///////////////////////////////////////////////

import java.awt.*;
import com.ms.ui.*;
import com.ms.util.Timer;
import com.ms.util.TimerEvent;
import com.ms.util.TimerListener;

public class MotionViewerApplet3 extends AwtUIApplet
{
    public MotionViewerApplet3()
    {
        super(new AppletImplementation());
    }
}

class AppletImplementation extends UIApplet
    implements TimerListener
{
    UIViewer viewer;
    int frameNum;
    UIGraphic graphic1;
    UIGraphic graphic2;
    UIGraphic graphic3;

    public void init()
    {
        UIBorderLayout layout = new UIBorderLayout();
        setLayout(layout);

        Image image1 = getImage(getCodeBase(), "image1.gif");
        Image image2 = getImage(getCodeBase(), "image2.gif");
        Image image3 = getImage(getCodeBase(), "image3.gif");
```

```
        graphic1 = new UIGraphic(image1);
        graphic2 = new UIGraphic(image2);
        graphic3 = new UIGraphic(image3);

        viewer = new UIViewer(graphic2);
        add(viewer, "Center");

        Timer timer = new Timer(this, 400, true);
        timer.start();

        frameNum = 0;

        setValid(true);
    }

    public void timeTriggered(TimerEvent te)
    {
        ++frameNum;
        if (frameNum == 3)
            frameNum = 0;

        UIGraphic frame = graphic1;
        if (frameNum == 1)
            frame = graphic2;
        else if (frameNum == 2)
            frame = graphic3;

        viewer.setContent(frame);
    }
}
```

## Figure 11.15

*MotionViewerApplet3, running in Applet Viewer.*

## Responding To Column Viewer Selections

When you create a column viewer and fill it with data, you may intend that the user be able to only view the data. However, in many cases, you may want the user to select an item in the table. To do so, your program must respond to the action events that users generate when they double-click an item in the viewer.

Listing 11.9, for example, presents an applet that creates a column viewer and fills the viewer with data. When you run the applet in Applet Viewer, you see the applet window; the top half displays the column viewer, and the bottom half displays a canvas control. If you double-click an item in the viewer, the item's text appears in the canvas control, as shown in Figure 11.16.

**Listing 11.9   Source code for ColumnViewerApplet2.**

```
//////////////////////////////////////////////////
// ColumnViewerApplet2.java
//
// An AFC applet that demonstrates how to respond
// to selections in a column viewer component.
//////////////////////////////////////////////////

import com.ms.ui.*;
import com.ms.ui.event.*;
import com.ms.fx.*;

public class ColumnViewerApplet2 extends AwtUIApplet
{
    public ColumnViewerApplet2()
    {
        super(new AppletImplementation());
    }
}

class AppletImplementation extends UIApplet
    implements IUIActionListener
{
    MessageCanvas canvas;

    public void init()
    {
        UIGridLayout layout = new UIGridLayout(2, 1);
        setLayout(layout);

        UIColumnHeader headings[] =
        {
```

```
            new UIColumnHeader("Last Name"),
            new UIColumnHeader("First Name"),
            new UIColumnHeader("Cust. #"),
    };

    UIRow rows[] = createRows();

    UIList list = new UIList();
    for (int x=0; x<12; ++x)
        list.add(rows[x]);

    UIColumnViewer colViewer = new UIColumnViewer(headings, list);
    colViewer.setWidth(0, 100);
    colViewer.setWidth(1, 100);
    colViewer.setWidth(2, 75);
    colViewer.addActionListener(this);

    add(colViewer);

    canvas = new MessageCanvas("", 36, 70, 90);
    add(canvas);

    setValid(true);
}

public UIRow[] createRows()
{
    UIRow rows[] = new UIRow[12];

    String rowData1[] = {"Needham", "Ted", "243567"};
    String rowData2[] = {"Wallace", "Stacy", "374859"};
    String rowData3[] = {"Burns", "Montgomery", "374895"};
    String rowData4[] = {"Johnson", "Nancy", "194837"};
    String rowData5[] = {"Rogers", "Gary", "398573"};
    String rowData6[] = {"Michaels", "Harold", "983745"};
    String rowData7[] = {"Kelly", "Ursula", "285740"};
    String rowData8[] = {"Daniels", "Ellen", "584932"};
    String rowData9[] = {"Anderson", "Jackie", "254894"};
    String rowData10[] = {"Landry", "Peter", "485734"};
    String rowData11[] = {"Jackson", "Redford", "584932"};
    String rowData12[] = {"Renfield", "Buster", "254894"};

    rows[0] = new UIRow(rowData1);
    rows[1] = new UIRow(rowData2);
    rows[2] = new UIRow(rowData3);
    rows[3] = new UIRow(rowData4);
    rows[4] = new UIRow(rowData5);
```

```
            rows[5] = new UIRow(rowData6);
            rows[6] = new UIRow(rowData7);
            rows[7] = new UIRow(rowData8);
            rows[8] = new UIRow(rowData9);
            rows[9] = new UIRow(rowData10);
            rows[10] = new UIRow(rowData11);
            rows[11] = new UIRow(rowData12);

            return rows;
        }

        public void actionPerformed(UIActionEvent event)
        {
            String msg = event.getActionCommand();
            canvas.showMessage(msg);
        }
    }

    class MessageCanvas extends UICanvas
    {
        String displayString;
        int pointSize;
        int col, row;

        public MessageCanvas(String msg, int points, int x, int y)
        {
            displayString = msg;
            pointSize = points;
            col = x;
            row = y;
            setBackground(FxColor.blue);
        }

        public void paint(FxGraphics graphics)
        {
            FxFont font =
                new FxFont("TimesRoman", FxFont.PLAIN, pointSize);
            graphics.setFont(font);
            graphics.setColor(FxColor.white);
            graphics.drawString(displayString, col, row);
        }

        public void showMessage(String str)
        {
            displayString = str;
            repaint();
        }
    }
```

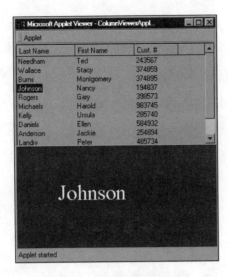

**Figure 11.16**

*ColumnViewerApplet2, displaying a selection.*

## Laying Out Components In Tab Viewer Pages

If you have the urge to create a tab viewer, you need to organize many components into a logical, but attractive, layout. Being able to divide the components into separate pages goes a long way toward reducing component clutter in your applet or application. However, you may have noticed that a tab-viewer page can hold only a single component.

Just as with other AFC containers that hold only a single component, there's no reason that single component can't also be a container. A **UIPanel** object is often a good choice as the container component, because it represents an empty area just waiting to be filled. So, to populate the pages of your tab viewer, create a custom panel for each page, organizing the components you want to display into each of the panels.

Listing 11.10 presents an applet that creates a tab viewer with two pages. When you run the applet in Applet Viewer, you see the window shown in Figure 11.17. The applet uses a border layout so that it can display both the tab viewer and a row of buttons. (The row of buttons also is a panel.) The buttons across the bottom of the applet stay in view no matter which tab-viewer page is displayed. To see that this is true, click Tab 2, and then you see the window shown in Figure 11.18.

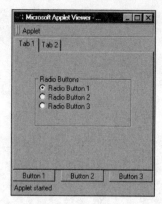

## Figure 11.17

*TabViewerApplet2, running in Applet Viewer.*

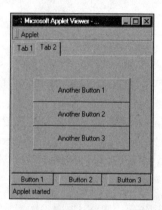

## Figure 11.18

*TabViewerApplet2, showing its second page of components.*

### Listing 11.10   Source code for TabViewerApplet2.

```
/////////////////////////////////////////////////
// TabViewerApplet2.java
//
// An AFC applet that demonstrates how to layout
// components in the pages of a tab viewer.
/////////////////////////////////////////////////

import com.ms.ui.*;
import java.awt.Insets;
```

```
public class TabViewerApplet2 extends AwtUIApplet
{
    public TabViewerApplet2()
    {
        super(new AppletImplementation());
    }
}


class AppletImplementation extends UIApplet
{
    public void init()
    {
        UIBorderLayout layout = new UIBorderLayout();
        setLayout(layout);

        UITabViewer viewer = new UITabViewer();

        Panel1 panel1 = new Panel1();
        Panel2 panel2 = new Panel2();

        viewer.add("Tab 1", panel1);
        viewer.add("Tab 2", panel2);

        add(viewer, "Center");

        ButtonPanel buttonPanel = new ButtonPanel();
        add(buttonPanel, "South");

        setValid(true);
    }
}


class Panel1 extends UIPanel
{
    public Panel1()
    {
        UIBorderLayout layout = new UIBorderLayout();
        setLayout(layout);

        UIRadioGroup group =
            new UIRadioGroup("Radio Buttons");

        UIRadioButton button1 =
            new UIRadioButton("Radio Button 1");
        button1.setChecked(true);
        group.add(button1);
```

```
                UIRadioButton button2 =
                    new UIRadioButton("Radio Button 2");
                group.add(button2);
                UIRadioButton button3 =
                    new UIRadioButton("Radio Button 3");
                group.add(button3);

                add(group, "Center");
            }

        public Insets getInsets()
        {
            return new Insets(35, 35, 70, 35);
        }
    }

class Panel2 extends UIPanel
{
    public Panel2()
    {
        UIGridLayout layout = new UIGridLayout(3, 1);
        setLayout(layout);

        UIPushButton button1 =
            new UIPushButton("Another Button 1", UIPushButton.RAISED);
        UIPushButton button2 =
            new UIPushButton("Another Button 2", UIPushButton.RAISED);
        UIPushButton button3 =
            new UIPushButton("Another Button 3", UIPushButton.RAISED);

        add(button1);
        add(button2);
        add(button3);
    }

    public Insets getInsets()
    {
        return new Insets(35, 35, 35, 35);
    }
}

class ButtonPanel extends UIPanel
{
    public ButtonPanel()
    {
        UIGridLayout layout = new UIGridLayout(1, 3);
        layout.setHgap(10);
        setLayout(layout);
```

```
    UIPushButton button1 =
        new UIPushButton("Button 1", UIPushButton.RAISED);
    UIPushButton button2 =
        new UIPushButton("Button 2", UIPushButton.RAISED);
    UIPushButton button3 =
        new UIPushButton("Button 3", UIPushButton.RAISED);

    add(button1);
    add(button2);
    add(button3);
}
}
```

# Chapter 12

## The Component, Container, Canvas, And Panel Classes

*The lie is the basic building block of good manners. That may seem mildly shocking to a moralist—but then what isn't?*
*—Quentin Crisp,*
*Manners from Heaven*

# Notes...

# Chapter 12

Components and containers are the basic building blocks for most of AFC. Thanks to this fact, it's no lie that (if you understand how the other classes relate to component and containers) you will better understand how those other classes work. If nothing else, you'll become aware of the huge number of methods that most classes inherit from these basic superclasses. After all, you can't build a sophisticated program without knowing about the tools with which you have to work.

In this chapter, you explore the **UIComponent**, **UIStateComponent**, **UIContainer**, **UIStateContainer**, and **UISingleContainer** classes. Most of the components you've worked with so far in this book can trace their ancestry back through one or more of these important base classes. You'll also take a closer look at the **UIPanel** and **UICanvas** classes, which are the first components in the AFC hierarchy that AFC programmers are likely to use to create their own custom components.

## The **UIComponent** Class

If you want to know where most of any AFC component or container class's methods come from, look no further than **UIComponent**. **UIComponent** is AFC's Big Daddy—the class to which every component and container can trace its ancestry. As such, **UIComponent** defines all the methods that provide the basic functionality required by all AFC components or containers—a big responsibility for a big class.

The **UIComponent** class defines methods that respond to events, register event listeners, manage child components, handle attributes and states, paint the object, and more. Although **UIComponent** defines a large set of methods, many of these methods must be overridden in classes that extend **UIComponent**. For example, if you were to extend a class from **UIComponent**, you would want to override the **paint()** method to draw your component; **UIComponent**'s **paint()** does nothing.

Only two AFC classes—**UIStateComponent** and **UIContainer**—directly extend **UIComponent**. The **UIStateComponent** class represents basic components that can manage states, such as being selected or checked. The **UIContainer** class represents components that can contain other components and is the class that all other container classes extend. You're not likely to ever create a **UIComponent** object; instead, you'll create objects from classes that have **UIComponent** as an ancestor.

Table 12.1 lists **UIComponent**'s methods along with their descriptions. As you can see, **UIComponent** defines more methods than any other AFC class. Most of these methods, however, act as placeholders for functionality implemented in other classes. A **UIComponent** object, for example, is a stateless object, but it still defines methods that manage component states, such as **isChecked()**, **isFocused()**, and **isSelected()**. These methods are meant to be overridden by extended classes that support states.

**Table 12.1  Methods of the UIComponent class.**

| Method | Description |
| --- | --- |
| action() | Handles action events |
| addFocusListener() | Registers a focus listener with the component |
| addKeyListener() | Registers a key listener with the component |
| addMouseListener() | Registers a mouse listener with the component |
| addMouseMotionListener() | Registers a mouse-motion listener with the component |
| addNotify() | Performs component initialization |
| adjustLayoutSize() | Adjusts the component's layout size |
| clone() | Returns a copy of the component |
| contains() | Returns **true** if the component contains the specified point |

*(continued)*

Table 12.1 Methods of the **UIComponent** class *(continued)*.

| Method | Description |
|---|---|
| createImage() | Creates an image |
| deliverEvent() | Dispatches events to the component |
| doDefaultAction() | Executes the component's default action |
| ensureVisible() | Ensures that the given area is visible |
| getBackground() | Gets the component's background color |
| getBounds() | Gets the component's bounding rectangle |
| getComponent() | Gets the component that contains the specified point |
| getCursor() | Gets the component's cursor |
| getDefaultAction() | Gets the component's default action |
| getDescription() | Gets the component's description |
| getFlags() | Gets the component's flags |
| getFont() | Gets the component's font |
| getFontMetrics() | Gets the component's font metrics |
| getForeground() | Gets the component's foreground color |
| getGraphics() | Gets the component's graphics object |
| getHelp() | Gets the component's help text |
| getID() | Gets the component's ID |
| getIndex() | Gets the component's index |
| getKeyboardShortcut() | Gets the component's keyboard shortcut |
| getLocation() | Gets the component's location |
| getMaximumSize() | Gets the component's maximum size |
| getMinimumSize() | Gets the component's minimum size |

*(continued)*

## Table 12.1  Methods of the **UIComponent** class (continued).

| Method | Description |
| --- | --- |
| getName() | Gets the component's name |
| getParent() | Gets the component's parent |
| getPeer() | Gets the component's root-container peer |
| getPreferredSize() | Gets the component's preferred size |
| getRoleCode() | Gets the component's role code |
| getRoot() | Gets the component's root object |
| getSize() | Gets the component's size |
| getStateCode() | Gets the component's state |
| getToolkit() | Gets the component's toolkit |
| getTreeLock() | Gets the component's locking object |
| getValueText() | Gets the component's value |
| gotFocus() | Called when the component receives the focus |
| handleEvent() | Handles the component's events |
| imageUpdate() | Draws the component's image |
| invalidateAll() | Invalidates the component and its children |
| isChecked() | Returns **true** if the component's check state is set |
| isEnabled() | Returns **true** if the component's enabled state is set |
| isFocused() | Returns **true** if the component's focused state is set |
| isHeightRelative() | Returns **true** if the component lays out children based on the container's height |
| isHot() | Returns **true** if the component's hot-tracking state is set |
| isIndeterminate() | Returns **true** if the component's indeterminate state is set |

*(continued)*

Table 12.1  Methods of the **UIComponent** class (continued).

| Method | Description |
| --- | --- |
| isInvalidating() | Returns **true** if the component has been invalidated |
| isKeyable() | Returns **true** if the component can receive keyboard input |
| isNotified() | Returns **true** if the component's notified state is set |
| isPressed() | Returns **true** if the component's pressed state is set |
| isRedrawing() | Returns **true** if component will be redrawn |
| isSelectable() | Returns **true** if the component can be selected |
| isSelected() | Returns **true** if the component's selected state is set |
| isValid() | Returns **true** if the component is valid |
| isVisible() | Returns **true** if the component is visible |
| isWidthRelative() | Returns **true** if the component lays out children based on the container's width |
| keyDown() | Handles key presses |
| keyUp() | Handles key releases |
| layout() | Lays out the component |
| lostFocus() | Called when the component loses the focus |
| mouseClicked() | Handles mouse clicks |
| mouseDown() | Handles mouse-down events |
| mouseDrag() | Handles mouse-drag events |
| mouseEnter() | Handles mouse-enter events |
| mouseExit() | Handles mouse-exit events |
| mouseMove() | Handles mouse-move events |
| mouseUp() | Handles mouse-up events |

(continued)

**Table 12.1  Methods of the UIComponent class (continued).**

| Method | Description |
| --- | --- |
| navigate() | Navigates from one component to another |
| notifyEvent() | Dispatches event notifications to child components |
| paint() | Draws the component |
| paintAll() | Draws the component and its children |
| postEvent() | Posts events to the component |
| prepareImage() | Prepares a component image |
| print() | Prints the component |
| printAll() | Prints the component and its children |
| relayout() | Requests component layout |
| removeFocusListener() | Unregisters a focus listener |
| removeKeyListener() | Unregisters a key listener |
| removeMouseListener() | Unregisters a mouse listener |
| removeMouseMotionListener() | Unregisters a mouse-motion listener |
| removeNotify() | Called when the component's graphics context is no longer available |
| repaint() | Requests the component to be redrawn |
| requestFocus() | Requests the focus on behalf of the component |
| setBackground() | Sets the component's background color |
| setBounds() | Sets the component's bounding rectangle |
| setChecked() | Toggles the component's checked state |
| setCursor() | Sets the component's cursor |
| setEnabled() | Toggles the component's enabled state |

*(continued)*

## Table 12.1 Methods of the **UIComponent** class (continued).

| Method | Description |
| --- | --- |
| setFlags() | Sets the component's flags |
| setFocused() | Toggles the component's focused state |
| setFont() | Sets the component's font |
| setForeground() | Sets the component's foreground color |
| setHot() | Toggles the component's hot-tracked state |
| setID() | Sets the component's ID |
| setIndeterminate() | Toggles the component's indeterminate state |
| setIndex() | Sets the component's index |
| setInvalidating() | Sets the component's invalidating state |
| setLocation() | Sets the component's location |
| setName() | Sets the component's name |
| setParent() | Sets the component's parent |
| setPressed() | Toggles the component's pressed state |
| setRedrawing() | Toggles the component's redrawing state |
| setSelected() | Toggles the component's selected state |
| setSize() | Sets the component's size |
| setValid() | Toggles the component's valid state |
| setValueText() | Sets the component's value |
| setVisible() | Toggles the component's visible state |
| toString() | Gets the component's text description |
| update() | Updates the component |

# The **UIContainer** Class

**UIContainer** is one of two classes that extend **UIComponent**, adding the capability to create components that contain child components. That is, any AFC class that represents a container must be able to trace its ancestry back to **UIContainer**. **UIContainer** overrides many of the methods defined by **UIComponent**. **UIContainer** also adds quite a few of its own methods, as shown in Table 12.2.

Notice that many methods original to **UIContainer** manage child components in some way. These methods include **getChildBounds()**, **getChildCount()**, **getChildIndex()**, **getChildSize()**, **removeAllChildren()**, **setChildSize()**, and others.

Only one AFC class—**UIStateContainer**—extends **UIContainer**. You will notice that none of **UIContainer**'s methods manages states, such as pressed, selected, or focused. Rather, the **UIStateContainer** class represents containers that can manage states.

As with **UIComponent**, you're not likely to ever create a **UIContainer** object directly; instead, you will create objects from classes that have **UIContainer** as an ancestor. These classes include **UIPanel**, **UIViewer**, **UIPropertyPage**, **UIRoot**, **UIScroll**, **UISplitViewer**, and **UITabViewer**, and also all classes that extend these classes.

**Table 12.2   Methods of the UIContainer class.**

| Method | Description |
|---|---|
| add() | Adds a component to the container |
| addContainerListener() | Registers a container listener with the component |
| addFocusListener() | Registers a focus listener with the component |
| addKeyListener() | Registers a key listener with the component |
| addMouseListener() | Registers a mouse listener with the component |
| addMouseMotionListener() | Registers a mouse-motion listener with the component |
| addNotify() | Performs component initialization |
| adjustLayoutSize() | Adjusts the component's layout size |
| continueInvalidate() | Returns **true** if the container should be invalidated |
| ensureVisible() | Ensures that the given area is visible |

*(continued)*

Table 12.2  Methods of the **UIContainer** class (continued).

| Method | Description |
|---|---|
| getChild() | Gets a child component |
| getChildBounds() | Gets a child component's bounding rectangle |
| getChildCount() | Gets the number of components in the container |
| getChildIndex() | Gets a child component's index |
| getChildLocation() | Gets a child component's location |
| getChildSize() | Gets a child component's size |
| getClientRect() | Gets the container's client rectangle |
| getComponent() | Gets the component that contains the specified point |
| getComponentCount() | Gets the number of components in the container |
| getComponentFromID() | Gets a component given its ID |
| getComponentIndex() | Gets a component's index |
| getComponents() | Gets all the container's components |
| getEdge() | Gets the container's edge style |
| getFloater() | Gets the container's floating component |
| getFocusComponent() | Gets the child component with the focus |
| getHeader() | Gets the container's header component |
| getID() | Gets the container's ID |
| getInsets() | Gets the container's insets |
| getLayout() | Gets the container's layout manager |
| getMinimumSize() | Gets the component's minimum size |
| getName() | Gets the component's name |
| getPreferredSize() | Gets the component's preferred size |

(continued)

**Table 12.2 Methods of the UIContainer class *(continued)*.**

| Method | Description |
|---|---|
| gotFocus() | Called when the component receives the focus |
| invalidateAll() | Invalidates the component and its children |
| isHeightRelative() | Returns **true** if the component lays out children based on the container's height |
| isOverlapping() | Returns **true** if child components overlap in the layout |
| isWidthRelative() | Returns **true** if the component lays out children based on the container's width |
| keyDown() | Handles key presses |
| layout() | Lays out the component |
| lostFocus() | Called when the component loses the focus |
| mouseEnter() | Handles mouse-enter events |
| mouseExit() | Handles mouse-exit events |
| move() | Moves a child component |
| navigate() | Navigates from one component to another |
| notifyEvent() | Dispatches event notifications to child components |
| paint() | Draws the component |
| paintAll() | Draws the component and its children |
| paintComponents() | Draws all of the container's components |
| passFocus() | Gets the component that will next receive the focus |
| printAll() | Prints the component and its children |
| remove() | Removes a component from the container |
| removeAll() | Removes all the container's components |
| removeAllChildren() | Removes all of the container's child components |

*(continued)*

**Table 12.2 Methods of the UIContainer class (continued).**

| Method | Description |
| --- | --- |
| removeContainerListener() | Unregisters a container listener |
| removeFocusListener() | Unregisters a focus listener |
| removeKeyListener() | Unregisters a key listener |
| removeMouseListener() | Unregisters a mouse listener |
| removeMouseMotionListener() | Unregisters a mouse-motion listener |
| removeNotify() | Called when the component's graphics context is no longer available |
| replace() | Replaces one component with another |
| setChildBounds() | Sets a child component's bounds |
| setChildLocation() | Sets a child component's location |
| setChildSize() | Sets a child component's size |
| setComponent() | Adds a child component to the container |
| setEdge() | Sets the container's edge style |
| setHeader() | Sets the container's header component |
| setID() | Set the component's ID |
| setLayout() | Sets the container's layout manager |
| setLocation() | Sets the component's location |
| setName() | Sets the component's name |
| setSize() | Sets the component's size |
| update() | Updates the component |

# The **UIStateContainer** Class

That no AFC class other than **UIStateContainer** directly extends **UIContainer** should tell you that all AFC container classes represent objects that can be set to various states. Exactly what states an object can be set to depends on the object. For example, although it makes sense to have a button with a pressed state, it doesn't make much sense to have a panel with a pressed state (unless it's a custom panel that has characteristics common to buttons).

So, **UIStateContainer** represents objects with states. Only two classes directly extend **UIStateContainer**: **UIPanel** and **UISingleContainer**. However, many AFC classes trace their ancestry back to **UIStateContainer**, including **UIPanel**, **UIViewer**, **UIPropertyPage**, **UIRoot**, **UIScroll**, **UISplitViewer**, **UITabViewer**, **UIThumb**, **UIButton**, **UIMenuLauncher**, **UIStatus**, and **UITab**, and also all classes that extend these classes. Still, you're not likely to create a **UIStateContainer** object in one of your AFC programs. The first class in this hierarchy that you're likely to use directly is **UIPanel**.

The various object states and their descriptions are shown in the following list:

- *Checked*—Indicates that the component has been checked; used most often with buttons, including check buttons and radio buttons

- *Enabled*—Indicates that the user is able to manipulate the component

- *Focused*—Indicates that the component will receive keyboard input

- *Hot-tracked*—Indicates that the mouse is over the component

- *Indeterminate*—The component's state cannot be determined, usually because of conflicting states

- *Notified*—Indicates that the component has been notified that the graphics context is available

- *Pressed*—Indicates that the mouse button was pressed while the mouse pointer was over the component

- *Redrawing*—Indicates that the component can be redrawn

- *Selected*—Indicates that the user has selected the component

- *Valid*—Indicates that the component's layout is up to date

- *Visible*—Indicates that the component is visible

Table 12.3 lists the methods defined in the **UIStateContainer** class. Many of these methods override methods in **UIComponent** and **UIContainer**. The most important of these overrides—to a component with states—are the methods that set and get the states, including **isEnabled()**, **isFocused()**, **isHot()**, **isPressed()**, **isSelected()**, **setPressed()**, **setSelected()**, **setVisible()**, and others.

**Table 12.3  Methods of the UIStateContainer class.**

| Method | Description |
|---|---|
| add() | Adds a component to the container |
| addContainerListener() | Registers a container listener with the component |
| addFocusListener() | Registers a focus listener with the component |
| addKeyListener() | Registers a key listener with the component |
| addMouseListener() | Registers a mouse listener with the component |
| addMouseMotionListener() | Registers a mouse-motion listener with the component |
| addNotify() | Performs component initialization |
| adjustLayoutSize() | Adjusts the component's layout size |
| disableEvents() | Disables the specified events |
| enableEvents() | Enables the specified events |
| getBackground() | Gets the component's background color |
| getCachedPreferredSize() | Gets the container's preferred size |
| getCursor() | Gets the component's cursor |
| getEdge() | Gets the container's edge style |
| getFlags() | Gets the container's flags |
| getFont() | Gets the container's font |
| getForeground() | Gets the component's foreground color |
| getIndex() | Gets the component's index |
| getParent() | Gets the component's parent |

*(continued)*

**Table 12.3  Methods of the UIStateContainer class** *(continued).*

| Method | Description |
| --- | --- |
| isChecked() | Returns **true** if the component's check state is set |
| isEnabled() | Returns **true** if the component's enabled state is set |
| isFocused() | Returns **true** if the component's focused state is set |
| isHot() | Returns **true** if the component's hot-tracking state is set |
| isIndeterminate() | Returns **true** if the component's indeterminate state is set |
| isInvalidating() | Returns **true** if the component was invalidated |
| isNotified() | Returns **true** if the component's notified state is set |
| isPressed() | Returns **true** if the component's pressed state is set |
| isRedrawing() | Returns **true** if component will be redrawn |
| isSelected() | Returns **true** if the component's selected state is set |
| isValid() | Returns **true** if the component is valid |
| isVisible() | Returns **true** if the component is visible |
| postEvent() | Posts events to the component |
| processContainerEvent() | Handles container events |
| processEvent() | Handles the specified event |
| processKeyEvent() | Handles key events |
| processMouseEvent() | Handles mouse events |
| processMouseMotionEvent() | Handles mouse-motion events |
| recalcPreferredSize() | Recalculates the container's preferred size |
| remove() | Removes a component from the container |
| removeContainerListener() | Unregisters a container listener |
| removeFocusListener() | Unregisters a focus listener |
| removeKeyListener() | Unregisters a key listener |

*(continued)*

Table 12.3  Methods of the **UIStateContainer** class *(continued)*.

| Method | Description |
|---|---|
| removeMouseListener() | Unregisters a mouse listener |
| removeMouseMotionListener() | Unregisters a mouse-motion listener |
| removeNotify() | Called when the component's graphics context is no longer available |
| setBackground() | Sets the component's background color |
| setChecked() | Toggles the component's checked state |
| setCursor() | Sets the component's cursor |
| setEdge() | Sets the container's edge style |
| setEnabled() | Toggles the component's enabled state |
| setFlags() | Sets the component's flags |
| setFocused() | Toggles the component's focused state |
| setFont() | Sets the component's font |
| setForeground() | Sets the component's foreground color |
| setHot() | Toggles the component's hot-tracked state |
| setIndeterminate() | Toggles the container's indeterminate |
| setIndex() | Sets the component's index |
| setInvalidating() | Sets the component's invalidating state |
| setParent() | Sets the component's parent |
| setPressed() | Toggles the component's pressed state |
| setRedrawing() | Toggles the component's redrawing state of the control |
| setSelected() | Toggles the component's selected state |
| setValid() | Toggles the component's valid state |
| setVisible() | Toggles the component's visible state |

# The **UISingleContainer** Class

The **UISingleContainer** class represents a special type of container, one that can hold only a single component, known as a *header component*. One example of this kind of container is a button, whose header component is the button's label. Other single-container components include scroll thumbs, menu items, status bars, and tabs, represented by the **UIScrollThumb**, **UIMenuItem**, **UIStatus**, and **UITab** classes, respectively.

Table 12.4 lists the methods defined in the **UISingleContainer** class. Many of these methods override methods in the **UIComponent** and **UIContainer** classes. Two methods defined for the first time in **UISingleContainer**—**getHeader()** and **setHeader()**— enable the container to access its header component. You're not likely to create a **UIStateContainer** object directly in your AFC programs; instead, you will create objects from the classes that extend **UISingleContainer**.

# The **UIPanel** Class

**UIPanel** is the first class in AFC's container hierarchy that you, as a programmer, will find most useful to extend in your programs. Using the **UIPanel** class, you can create custom components that contain the child-component layouts needed to implement your applet or application's user interface. **UIPanel** extends **UIStateContainer** and so represents a container that can manage states. Moreover, unlike a class extended from **UISingleContainer**, a **UIPanel** object can contain any number of child components.

Many useful AFC components are extended from **UIPanel**. These classes include **UIApplet**, **UIGroup**, **UIChoice**, **UIScrollViewer**, **UIRow**, **UISelector**, **UIViewer**, **UIPropertyPage**, **UIRoot**, **UIScroll**, **UISplitViewer**, and **UITabViewer**. Many other classes can trace their ancestry back to **UIPanel**, including **UICheckGroup**, **UIRadioGroup**, **UIEditChoice**, **UIColumnViewer**, **UIList**, **UIMenuList**, **UIBandBox**, **UITree**, **UIMarquee**, **UIWindow**, **UIDialog**, and **UIFrame**. In fact, most AFC components are actually panels in one form or another.

Table 12.5 lists the methods defined in the **UIPanel** class. All of these methods override methods defined in **UIComponent** or **UIContainer** (mostly **UIContainer**).

To create a **UIPanel** object, call the class's constructor through the **new** operator, like this:

```
UIPanel panel = new UIPanel();
```

**Table 12.4  Methods of the UISingleContainer class.**

| Method | Description |
| --- | --- |
| add() | Adds a component to the container |
| getChild() | Gets a child component |
| getChildBounds() | Gets a child component's bounding rectangle |
| getChildCount() | Gets the number of components in the container |
| getChildLocation() | Gets a child component's location |
| getChildSize() | Gets a child component's size |
| getComponent() | Gets the component that contains the specified point |
| getComponentCount() | Gets the number of components in the container |
| getHeader() | Gets the container's header component |
| layout() | Lays out the component |
| mouseExit() | Handles mouse-exit events |
| relayout() | Requests layout for the container |
| remove() | Removes a component from the container |
| setFocused() | Toggles the component's focused state |
| setHeader() | Sets the container's header component |
| setID() | Set the component's ID |
| setName() | Sets the component's name |

**Table 12.5  Methods of the UIPanel class.**

| Method | Description |
| --- | --- |
| add() | Adds a component to the container |
| getChild() | Gets a child component |

*(continued)*

**Table 12.5  Methods of the UIPanel class** *(continued).*

| Method | Description |
|---|---|
| getChildBounds() | Gets a child component's bounding rectangle |
| getChildCount() | Gets the number of components in the container |
| getChildLocation() | Gets a child component's location |
| getChildSize() | Gets a child component's size |
| getComponent() | Gets the component that contains the specified point |
| getComponentCount() | Gets the number of components in the container |
| getHeader() | Gets the container's header component |
| getID() | Gets the container's ID |
| getLayout() | Gets the container's layout manager |
| getName() | Gets the component's name |
| getRoleCode() | Gets the panel's role code, which is **ROLE_SYSTEM_PANE** |
| move() | Moves a child component |
| paintAll() | Draws the component and its children |
| remove() | Removes a component from the container |
| setChildBounds() | Sets a child component's bounds |
| setChildLocation() | Sets a child component's location |
| setChildSize() | Sets a child component's size |
| setHeader() | Sets the container's header component |
| setID() | Set the component's ID |
| setLayout() | Sets the container's layout manager |
| setName() | Sets the component's name |
| setRedrawing() | Toggles the component's redrawing state |

**UIPanel** overloads it constructor, giving you two ways to create a panel. The second constructor takes an edge style as its single argument:

```
UIPanel panel = new UIPanel(IFxGraphicsConstants.BDR_RAISED);
```

You'll learn more about the edge styles in this chapter's Practical Guide.

After creating the panel, you can add it to your applet's layout just as you add any other component. However, an empty panel isn't very useful. Before adding the panel to your program's layout, you need to place components in the panel. The most elegant way to accomplish this task is to create custom panel classes, something you learn about in this chapter's Practical Guide.

## The **UIStateComponent** Class

Not all AFC components act as containers. Some are perfectly happy acting like just plain ol' components. These types of components include canvases and edit boxes, as well as static graphics, text, item, and line components. All these components have one thing in common: Their classes are derived from, or can trace their way back to, the **UIStateComponent** class.

**UIStateComponent** is one of two classes (the other being **UIContainer**) that directly extend **UIComponent**. Obviously, **UIStateComponent** inherits **UIComponent**'s impressive list of methods. It also defines a large set of its own, most of which override **UIComponent** methods to provide support for component states. The component states in question are the same states that are described in the **UIStateContainer** section of this chapter. Table 12.6 lists the methods defined in the **UIStateComponent** class.

You're not likely ever to create an object directly from **UIStateComponent**. Instead, you'll create (as you've done previously in this book) objects from the classes that have **UIStateComponent** as a superclass. These classes include **UICanvas**, **UIDrawText**, **UIEdit**, **UIStatic**, **UIGraphic**, **UIItem**, **UIText**, and **UILine**.

## The **UICanvas** Class

**UICanvas** is the first class in AFC's container hierarchy that most programmers will want to extend in their programs. Using the **UICanvas** class, you can create custom components on which the applet can draw by using the methods defined in the

## Table 12.6  Methods of the **UIStateComponent** class.

| Method | Description |
| --- | --- |
| addFocusListener() | Registers a focus listener with the component |
| addKeyListener() | Registers a key listener with the component |
| addMouseListener() | Registers a mouse listener with the component |
| addMouseMotionListener() | Registers a mouse-motion listener with the component |
| addNotify() | Performs component initialization |
| adjustLayoutSize() | Adjusts the component's layout size |
| disableEvents() | Disables the specified events |
| enableEvents() | Enables the specified events |
| getBackground() | Gets the component's background color |
| getCursor() | Gets the component's cursor |
| getFlags() | Gets the component's flags |
| getFont() | Gets the component's font |
| getForeground() | Gets the component's foreground color |
| getIndex() | Gets the component's index |
| getParent() | Gets the component's parent |
| isChecked() | Returns **true** if the component's check state is set |
| isEnabled() | Returns **true** if the component's enabled state is set |
| isFocused() | Returns **true** if the component's focused state is set |
| isHot() | Returns **true** if the component's hot-tracking state is set |
| isIndeterminate() | Returns **true** if the component's indeterminate state is set |
| isInvalidating() | Returns **true** if the component has been invalidated |
| isNotified() | Returns **true** if the component's notified state is set |

*(continued)*

**Table 12.6   Methods of the UIStateComponent class *(continued)*.**

| Method | Description |
|---|---|
| isPressed() | Returns **true** if the component's pressed state is set |
| isRedrawing() | Returns **true** if the component will be redrawn |
| isSelected() | Returns **true** if the component's selected state is set |
| isValid() | Returns **true** if the component is valid |
| isVisible() | Returns **true** if the component is visible |
| processEvent() | Handles the specified event |
| processFocusEvent() | Handles the specified event |
| processKeyEvent() | Handles key events |
| processMouseEvent() | Handles mouse events |
| processMouseMotionEvent() | Handles mouse-motion events |
| recalcPreferredSize() | Recalculates the container's preferred size |
| removeFocusListener() | Unregisters a focus listener |
| removeKeyListener() | Unregisters a key listener |
| removeMouseListener() | Unregisters a mouse listener |
| removeMouseMotionListener() | Unregisters a mouse-motion listener |
| removeNotify() | Called when the component's graphics context is no longer available |
| setBackground() | Sets the component's background color |
| setChecked() | Toggles the component's checked state |
| setCursor() | Sets the component's cursor |
| setEnabled() | Toggles the component's enabled state |
| setFlags() | Sets the component's flags |

*(continued)*

Table 12.6   Methods of the **UIStateComponent** class *(continued)*.

| Method | Description |
| --- | --- |
| setFocused() | Toggles the component's focused state |
| setFont() | Sets the component's font |
| setForeground() | Sets the component's foreground color |
| setHot() | Toggles the component's hot-tracked state |
| setIndeterminate() | Toggles the component's indeterminate state |
| setInvalidating() | Sets the component's invalidating state |
| setParent() | Sets the component's parent |
| setPressed() | Toggles the component's pressed state |
| setRedrawing() | Toggles the component's redrawing state |
| setSelected() | Toggles the component's selected state |
| setValid() | Toggles the component's valid state |
| setVisible() | Toggles the component's visible state |

**FxGraphics** class, such as **draw3DRect()**, **drawImage()**, **drawString()**, **drawPixels()**, and **drawPolyline()**. **UICanvas** extends **UIStateContainer** and so represents a component (not a container) that can manage states.

Some handy AFC classes, such as **UIDrawText()** and **UIStatic()**, extend **UIPanel**. Other classes can trace their ancestry back to **UIPanel**, including **UIEdit**, **UIGraphic**, **UIItem**, and **UIText**. All these classes inherit their basic functionality from **UICanvas**. Table 12.7 lists the methods defined in the **UICanvas** class. All these methods override methods defined in **UIComponent**.

To create a **UICanvas** object, call the class's constructor through the **new** operator, as in the following example:

```
UICanvas canvas = new UICanvas();
```

**Table 12.7   Methods of the UICanvas class.**

| Method | Description |
|---|---|
| getID() | Gets the component's ID |
| getName() | Gets the component's name |
| setID() | Sets the component's ID |
| setName() | Sets the component's name |

After creating the canvas, you can add it to your applet's layout just as you add any other component. However, an empty canvas isn't very useful. To display anything on the canvas's surface, you must at least override the class's **paint()** method. Also, to override **paint()**, you have to extend **UICanvas** with your own custom canvas class. You learn more about extending **UICanvas** in this chapter's Practical Guide.

# Practical Guide To

# Using Panels And Canvases

- Using Panels As Component Containers

- Accessing Child Components In A Panel

- Creating Custom Panel Classes

- Dynamically Removing And Adding Panel Components

- Displaying Panels With Different Edge Styles

- Creating Custom Canvas Classes

# Using Panels As Component Containers

Panels weren't named panels just because someone couldn't come up with a better name. Panels get their name from the way you use them. Specifically, panels in Java, just like panels in the real world, represent a surface on which you can install controls. Consider, for example, the control panel on your microwave oven or CD player. Java panels, too, contain controls (usually), although these controls are Java components rather than buttons and knobs that you can actually touch.

Because a **UIApplet** object is a special kind of panel, it can contain Java components. How many components it can hold and how they're positioned depend on the current layout manager. (See Chapter 9 for more information on component layouts.) But the important thing to remember is that an AFC applet's display area is a panel, which means that often you can create the component layout you need without being forced to create additional panels.

However, a panel—even of the applet variety—can be associated with only one layout manager, and occasionally, no single layout manager will give you the flexibility you need to create your desired layout. In this case, you can break down your layout into multiple panels, with each panel containing its own layout manager. By combining several layouts in this way, you can devise nearly any component arrangement imaginable. For really complex layouts, you can even nest panels inside panels. The combinations are endless.

To use multiple panels as control containers in your applet, you must perform the following steps:

1. Set the applet's layout manager to the layout that will hold the number of needed panels. If you need to stack three panels vertically, for example, you may want to create a grid layout with three vertical cells.

2. Create a **UIPanel** object for each panel in the layout.

3. Set each panel's layout manager as appropriate for your applet. Each panel can have a different type of layout manager.

4. Add components to each of the panels.

5. Add the panels to the applet's layout.

Listing 12.1 presents an applet that uses the previously discussed techniques to create the component layout shown in Figure 12.1. When you click one of the buttons in the layout, the button's label appears in the text box located at the bottom of the

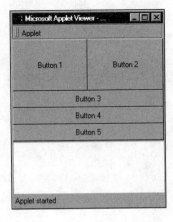

**Figure 12.1**

*PanelCompApplet, running in Applet Viewer.*

applet. As you can see, although the buttons are located in panels, they can still report their events back to the applet for handling.

**Listing 12.1  Source code for PanelCompApplet.**

```
///////////////////////////////////////////////
// PanelCompApplet.java
//
// An AFC applet that demonstrates how to use
// multiple panels to create component layouts.
///////////////////////////////////////////////

import com.ms.ui.*;
import com.ms.ui.event.*;

public class PanelCompApplet extends AwtUIApplet
{
    public PanelCompApplet()
    {
        super(new AppletImplementation());
    }
}

class AppletImplementation extends UIApplet
    implements IUIActionListener
{
    UIEdit edit;

    public void init()
    {
```

```
        UIGridLayout layout = new UIGridLayout(3, 1);
        setLayout(layout);

        UIPanel upperPanel = new UIPanel();
        UIGridLayout panelLayout1 = new UIGridLayout(1, 2);
        upperPanel.setLayout(panelLayout1);
        UIPushButton button1 =
            new UIPushButton("Button 1", UIPushButton.RAISED);
        button1.addActionListener(this);
        upperPanel.add(button1);
        UIPushButton button2 =
            new UIPushButton("Button 2", UIPushButton.RAISED);
        button2.addActionListener(this);
        upperPanel.add(button2);

        UIPanel middlePanel = new UIPanel();
        UIGridLayout panelLayout2 = new UIGridLayout(3, 1);
        middlePanel.setLayout(panelLayout2);
        UIPushButton button3 =
            new UIPushButton("Button 3", UIPushButton.RAISED);
        button3.addActionListener(this);
        middlePanel.add(button3);
        UIPushButton button4 =
            new UIPushButton("Button 4", UIPushButton.RAISED);
        button4.addActionListener(this);
        middlePanel.add(button4);
        UIPushButton button5 =
            new UIPushButton("Button 5", UIPushButton.RAISED);
        button5.addActionListener(this);
        middlePanel.add(button5);

        edit = new UIEdit();

        add(upperPanel);
        add(middlePanel);
        add(edit);

        setValid(true);
    }

    public void actionPerformed(UIActionEvent event)
    {
        String label = event.getActionCommand();
        edit.setValueText(label);
    }
}
```

# Accessing Child Components In A Panel

Commonly, components placed in an applet's layout are declared as data fields of the class. When you declare child components in this way, you can access the components by name anywhere in the applet. If you don't declare the components as data fields, you cannot access them (outside of the method in which they're created) by the object's name.

For example, in Listing 12.2, the **UIPanel** object named **panel** cannot be accessed by name outside of the **init()** method. This problem occurs because the **panel** identifier is in scope only inside the **init()** method. That is, even though the **panel** object exists as long as the applet is running, its object name ceases to exist when **init()** exits.

**Listing 12.2   Component scope limited to the init() method.**

```
import com.ms.ui.*;

public class PanelChildApplet extends AwtUIApplet
{
    public PanelChildApplet()
    {
        super(new AppletImplementation());
    }
}

class AppletImplementation extends UIApplet
{
    public void init()
    {
        // This panel object cannot be accessed by
        // name outside of init().
        UIPanel panel = new UIPanel();
    }
}
```

The most common way around this scope problem is to define the components you need to access as data fields of the class. Listing 12.3 shows how you can change Listing 12.2 so that the **panel** identifier will be accessible in other methods in the applet.

**Listing 12.3   Component scope not limited to the init() method.**

```
import com.ms.ui.*;

public class PanelChildApplet extends AwtUIApplet
{
    public PanelChildApplet()
    {
```

```
            super(new AppletImplementation());
        }
    }

class AppletImplementation extends UIApplet
{
    UIPanel panel;

    public void init()
    {
        panel = new UIPanel();
    }
}
```

There is, however, another way to access the components in a panel, a way that doesn't require that you declare the components as data fields. Just call the panel's **getChild()** method with the zero-based index for the component you want to access. Then, with a little casting trickery, you can access the component and its methods. (A component's index is based on the order in which the component appears in the layout.)

Listing 12.4 presents a short applet that demonstrates this programming technique. When you run the applet in Applet Viewer, you see the window shown in Figure 12.2. Click the Set Edit Text button, and a line of text appears in the edit box. Click the Set Button Text button, and the button's label changes. If you look at the listing, you will see that none of the components—not even the panel—has names that remain in scope outside of **init()**, yet the **actionPerformed()** method has no problem finding the components and calling their methods.

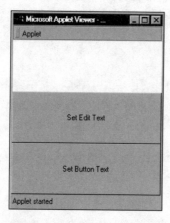

**Figure 12.2**

*PanelChildApplet, running in Applet Viewer.*

## Listing 12.4  Source code for PanelChildApplet.

```
//////////////////////////////////////////////////
// PanelChildApplet.java
//
// An AFC applet that demonstrates how to access
// child components in a panel.
//////////////////////////////////////////////////

import com.ms.ui.*;
import com.ms.ui.event.*;

public class PanelChildApplet extends AwtUIApplet
{
    public PanelChildApplet()
    {
        super(new AppletImplementation());
    }
}

class AppletImplementation extends UIApplet
    implements IUIActionListener
{
    public void init()
    {
        UIBorderLayout layout = new UIBorderLayout();
        setLayout(layout);

        UIPanel panel = new UIPanel();
        UIGridLayout panelLayout = new UIGridLayout(3, 1);
        panel.setLayout(panelLayout);
        UIEdit edit = new UIEdit();
        panel.add(edit);
        UIPushButton button1 =
            new UIPushButton("Set Edit Text",
            UIPushButton.RAISED);
        button1.addActionListener(this);
        panel.add(button1);
        UIPushButton button2 =
            new UIPushButton("Set Button Text",
            UIPushButton.RAISED);
        button2.addActionListener(this);
        panel.add(button2);
        add(panel, "Center");

        setValid(true);
    }

    public void actionPerformed(UIActionEvent event)
    {
```

```
        String label = event.getActionCommand();
        if (label == "Set Edit Text")
        {
            IUIComponent panel = getChild(0);
            IUIComponent edit = ((UIPanel)panel).getChild(0);
            ((UIEdit)edit).setValueText("New Edit Box Text!");
        }
        else if (label == "Set Button Text")
        {
            IUIComponent panel = getChild(0);
            IUIComponent button = ((UIPanel)panel).getChild(2);
            ((UIButton)button).setName("New Button Text!");
        }
    }
}
```

You may be a little thrown by the syntax used to cast the **IUIComponent** object returned by **getChild()** to the proper object type. Look, for example, at the body of **actionPerformed()**'s first **if** statement. First, the program gets the panel component:

```
IUIComponent panel = getChild(0);
```

Because the panel is the first component in the applet's layout, its index is zero. However, **getChild()** returns an **IUIComponent** object. You can't access the panel's methods through an **IUIComponent** object; you must access the panel's methods through a **UIPanel** object. The next line in the program both casts **panel** from **IUIComponent** to **UIPanel** and calls the panel's **getChild()** method to obtain the panel's first component, which is the edit control:

```
IUIComponent edit = ((UIPanel)panel).getChild(0);
```

A different way to write the code lines you examined so far might be as follows:

```
// Get the panel component.
IUIComponent comp = getChild(0);

// Cast to a UIPanel object.
UIPanel panel = (UIPanel) comp;

// Get the panel's edit component.
IUIComponent edit = panel.getChild(0);
```

Here, you can more easily see the way the cast from **IUIComponent** to **UIPanel** works. You could, in fact, rewrite the **actionPerformed()** method as shown in Listing 12.5.

## Listing 12.5   Modified source code for **actionPerformed()**.

```
public void actionPerformed(UIActionEvent event)
{
    String label = event.getActionCommand();
    if (label == "Set Edit Text")
    {
        IUIComponent comp = getChild(0);
        UIPanel panel = (UIPanel) comp;
        comp = panel.getChild(0);
        UIEdit edit = (UIEdit)comp;
        edit.setValueText("New Edit Box Text!");
    }
    else if (label == "Set Button Text")
    {
        IUIComponent comp = getChild(0);
        UIPanel panel = (UIPanel)comp;
        comp = panel.getChild(2);
        UIButton button = (UIButton)comp;
        button.setName("New Button Text!");
    }
}
```

## Creating Custom Panel Classes

So far in this chapter's programs, you created and populated your panel objects all within the applet's **init()** method. Although this technique works fine for simple layouts, things can become very confusing when you start creating many panels or even, heaven forbid, nesting panels. Before you know it, your **init()** method will be almost unreadable and as lengthy as your neighbor's home movies. The solution to this dilemma is to create your own panel classes, taking all the details out of **init()** and placing them inside the panel class's constructor, where they belong.

Creating a custom panel class requires only extending the class from **UIPanel** and providing a suitable constructor. In the constructor, you create the panel's layout, all hidden from the main applet. If you need your applet to respond to events generated by components in the panel, simply pass a reference to the applet to the panel's constructor. You can then add the applet as an event listener to whatever event generators you create in the panel.

Listing 12.6 is an applet that demonstrates how to create and manage custom panel classes. For comparison purposes, this applet is much like PanelCompApplet in Listing 12.1. The applet was rewritten to organize the panels into their own classes. Additionally, the applet adds a third panel for the edit control, using the panel's insets to force

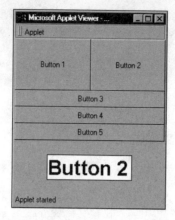

**Figure 12.3**

*PanelClassApplet, running in Applet Viewer.*

the edit control to a more appropriate size. When you run the applet in Applet Viewer, click a button. The button's label appears in the edit box, as shown in Figure 12.3.

### Listing 12.6   Source code for PanelClassApplet.

```
/////////////////////////////////////////////////
// PanelClassApplet.java
//
// An AFC applet that demonstrates how to create
// custom panel classes to organize layouts.
/////////////////////////////////////////////////

import com.ms.ui.*;
import com.ms.fx.FxFont;
import com.ms.ui.event.*;
import java.awt.Insets;

public class PanelClassApplet extends AwtUIApplet
{
    public PanelClassApplet()
    {
        super(new AppletImplementation());
    }
}

class AppletImplementation extends UIApplet
    implements IUIActionListener
{
    public void init()
    {
```

```java
        UIGridLayout layout = new UIGridLayout(3, 1);
        setLayout(layout);

        UpperPanel upperPanel = new UpperPanel(this);
        MiddlePanel middlePanel = new MiddlePanel(this);
        LowerPanel lowerPanel = new LowerPanel();

        add(upperPanel);
        add(middlePanel);
        add(lowerPanel);

        setValid(true);
    }

    public void actionPerformed(UIActionEvent event)
    {
        String label = event.getActionCommand();
        IUIComponent panel = getChild(2);
        ((LowerPanel)panel).edit.setValueText(label);
    }
}

class UpperPanel extends UIPanel
{
    public UpperPanel(IUIActionListener applet)
    {
        UIGridLayout panelLayout = new UIGridLayout(1, 2);
        setLayout(panelLayout);

        UIPushButton button1 =
            new UIPushButton("Button 1", UIPushButton.RAISED);
        button1.addActionListener(applet);
        add(button1);

        UIPushButton button2 =
            new UIPushButton("Button 2", UIPushButton.RAISED);
        button2.addActionListener(applet);
        add(button2);
    }
}

class MiddlePanel extends UIPanel
{
    public MiddlePanel(IUIActionListener applet)
    {
        UIGridLayout panelLayout = new UIGridLayout(3, 1);
        setLayout(panelLayout);
```

```
        UIPushButton button3 =
            new UIPushButton("Button 3", UIPushButton.RAISED);
        button3.addActionListener(applet);
        add(button3);

        UIPushButton button4 =
            new UIPushButton("Button 4", UIPushButton.RAISED);
        button4.addActionListener(applet);
        add(button4);

        UIPushButton button5 =
            new UIPushButton("Button 5", UIPushButton.RAISED);
        button5.addActionListener(applet);
        add(button5);
    }
}

class LowerPanel extends UIPanel
{
    UIEdit edit;

    public LowerPanel()
    {
        UIBorderLayout panelLayout = new UIBorderLayout();
        setLayout(panelLayout);

        edit = new UIEdit();
        FxFont font = new FxFont("Arial", FxFont.BOLD, 32);
        edit.setFont(font);
        edit.setBordered(true);
        add(edit, "Center");
    }

    public Insets getInsets()
    {
        return new Insets(20, 52, 20, 52);
    }
}
```

## Dynamically Removing And Adding Panel Components

You may run into situations where you want to display different components in your applet, based on user input. For example, you may have some options that are available only when the user selects a particular command. You can easily remove and add components to a layout by calling the panel's **remove()** and **add()** methods.

Listing 12.7 presents an applet that lets you experiment with removing and adding components. When you run the applet in Applet Viewer, you see the window shown in Figure 12.4. Click the Add button to add components to the layout, and click the Remove button to remove components. Figure 12.5, for example, shows the applet after the user has clicked the Add button four times.

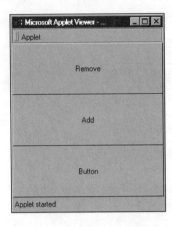

**Figure 12.4**

*PanelRemoveApplet, running in Applet Viewer.*

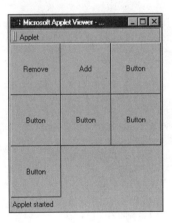

**Figure 12.5**

*PanelRemoveApplet after adding four components.*

**Listing 12.7  Source code for PanelRemoveApplet.**

```java
//////////////////////////////////////////////////
// PanelRemoveApplet.java
//
// An AFC applet that demonstrates removing
// and adding components from and to a panel.
//////////////////////////////////////////////////

import com.ms.ui.*;
import com.ms.ui.event.*;

public class PanelRemoveApplet extends AwtUIApplet
{
    public PanelRemoveApplet()
    {
        super(new AppletImplementation());
    }
}

class AppletImplementation extends UIApplet
    implements IUIActionListener
{
    public void init()
    {
        UIBorderLayout layout = new UIBorderLayout();
        setLayout(layout);

        ButtonPanel panel = new ButtonPanel(this);
        add(panel);

        setValid(true);
    }

    public void actionPerformed(UIActionEvent event)
    {
        String label = event.getActionCommand();
        if (label == "Remove")
        {
            IUIComponent panel = getChild(0);
            ((ButtonPanel)panel).remove(2);
        }
        else
        {
            UIPushButton button =
                new UIPushButton("Button",
                UIPushButton.RAISED);
```

```
            IUIComponent panel = getChild(0);
            ((ButtonPanel)panel).add(button);
        }
    }
}

class ButtonPanel extends UIPanel
{
    public ButtonPanel(IUIActionListener applet)
    {
        UIGridLayout panelLayout = new UIGridLayout(3, 1);
        setLayout(panelLayout);

        UIPushButton removeButton =
            new UIPushButton("Remove", UIPushButton.RAISED);
        removeButton.addActionListener(applet);
        add(removeButton);

        UIPushButton addButton =
            new UIPushButton("Add", UIPushButton.RAISED);
        addButton.addActionListener(applet);
        add(addButton);

        UIPushButton button =
            new UIPushButton("Button", UIPushButton.RAISED);
        add(button);
    }
}
```

## Displaying Panels With Different Edge Styles

As was hinted at previously in this chapter, you can create panels that use different edge styles. This extra graphical pizzazz can make a big difference in your applet's appearance. To add an edge style, simply call the version of the **UIPanel** constructor that accepts the edge style as its single argument:

```
UIPanel panel = new UIPanel(style);
```

Here, **style** can be one of fourteen values, as follows:

- **0** (no style)

- **IFxGraphicsConstants.BDR_RAISED**

- **IFxGraphicsConstants.BDR_SUNKEN**

- **IFxGraphicsConstants.BDR_OUTER**

- **IFxGraphicsConstants.BDR_INNER**

- **IFxGraphicsConstants.BDR_RAISEDOUTER**

- **IFxGraphicsConstants.BDR_RAISEDINNER**

- **IFxGraphicsConstants.BDR_SUNKENOUTER**

- **IFxGraphicsConstants.BDR_SUNKENINNER**

- **IFxGraphicsConstants.BDR_FLAT**

- **IFxGraphicsConstants.EDGE_RAISED**

- **IFxGraphicsConstants.EDGE_SUNKEN**

- **IFxGraphicsConstants.EDGE_ETCHED**

- **IFxGraphicsConstants.EDGE_BUMP**

As you can see, the styles are defined in the **IFxGraphicsConstants** interface, so make sure that you add **com.ms.fx.IFxGraphicsConstants** to your applet's other include files.

Listing 12.8 presents an applet that displays all the different panel styles. When you run the applet in Applet Viewer, you see the window shown in Figure 12.6. Click the Change Style button to switch to a different panel style. The new panel appears, containing a text string that describes the current style. Figure 12.7 shows the panel with a raised style, and Figure 12.8 shows the panel with a sunken style.

**Figure 12.6**

*PanelStyleApplet, running in Applet Viewer.*

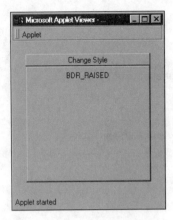

**Figure 12.7**

*PanelStyleApplet with a raised panel.*

**Figure 12.8**

*PanelStyleApplet with a sunken panel.*

### Listing 12.8   Source code for PanelStyleApplet.

```
///////////////////////////////////////////////
// PanelStyleApplet.java
//
// An AFC applet that shows the different panel
// edge styles.
///////////////////////////////////////////////

import com.ms.ui.*;
import com.ms.fx.IFxGraphicsConstants;
import com.ms.ui.event.*;
import java.awt.Insets;
```

```
public class PanelStyleApplet extends AwtUIApplet
{
    public PanelStyleApplet()
    {
        super(new AppletImplementation());
    }
}

class AppletImplementation extends UIApplet
    implements IUIActionListener
{
    int styleNum;
    int styles[];
    String names[];

    public void init()
    {
        UIBorderLayout layout = new UIBorderLayout();
        setLayout(layout);

        UIPushButton button =
            new UIPushButton("Change Style", UIPushButton.RAISED);
        button.addActionListener(this);
        add(button, "North");

        styles = new int[14];
        names = new String[14];
        styleNum = 0;

        styles[0] = 0;
        names[0] = "No Style";
        styles[1] = IFxGraphicsConstants.BDR_RAISED;
        names[1] = "BDR_RAISED";
        styles[2] = IFxGraphicsConstants.BDR_SUNKEN;
        names[2] = "BDR_SUNKEN";
        styles[3] = IFxGraphicsConstants.BDR_OUTER;
        names[3] = "BDR_OUTER";
        styles[4] = IFxGraphicsConstants.BDR_INNER;
        names[4] = "BDR_INNER";
        styles[5] = IFxGraphicsConstants.BDR_RAISEDOUTER;
        names[5] = "BDR_RAISEDOUTER";
        styles[6] = IFxGraphicsConstants.BDR_RAISEDINNER;
        names[6] = "BDR_RAISEDINNER";
        styles[7] = IFxGraphicsConstants.BDR_SUNKENOUTER;
        names[7] = "BDR_SUNKENOUTER";
        styles[8] = IFxGraphicsConstants.BDR_SUNKENINNER;
        names[8] = "BDR_SUNKENINNER";
        styles[9] = IFxGraphicsConstants.BDR_FLAT;
```

```
    names[9] = "BDR_FLAT";
    styles[10] = IFxGraphicsConstants.EDGE_RAISED;
    names[10] = "EDGE_RAISED";
    styles[11] = IFxGraphicsConstants.EDGE_SUNKEN;
    names[11] = "EDGE_SUNKEN";
    styles[12] = IFxGraphicsConstants.EDGE_ETCHED;
    names[12] = "EDGE_ETCHED";
    styles[13] = IFxGraphicsConstants.EDGE_BUMP;
    names[13] = "EDGE_BUMP";

    UIPanel panel = new UIPanel(0);
    UIText text = new UIText("No Style");
    panel.add(text);
    add(panel);

    setValid(true);
}

public void actionPerformed(UIActionEvent event)
{
    remove(1);

    ++styleNum;
    if (styleNum == 14)
        styleNum = 0;

    int style = styles[styleNum];
    String name = names[styleNum];
    UIPanel panel = new UIPanel(style);
    UIText text = new UIText(name);
    panel.add(text);
    add(panel, "Center");
}

public Insets getInsets()
{
    return new Insets(20, 20, 20, 20);
}
}
```

## Creating Custom Canvas Classes

As you know, several AFC classes—including **UIDrawText**, **UIEdit**, and **UIText**—are really just special types of canvases. You also can extend the **UICanvas** class to create your own special displays. Just extend your custom class from **UICanvas** and provide at least a constructor and a **paint()** method. In the **paint()** method, you draw what you want to appear on the canvas. Keep in mind, however, that a canvas is not a container, and so cannot host other components.

Listing 12.9 presents an applet that creates and displays a custom canvas object. The **ImageCanvas** class displays, in a 3D frame, any image that's passed to its constructor. Figure 12.9 shows the applet when you run it in Applet Viewer. Notice how the canvas not only displays the image, but also paints a 3D border around the image. The size of this border must change when the image size changes, which it does, as you can see in Figure 12.10. Notice the use of a **MediaTracker** object in the applet's **init()** method to ensure that the image is fully loaded before it's passed to the canvas for display.

**Figure 12.9**

*CanvasApplet, running in Applet Viewer.*

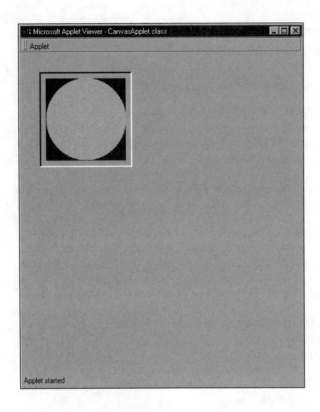

**Figure 12.10**

*CanvasApplet, displaying a different image.*

**Listing 12.9  Source code for CanvasApplet.**

```
/////////////////////////////////////////////////
// CanvasApplet.java
//
// An AFC applet that demonstrates how to create
// a custom canvas component.
/////////////////////////////////////////////////

import com.ms.ui.*;
import com.ms.fx.*;
import java.awt.*;
import java. applet.*;

public class CanvasApplet extends AwtUIApplet
{
    public CanvasApplet()
    {
```

```
            super(new AppletImplementation());
    }
}

class AppletImplementation extends UIApplet
{
    public void init()
    {
        UIBorderLayout layout = new UIBorderLayout();
        setLayout(layout);

        Applet applet = getApplet();
        MediaTracker tracker = new MediaTracker(applet);
        Image image = getImage(getCodeBase(), "sunset.git");
        tracker.addImage(image, 0);

        try
        {
            tracker.waitForAll();
        }
        catch (InterruptedException e)
        {
        }

        ImageCanvas canvas = new ImageCanvas(image);
        add(canvas, "Center");
    }

    public Insets getInsets()
    {
        return new Insets(20, 20, 20,20);
    }
}

class ImageCanvas extends UICanvas
{
    Image image;

    public ImageCanvas(Image image)
    {
        this.image = image;
    }

    public void paint(FxGraphics graphics)
    {
        int width = image.getWidth(this);
        int height = image.getHeight(this);
```

```
        graphics.drawImage(image, 20, 20, width, height, this);

        graphics.drawLine(10, 10, width+29, 10);
        graphics.drawLine(10, 10, 10, height+29);
        graphics.drawLine(11, 11, width+28, 11);
        graphics.drawLine(11, 11, 11, height+28);

        graphics.setColor(FxColor.white);

        graphics.drawLine(10, height+29, width+29, height+29);
        graphics.drawLine(width+29, height+29, width+29, 10);
        graphics.drawLine(11, height+28, width+28, height+28);
        graphics.drawLine(width+28, height+28, width+28, 11);
    }
}
```

# Chapter 13

# The General And Font Fx Classes

# Notes…

*Chapter*

# 13

If Robert M. Pirsig ever had a chance to sit down and try writing a computer program, I wonder whether he might have removed digital computers from his list of spiritual things. At least with a motorcycle, you can see the gears, and so watch what goes on inside. Last I heard, no one has come up with a way to take the hood off a microprocessor. But then, bits are so much smaller than gears, eh? Speaking of gears, up to this point in the book, you concentrated on the user interface classes that make up the bulk of AFC. Now, it's time to switch gears (talk about a sloppy segue) and spend the last few chapters looking at some of the other useful classes that make up AFC.

In this chapter, you explore a few of the classes defined in the **com.ms.fx** package, which extend the graphical capabilities of Java. The most important of these classes, **FxGraphics**, directly extends Java AWT's **Graphics** class, adding handy capabilities sure to make your AFC programs special. A couple of font classes and a class for managing ellipses round out this chapter's discussion. You can also trace the ancestry of these classes back to Java AWT classes.

## The **FxGraphics** Class

**FxGraphics** is the AFC counterpart to Java's **Graphics** class. If you've done any Java graphics programming, you know that the **Graphics** class provides the methods needed to draw lines, shapes, and text in an applet's display area. **FxGraphics**, actually, directly extends Java's **Graphics** class, which means that you can access, through **FxGraphics**, the same methods you're used to using with **Graphics**. **FxGraphics**, however, adds a few special twists, including methods such as **drawPixels()** and **drawPolyline()**, as well as enables you to perform actions such as drawing text at any angle. Table 13.1 lists the methods in the **FxGraphics** class. Some of these methods, like **drawString()**, override Java **Graphics** methods, extending the method to provide new features.

**Table 13.1  Methods of the FxGraphics class.**

| Method | Description |
|---|---|
| **draw3DRect()** | Draws a 3D rectangle |
| **drawBezier()** | Draws a Bezier curve |
| **drawBorder()** | Draws the 3D rectangle's border |
| **drawChars()** | Draws a character array |
| **drawEdge()** | Draws a 3D rectangle's edges |
| **drawImage()** | Draws an image |
| **drawOutlineChar()** | Draws an outline character |
| **drawOutlinePolygon()** | Draws a character's outline polygon |
| **drawPixels()** | Draws a set of pixels |
| **drawPolyline()** | Draws multiple lines at one time |
| **drawScanLines()** | Draws fast lines, either horizontally or vertically |
| **drawString()** | Draws the given string using the supplied advancement lists |
| **drawStringFormatted()** | Draws a formatted text string |
| **drawT2Curve()** | Draws a true-type curve |
| **excludeClip()** | Disables clipping in a rectangle |
| **fill3DRect()** | Draws a solid 3D rectangle |
| **getClip()** | Gets the clipping area |

*(continued)*

**Table 13.1  Methods of the FxGraphics class** *(continued).*

| Method | Description |
| --- | --- |
| **getClipBounds()** | Gets the clipping area's bounds |
| **getClipRegion()** | Gets the clipping area in the form of a region |
| **getExtendedGraphics()** | Gets an extended graphics object |
| **getGlyphOutline()** | Gets a character's outline |
| **getTextBackgroundColor()** | Gets the text's background color |
| **getTranslation()** | Gets the translation origin point |
| **intersectClip()** | Sets the clipping area |
| **setClip()** | Sets the clipping area |
| **setColor()** | Sets the color for drawing operations |
| **setTextBackgroundColor()** | Sets the text's background color |

# The **FxFont** Class

The **FxFont** class, as you may have guessed, represents fonts in an AFC program. **FxFont** extends directly from Java's **Font**, so you can use it just as you use the **Font** class. **FxFont**, however, overrides the **getFont()** method to provide extra features, and it also defines some new methods such as **getEmboldenedFont()**, **getAttributeList()**, and **getStyleVal()**. Table 13.2 lists the methods defined in the **FxFont** class.

You can create a font with **FxFont** just as you did with **Font**, as shown in the following example:

```
FxFont font = new FxFont("TimesRoman", FxFont.PLAIN, 36);
```

Here, the example creates a 36-point, plain (not bold or italic) Times Roman font. The constructor's three arguments are described as follows:

- The font's name

- The font's style (can be **PLAIN**, **BOLD**, or **ITALIC**)

- The font's size in points

## Table 13.2   Methods of the **FxFont** class.

| Method | Description |
| --- | --- |
| drawBytesCallback() | Draws an array of bytes; for internal use only |
| drawCharsCallback() | Draws an array of characters; for internal use only |
| drawOutlineCharCallback() | Draws an outline character; for internal use only |
| drawStringCallback() | Draws a string; for internal use only |
| getAttributeList() | Gets a list of the font's generic attributes |
| getEmboldenedFont() | Gets a bold version of the font |
| getFlags() | Gets the font's extra flags |
| getFlagsVal() | Gets a flag's value |
| getFont() | Gets a font |
| getFontList() | Gets a list of the font's faces |
| getFontMetricsCallback() | Gets the font metrics; for internal use only |
| getGlyphOutlineCallback() | Gets a character glyph outline; for internal use only |
| getStyleVal() | Gets a style's value |
| setBackgroundCallback() | Sets the text background color; for internal use only |
| setColorCallback() | Sets the font's foreground color; for internal use only |
| setFontCallback() | Sets the font; for internal use only |

You can also create a font by adding an additional style flag to the constructor, as follows:

```
FxFont font = new FxFont("TimesRoman",
    FxFont.PLAIN, 72, FxFont.UNDERLINE);
```

Here, the last argument is a style flag, which supposedly can be **STRIKEOUT**, **UNDERLINE**, or **EMBEDDED**. If you try to use the **EMBEDDED** style, however, your program won't compile. For some reason, Microsoft gave the **EMBEDDED** style flag private access. It looks like they don't want us to use it.

**Figure 13.1**

*FontApplet, running in Applet Viewer.*

Listing 13.1 presents a short applet that creates a font and displays a line of text with the font. When you run the applet in Applet Viewer, you see the window shown in Figure 13.1.

**Listing 13.1   Source code for FontApplet.**

```
/////////////////////////////////////////////////
// FontApplet.java
//
// An AFC applet that demonstrates how to create
// an AFC font.
/////////////////////////////////////////////////

import com.ms.ui.*;
import com.ms.fx.*;

public class FontApplet extends AwtUIApplet
{
    public FontApplet()
    {
        super(new AppletImplementation());
    }
}

class AppletImplementation extends UIApplet
{
    public void init()
    {
        setValid(true);
    }
```

```
    public void paint(FxGraphics graphics)
    {
        FxFont font = new FxFont("TimesRoman",
            FxFont.PLAIN, 36, FxFont.UNDERLINE);
        graphics.setFont(font);
        graphics.drawString("An AFC Font", 22, 100);
    }
}
```

# The **FxSystemFont** Class

The **FxSystemFont** class gives you easy access to the fonts that AFC uses for system purposes, such as menu items and message-box text. **FxSystemFont** extends **FxFont** and so inherits all of **FxFont**'s methods. **FxSystemFont** also defines a few methods of its own, as shown in Table 13.3.

**FxSystemFont** is a bit unusual in that the class has no constructor. Rather, all of its methods are declared as **static**, which means that you can call them without creating an **FxSystemFont** object. For example, to get the font that AFC uses in message boxes, you might write the following line:

```
Font sysFont = FxSystemFont.getMessageBoxFont();
```

**Table 13.3  Methods of the FxSystemFont class.**

| Method | Description |
| --- | --- |
| **getAttributeList()** | Gets a list of the font's generic attributes |
| **getCaptionFont()** | Gets the caption font |
| **getFont()** | Gets a font, given the face, vector, and size |
| **getFontList()** | Gets a list of the font's faces |
| **getIconTitleFont()** | Gets the icon title font |
| **getMenuFont()** | Gets the menu font |
| **getMessageBoxFont()** | Gets the message-box font |
| **getSmallCaptionFont()** | Gets the small caption font |
| **getStatusFont()** | Gets the status font |
| **matchFaceToFont()** | Matches a face to the font |

## Figure 13.2

*MenuFontApplet, running in Applet Viewer.*

Listing 13.2 presents a short applet that creates a system menu font and displays a line of text with the font. When you run the applet in Applet Viewer, you see the window shown in Figure 13.2.

## Listing 13.2   Source code for MenuFontApplet.

```
//////////////////////////////////////////////////
// MenuFontApplet.java
//
// An AFC applet that demonstrates how to create
// and use a system font.
//////////////////////////////////////////////////

import com.ms.ui.*;
import com.ms.fx.*;
import java.awt.*;

public class MenuFontApplet extends AwtUIApplet
{
    public MenuFontApplet()
    {
        super(new AppletImplementation());
    }
}

class AppletImplementation extends UIApplet
{
    public void init()
    {
        setValid(true);
    }
```

```
    public void paint(FxGraphics graphics)
    {
        Font sysFont = FxSystemFont.getMenuFont();
        graphics.setFont(sysFont);
        graphics.drawString("The menu Font", 70, 100);
    }
}
```

# The **FxEllipse** Class

Many modern programming languages provide a class for manipulating rectangles because rectangles are so prevalent in a windowed operating system. Even Java has the **Rectangle** class, which enables a program to manage a rectangle in many ways, including comparing, translating, and resizing rectangles. Java even includes a **Polygon** class for managing shapes with three or more edges. AFC adds to the shape classes by providing the **FxEllipse** class, which enables programs to—you guessed it—manipulate ellipses.

**FxEllipse** extends AFC's **FxCurve** class (it's currently the only class that extends **FxCurve**), which itself indirectly extends Java's **Shape** class through the **IFxShape** interface. **FxCurve** is an abstract class that implements none of the methods declared in the **IFxShape** interface, which leaves it up to **FxEllipse** to implement these methods (listed in Table 13.4). Unfortunately, although the methods are defined in the class (they have to be to satisfy the **IFxShape** interface), many of these methods are not yet fully implemented.

To create an ellipse object, call the **FxEllipse** constructor, as follows:

```
FxEllipse ellipse = new FxEllipse(20, 20, 100, 100);
```

**Table 13.4  Methods of the FxEllipse class.**

| Method | Description |
|---|---|
| **contains()** | Returns **true** if the given point is inside the curve's boundary |
| **draw()** | Draws the ellipse |
| **getBorderLength()** | Gets the border's length |
| **getBounds()** | Gets the ellipse's bounds |

*(continued)*

## Table 13.4   Methods of the **FxEllipse** class *(continued).*

| Method | Description |
|---|---|
| getOrigin() | Gets the origin |
| getPoint() | Gets a point on the curve |
| getPointAndAngle() | Gets a point on the curve and the angle of a perpendicular line |
| getPointAngle() | Gets the angle of a line perpendicular to the curve |
| getPointPos() | Gets a point from a position |
| setOrigin() | Sets the curve's origin |
| translate() | Translates the ellipse |
| updateBounds() | Updates the ellipse's bounding rectangle |

The constructor's four arguments are described as:

- The upper left X coordinate of the ellipse's bounding rectangle
- The upper left Y coordinate of the ellipse's bounding rectangle
- The ellipse's width
- The ellipse's height

**FxEllipse** objects are used as arguments for some AFC method calls. You also can draw an ellipse after creating it, by calling the object's **draw()** method. Listing 13.3, for example, presents a short applet that creates and displays an ellipse object. Figure 13.3 shows the applet running in Applet Viewer.

### Listing 13.3   Source code for EllipseApplet.

```
///////////////////////////////////////////////
// EllipseApplet.java
//
// An AFC applet that demonstrates how to create
// and display an FxEllipse object.
///////////////////////////////////////////////

import com.ms.ui.*;
import com.ms.fx.*;
```

```
public class EllipseApplet extends AwtUIApplet
{
    public EllipseApplet()
    {
        super(new AppletImplementation());
    }
}

class AppletImplementation extends UIApplet
{
    public void init()
    {
        setValid(true);
    }

    public void paint(FxGraphics graphics)
    {
        FxEllipse ellipse = new FxEllipse(20, 20, 100, 100);
        ellipse.draw(graphics);
    }
}
```

**Figure 13.3**

*EllipseApplet, running in Applet Viewer.*

# Practical Guide To

# Graphics And Font Classes

- Using Extended Graphics In An AWT Program
- Drawing Shapes With **FxGraphics**
- Creating User-Defined Fonts
- Creating System Fonts

## Using Extended Graphics In An AWT Program

The classes in the **com.ms.fx** package are compatible with Java's AWT, so you can access these classes even in conventional Java programs. This is even true of **FxGraphics**, although you first need to convert the **Graphics** object your **paint()** method receives to an extended **FxGraphics** object. Accomplishing this task is as easy as calling the static **FxGraphics.getExtendedGraphics()** function.

Listing 13.4 presents a short applet that shows how to create an extended graphics object in a traditional AWT Java program. In the **paint()** method, the program first draws some text with the standard **Graphics** object. The program then converts the **Graphics** object to an **FxGraphics** object and uses the extended graphics object to call two AFC methods, an AFC version of **drawString()** and the **drawPolyline()** method. Figure 13.4 shows the applet running in Applet Viewer.

### Listing 13.4   Source code for ExGraphicsApplet.

```
//////////////////////////////////////////////////
// ExGraphicsApplet.java
//
// An AWT applet that creates an extended AFC
// graphics object in order to access extended
// graphics capabilities.
//////////////////////////////////////////////////

import java.awt.*;
import java.applet.*;
import com.ms.fx.*;

public class ExGraphicsApplet extends Applet
{
    public void init()
    {
    }

    public void paint(Graphics graphics)
    {
        Font font = new Font("TimesRoman", Font.PLAIN, 24);
        graphics.setFont(font);
        graphics.drawString("AWT Text", 20, 40);

        FxGraphics fxGraphics =
            FxGraphics.getExtendedGraphics(graphics);
        fxGraphics.drawString("AFC Text", 20, 150, 20);
```

```
      int xPoints[] = {30, 200, 45, 10, 190, 25};//, 20, 30, 40};
      int yPoints[] = {40, 200, 180, 10, 20, 210};//, 200, 150, 90};
      fxGraphics.drawPolyline(xPoints, yPoints, 6);
   }
}
```

## Drawing Shapes With FxGraphics

Because **FxGraphics** extends Java's **Graphics** class, you get the best of both worlds. You can call the **Graphics** methods you're accustomed to using, and also take advantage of the extended and new methods provided by **FxGraphics**. These extended and new methods enable you to perform actions such as drawing text from a character array, drawing angled and formatted text, drawing polylines, and drawing a set of pixels.

Listing 13.5 presents an applet, named ShapesApplet, that shows how to draw with some of the **FxGraphics** object's more interesting methods. The program calls both standard methods, such as **drawLine()** and the new methods. Figure 13.5 shows the applet running in Applet Viewer. Click the Change Shape button to see the next drawing in the series. Each screen includes a text label at the bottom that tells you the drawing function that was called to produce the screen. Figure 13.6, for example, shows the polyline screen, whereas Figure 13.7 shows the formatted-text screen.

Using the various drawing methods is mostly straightforward; you can find descriptions of each method's arguments in the AFC documentation. Moreover, by experimenting

### Figure 13.4

*ExGraphicsApplet, running in Applet Viewer.*

**Figure 13.5**

*ShapesApplet, running in Applet Viewer.*

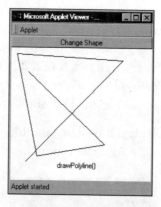

**Figure 13.6**

*ShapesApplet, displaying polylines.*

with ShapesApplet, you should be able to master any of the methods called in Listing 13.5. Only two of these methods are particularly tricky. For **drawPolyline()**, keep in mind that the first line drawn requires both the starting and the ending points. Subsequently, each point in the point arrays becomes the ending point of the next line, and the method sees that the starting point for the line is now the end point of the previous line. That is, the number of lines drawn will always be the number of points in the arrays, minus 1.

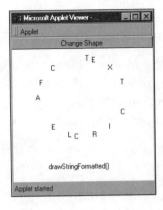

**Figure 13.7**

*ShapesApplet, displaying formatted text.*

The **drawStringFormatted()** method also requires further explanation because of its many arguments and poor documentation. The method's prototype looks as follows:

```
public FxFormattedText drawStringFormatted(String str,
    Rectangle rect, int hta, int vta, int ww,
    boolean bordered, int tabOrigin, int tabs[],
    IFxShape outline, boolean mnem);
```

The method's arguments are described as:

- *str*—The text to display.

- *rect*—The text's bounding rectangle. Anything outside of this rectangle will be clipped.

- *hta*—The horizontal text alignment. These alignments are defined in the **IFxTextConstants** interface, and can be **htaLeft, htaCenter, htaRight, htaStretch, htaJustified**, and **htaScriptDefault**. You can bring these constants into your class by declaring the class as implementing the **IFxTextConstants** interface. You need to experiment with the different alignments, but if you want the text to fill the outline you specify, you should use the **htaStretch** style.

- *vta*—The vertical text alignment, the constants for which are also defined in the **IFxTextConstants** interface. This value can be **vtaTop, vtaCenter, vtaBaseline, vtaBottom, vtaStretch**, or **vtaScriptDefault**.

Again, you need to experiment, but the vertical alignment seems to have little or no effect on the text display.

- *ww*—The word wrapping to use. This value, also defined in **IFxTextConstants**, can be **wwCleanEdges**, **wwKeepWordIntact**, **wwNone**, **wwVirtualRectEnd**, **wwVirtualRectSide**, or **wwWrap**. In most cases, word wrapping is inappropriate, so you'll use **wwNone**.

- *bordered*—A flag that specifies whether the text should be bordered. This flag seems to have no effect on the output.

- *tabOrigin*—The starting point for determining how to expand tabs. For example, in a straight line of text, the tab origin usually is the beginning of the text line. You probably won't use tabs with the **drawStringFormatted()** method, so you'll likely use 0 for this argument.

- *tabs*—An array of tab positions. Again, you probably won't use tabs, so you can just set this argument to **null**.

- *outline*—The shape on which the text layout is based. Because this argument requires an **IFxShape** object, and only **FxEllipse** currently implements **IFxShape**, this argument must be an **FxEllipse** object or **null**. If you use **null**, you get a straight line of normal text. If you use an ellipse, the text positions itself around the shape's outline.

- *mnem*—A flag that specifies whether mnemonic drawing should be used. *Mnemonic drawing* causes a character in the text to be underlined as a hot key. Only a value of **false** works here if you want formatted text. A value of **true** results in a straight line of text, with one character underlined.

## Listing 13.5  Source code for ShapesApplet.

```
///////////////////////////////////////////////////
// ShapesApplet.java
//
// An AFC applet that demonstrates how to draw
// with the FxGraphics object.
///////////////////////////////////////////////////

import com.ms.ui.*;
import com.ms.ui.event.*;
import com.ms.fx.*;
import java.awt.*;
```

```
public class ShapesApplet extends AwtUIApplet
{
    public ShapesApplet()
    {
        super(new AppletImplementation());
    }
}

class AppletImplementation extends UIApplet
    implements IUIActionListener
{
    int shapeNum;
    DrawCanvas canvas;

    public void init()
    {
        UIBorderLayout layout = new UIBorderLayout();
        setLayout(layout);

        UIPushButton button =
            new UIPushButton("Change Shape",
            UIPushButton.RAISED);
        button.addActionListener(this);
        add(button, "North");

        canvas = new DrawCanvas();
        add(canvas, "Center");

        shapeNum = 0;
        setValid(true);
    }

    public void actionPerformed(UIActionEvent event)
    {
        ++shapeNum;
        if (shapeNum == 9)
            shapeNum = 0;

        canvas.drawShape(shapeNum);
    }
}

class DrawCanvas extends UICanvas
    implements IFxTextConstants
{
    int shapeNum;
```

```
public DrawCanvas()
{
    shapeNum = 0;
    setBackground(FxColor.white);
}

public void drawShape(int shape)
{
    shapeNum = shape;
    if ((shapeNum > 8) || (shapeNum < 0))
        shapeNum = 0;

    repaint();
}

public void paint(FxGraphics graphics)
{
    switch(shapeNum)
    {
        case 0:
            graphics.draw3DRect(30, 30, 180, 150, true);
            graphics.drawString("draw3DRect()", 80, 200);
            break;
        case 1:
            char c[] = {'T','E','S','T','I','N','G'};
            graphics.drawChars(c, 0, 7, 90, 90);
            graphics.drawString("drawChars()", 80, 200);
            break;
        case 2:
            graphics.drawLine(20, 20, 200, 200);
            graphics.drawString("drawLine()", 80, 200);
            break;
        case 3:
            int pixels[] = {10, 10, 15, 25, 34, 32,
                16, 189, 78, 92, 200, 200, 120, 140,
                180, 150, 150, 75, 160, 180, 210, 160,
                75, 75, 98, 130, 160, 155, 90, 88,
                150, 20, 180, 30, 190, 40, 200, 60};
            graphics.drawPixels(pixels, 19);
            graphics.drawString("drawPixels()", 80, 200);
            break;
        case 4:
            int xPoints[] = {30, 160, 45, 10, 190, 25};
            int yPoints[] = {40, 160, 180, 10, 20, 190};
            graphics.drawPolyline(xPoints, yPoints, 6);
            graphics.drawString("drawPolyline()", 80, 200);
            break;
```

```
case 5:
    FxEllipse ellipse = new FxEllipse(20, 20, 195, 150);
    ellipse.draw(graphics);
    graphics.drawString("FxEllipse.draw()", 80, 200);
    break;
case 6:
    graphics.drawString("Angled Text", 50, 150, 45);
    graphics.drawString("drawString()", 80, 200);
    break;
case 7:
    ellipse = new FxEllipse(40, 20, 150, 130);
    Rectangle rect = new Rectangle(40, 10, 160, 140);
    graphics.drawStringFormatted("AFC TEXT CIRCLE ",
        rect, htaStretch, vtaTop, wwNone,
        true, 0, null, ellipse, false);
    graphics.drawString("drawStringFormatted()", 60, 200);
    break;
case 8:
    graphics.setColor(FxColor.lightGray);
    graphics.fill3DRect(30, 30, 180, 150, false);
    graphics.setColor(FxColor.black);
    graphics.drawString("fill3DRect()", 90, 200);
    break;
    }
  }
}
```

## Creating User-Defined Fonts

The **FxFont** class extends Java's standard **Font** class, and so works much in the same way as **Font**. However, **FxFont** enables you to create underlined and strikeout fonts by adding a fourth argument to the constructor. **FxFont** also supplies additional methods, such as **getEmboldenedFont()**, which returns a bold version of the current font. You can use **FxFont** exactly as you used **Font**, or you can take advantage of the new **FxFont** features.

Listing 13.6 presents an applet, named UserFontApplet, that shows how to create and display text with **FxFont** objects. When you run the applet in Applet Viewer, you see the window shown in Figure 13.8. As you can see, the applet displays text in various fonts, using the different **FxFont** constructors to create the fonts.

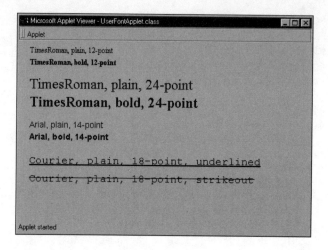

**Figure 13.8**

*UserFontApplet, running in Applet Viewer.*

### Listing 13.6   Source code for UserFontApplet.

```
/////////////////////////////////////////////////
// UserFontApplet.java
//
// An AFC applet that demonstrates how to create
// and display text with FxFont objects.
/////////////////////////////////////////////////

import com.ms.ui.*;
import com.ms.fx.*;

public class UserFontApplet extends AwtUIApplet
{
    public UserFontApplet()
    {
        super(new AppletImplementation());
    }
}

class AppletImplementation extends UIApplet
{
    public void init()
    {
        setValid(true);
    }
```

```
public void paint(FxGraphics graphics)
{
    FxFont font = new FxFont("TimesRoman", FxFont.PLAIN, 12);
    graphics.setFont(font);
    graphics.drawString("TimesRoman, plain, 12-point", 20, 20);
    FxFont boldFont = font.getEmboldenedFont();
    graphics.setFont(boldFont);
    graphics.drawString("TimesRoman, bold, 12-point", 20, 40);

    font = new FxFont("TimesRoman", FxFont.PLAIN, 24);
    graphics.setFont(font);
    graphics.drawString("TimesRoman, plain, 24-point", 20, 80);
    boldFont = font.getEmboldenedFont();
    graphics.setFont(boldFont);
    graphics.drawString("TimesRoman, bold, 24-point", 20, 110);

    font = new FxFont("Arial", FxFont.PLAIN, 14);
    graphics.setFont(font);
    graphics.drawString("Arial, plain, 14-point", 20, 145);
    boldFont = font.getEmboldenedFont();
    graphics.setFont(boldFont);
    graphics.drawString("Arial, bold, 14-point", 20, 165);

    font = new FxFont("Courier", FxFont.PLAIN, 18,
        FxFont.UNDERLINE);
    graphics.setFont(font);
    graphics.drawString("Courier, plain, 18-point, underlined",
        20, 205);

    font = new FxFont("Courier", FxFont.PLAIN, 18,
        FxFont.STRIKEOUT);
    graphics.setFont(font);
    graphics.drawString("Courier, plain, 18-point, strikeout",
        20, 235);
    }
}
```

## Creating System Fonts

There's not a lot to say about the **FxSystemFont** class, except that its static methods
enable you to access and display text with system fonts that are used for captions,
menu items, message box text, and so on. **FxSystemFont** gives you access to six fonts:
caption, icon title, menu, message box, small caption, and status (although, many of
these fonts actually may be the same font). Because all of **FxSystemFont**'s methods

are static, you can call them without creating an **FxSystemFont** object. You couldn't create an **FxSystemFont** object if you wanted to because the class has no constructor!

Listing 13.7 presents an applet, named SystemFontApplet, that shows how to create and display text with fonts obtained from the **FxSystemFont** class. When you run the applet in Applet Viewer, you see the window shown in Figure 13.9. As you can see, the applet displays text in all the system fonts obtainable through **FxSystemFont**.

**Listing 13.7   Source code for SystemFontApplet.**

```
/////////////////////////////////////////////////
// SystemFontApplet.java
//
// An AFC applet that demonstrates how to
// display text with the FxSystemFont class.
/////////////////////////////////////////////////

import com.ms.ui.*;
import com.ms.fx.*;
import java.awt.Font;

public class SystemFontApplet extends AwtUIApplet
{
    public SystemFontApplet()
    {
        super(new AppletImplementation());
    }
}

class AppletImplementation extends UIApplet
{
    public void init()
    {
        setValid(true);
    }

    public void paint(FxGraphics graphics)
    {
        Font captionFont =
            FxSystemFont.getCaptionFont();
        graphics.setFont(captionFont);
        graphics.drawString("Caption Font", 75, 50);

        Font menuFont = FxSystemFont.getMenuFont();
        graphics.setFont(menuFont);
        graphics.drawString("Menu Font", 75, 70);
```

```
        Font messageBoxFont =
            FxSystemFont.getMessageBoxFont();
        graphics.setFont(messageBoxFont);
        graphics.drawString("Message Box Font", 75, 90);

        Font smallCaptionFont =
            FxSystemFont.getSmallCaptionFont();
        graphics.setFont(smallCaptionFont);
        graphics.drawString("Small Caption Font", 75, 110);

        Font statusFont = FxSystemFont.getStatusFont();
        graphics.setFont(statusFont);
        graphics.drawString("Status Font", 75, 130);

        Font iconTitleFont =
            FxSystemFont.getIconTitleFont();
        graphics.setFont(iconTitleFont);
        graphics.drawString("Icon Title Font", 75, 150);
    }
}
```

**Figure 13.9**

*SystemFontApplet, running in Applet Viewer.*

# The Color, Texture, And Text Classes

*Mere colour, unspoiled by meaning, and unallied with definite form, can speak to the soul in a thousand different ways.*
—Oscar Wilde,
*The Critic as Artist*

# Notes...

*Chapter*

# 14

Throughout most of this book, you created applets by arranging components in layouts. In many cases, components are all you need to create your applet's user interface, enabling the program and the user to exchange information efficiently. Sometimes, however, you want to get right down to the nitty-gritty and *draw* something. This is where the classes in AFC's **com.ms.fx** package come in handy. These classes give you extra control over Java's already capable drawing tools.

In Chapter 13, you got a look at a few of the **com.ms.fx** package's most important classes, especially **FxGraphics**, which extends Java's **Graphics** class. In this chapter, you explore the color, texture, and text classes, which give you even more drawing power. The color classes include not only **FxColor**, but also some classes that you wouldn't usually think of as colors. These special classes include **FxPen** and **FxTexture**, which enable your programs to draw with thick or textured lines. AFC even includes classes for rubber lines and styled lines. If you don't know what these lines are, you soon will!

## The **FxColor** Class

**FxColor** is AFC's version of Java's **Color** class. Although it defines fewer methods than the original **Color** class, it does support the original **Color** methods, including **brighter()**, **darker()**, and **getRGB()**. More importantly, **FxColor** acts as a base class for other, more powerful AFC classes, such as **FxPen**, **FxBrushPen**, **FxRubberPen**,

**FxStyledPen**, and **FxTexture**. Yet, you can use the **FxColor** class in much the same way you used **Color** in a traditional Java program, selecting colors to use with drawing tools. The class not only defines commonly used colors, it also provides methods for manipulating the current color in various way. Table 14.1 shows the **FxColor** class's methods.

To create an **FxColor** object, call one of its constructors. One example might be the following:

```
FxColor color = new FxColor(255,0,0);
```

Here the constructor's three arguments are the red, green, and blue elements of the color. These arguments can be integer values from 0 to 255, with 255 yielding the brightest color element. In the preceding example, the code line creates the brightest possible red color object.

The **FxColor** class overloads its constructor, giving you three ways to create a color object. You've already seen one version of the constructor. The other two constructors' signatures look as follows:

```
public FxColor(int rgb);
public FxColor(float red, float green, float blue);
```

The constructors' arguments are:

- *rgb*—An integer containing the combined red, green, and blue color elements

**Table 14.1   Methods of the FxColor class.**

| Method | Description |
| --- | --- |
| **brightenColor()** | Gets a brighter version of the color |
| **darkenColor()** | Gets a darker version of the color |
| **getDarkShadow()** | Gets the color's dark shadow color |
| **getHilight()** | Gets the color's highlight color |
| **getLightHilight()** | Gets the color's light highlight color |
| **getShadow()** | Gets the color's shadow color |

- *red*—The red color element as a floating-point value

- *green*—The green color element as a floating-point value

- *blue*—The blue color element as a floating-point value

In Listing 14.1, you see a short applet that demonstrates creating a color object, using the color object to set the current color, and drawing a rectangle. When you run the applet in Applet Viewer, you see the window shown in Figure 14.1. What you can't see in the figure is that the rectangle is red.

### Listing 14.1  Source code for ColorApplet.

```
/////////////////////////////////////////////////
// ColorApplet.java
//
// An AFC applet that demonstrates how to create
// and draw with FxColor objects.
/////////////////////////////////////////////////

import com.ms.ui.*;
import com.ms.fx.*;

public class ColorApplet extends AwtUIApplet
{
    public ColorApplet()
    {
        super(new AppletImplementation());
    }
}

class AppletImplementation extends UIApplet
{
    public void init()
    {
        setValid(true);
    }

    public void paint(FxGraphics graphics)
    {
        FxColor color = new FxColor(255,0,0);
        graphics.setColor(color);
        graphics.drawRect(40, 40, 160, 160);
    }
}
```

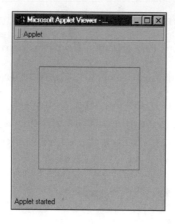

**Figure 14.1**

*ColorApplet, running in Applet Viewer.*

## The **FxFill** Class

The **FxFill** class is of only passing interest to AFC programmers. It's an abstract class that sits between **FxColor** and the other color-related classes like **FxPen**, **FxBrushPen**, and **FxTexture**. **FxFill** declares a set of callback methods, shown in Table 14.2, used internally by AFC. You'll never call these methods in your programs, nor will you ever create an **FxFill** object in a program. **FxFill** is included in this chapter's discussion only because of its position in the AFC class hierarchy between **FxColor** and other color classes.

**Table 14.2  Methods of the FxFill class.**

| Method | Description |
|---|---|
| draw3DRectCallback() | Draws a three-dimensional rectangle; for internal use only |
| drawArcCallback() | Draws an arc; for internal use only |
| drawBytesCallback() | Draws a byte array; for internal use only |
| drawCharsCallback() | Draws a character array; for internal use only |
| drawLineCallback() | Draws a line; for internal use only |
| drawOvalCallback() | Draws an oval; for internal use only |

*(continued)*

**Table 14.2   Methods of the FxFill class (continued).**

| Method | Description |
| --- | --- |
| drawPolygonCallback() | Draws a polygon; for internal use only |
| drawPolylineCallback() | Draws polylines; for internal use only |
| drawRectCallback() | Draws a rectangle; for internal use only |
| drawRoundRectCallback() | Draws a rounded rectangle; for internal use only |
| drawScanLinesCallback() | Draws scan lines; for internal use only |
| drawStringCallback() | Draws a string; for internal use only |
| fill3DRectCallback() | Draws a filled 3D rectangle; for internal use only |
| fillArcCallback() | Draws a filled arc; for internal use only |
| fillOvalCallback() | Draws a filled oval; for internal use only |
| fillPolygonCallback() | Draws a filled polygon; for internal use only |
| fillRectCallback() | Draws a filled rectangle; for internal use only |
| fillRoundRectCallback() | Draws a filled rounded rectangle; for internal use only |

# The **FxTexture** Class

An **FxTexture** object is a special color object that you can use to specify textures for drawing operations. That is, you can use an **FxTexture** object almost anywhere you would specify a color for a drawing operation. This operation then would draw with the texture rather than with a solid color. A glance at Table 14.3, which lists **FxTexture**'s methods, may make you think the class is too complex to bother with. The truth is that AFC uses many of the methods internally, and the others aren't needed to use **FxTexture** objects in your drawing operations.

To create an **FxTexture** object, call its constructor, as the following example shows:

```
FxTexture texture = new FxTexture(image);
```

Here, **image** is an image you have loaded with the **getImage()** method. The **FxTexture** object uses the image as the texture that will be displayed in drawing operations.

## Table 14.3   Methods of the **FxTexture** class.

| Method | Description |
| --- | --- |
| drawScanLinesCallback() | Draws scan lines with an image fill; for internal use only |
| fillArcCallback() | Draws a filled arc; for internal use only |
| fillOvalCallback() | Draws a filled oval; for internal use only |
| fillPolygonCallback() | Draws a filled polygon; for internal use only |
| fillRectCallback() | Draws a filled rectangle; for internal use only |
| fillRoundRectCallback() | Draws a filled rectangle with rounded edges; for internal use only |
| getBottomAxis() | Gets the stretch and repeat factors' bottom bound |
| getImage() | Gets the texture's image |
| getInner() | Gets the inner rectangle's bounds |
| getLeftAxis() | Gets the stretch and repeat factors' left bound |
| getPinOrigin() | Returns **true** if the image is pinned |
| getRightAxis() | Gets the stretch and repeat factors' right bound |
| getSnapDraw() | Returns **true** if there will be repeated partial images |
| getStretch() | Returns **true** if the image is stretched rather than repeated |
| getTopAxis() | Gets the stretch and repeat factors' top bound |
| getUpdatedAreasMask() | Gets a drawing mask |
| imageUpdate() | Determines when to draw an image |
| setAxis() | Sets the stretch and repeat factors' bounds |
| setPinOrigin() | Sets the image's pinned attribute |
| setSnapDraw() | Sets partial-images repeats |
| setStretch() | Sets the stretch or the repeat value |
| setUpdatedAreasMask() | Sets a mask for visible areas |
| size() | Gets the size of the texture's image |

The **FxTexture** class overloads its constructor, giving you five ways to create an **FxTexture** object. You already saw one **FxTexture** constructor. The remaining constructors' signatures look as follows:

```
public FxTexture(Image image, int stretch, int left,
    int top, int right, int bottom, boolean pin, int red,
    int green, int blue);
public FxTexture(Image image, int stretch, int left,
    int top, int right, int bottom, boolean pin, Color base);
public FxTexture(Image image, int stretch, int left,
    int top, int right, int bottom, boolean pin, FxFill base);
public FxTexture(Image image, int stretch, int left,
    int top, int right, int bottom, boolean pin);
```

The arguments in the previous constructor signatures are as follows:

- *image*—The image to use for the texture

- *stretch*—A flag specifying the stretch operation to use

- *left*—The left image boundary

- *top*—The top image boundary

- *right*—The right image boundary

- *bottom*—the bottom image boundary

- *pin*—A flag specifying whether the image is pinned

- *red*—The red element of the default color if the image can't be used

- *green*—The green element of the default color if the image can't be used

- *blue*—The blue element of the default color if the image can't be used

- *base*—The default color object

## The **FxPen** Class

The **FxPen** class represents an object that is sorely missed in Java's AWT classes—a pen that can draw lines of various widths. In straight Java, if you want to draw a line four pixels thick, you must draw four lines. AFC's **FxPen** class changes this, giving you better control over the way programs draw lines. The **FxPen** class defines a set of methods (Table 14.4), most of which AFC uses internally. You can call only two methods—**getWidth()** and **setWidth()**.

## Table 14.4   Methods of the **FxPen** class.

| Method | Description |
|---|---|
| drawLineCallback() | Draws a wide line; for internal use only |
| drawOvalCallback() | Draws an oval; for internal use only |
| drawPolygonCallback() | Draws a polygon; for internal use only |
| drawRectCallback() | Draws a rectangle; for internal use only |
| drawRoundRectCallback() | Draws a rounded rectangle; for internal use only |
| drawScanLinesCallback() | Draws scan lines; for internal use only |
| fillRectCallback() | Draws a filled rectangle; for internal use only |
| getWidth() | Gets the pen's width |
| setWidth() | Sets the pen's width |

When using the **FxPen** class, keep in mind that an **FxPen** is just a color, and you can use the object as you use color objects. For example, you can use an **FxPen** object as the argument in a call to **setColor()**, rather than the **Color** or **FxColor** object that you're accustomed to using. After you use the pen to set the color, AFC will draw all lines with the specified pen.

To create an **FxPen** object, call its constructor, as shown in the following example:

```
FxPen pen = new FxPen(20, 0, 255, 0);
```

Here, the constructor's four arguments are the pen's width and the values for the red, green, and blue elements of the pen's color. In this case, the constructor creates a bright-green pen 20 pixels thick.

**FxPen** overloads its constructor, giving you five ways to create a pen. You've already seen one constructor. The remaining constructors' signatures look as follows:

```
public FxPen();
public FxPen(int width, int rgb);
public FxPen(int width, FxColor color);
public FxPen(int width, Color color);
```

The following list describes the constructors' arguments:

- *width*—The pen's width

- *rgb*—An integer containing the combined red, green, and blue elements of the pen's color

- *color*—The pen's color as an **FxColor** or **Color** object

Listing 14.2 presents a short applet that demonstrates creating a pen object, using the pen to set the current color, and drawing a rectangle. When you run the applet in Applet Viewer, you see the window shown in Figure 14.2. What you can't see in this figure is that the rectangle's border is blue.

## Listing 14.2   Source code for PenApplet.

```
/////////////////////////////////////////////////
// PenApplet.java
//
// An AFC applet that demonstrates how to create
// and draw with FxPen objects.
/////////////////////////////////////////////////

import com.ms.ui.*;
import com.ms.fx.*;

public class PenApplet extends AwtUIApplet
{
    public PenApplet()
    {
        super(new AppletImplementation());
    }
}

class AppletImplementation extends UIApplet
{
    public void init()
    {
        setValid(true);
    }

    public void paint(FxGraphics graphics)
    {
        FxPen pen = new FxPen(20, FxColor.blue);
        graphics.setColor(pen);
        graphics.drawRect(40, 40, 160, 160);
    }
}
```

**Figure 14.2**

*PenApplet, running in Applet Viewer.*

# The **FxRubberPen** Class

**FxRubberPen** is a specialized pen for drawing rubber lines. You've probably seen these rubber lines in paint programs when you draw shapes such as lines or circles. Essentially, a rubber pen draws shapes in a mode that enables the pen to remove the shape from the screen without disturbing what was previously drawn. Using an **FxRubberPen** object, for example, you can create lines and shapes that follow the mouse pointer on the display, enabling the user to position the shape exactly as he wants it. Rubber lines get their name from the way they stretch and shrink with the mouse pointer's movement.

Because **FxRubberPen** extends the **FxPen** class, it inherits all of **FxPen**'s methods. The class also defines its own set of methods, as shown in Table 14.5. However, AFC uses all but one of the methods internally. The only method you can call in your program is **drawLast()**, which automatically erases the last lines the rubber pen drew.

You create a rubber pen by calling the **FxRubberPen** class's constructor, as follows:

```
FxRubberPen rubberPen = new FxRubberPen(FxColor.red);
```

As you can see, the constructor's single argument is a color object. You can use either a **Color** or **FxColor** object for this color argument. Because an **FxPen** object is also a color object, you can use a pen as **FxRubberPen**'s color. This technique enables you to create rubber pens that draw with wide lines.

Table 14.5    Methods of the **FxRubberPen** class.

**Table 14.5    Methods of the FxRubberPen class.**

| Method | Description |
|---|---|
| drawLast() | Erases the last drawing |
| drawLineCallback() | Draws a temporary line; for internal use only |
| drawOvalCallback() | Draws a temporary ellipse; for internal use only |
| drawPolygonCallback() | Draws a temporary polygon; for internal use only |
| drawRectCallback() | Draws a temporary rectangle; for internal use only |
| drawRoundRectCallback() | Draws a temporary rounded rectangle; for internal use only |

Listing 14.3 presents a short applet that demonstrates how to create and draw with a rubber pen. When you run the applet in Applet Viewer, you will see a blank window, because, in the applet's **paint**() method, the program creates a rubber pen, uses it to draw a rectangle, and then calls the pen's **drawLast**() method, which erases the rectangle. If you want to see the rubber line before it gets erased, comment out the call to **drawLast**(). You'll then see the window shown in Figure 14.3. You see how to do more useful things with rubber pens in this chapter's Practical Guide.

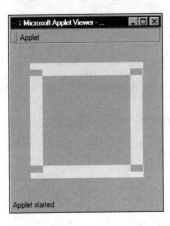

**Figure 14.3**

*RubberPenApplet, before erasing its rubber lines.*

**Listing 14.3   Source code for RubberPenApplet.**

```java
//////////////////////////////////////////////////
// RubberPenApplet.java
//
// An AFC applet that demonstrates how to create
// and draw with FxRubberPen objects.
//////////////////////////////////////////////////

import com.ms.ui.*;
import com.ms.fx.*;

public class RubberPenApplet extends AwtUIApplet
{
    public RubberPenApplet()
    {
        super(new AppletImplementation());
    }
}


class AppletImplementation extends UIApplet
{
    public void init()
    {
        setValid(true);
    }

    public void paint(FxGraphics graphics)
    {
        FxPen pen = new FxPen(20, FxColor.blue);
        FxRubberPen rubberPen = new FxRubberPen(pen);
        graphics.setColor(rubberPen);
        graphics.drawRect(40, 40, 160, 160);
        rubberPen.drawLast(graphics);
    }
}
```

# The **FxStyledPen** Class

Most operating systems' graphics primitives include styled lines, which are lines that are drawn with dashes and dots. Java offers no such lines, but AFC adds them to your graphics toolkit through the **FxStyledPen** class. This class extends **FxPen**, but defines only three methods of its own—**drawLineCallback()**, **drawPolygonCallback()**, and **drawRectCallback()**—all of which AFC uses internally. You'll never call these methods in your programs.

To create a styled pen, call the **FxStyledPen** class's constructor, as follows:

```
FxStyledPen pen = new FxStyledPen(FxStyledPen.DOT, 1);
```

Here, the constructor's two arguments are the pen's style (which can be **PLAIN**, **DOT**, or **DASH**) and the pen width. Currently, styled pens always have a width of 1.

Listing 14.4 shows a short applet that demonstrates how to create and draw with styled pens. When you run the applet in Applet Viewer, you see the window shown in Figure 14.4.

### Listing 14.4  Source code for StyledPenApplet.

```
/////////////////////////////////////////////////
// StyledPenApplet.java
//
// An AFC applet that demonstrates how to create
// and draw with an FxStyledPen object.
/////////////////////////////////////////////////

import com.ms.ui.*;
import com.ms.fx.*;

public class StyledPenApplet extends AwtUIApplet
{
    public StyledPenApplet()
    {
        super(new AppletImplementation());
    }
}

class AppletImplementation extends UIApplet
{
    public void init()
    {
        setValid(true);
    }

    public void paint(FxGraphics graphics)
    {
        FxStyledPen pen =
            new FxStyledPen(FxStyledPen.DOT, 1);
        graphics.setColor(pen);
        graphics.drawRect(40, 40, 160, 160);
    }
}
```

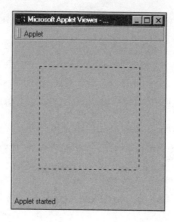

**Figure 14.4**

*StyledPenApplet, running in Applet Viewer.*

# The **FxBrushPen** Class

In conventional applications, programs use pen objects to draw lines and brush objects to fill shapes. For example, when you program under Windows and draw a normal rectangle, the system draws the rectangle's edges with the currently selected pen, which controls the color and width of the lines. On the other hand, when you draw a filled rectangle in a Windows program, the system fills the rectangle with the currently selected brush, which controls the color (and sometimes the pattern) of the filled area.

Java doesn't directly support the idea of pens and brushes. Instead, with Java, you set the current drawing color before each operation that needs a new color. As you've just learned, AFC adds the concept of pens to Java programming, by providing the **FxPen**, **FxRubberPen**, and **FxStyledPen** classes. AFC also provides the **FxBrushPen** class, which adds brushes to the mix. Using the **FxBrushPen** class, you can define colors for both lines and fills at the same time.

**FxBrushPen** extends **FxFill** and so also counts **FxColor** as a superclass. Although **FxBrushPen** inherits methods from its superclasses, it defines only its own callback methods (see Table 14.6), which AFC uses internally. You'll never call these methods in your programs.

To create a pen/brush object, call the **FxBrushPen** class's constructor, as follows:

```
FxBrushPen brushPen = new FxBrushPen(FxColor.red, FxColor.blue);
```

## Table 14.6 Methods of the FxBrushPen class.

| Method | Description |
|---|---|
| draw3DRectCallback() | Draws a 3D rectangle; for internal use only |
| drawArcCallback() | Draws an arc; for internal use only |
| drawBytesCallback() | Draws a byte array; for internal use only |
| drawCharsCallback() | Draws a character array; for internal use only |
| drawLineCallback() | Draws a line; for internal use only |
| drawOvalCallback() | Draws an oval; for internal use only |
| drawPolygonCallback() | Draws a polygon; for internal use only |
| drawRectCallback() | Draws a rectangle; for internal use only |
| drawRoundRectCallback() | Draws a rounded rectangle; for internal use only |
| drawScanLinesCallback() | Draws scan lines; for internal use only |
| drawStringCallback() | Draws a string; for internal use only |
| fill3DRectCallback() | Draws a filled 3D rectangle; for internal use only |
| fillArcCallback() | Draws a filled arc; for internal use only |
| fillOvalCallback() | Draws a filled oval; for internal use only |
| fillPolygonCallback() | Draws a filled polygon; for internal use only |
| fillRectCallback() | Draws a filled rectangle; for internal use only |
| fillRoundRectCallback() | Draws a filled rounded rectangle; for internal use only |

Here, the constructor's two arguments are the color for the pen (the line color) and the color for the brush (the fill color). You can use either **FxColor** or **Color** objects for these arguments.

Listing 14.5 presents a short applet that demonstrates how to create **FxBrushPen** objects and how to use them in drawing operations. When you run the applet in Applet Viewer, you see the window shown in Figure 14.5. Notice in the **paint()** method

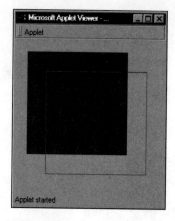

**Figure 14.5**

*BrushPenApplet, running in Applet Viewer.*

that the applet draws a regular rectangle and a filled rectangle. AFC draws the regular rectangle's lines with the pen and draws the filled rectangle with the brush.

**Listing 14.5   Source code for BrushPenApplet.**

```
/////////////////////////////////////////////////
// BrushPenApplet.java
//
// An AFC applet that demonstrates how to create
// and draw with an FxBrushPen object.
/////////////////////////////////////////////////

import com.ms.ui.*;
import com.ms.fx.*;

public class BrushPenApplet extends AwtUIApplet
{
    public BrushPenApplet()
    {
        super(new AppletImplementation());
    }
}

class AppletImplementation extends UIApplet
{
    public void init()
    {
        setValid(true);
    }
```

```
public void paint(FxGraphics graphics)
{
    FxBrushPen brushPen =
        new FxBrushPen(FxColor.red, FxColor.blue);
    graphics.setColor(brushPen);
    graphics.fillRect(20, 20, 160, 160);
    graphics.drawRect(50, 50, 160, 160);
}
}
```

# The FxText Class

The **FxText** class enables your programs to manipulate text in various ways, including inserting and deleting characters from the text buffer. This class is similar to Java's **StringBuffer** class, but, for efficiency's sake, it doesn't employ synchronization. This lack of synchronization, though, means that the **FxText** class is not suitable for use in threaded applications, where multiple threads may try to access the text buffer simultaneously. Table 14.7 lists the methods defined in the **FxText** class.

**Table 14.7  Methods of the FxText class.**

| Method | Description |
|---|---|
| **append()** | Adds a character to the end of the text |
| **ensureResize()** | Ensures that the text buffer has room to handle text operations that add characters |
| **getChar()** | Gets a character |
| **getLength()** | Gets the length of the text |
| **getWordBreak()** | Gets the next word's length |
| **insert()** | Inserts a character into the text |
| **isDelimiter()** | Returns **true** if a character is a delimiter |
| **isWhite()** | Returns **true** if a character is a white space |
| **remove()** | Removes characters from the text buffer |
| **setText()** | Replaces the text in the buffer |

You create an object of the **FxText** class by calling its constructor, as follows:

```
FxText text = new FxText("Text String");
```

The constructor's single argument is the string to be copied into the **FxText** object's text buffer. You can also create an **FxText** object from a character array. However, because **FxText** provides no methods for extracting string data from the text buffer, you probably want to use the **FxFormattedText** class, which extends **FxText**, for your text-handling chores.

## The **FxFormattedText** Class

The **FxFormattedText** class extends the **FxText** superclass with many new methods, providing all the functionality you need to manipulate text data in your programs. This functionality includes getting and setting text attributes, screen locations, and password characters. **FxFormattedText** inherits all of **FxText**'s methods, as well as defines a large set of its own. Table 14.8 lists the methods defined in the **FxFormattedText** class.

**Table 14.8 Methods of the FxFormattedText class.**

| Method | Description |
|---|---|
| dropTail() | Creates a new **FxFormattedText** object without the text that falls after the given offset |
| ensureNotDirty() | Updates the text formatting |
| getBounding() | Gets the text's bounding box |
| getClosestOffset() | Finds the character closest to the given screen coordinates |
| getFont() | Gets the **FxFormattedText** object's font |
| getHeight() | Gets the text height |
| getHorizAlign() | Gets the text's horizontal alignment |
| getKerning() | Returns **true** if kerning is in use |
| getLocale() | Gets the text's locale |

*(continued)*

Table 14.8  Methods of the **FxFormattedText** class *(continued).*

| Method | Description |
|---|---|
| getLocaleFormattingOverride() | Returns **true** if text formatting override features are based on locale |
| getMnemonicDrawing() | Returns **true** if the text uses hot-key underlining |
| getNextStartPoint() | Gets the next drawing position following the text |
| getOffsetFromPos() | Gets the offset of the character closest to a given screen coordinate |
| getOutline() | Gets the current shape's outline |
| getPasswordChar() | Gets the password character |
| getScrnLocation() | Gets a character's screen location |
| getStartPoint() | Gets the text's starting point |
| getText() | Gets the text as a **String** object |
| getTextDirection() | Gets the text direction |
| getVertAlign() | Gets the text's vertical alignment |
| getWidth() | Gets the text buffer's width |
| getWordWrap() | Gets the text's word-wrap style |
| insert() | Inserts characters into the text |
| isBodyLocationDetermined() | Returns **true** if a character's screen position can be determined |
| isDirty() | Returns **true** if the text needs reformatting |
| paint() | Paints characters in the text |
| remove() | Deletes characters from the text |
| setBounding() | Sets the text's bounding box |
| setCallback() | Sets the callback interface |

*(continued)*

## Table 14.8  Methods of the **FxFormattedText** class *(continued)*.

| Method | Description |
| --- | --- |
| setFont() | Sets the text's font |
| setHorizAlign() | Sets the text's horizontal alignment |
| setKerning() | Specifies whether the text will use kerning |
| setLocale() | Sets the text's locale |
| setLocaleFormattingOverride() | Sets whether the format overriding features are based on locale |
| setMnemonicDrawing() | Sets whether the text underlines hot keys |
| setOutline() | Sets the text outline |
| setPasswordChar() | Sets the password character |
| setStartPoint() | Sets the text's start point |
| setStartPointAtOrigin() | Sets the text's starting point when a bounding box is associated with text |
| setTabs() | Sets the text's tabs |
| setText() | Sets the text |
| setTextDirection() | Sets the direction of text flow |
| setVertAlign() | Sets the text's vertical alignment |
| setWordWrap() | Sets the text's word-wrap style |
| shrinkBound() | Shrinks the text's bounding rectangle to its minimum size |

You create an object of the **FxFormattedText** class by calling its constructor, as follows:

```
FxFormattedText text = new FxFormattedText("Text String");
```

The constructor's single argument is the string to be copied into the **FxFormattedText** object's text buffer. You can also create an **FxFormattedText** object from a character array. After you create the **FxFormattedText** object, you manipulate the text by using the class's methods. When the time comes to display the text, you can extract the text buffer as a string by calling the class's **getText()** method.

Listing 14.6 presents the source code for a short applet that creates an **FxFormattedText** object, extracts the text using **getText()**, and then displays the result on the screen. When you run the applet under Applet Viewer, you see the window shown in Figure 14.6.

### Listing 14.6   Source code for FormattedTextApplet.

```java
///////////////////////////////////////////////////
// FormattedTextApplet.java
//
// An AFC applet that demonstrates how to create
// and display an FxFormattedText object.
///////////////////////////////////////////////////

import com.ms.ui.*;
import com.ms.fx.*;

public class FormattedTextApplet extends AwtUIApplet
{
    public FormattedTextApplet()
    {
        super(new AppletImplementation());
    }
}

class AppletImplementation extends UIApplet
{
    public void init()
    {
        setValid(true);
    }

    public void paint(FxGraphics graphics)
    {
        FxFont font =
            new FxFont("TimesRoman", FxFont.PLAIN, 24);
        graphics.setFont(font);

        FxFormattedText text =
            new FxFormattedText("Text String");
        String str = text.getText();
        graphics.drawString(str, 60, 100);
    }
}
```

**Figure 14.6**

*FormattedTextApplet, running in Applet Viewer.*

# Practical Guide To

# Color And Texture Classes

- Creating Sets Of Related Colors
- Using Textures In Drawing Operations
- Getting And Setting Pen Widths
- Manipulating Rubber Pens

## Creating Sets Of Related Colors

One of the handiest things about the **FxColor** class is its capability to create related colors that you can use when creating your displays. For example, when drawing 3D shapes, you can call the **FxColor** class's **getHilight()** and **getShadow()** methods to obtain the perfect colors for drawing the borders and main body of the shape. Moreover, the **brightenColor()** and **darkenColor()** methods let you get almost any shade of the original color (by specifying the percentage by which the color should be changed) that you want.

This color-management programming technique is better seen than described, so Listing 14.7 presents an applet that creates an **FxColor** object and calls its methods to generate various shades of the original color. When you run the applet, you see the window shown in Figure 14.7 (in this figure, you see only the shades of the colors). You can compare the labeled color bars in the display with the method calls in the source code that produce the color bars. The last image (in the lower right corner) is a 3D rectangle that illustrates one way that you may want to use the colors returned from **FxColor**'s **getHilight()** and **getShadow()** methods. To see different sets of related colors, click the Change Color button. The applet displays color sets for the basic red, green, and blue colors.

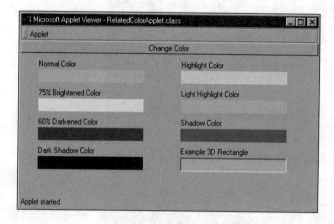

**Figure 14.7**

RelatedColorApplet, running in Applet Viewer.

## Listing 14.7   Source code for RelatedColorApplet.

```java
/////////////////////////////////////////////////
// RelatedColorApplet.java
//
// An AFC applet that demonstrates how to create
// colors related to an FxColor object.
/////////////////////////////////////////////////

import com.ms.ui.*;
import com.ms.ui.event.*;
import com.ms.fx.*;
import java.awt.*;

public class RelatedColorApplet extends AwtUIApplet
{
    public RelatedColorApplet()
    {
        super(new AppletImplementation());
    }
}

class AppletImplementation extends UIApplet
    implements IUIActionListener
{
    int colorNum;

    public void init()
    {
        UIBorderLayout layout = new UIBorderLayout();
        setLayout(layout);

        UIPushButton button =
            new UIPushButton("Change Color",
            UIPushButton.RAISED);
        button.addActionListener(this);
        add(button, "North");

        colorNum = 0;

        setValid(true);
    }

    public void paint(FxGraphics graphics)
    {
        FxColor fxColor;
```

```
switch (colorNum)
{
    case 0:
        fxColor = new FxColor(255,0,0);
        break;

    case 1:
        fxColor = new FxColor(0,255,0);
        break;

    default:
        fxColor = new FxColor(0,0,255);
        break;
}

graphics.drawString("Normal Color", 30, 40);
FxPen pen = new FxPen(20, fxColor);
graphics.setColor(pen);
graphics.drawLine(30, 55, 200, 55);

graphics.setColor(FxColor.black);
graphics.drawString("75% Brightened Color", 30, 85);
Color color = fxColor.brightenColor(75);
pen = new FxPen(20, color);
graphics.setColor(pen);
graphics.drawLine(30, 100, 200, 100);

graphics.setColor(FxColor.black);
graphics.drawString("60% Darkened Color", 30, 130);
color = fxColor.darkenColor(60);
pen = new FxPen(20, color);
graphics.setColor(pen);
graphics.drawLine(30, 145, 200, 145);

graphics.setColor(FxColor.black);
graphics.drawString("Dark Shadow Color", 30, 175);
color = fxColor.getDarkShadow();
pen = new FxPen(20, color);
graphics.setColor(pen);
graphics.drawLine(30, 190, 200, 190);

graphics.setColor(FxColor.black);
graphics.drawString("Highlight Color", 260, 40);
Color hilightColor = fxColor.getHilight();
pen = new FxPen(20, hilightColor);
graphics.setColor(pen);
graphics.drawLine(260, 55, 430, 55);
```

```
        graphics.setColor(FxColor.black);
        graphics.drawString("Light Highlight Color", 260, 85);
        color = fxColor.getLightHilight();
        pen = new FxPen(20, color);
        graphics.setColor(pen);
        graphics.drawLine(260, 100, 430, 100);

        graphics.setColor(FxColor.black);
        graphics.drawString("Shadow Color", 260, 130);
        Color shadowColor = fxColor.getShadow();
        pen = new FxPen(20, shadowColor);
        graphics.setColor(pen);
        graphics.drawLine(260, 145, 430, 145);

        graphics.setColor(FxColor.black);
        graphics.drawString("Example 3D Rectangle", 260, 175);
        graphics.setColor(shadowColor);
        graphics.drawRect(260, 180, 170, 20);
        graphics.drawRect(261, 181, 169, 19);
        graphics.setColor(fxColor);
        graphics.fillRect(262, 182, 168, 18);
        graphics.setColor(hilightColor);
        graphics.drawLine(430, 181, 430, 200);
        graphics.drawLine(431, 180, 431, 200);
        graphics.drawLine(261, 200, 430, 200);
        graphics.drawLine(260, 201, 430, 201);
    }

    public void actionPerformed(UIActionEvent event)
    {
        ++colorNum;
        if (colorNum == 3)
            colorNum = 0;

        repaint();
    }
}
```

## Using Textures In Drawing Operations

Most operating systems' graphics libraries support the use of images as brushes,
enabling a program to draw wide lines or filled shapes with a pattern that's either
predefined by the system or defined by the programmer. Java applets and applications can display filled shapes (Java can't draw thick lines at all) only with solid
colors, which is where AFC's **FxTexture** class comes in. By creating an **FxTexture**

object and passing it as a color to drawing operations, your programs can paint shapes with patterns.

Moreover, you can tell AFC to use the texture to tile an area with the image or to stretch the image to fit the area. To tile an area, you simply create the texture object using the constructor that takes a reference to the image as its only argument. To stretch a texture image, you pass the **STRETCH_ALL** flag to the **FxTexture** constructor.

Listing 14.8 presents an applet that demonstrates using both tiled and stretched texture images in a drawing operation. When you run the applet, you see the window shown in Figure 14.8. Click the Change Size button to enlarge the drawing area. The bigger the area becomes, the more copies of the texture are required to fill the rectangle. Click the Toggle Stretch Mode button to turn on the stretch mode. When you do, no matter what size you make the rectangle, the image shrinks or stretches to fit. Figure 14.9 shows the tiled image at its largest size, whereas Figure 14.10 shows the image stretched to fit the same area.

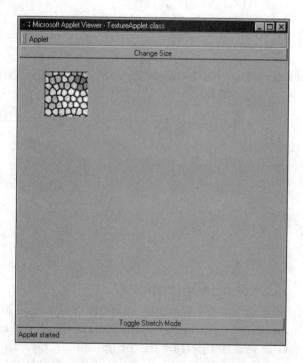

**Figure 14.8**

*TextureApplet, running in Applet Viewer.*

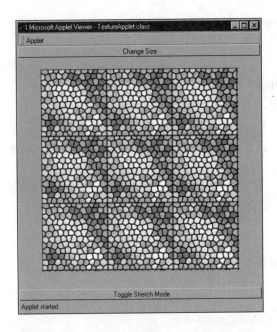

**Figure 14.9**

*TextureApplet, tiling the image to fill the rectangle.*

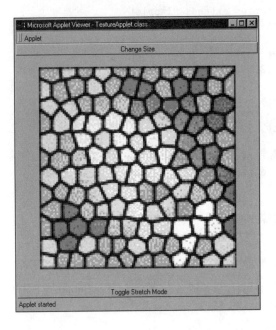

**Figure 14.10**

*TextureApplet, stretching the image to fill the rectangle.*

## Listing 14.8 Source code for TextureApplet.

```java
///////////////////////////////////////////////////
// TextureApplet.java
//
// An AFC applet that shows how to create an
// FxTexture object and use it in drawing
// operations.
///////////////////////////////////////////////////

import com.ms.ui.*;
import com.ms.ui.event.*;
import com.ms.fx.*;
import java.awt.*;
import java.applet.*;
import java.net.*;

public class TextureApplet extends AwtUIApplet
{
    public TextureApplet()
    {
        super(new AppletImplementation());
    }
}

class AppletImplementation extends UIApplet
    implements IUIActionListener
{
    FxTexture texture1;
    FxTexture texture2;
    FxTexture curTexture;
    int shapeNum;

    public void init()
    {
        UIBorderLayout layout = new UIBorderLayout();
        setLayout(layout);

        UIPushButton button =
            new UIPushButton("Change Size",
            UIPushButton.RAISED);
        button.addActionListener(this);
        add(button, "North");

        button = new UIPushButton("Toggle Stretch Mode",
            UIPushButton.RAISED);
```

```
        button.addActionListener(this);
        add(button, "South");

        Applet applet = getApplet();
        MediaTracker tracker = new MediaTracker(applet);
        URL url = getCodeBase();
        Image image = getImage(url, "sglass.gif");
        tracker.addImage(image, 0);

        try
        {
            tracker.waitForAll();
        }
        catch (InterruptedException e)
        {
        }

        texture1 = new FxTexture(image);
        texture2 = new FxTexture(image, FxTexture.STRETCH_ALL,
            0, 0, -1, -1, false);
        curTexture = texture1;
        shapeNum = 1;

        setValid(true);
    }

    public void paint(FxGraphics graphics)
    {
        graphics.setColor(curTexture);
        graphics.fillRect(40, 40, shapeNum*70, shapeNum*70);
    }

    public void actionPerformed(UIActionEvent event)
    {
        String str = event.getActionCommand();
        if (str == "Change Size")
        {
            ++shapeNum;
            if (shapeNum == 6)
                shapeNum = 1;
        }
        else if (str == "Toggle Stretch Mode")
        {
            if (curTexture == texture1)
                curTexture = texture2;
```

```
        else
            curTexture = texture1;
        }

        repaint();
    }
}
```

You should notice a couple of things about Listing 14.8. First, the applet's **init()** method uses a **MediaTracker** object to ensure that the image is fully loaded before the program creates the texture. Often in AFC, if you don't wait for an image to load, you get unpredictable results. Second, notice how the stretching mode is determined at the time the program constructs the **FxTexture** objects. This was done to show you two ways to create a texture object. In Listing 14.8, you could use a single texture object and call its **setStretch()** method to change the stretch mode. For example, without modifying any other part of the program, you can change the **actionPerformed()** method's **else if** clause to look as follows:

```
else if (str == "Toggle Stretch Mode")
{
    int stretch = curTexture.getStretch();
    if (stretch == FxTexture.STRETCH_NONE)
        curTexture.setStretch(FxTexture.STRETCH_ALL);
    else
        curTexture.setStretch(FxTexture.STRETCH_NONE);
}
```

## Getting And Setting Pen Widths

Previously in this chapter, you learned to create an AFC pen by specifying a width and a color as the constructor's arguments. After you create this pen, however, you're not stuck with its size. You can change the pen's width by calling the class's **setWidth()** method. Not surprisingly, you can inquire about the pen width by calling the **getWidth()** method.

In Listing 14.9, you see an applet that demonstrates getting and setting the width of an existing pen so that it responds to user input. When you run the applet, you see the window shown in Figure 14.11. Click the Change Width button to enlarge the pen. You can keep increasing the pen thickness up to 30 pixels wide, after which the pen returns to 2 pixels wide. Figure 14.12 shows a 20 pixel-thick pen drawing the rectangle.

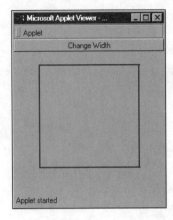

**Figure 14.11**

*PenWidthApplet, running in Applet Viewer.*

**Figure 14.12**

*PenWidthApplet, displaying its rectangle using a 20 pixel-thick pen.*

### Listing 14.9   Source code for PenWidthApplet.

```
///////////////////////////////////////////////
// PenWidthApplet.java
//
// An AFC applet that shows how to create get and
// set a pen's width.
///////////////////////////////////////////////

import com.ms.ui.*;
import com.ms.ui.event.*;
import com.ms.fx.*;
```

```
public class PenWidthApplet extends AwtUIApplet
{
    public PenWidthApplet()
    {
        super(new AppletImplementation());
    }
}

class AppletImplementation extends UIApplet
    implements IUIActionListener
{
    FxPen pen;

    public void init()
    {
        UIBorderLayout layout = new UIBorderLayout();
        setLayout(layout);

        UIPushButton button =
            new UIPushButton("Change Width",
            UIPushButton.RAISED);
        button.addActionListener(this);
        add(button, "North");

        pen = new FxPen(2, FxColor.blue);

        setValid(true);
    }

    public void paint(FxGraphics graphics)
    {
        graphics.setColor(pen);
        graphics.drawRect(40, 40, 160, 160);
    }

    public void actionPerformed(UIActionEvent event)
    {
        int width = pen.getWidth();
        width += 2;
        if (width == 30)
            width = 2;
        pen.setWidth(width);

        repaint();
    }
}
```

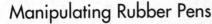

## Manipulating Rubber Pens

Because rubber pens must respond to user mouse input, they can be a little tricky to add to a program. For example, if you were writing a painting program in Java, you'd want to use rubber lines to enable the user to size and position shapes before they're drawn permanently. To do so, the program must track mouse-down, mouse-drag, and mouse-up events. To implement a rubber pen for the program, you'd perform the following steps:

1. Declare data fields for an **FxGraphics** object, for an **FxRubberPen** object, and for the coordinates needed to draw the shape that the rubber pen will represent. For example, if you're going to use a rubber pen to draw a line, you need variables for the starting and ending coordinates of the line.

2. In the applet's **init()** method, create the **FxRubberPen** object.

3. In your mouse-down event handler, call **getGraphics()** to initialize the **FxGraphics** object, record the mouse position as the starting shape coordinates, set the ending shape coordinates to **0** (zero), and set the **FxGraphics** object's color to the **FxRubberPen** object.

4. In your mouse-drag event handler, call the appropriate **FxGraphics** drawing method for the shape, using the coordinates you recorded in the mouse-down event handler as the starting coordinates and using the current mouse position as the ending coordinates. If you were drawing a line shape, for example, you would call the **FxGraphics** object's **drawLine()** function with the coordinates from the mouse-down handler as the method's first two arguments and the current mouse position as the last two arguments. The method call may look something like this: **graphics.drawLine(startX, startY, x, y)**.

5. In your mouse-up event handler, call the **FxRubberPen** object's **drawLast()** method to erase the last rubber line drawn. Then, record the mouse position as the ending coordinates for the shape.

6. Use the final starting and ending coordinates to draw the permanent shape.

Listing 14.10 presents an applet that demonstrates the previously outlined programming technique. As you examine the source code, you'll see that the process isn't as complicated as it first seems. It's one of those things that is easier to implement than it is to explain. To test the applet, run it in Applet Viewer. When the applet appears, click and hold down the mouse button with the pointer over the applet and start dragging the mouse. As you move the mouse around the window, the rubber line

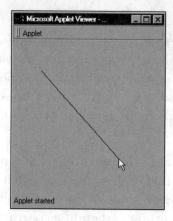

**Figure 14.13**

*RubberPenApplet2, as the user drags the rubber line.*

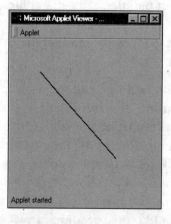

**Figure 14.14**

*RubberPenApplet2, displaying the final line.*

follows your movements (Figure 14.13). When you release the mouse button, the applet draws the line in the final position you selected, as shown in Figure 14.14.

### Listing 14.10   Source code for RubberPenApplet2.

```
/////////////////////////////////////////////////
// RubberPenApplet2.java
//
// An AFC applet that demonstrates how to create
// and manipulate a rubber pen.
/////////////////////////////////////////////////
```

```
import com.ms.ui.*;
import com.ms.fx.*;
import java.awt.Event;

public class RubberPenApplet2 extends AwtUIApplet
{
    public RubberPenApplet2()
    {
        super(new AppletImplementation());
    }
}

class AppletImplementation extends UIApplet
{
    FxGraphics graphics;
    FxRubberPen rubberPen;
    int startX;
    int startY;
    int endX;
    int endY;

    public void init()
    {
        rubberPen = new FxRubberPen(FxColor.white);

        startX = 0;
        startY = 0;
        endX = 0;
        endY = 0;

        setValid(true);
    }

    public void paint(FxGraphics graphics)
    {
        FxPen pen = new FxPen(2, FxColor.black);
        graphics.setColor(pen);
        graphics.drawLine(startX, startY, endX, endY);
    }

    public boolean mouseDown(Event evt, int x, int y)
    {
        startX = x;
        startY = y;
        endX = 0;
        endY = 0;
        graphics = getGraphics();
        graphics.setColor(rubberPen);
```

```
        return true;
    }

    public boolean mouseDrag(Event evt, int x, int y)
    {
        graphics.drawLine(startX, startY, x, y);

        return true;
    }

    public boolean mouseUp(Event evt, int x, int y)
    {
        endX = x;
        endY = y;
        rubberPen.drawLast(graphics);
        repaint();

        return true;
    }
}
```

# Chapter 15

# The Event Classes

*No great inner event befalls those who summon it not.*
*—Maurice Maeterlinck,*
*Wisdom and Destiny*

# Notes...

# Chapter

# 15

Throughout this book, you examined many AFC applets, most of which employed some form of event handling. If you weren't very knowledgeable about Java events, you now probably know a lot more. In any case, this final chapter will close most of the gaps in your AFC event education. Here, you not only review the basic concepts behind the propagation and delegation event models, but you also see how to write AFC programs that can respond to virtually any event that they receive.

## A Java Event Overview

If you've gotten this far with your Java programming, you're probably already comfortable with at least one type of Java event handling. However, the Java language actually gives you two event-handling models from which to choose—the original Java 1.0 model (now known as the propagation event model) and the Java 1.1 model (now known as the delegation event model). Most Java programmers feel right at home with the propagation event model. However, you, as a programmer should start using the new delegation event model to get the most out of Java events. For example, the delegation event model is used with Java Beans, which enables you to create ActiveX-type controls.

When it uses the propagation event model, Java broadcasts events by propagating them up through the class hierarchy. That is, Java passes the events from one class to the next, up the chain of superclasses until the event is either ignored or handled. How a class handles an event depends on the type of event. For example, to respond to an action event—which is the type of event generated by a pushbutton control— a class implements the **action()** method, as shown in Listing 15.1.

In Listing 15.1, when the user clicks the button, the program's **action()** method gets called, with the button's label stored in the **object** parameter. By accessing the **event** parameter, the **action()** method can acquire additional information about the event, although the button's label usually is enough information to process the command. Notice how the **action()** method returns **true** if the event is handled and returns **false** if it's not. Returning **true** from **action()** is the mechanism that informs Java that the event was handled and doesn't need to be propagated further up the class hierarchy.

## Listing 15.1   Source code for ButtonApplet.

```
//////////////////////////////////////////////////
// ButtonApplet.java
//
// An applet that demonstrates the propagation
// event model.
//////////////////////////////////////////////////

import java.awt.*;
import java.applet.*;

public class ButtonApplet extends Applet
{
    private Button button;
    String displayString;

    public void init()
    {
        button = new Button("Test Button");
        add(button);
        displayString = "";
    }

    public void paint(Graphics g)
    {
        g.drawString(displayString, 20, 100);
    }

    public boolean action(Event event, Object object)
    {
```

```
        if (object == "Test Button")
        {
            displayString = "Button clicked!";
            repaint();
            return true;
        }
        return false;
    }
}
```

While, at first, the propagation model may seem to work mysteriously, it's actually easy to understand. Every class that can handle events inherits a **handleEvent()** method, which dispatches the events. Listing 15.2 presents the **handleEvent()** method. Every event that an applet can receive is represented in **handleEvent()**. Notice how the **case** clause for the **ACTION_EVENT** event results in a call to the **action()** method. When using the propagation event model, you can even override **handleEvent()** in your class and call any one or more of the functions you want for each event.

## Listing 15.2  Source code for the **handleEvent()** method.

```
public boolean handleEvent(Event evt) {
    switch (evt.id) {
        case Event.MOUSE_ENTER:
            return mouseEnter(evt, evt.x, evt.y);

        case Event.MOUSE_EXIT:
            return mouseExit(evt, evt.x, evt.y);

        case Event.MOUSE_MOVE:
            return mouseMove(evt, evt.x, evt.y);

        case Event.MOUSE_DOWN:
            return mouseDown(evt, evt.x, evt.y);

        case Event.MOUSE_DRAG:
            return mouseDrag(evt, evt.x, evt.y);

        case Event.MOUSE_UP:
            return mouseUp(evt, evt.x, evt.y);

        case Event.KEY_PRESS:
        case Event.KEY_ACTION:
            return keyDown(evt, evt.key);

        case Event.KEY_RELEASE:
        case Event.KEY_ACTION_RELEASE:
            return keyUp(evt, evt.key);
```

```
        case Event.ACTION_EVENT:
            return action(evt, evt.arg);
        case Event.GOT_FOCUS:
            return gotFocus(evt, evt.arg);
        case Event.LOST_FOCUS:
            return lostFocus(evt, evt.arg);
    }
    return false;
}
```

The delegation event model works very differently from the propagation event model. Rather than send events willy-nilly up a class hierarchy with no idea of whether the events will ever be handled, the delegation event model broadcasts events only to classes that request them. Classes that request events are called *event listeners* and are required to implement the appropriate interfaces for the events they plan to handle. For example, an applet that needs to manage action events must implement the **ActionListener** interface, which declares the **actionPerformed()** method. (In AFC, the interface is known as **IUIActionListener**.)

To make a class an event listener, you must perform several tasks, as follows:

1.  Declare the class as implementing the appropriate event-listener interfaces for the events it plans to handle. For example, if the class is to handle action events, it must declare itself as implementing the **ActionListener** (or, in AFC, the **IUIActionListener**) interface.

2.  Register the class with the component for whose events the class will be a listener. For example, to register a class to receive action events from a pushbutton, the class must call the button's **addActionListener()** method.

3.  Implement the methods declared in the event-listener interfaces. For example, to complete the action-event button scenario, the class must implement the **actionPerformed()** method, which the button object will call when the button is clicked. Other interfaces may have several methods that must be implemented.

Listing 15.3 shows how you might convert Listing 15.1 to manage action events by using the delegation event model. The shaded areas in the listing indicate where the program was changed. In the first change, the program brings in the declarations in the **java.awt.event** classes. In the second shaded line, the program declares itself as implementing the **ActionListener** interface. In the third shaded line, the class registers itself as an action listener. Because the button control generates the action events the class wants to handle, it's the button object's **addActionListener()** method that the program calls. If there had been two buttons, the class would have registered with them both. Finally, the last shaded area is the **actionPerformed()** method's implementation.

## Listing 15.3  Source code for ButtonApplet2.

```java
//////////////////////////////////////////////////
// ButtonApplet2.java
//
// An applet that demonstrates the delegation
// event model.
//////////////////////////////////////////////////

import java.awt.*;
import java.applet.*;
import java.awt.event.*;

public class ButtonApplet2 extends Applet
    implements ActionListener
{
    private Button button;
    String displayString;

    public void init()
    {
        button = new Button("Test Button");
        add(button);
        button.addActionListener(this);
        displayString = "";
    }

    public void paint(Graphics g)
    {
        g.drawString(displayString, 20, 100);
    }

    public void actionPerformed(ActionEvent event)
    {
        String str = event.getActionCommand();
        if (str == "Test Button")
        {
            displayString = "Button clicked!";
            repaint();
        }
    }
}
```

# AFC And Event Handling

In the preceding section, you reviewed how to handle events in a conventional Java program. You'll be glad to know that you can apply almost everything you learned there to AFC programming. Using the propagation event model in an AFC program is exactly the same process as using it in a Java AWT program. For this reason, the rest of this chapter, including the Practical Guide, covers the AFC delegation event model, as defined in the **com.ms.ui.event** package.

The only real difference between Java's implementation of the delegation event model and AFC's implementation is in the name of the interfaces needed to declare the various types of listeners and the names of the event classes those interfaces handle. All the event listener interfaces in AFC begin with the **IUI** prefix, after which the name of the interface is the same as the regular Java version. So, Java's **ActionListener** interface becomes **IUIActionListener** in AFC. Likewise, **ItemListener** becomes **IUIItemListener**, **MouseListener** becomes **IUIMouseListener**, **KeyListener** becomes **IUIKeyListener**, and so on.

All of AFC's event classes also have slightly different names from the standard Java event classes. In this case, each AFC class prefixes its name with a **UI**. So, Java's **ActionEvent** class becomes **UIActionEvent** in AFC. Likewise, **AdjustmentEvent** becomes **UIAdjustmentEvent**, **FocusEvent** becomes **UIFocusEvent**, **MouseEvent** becomes **UIMouseEvent**, and so on. In the remainder of this chapter, you see how—using the delegation event model—to use the various event interfaces and classes in your AFC programs.

# Practical Guide To

# AFC Event Handling

- Handling Action Events
- Handling Adjustment Events
- Handling Focus Events
- Handling Item Events
- Handling Key Events
- Handling Mouse Events
- Handling Mouse-Motion Events
- Handling Text Events
- Handling Window Events

## Handling Action Events

AFC programs manage action events (which are generated by pushbuttons, list, and menu-item components) by implementing the **IUIActionListener** interface. This interface declares only a single method, **actionPerformed()**, that must be implemented in any class that registers with a component as an action listener (by calling the component's **addActionListener()** method). The **actionPerformed()** method receives a **UIActionEvent** object as its single parameter. The **UIActionEvent** class defines four methods that a program can call to get more information about the event. The following list describes these methods:

- **getActionCommand()**—Gets the command name, which is often the text label of the component that generated the event

- **getActionItem()**—Gets the component that generated the event

- **getModifiers()**—Gets the command's modifiers (keyboard or mouse buttons pressed), which can be one or more of **SHIFT_MASK**, **CTRL_MASK, META_MASK, ALT_MASK , BUTTON1_MASK, BUTTON2_MASK**, and **BUTTON3_MASK**

- **paramString()**—Gets a string that lists all this event's attributes

Listing 15.4 presents a short applet that demonstrates how to respond to action events in an AFC applet. When you run the applet, click the button to generate action events, which are reported in the DOS window. Figure 15.1 shows the applet running in Applet Viewer, and Figure 15.2 shows the DOS window reporting the events.

**Figure 15.1**

*ActionListenerApplet, running in Applet Viewer.*

## Figure 15.2

*The DOS window, reporting ActionListenerApplet's action events.*

## Listing 15.4   Source code for ActionListenerApplet.

```
//////////////////////////////////////////////////
// ActionListenerApplet.java
//
// An AFC applet that demonstrates how to handle
// action events with the delegation event model.
//////////////////////////////////////////////////

import com.ms.ui.*;
import com.ms.ui.event.*;

public class ActionListenerApplet extends AwtUIApplet
{
    public ActionListenerApplet()
    {
        super(new AppletImplementation());
    }
}

class AppletImplementation extends UIApplet
    implements IUIActionListener
{
    public void init()
    {
```

```
            UIBorderLayout layout = new UIBorderLayout();
            setLayout(layout);
            UIPushButton button = new UIPushButton("Click Me");
            button.addActionListener(this);
            add(button, "Center");

            setValid(true);
        }

        public void actionPerformed(UIActionEvent e)
        {
            String str = "actionPerformed: " +
                e.paramString() + '\n';
            System.out.println(str);
        }
    }
```

## Handling Adjustment Events

AFC programs manage adjustment events (generated by scroll, slider, and spinner components) by implementing the **IUIAdjustmentListener** interface. This interface declares only a single method, **adjustmentValueChanged()**, that must be implemented in any class that registers with a component as an action listener (by calling the component's **addAdjustmentListener()** method).

The **adjustmentValueChanged()** method receives a **UIAdjustmentEvent** object as its only parameter. The **UIAdjustmentEvent** class defines three methods a program can call to get more information about the event. The following list describes these methods:

- **getAdjustmentType()**—Gets the event's adjustment type, which can be one of **UNIT_INCREMENT**, **UNIT_DECREMENT**, **BLOCK_INCREMENT**, **BLOCK_DECREMENT**, or **TRACK**

- **getValue()**—Gets the new adjustment value, which is usually the component's new position

- **paramString()**—Gets a string that lists all of this event's attributes

Listing 15.5 presents a short applet that demonstrates how to respond to adjustment events in an AFC applet. When you run the applet, manipulate the scroller to generate adjustment events, which are reported in the DOS window. Figure 15.3 shows the applet running in Applet Viewer, and Figure 15.4 shows the DOS window reporting the events.

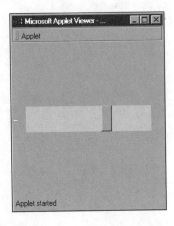

**Figure 15.3**

*AdjustmentListenerApplet, running in Applet Viewer.*

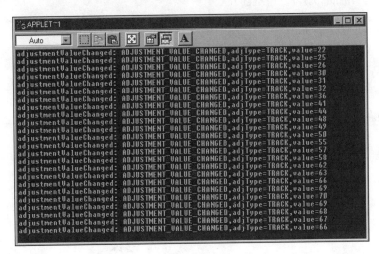

**Figure 15.4**

*The DOS window, reporting AdjustmentListenerApplet's adjustment events.*

**Listing 15.5   Source code for AdjustmentListenerApplet.**

```java
///////////////////////////////////////////////
// AdjustmentListenerApplet.java
//
// An AFC applet that demonstrates how to handle
// adjustment events with the delegation event
// model.
///////////////////////////////////////////////

import com.ms.ui.*;
import com.ms.ui.event.*;
import java.awt.Insets;

public class AdjustmentListenerApplet extends AwtUIApplet
{
    public AdjustmentListenerApplet()
    {
        super(new AppletImplementation());
    }
}

class AppletImplementation extends UIApplet
    implements IUIAdjustmentListener
{
    public void init()
    {
        UIScroll scroller = new UIScroll();
        scroller.addAdjustmentListener(this);
        add(scroller);

        setValid(true);
    }

    public void adjustmentValueChanged(UIAdjustmentEvent e)
    {
        String str = "adjustmentValueChanged: "
            + e.paramString() + '\n';
        System.out.println(str);
    }

    public Insets getInsets()
    {
        return new Insets(100, 20, 100, 20);
    }
}
```

## Handling Focus Events

AFC programs manage focus events (generated by most components) by implementing the **IUIFocusListener** interface. This interface declares two methods, **focusGained()** and **focusLost()**, that must be implemented in any class that registers with a component as a focus listener (by calling the component's **addFocusListener()** method). The **focusGained()** and **focusLost()** methods receive a **UIFocusEvent** object as their single parameter. The **UIFocusEvent** class defines three methods a program can call to get more information about the event. The following list describes these methods:

- **getArg()**—Gets the event's target component, which is the component losing or gaining the focus

- **isTemporary()**—Returns **true** if the focus change is temporary, such as when the user drags a scroll bar

- **paramString()**—Gets a string that lists all this event's attributes

Listing 15.6 presents a short applet that demonstrates how to respond to focus events in an AFC applet. When you run the applet, switch between Applet Viewer's window and the DOS window, by clicking the windows with your mouse. As the windows become activated and deactivated, the DOS window reports the applet's focus events. Figure 15.5 shows the applet running in Applet Viewer, Figure 15.6 shows the DOS window reporting the events.

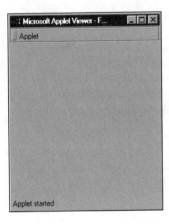

**Figure 15.5**

*FocusListenerApplet, running in Applet Viewer.*

**Figure 15.6**

*The DOS window, reporting FocusListenerApplet's events.*

**Listing 15.6   Source code for FocusListenerApplet.**

```java
//////////////////////////////////////////////////
// FocusListenerApplet.java
//
// An AFC applet that demonstrates how to handle
// focus events with the delegation event model.
//////////////////////////////////////////////////

import com.ms.ui.*;
import com.ms.ui.event.*;

public class FocusListenerApplet extends AwtUIApplet
{
    public FocusListenerApplet()
    {
        super(new AppletImplementation());
    }
}

class AppletImplementation extends UIApplet
    implements IUIFocusListener
{
    public void init()
    {
        addFocusListener(this);
```

```
        setValid(true);
    }

    public void focusGained(UIFocusEvent e)
    {
        String str = "focusGained: " +
            e.paramString() + '\n';
        System.out.println(str);
    }

    public void focusLost(UIFocusEvent e)
    {
        String str = "focusLost: " +
            e.paramString() + '\n';
        System.out.println(str);
    }
}
```

## Handling Item Events

AFC programs manage item events (generated by check buttons and radio buttons) by implementing the **IUIItemListener** interface. This interface declares only one method, **itemStateChanged()**, that must be implemented in any class that registers with a component as an item listener (by calling the component's **addItemListener()** method). The **itemStateChanged()** method receives a **UIItemEvent** object as its single parameter. The **UIItemEvent** class defines four methods a program can call to get more information about the event. The following list describes these methods:

- **getItem()**—Gets the object that generated the event

- **getItemSelectable()**—Gets the component that generated the event

- **getStateChange()**—Gets the type of item event, which can be **SELECTED** or **DESELECTED**

- **paramString()**—Gets a string that lists all of this event's attributes

Listing 15.7 presents a short applet that demonstrates how to respond to item events in an AFC applet. When you run the applet, click the check box and watch as the DOS window reports the event. Figure 15.7 shows the applet running in Applet Viewer, and Figure 15.8 shows the DOS window reporting the events.

**Figure 15.7**

*ItemListenerApplet, running in Applet Viewer.*

**Figure 15.8**

*The DOS window, reporting ItemListenerApplet's events.*

### Listing 15.7   Source code for ItemListenerApplet.

```
//////////////////////////////////////////////////
// ItemListenerApplet.java
//
// An AFC applet that demonstrates how to handle
// item events with the delegation event model.
//////////////////////////////////////////////////
```

```
import com.ms.ui.*;
import com.ms.ui.event.*;
import java.awt.Insets;

public class ItemListenerApplet extends AwtUIApplet
{
    public ItemListenerApplet()
    {
        super(new AppletImplementation());
    }
}

class AppletImplementation extends UIApplet
    implements IUIItemListener
{
    public void init()
    {
        UIBorderLayout layout = new UIBorderLayout();
        setLayout(layout);
        UICheckButton button = new UICheckButton("Click Me");
        button.addItemListener(this);
        add(button, "Center");

        setValid(true);
    }

    public void itemStateChanged(UIItemEvent e)
    {
        String str = "itemStateChanged: " +
            e.paramString() + '\n';
        System.out.println(str);
    }

    public Insets getInsets()
    {
        return new Insets(0, 90, 0, 0);
    }
}
```

 ## Handling Key Events

AFC programs manage key events (generated by edit boxes and any control that can respond to the keyboard) by implementing the **IUIKeyListener** interface. This interface declares three methods—**keyPressed()**, **keyReleased()**, and **keyTyped()**—that must be implemented in any class that registers with a component as a key listener (by calling the component's **addKeyListener()** method). These methods receive a **UIKeyEvent** object as their single parameter. The **UIKeyEvent** class defines four methods a program can call to get more information about the event. The following list describes these methods:

- **getKeyChar()**—Gets the character typed or **CHAR_UNDEFINED**
- **getKeyCode()**—Gets the key code of the key pressed
- **isActionKey()**—Returns **true** if the typed key is an action key
- **paramString()**—Gets a string that lists all this event's attributes

Listing 15.8 presents a short applet that demonstrates how to respond to key events in an AFC applet. When you run the applet, click the applet's display area to make sure that the component has the input focus, and then type on your keyboard. Watch as the key events appear in the DOS window. Figure 15.9 shows the applet running in Applet Viewer, whereas Figure 15.10 shows the DOS window reporting the events.

### Listing 15.8   Source code for KeyListenerApplet.

```
/////////////////////////////////////////////////
// KeyListenerApplet.java
//
// An AFC applet that demonstrates how to handle
// key events with the delegation event model.
/////////////////////////////////////////////////

import com.ms.ui.*;
import com.ms.ui.event.*;

public class KeyListenerApplet extends AwtUIApplet
{
    public KeyListenerApplet()
    {
        super(new AppletImplementation());
    }
}

class AppletImplementation extends UIApplet
    implements IUIKeyListener
{
```

```
    public void init()
    {
        addKeyListener(this);

        setValid(true);
    }

    public void keyPressed(UIKeyEvent e)
    {
        String str = "keyPressed: " +
            e.paramString() + '\n';
        System.out.println(str);
    }

    public void keyReleased(UIKeyEvent e)
    {
        String str = "keyReleased: " +
            e.paramString() + '\n';
        System.out.println(str);
    }

    public void keyTyped(UIKeyEvent e)
    {
        String str = "keyTyped: " +
            e.paramString() + '\n';
        System.out.println(str);
    }
}
```

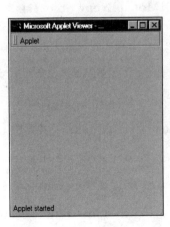

**Figure 15.9**

*KeyListenerApplet, running in Applet Viewer.*

**Figure 15.10**

*The DOS window, reporting KeyListenerApplet's events.*

## Handling Mouse Events

AFC programs manage mouse events (generated by the interaction of the mouse with a component) by implementing the **IUIMouseListener** interface. This interface declares five methods—**mouseClicked()**, **mouseEntered()**, **mouseExited()**, **mousePressed()**, and **mouseReleased()**—that must be implemented in any class that registers with a component as a mouse listener (by calling the component's **addMouseListener()** method). These methods receive a **UIMouseEvent** object as their single parameter. The **UIMouseEvent** class defines six methods a program can call to get more information about the event. The following list describes these methods:

- **getClickCount()**—Gets the number of mouse-button clicks

- **getPoint()**—Gets the mouse location at the time of the event

- **getX()**—Gets the mouse's X coordinate at the time of the event

- **getY()**—Gets the mouse's Y coordinate at the time of the event

- **isPopupTrigger()**—Returns **true** if the event is the pop-up menu trigger

- **paramString()**—Gets a string that lists all this event's attributes

Listing 15.9 presents a short applet that demonstrates how to respond to mouse events in an AFC applet. When you run the applet, click the mouse within the window and watch as the mouse events appear in the DOS window. Also, try moving the mouse off the window and back on to see the mouse-exit and mouse-enter events. Figure 15.11 shows the applet running in Applet Viewer, whereas Figure 15.12 shows the DOS window reporting the events.

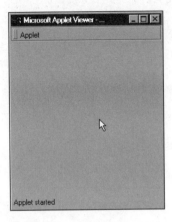

**Figure 15.11**

*MouseListenerApplet, running in Applet Viewer.*

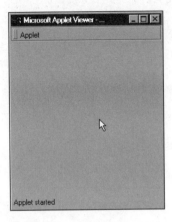

**Figure 15.12**

*The DOS window, reporting MouseListenerApplet's events.*

**Listing 15.9  Source code for MouseListenerApplet.**

```
///////////////////////////////////////////////
// MouseListenerApplet.java
//
// An AFC applet that demonstrates how to handle
// mouse events with the delegation event model.
///////////////////////////////////////////////

import com.ms.ui.*;
import com.ms.ui.event.*;

public class MouseListenerApplet extends AwtUIApplet
{
    public MouseListenerApplet()
    {
        super(new AppletImplementation());
    }
}

class AppletImplementation extends UIApplet
    implements IUIMouseListener
{
    public void init()
    {
        addMouseListener(this);
        setValid(true);
    }

    public void mouseClicked(UIMouseEvent e)
    {
        String str = "mouseClicked: " +
            e.paramString() + '\n';
        System.out.println(str);
    }

    public void mouseEntered(UIMouseEvent e)
    {
        String str = "mouseEntered: " +
            e.paramString() + '\n';
        System.out.println(str);
    }

    public void mouseExited(UIMouseEvent e)
    {
```

```
        String str = "mouseExited: " +
            e.paramString() + '\n';
        System.out.println(str);
    }

    public void mousePressed(UIMouseEvent e)
    {
        String str = "mousePressed: " +
            e.paramString() + '\n';
        System.out.println(str);
    }

    public void mouseReleased(UIMouseEvent e)
    {
        String str = "mouseReleased: " +
            e.paramString() + '\n';
        System.out.println(str);
    }
}
```

## Handling Mouse-Motion Events

AFC programs manage mouse-motion events (generated by the interaction of the mouse with a component) by implementing the **IUIMouseMotionListener** interface. This interface declares two methods—**mouseDragged()** and **mouseMoved()**—that must be implemented in any class that registers with a component as a mouse-motion listener (by calling the component's **addMouseMotionListener()** method). These methods receive a **UIMouseEvent** object as their single parameter. As you already know from the preceding section, the **UIMouseEvent** class defines six methods that a program can call to get more information about the event.

Listing 15.10 presents a short applet that demonstrates how to respond to mouse-motion events in an AFC applet. When you run the applet, move the mouse over the window and watch as the mouse events appear in the DOS window. Also, try dragging the mouse across the window to see how this action changes the events. Figure 15.13 shows the applet running in Applet Viewer, and Figure 15.14 shows the DOS window reporting the events.

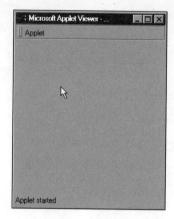

**Figure 15.13**

*MouseMotionListenerApplet, running in Applet Viewer.*

**Figure 15.14**

*The DOS window, reporting MouseMotionListenerApplet's events.*

### Listing 15.10   Source code for MouseMotionListenerApplet.

```
/////////////////////////////////////////////////
// MouseMotionListenerApplet.java
//
// An AFC applet that demonstrates how to handle
// mouse-motion events with the delegation event
// model.
/////////////////////////////////////////////////
```

```
import com.ms.ui.*;
import com.ms.ui.event.*;

public class MouseMotionListenerApplet extends AwtUIApplet
{
    public MouseMotionListenerApplet()
    {
        super(new AppletImplementation());
    }
}

class AppletImplementation extends UIApplet
    implements IUIMouseMotionListener
{
    public void init()
    {
        addMouseMotionListener(this);
        setValid(true);
    }

    public void mouseDragged(UIMouseEvent e)
    {
        String str = "mouseDragged: " +
            e.paramString() + '\n';
        System.out.println(str);
    }

    public void mouseMoved(UIMouseEvent e)
    {
        String str = "mouseMoved: " +
            e.paramString() + '\n';
        System.out.println(str);
    }
}
```

## Handling Text Events

AFC programs manage text events (generated by edit boxes) by implementing the
**IUITextListener** interface. This interface declares one method—**textValueChanged()**—
that must be implemented in any class that registers with a component as a text listener
(by calling the component's **addTextListener()** method). This method receives a
**UITextEvent** object as its single parameter. The **UITextEvent** class defines one method a
program can call to get more information about the event. This method is **paramString()**,
which gets a string that lists the event's attributes.

Listing 15.11 presents a short applet that demonstrates how to respond to text events in an AFC applet. When you run the applet, click within the edit box and start typing, watching as the text events appear in the DOS window. Figure 15.15 shows the applet running in Applet Viewer, whereas Figure 15.16 shows the DOS window reporting the events.

**Figure 15.15**

*TextListenerApplet, running in Applet Viewer.*

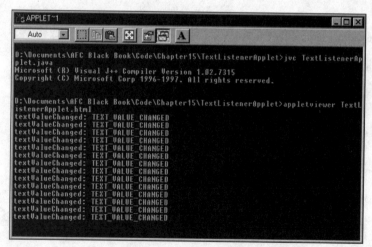

**Figure 15.16**

*The DOS window, reporting TextListenerApplet's events.*

## Listing 15.11   Source code for TextListenerApplet.

```
//////////////////////////////////////////////////
// TextListenerApplet.java
//
// An AFC applet that demonstrates how to handle
// text events with the delegation event model.
//////////////////////////////////////////////////

import com.ms.ui.*;
import com.ms.ui.event.*;
import com.ms.fx.*;
import java.awt.Insets;

public class TextListenerApplet extends AwtUIApplet
{
    public TextListenerApplet()
    {
        super(new AppletImplementation());
    }
}

class AppletImplementation extends UIApplet
    implements IUITextListener, IFxTextConstants
{
    public void init()
    {
        UIBorderLayout layout = new UIBorderLayout();
        setLayout(layout);
        UIEdit edit = new UIEdit();
        edit.setBordered(true);
        edit.setSingleLine(false);
        edit.setWordWrap(wwKeepWordIntact);
        edit.addTextListener(this);
        add(edit, "Center");

        setValid(true);
    }

    public void textValueChanged(UITextEvent e)
    {
        String str = "textValueChanged: " +
            e.paramString() + '\n';
        System.out.println(str);
    }
```

```
    public Insets getInsets()
    {
        return new Insets(20, 20, 20, 20);
    }
}
```

## Handling Window Events

AFC programs manage window events (generated by window components) by implementing the **IUIWindowListener** interface. This interface declares seven methods—**windowActivated()**, **windowClosed()**, **windowClosing()**, **windowDeactivated()**, **windowDeiconified()**, **windowIconified()**, and **windowOpened()**—that must be implemented in any class that registers with a component as a window listener (by calling the component's **addWindowListener()** method). These methods receive a **UIWindowEvent** object as their single parameter. The **UIWindowEvent** class defines two methods a program can call to get more information about the event:

- **getWindow()**—Gets the window that generated the event

- **paramString()**—Gets a string that lists all this event's attributes

Listing 15.12 presents a short, standalone application that demonstrates how to respond to window events in an AFC program. When you run the program, minimize and restore the window, as well as start and stop the application, watching as the window events appear in the DOS window. Figure 15.17 shows the application, whereas Figure 15.18 shows the DOS window reporting the events.

### Figure 15.17

*WindowListenerApp, running as a standalone application.*

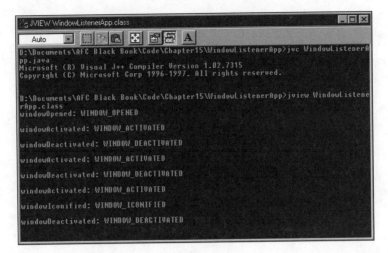

## Figure 15.18

*The DOS window, reporting WindowListenerApp's events.*

## Listing 15.12 Source code for WindowListenerApp.

```
/////////////////////////////////////////////////
// WindowListenerApp.java
//
// An AFC application that demonstrates how to
// handle window events with the delegation event
// model.
/////////////////////////////////////////////////

import com.ms.ui.*;
import com.ms.ui.event.*;

public class WindowListenerApp
{
    public static void main(String args[])
    {
        AFCFrame frame =
            new AFCFrame("Window Listener");
        frame.setSize(240, 240);
        frame.setVisible(true);
    }
}

class AFCFrame extends UIFrame
    implements IUIWindowListener
{
```

```java
public AFCFrame(String title)
{
    super(title);
    addWindowListener(this);

    setValid(true);
}

public void windowActivated(UIWindowEvent e)
{
    String str = "windowActivated: " +
        e.paramString() + '\n';
    System.out.println(str);
}

public void windowClosed(UIWindowEvent e)
{
    String str = "windowClosed: " +
        e.paramString() + '\n';
    System.out.println(str);
}

public void windowClosing(UIWindowEvent e)
{
    String str = "windowClosing: " +
        e.paramString() + '\n';
    System.out.println(str);

    System.exit(0);
}

public void windowDeactivated(UIWindowEvent e)
{
    String str = "windowDeactivated: " +
        e.paramString() + '\n';
    System.out.println(str);
}

public void windowDeiconified(UIWindowEvent e)
{
    String str = "windowDeiconified: " +
        e.paramString() + '\n';
    System.out.println(str);
}
```

```
public void windowIconified(UIWindowEvent e)
{
    String str = "windowIconified: " +
        e.paramString() + '\n';
    System.out.println(str);
}

public void windowOpened(UIWindowEvent e)
{
    String str = "windowOpened: " +
        e.paramString() + '\n';
    System.out.println(str);
}
}
```

# Index